The Matter of Wonder

The Matter of Wonder

Abhinavagupta's Panentheism and the New Materialism

Loriliai Biernacki

OXFORD
UNIVERSITY PRESS

OXFORD
UNIVERSITY PRESS

Oxford University Press is a department of the University of Oxford. It furthers the University's objective of excellence in research, scholarship, and education by publishing worldwide. Oxford is a registered trade mark of Oxford University Press in the UK and certain other countries.

Published in the United States of America by Oxford University Press
198 Madison Avenue, New York, NY 10016, United States of America.

Library of Congress Cataloging-in-Publication Data
Names: Biernacki, Loriliai, author.
Title: The matter of wonder : Abhinavagupta's panentheism and
the new materialism /Loriliai Biernacki.
Description: New York : Oxford University Press, 2023. |
Includes bibliographical references and index.
Identifiers: LCCN 2022040694 (print) | LCCN 2022040695 (ebook) |
ISBN 9780197643075 (hardback) | ISBN 9780197643099 (epub)
Subjects: LCSH: Abhinavagupta, Rājānaka. | Materialism—Religious aspects—Hinduism. |
Kashmir Śaivism. | Panentheism.
Classification: LCC B133.A354 B54 2023 (print) | LCC B133.A354 (ebook) |
DDC 294.5/2—dc23/eng/20221021
LC record available at https://lccn.loc.gov/2022040694
LC ebook record available at https://lccn.loc.gov/2022040695

DOI: 10.1093/oso/9780197643075.001.0001

Printed by Integrated Books International, United States of America

For Mary Biernacki and Ivan Biernacki,
my mother and father, and for John Shanks.

Acknowledgments

Every book is really the product of many minds fermenting the ideas that come forth. Here I would particularly like to express my gratitude to Sthaneshwar Timalsina for his thoughtful conversations, Fred Smith for his deep knowledge, and David Lawrence for his insight. Much appreciation to Mike Murphy, Jeff Kripal, and Catherine Keller for encouraging me to think outside the box. Also thanks go to Vasudha Narayanan, for her encouragement, Greg Shaw, Bill Barnard, Glen Hayes, John Nemec, Karen Pechilis and NBs Carol Anderson, Whitney Sanford, Robin Rinehart, Corinne Dempsey, Rebecca Manring, Phyllis Herman, and Nancy Martin. A special thanks to Ramdas Lamb for his inspiration. Thanks go also to my colleagues at the University of Colorado, especially Susan Kent and Terry Kleeman and my students there, particularly James Batten. Particular thanks also to John Lauer and Radhika Miles and Trupti Manina for her work on the cover. Also, thanks go to Cynthia Read at Oxford University Press and to Theo Calderara and the team there in the production of the book. I want to thank also my parents Mary and Ivan Biernacki, and especially my thanks go to John Shanks for his loving patience and support through the process.

Contents

Introduction: The Matter of Wonder: Abhinavagupta's Panentheism and New Materialism 1

1. Abhinavagupta's Panentheism and New Materialism 12

2. The Matter of Wonder 46

3. The Subtle Body 71

4. Panentheism, Panpsychism, Theism: Abhinavagupta on Consciousness, Sentience, and the Paperclip Apocalypse 95

5. It from Bit, It from *Cit*: Information and Meaning 123

Notes *155*
Bibliography *221*
Index *241*

Introduction

The Matter of Wonder: Abhinavagupta's Panentheism and New Materialism

> I bow to him who pierces through and pervades with his own essence this whole, from top to bottom, and makes this whole world to consist of *Śiva*, himself.[1]
>
> **—Abhinavagupta**

> We may someday have to enlarge the scope of what we mean by a "who."
>
> **—John Archibald Wheeler**

> Even down to a worm—when they do their own deeds, that which is to be done first stirs in the heart.[2]
>
> **—Abhinavagupta**

> If thou be'st born to strange sights, Things invisible to see, Ride ten thousand days and nights, Till age snow white hairs on thee, Thou, when thou return'st, wilt tell me, All strange wonders that befell thee
>
> **—John Donne**

In this book I argue that the panentheism of an 11th-century medieval Indian Hindu thinker can help us to rethink our current relationship to matter. Writing in northern India from 975 to 1025 CE, the Kashmiri philosopher Abhinavagupta (950–1016) articulated a panentheism—*both* seeing the divine as immanent in the world and at the same time as transcendent—as a way of reclaiming the solidity, the realness of the material world.[3] His theology understood the world itself, with its manifold inhabitants, from gods to humans to insects down to the merest rock as part of the unfolding of a single conscious reality, *Śiva*. This conscious singularity—the word "god" here does not

The Matter of Wonder. Lorilai Biernacki, Oxford University Press. © Oxford University Press 2023.
DOI: 10.1093/oso/9780197643075.003.0001

quite do justice to the pervasive panentheism involved—this consciousness, with its capacity to choose and will, pervades all through, from top to bottom; human and nonhuman, as Abhinavagupta tells us, "even down to a worm—when they do their own deeds, that which is to be done first stirs in the heart."[4] His panentheism proposed an answer to a familiar conundrum, one we still grapple with today—that is: consciousness is so unlike matter; how does it actually connect to the materiality of our world? To put this question in more familiar 21st-century terms, how does mind connect to body? This particular question drives the comparative impetus for this book.

Abhinavagupta

A towering figure in India's philosophical landscape, influential far beyond the boundaries of his native Kashmir in the thousand years since his death, Abhinavagupta wrote extensively on Tantra, an innovative religious movement that began in India in the first half of the first millennium.[5] Tantra as a religious system cut across religious boundaries, steering Buddhist groups and sectarian Hindu groups, Śaiva and Vaiṣṇava, and even an abstinency-minded Jainism[6] away from an earlier ascendant asceticism to a philosophy and a praxis more keenly focused on the body as part of the path of enlightenment and on ritual, especially ritual involving the body.[7] Perhaps in keeping with Tantra's attention to the body, it may not be surprising to find Abhinavagupta exercising his keen intellect as well in the domain of the senses, writing also on aesthetic theory.[8] And while Abhinavagupta is especially well known today for his writing on Tantric philosophy and ritual, it is probably fair to suggest that historically in India his pan-India fame rests especially on his writings on aesthetics, where his theoretical interventions shaped aesthetic understanding through the following centuries.[9] This material, sensual orientation shapes a physical portrait we have of him as well. One of his devotees, as Pandey tells us, a disciple who studied directly with Abhinavagupta, Madhurāja Yogin, gives us a visualization of Abhinavagupta.[10] Certainly, the intervening centuries make it hard to accord it any genuine accuracy; still the image we have is evocative, redolent of a sensual, physical embrace of the world. His long hair tied with a garland of flowers, bearing the insignia of a devotee of the god Śiva, *rudrākṣa* beads, and three lines of ash on his forehead, he plays a musical instrument, the *vīna*, and in an anticipated Tantric gesture, two women are at his side holding lotus flowers and the aphrodisiac betel nut.[11] Portraits aside, Abhinavagupta's writing is compelling and fresh even after these ten centuries precisely because of Abhinavagupta's ability to weave philosophy within a mundane material awareness.[12] Keen in its psychological comprehension, his acute sensibility of how the mind works can help us navigate our own contemporary engagement with the matter all around us.

My Argument

Particularly for a New Materialism, I propose that Abhinavagupta's articulation of panentheism, centered around a foundational subjectivity, gives us a first-person perspective that may offer a helpful intervention for our world today as we rethink our own relationship to matter, to the natural world around us, other humans and nonhumans, and the rapidly disappearing insects and worms that cross our paths.[13] Abhinavagupta's panentheism postulates a single reality, *Śiva*, which unfolds out of itself the wonderful diversity of our world. He tells us that

> the category called *Śiva* is itself the body of all things. "On the wall [of the world which is itself *Śiva*] the picture of all beings appears, shining forth"—This statement indicates the way that all these appear.[14]

His panentheism aims to keep our sights on the world, with all its matter and multiplicity, as real. A tricky endeavor for a singular reality, *Śiva*, a nondualism.[15] Classical, familiar attempts at nondualism try mostly to show us how our idea of the multiplicity of the world as real is just a mistake in judgment. Abhinavagupta's panentheism instead reformulates the relationship between matter and consciousness. He draws on psychological, linguistic modes, the idea of subject and object, to tell us that we find nested within materiality the possibility of a first-person perspective, even in a mere rock.[16] We find consciousness at the heart of matter. Rethinking the boundaries of life, matter, and consciousness, his strategy offers a way to think through materiality, for a New Materialism in particular, compelling in its decentering of the human.

I focus on key elements of Abhinavagupta's panentheism to address central issues for a New Materialism. First, his use of wonder (*camatkāra*), I propose, serves to alter our vision of matter, pointing to its essential liveliness. Moreover, it reinscribes transcendence within a bodily subjectivity. Second, I suggest his use of the term *vimarśa*, a kind of active awareness, can help us think through how we get the idea of sentience, that is, to think through the relationship between what is living and what is not. Third, I propose that he uses his inherited cosmological map of what there is (familiar to students of

India as the *tattva* system) to map phenomenologically how this originary consciousness, *Śiva*, progressively transforms its original subjectivity in stages to become objects, the materiality of earth and water that make up our world. Fourth, in addition, I suggest that he draws on the *tattva* system to chart how we get the many out of the One. Fifth, I propose that we may read the theology he gives us of the subtle body as a way of affording intentionality to the affective processes of the body, outside of human egoic intentions.

Finally, I propose that Abhinavagupta's strategy for connecting consciousness to materiality can instruct our own century's adoptions of panpsychism and dual-aspect monisms, models that contemporary philosophers and scientists use to solve the problem of how life and consciousness relate to mere matter—particularly in terms of our current enthusiasm for ideas of information. In this, I use Abhinavagupta's philosophy to address issues relevant for us today, and I do so comparatively, drawing on our own current cultural preoccupations to frame his panentheism.[17] In sum, I argue that Abhinavagupta's panentheism is too important a resource to not be used in our current construction of our world, particularly in the face of our rapidly increasing capacity to manipulate matter—and, indeed, in view of the consequent ecological results.

In the five chapters that follow I present an outline of Abhinavagupta's panentheism, charting how his panentheism maps the relationship between materiality and consciousness, between immanence and transcendence. But my particular focus is on the material side of the equation. Abhinavagupta's nondualist panentheism has, assuredly, been invoked more generally in the context of an idealism, that is, more on the consciousness side of things.[18] Here, I contend that paying attention to his sophisticated articulation of materiality can help us in our own understanding of what matter is and how it matters. To get a feeling for the importance of matter in his nondualism, we can compare him with another nondualist, the great nondual mystic of the 20th century, the South Indian Ramana Maharshi (1879–1950). Ramana Maharshi's philosophy is often aligned with the nondualism of Advaita Vedānta, the well-known Indian philosophical conception, in a nutshell (though this is perhaps too brief), that the world we experience here is illusory, is *Māyā*. Ramana Maharshi instructs us to ignore the world. We do not need to know about the world, he tells us; we just need to know about the Self.[19] He instructs us

> [t]o keep the mind constantly turned inwards and to abide thus in the Self is the only Self-enquiry. Just as it is futile to examine the rubbish that has to be swept up only to be thrown away, so it is futile for him who seeks to know the Self to set to work enumerating the *tattvas* that envelop the Self and examining them instead of casting them away.[20]

In other words, we do not need to know what our world is made of in order to get enlightened. It is rubbish, futile knowledge; simply toss it out. In contrast, Abhinavagupta tells us:

> Now, it would not be correct to say that for our present topic—i.e., to convey the recognition of the Lord—it is not necessary to ascertain the world as object to be known; [this is not correct, because] only to the extent that one makes the world into an object, to the extent that it is known, can one then transcend the level of object, of thing to be known and allow the true sense of the knower to take root in the heart, its fullness being grasped by mind, intellect and ego.[21]

Abhinavagupta addresses head on the assumption that enlightenment means we drop the idea of a world out there. Even if his readers might think that the path to enlightenment means concerning ourselves only with the highest, the recognition (*pratyabhijñā*) of the Lord, as we hear in the echoes of Ramana Maharshi's advice, Abhinavagupta instead reminds us that the fullness of insight also includes the materiality of the world. Only by knowing the world do we allow the real sense of the knower to blossom in the heart. It is, of course, important not to understate the legacy of transcendence and idealism that Abhinavagupta inherits and embraces. However, in this book I will focus especially on the materialist side of Abhinavagupta's thought. Rather than on the wall of the world that is *Śiva*, my center of attention is instead on the fantastic diversity of the picture, which has mostly been neglected in much of the excellent work on this thinker.[22]

My Primary Source Material

My thinking on Abhinavagupta and his perspective on the materiality side of things has been especially influenced by my primary source material. I have worked particularly with the third section of one of Abhinavagupta's last works, his massive *Īśvara Pratyabhijñā Vivṛti Vimarśinī* (*Ipvv*), the *Long Commentary on the Elucidation of Recognition of the Lord*, composed in 1015 CE.[23] The Sanskrit text, handed down in manuscript form through generations from Abhinavagupta's time, was first published in Kashmir in three volumes from 1938 to 1943; I draw primarily from the third section, titled the *Āgamādhikāra*, comprising 100 pages of Sanskrit.[24] Abhinavagupta's text is a commentary; he provides explanatory notes to a text written approximately 50 years earlier by his great grand teacher Utpaladeva, the *Īśvarapratyabhijñāv ivṛti* (*Elucidation of Recognition of the Lord*), which is itself a commentary on a shorter set of verses composed by Utpaladeva, *Īśvarapratyabhijñākārikā* (*The Verses on Recognition of the Lord*). Thus, we have a commentary on a commentary on an original set of verses. Abhinavagupta also wrote a shorter commentary on Utpaladeva's compelling verses, and Utpaladeva wrote his own autocommentary as well.[25]

The *Āgamādhikāra* deals particularly with received knowledge, what the tradition has passed down. *Āgama* is typically translated as "scripture" or "revealed text." Abhinavagupta and Utpaladeva, however, use the term not so much to focus on particular scriptures or textual sources, but rather to discuss knowledge of the cosmos, the cosmology that we find in the *tattva* system, the classification of all that exists, handed down by tradition.[26] Abhinavagupta explicates the received tradition of cosmology, the *tattva* system, within his understanding of a subject–object continuum, offering us a map of how an originary consciousness, *Śiva*, unfolds to become the myriad objects that make up our world. The two chapters of the *Āgamādhikāra* chart out what the world is made of, following Abhinavagupta's Tantric classificatory scheme of cosmology, the *tattvas*, and then addresses the tradition's understanding of different modes of subjectivity in relation to the objects we find in the world. Describing these two chapters, Abhinavagupta tells us:

> So far [Utpaladeva] has explained how the group of *tattvas* exist as object and immediately preceding that he explained the nature of the subject also. Here, because of its importance, the text reveals the essence of the object because it is helpful for the recognition of one's own divinity. So it is a topic worth delineating in detail.[27]

Again, we see Abhinavagupta telling us that we need to know the world; we need to know the essence of the objects we encounter if we want to achieve our own enlightenment. The *Āgamādhikāra* charts out the nature of the world, the materiality all around us.

Abhinavagupta's *Long Commentary* is interesting and helpful because he at times offers long and insightful expositions on various ideas that we do not find anywhere else; it is also difficult because Utpaladeva's autocommentary, the *Elucidation* (*vivṛti*), has been lost. As a result, Abhinavagupta's *Long Commentary* makes reference throughout to particular specific words whose source is no longer extant. Still, many of his long excursions are coherent and compelling without recourse to Utpaladeva's lost text; the situation is also remedied to some extent by the availability of Abhinavagupta's earlier shorter commentary (*Ipv*). A translation for the *Long Commentary* as a whole and for this third section, the text of the *Āgamādhikāra*, is not yet available.[28] For this reason, when I offer translations drawing from Abhinavagupta's writing and particularly this text, the *Āgamādhikāra*, to explicate Abhinavagupta's thought, I give the passages of Sanskrit in the notes section at the end of each chapter. All translations are my own.

Panentheism and the New Materialism

Abhinavagupta's panentheism maps out the nature of matter, telling us we need to understand matter if we want to understand ourselves and our own enlightened divinity. This focus on what matter is, I suggest, can help steer our own thinking as we face a rapidly crashing environment and help to rethink how we relate to our material world. For a nascent New Materialism in particular, keenly attuned to how the way we think about matter directs what we do, Abhinavagupta's panentheism with its sophisticated articulation of subjectivity in relation to the matter of our world may help to refine our contemporary attitudes toward the rocks and insects and worms all around us. Of course, I am premising this suggestion on the provocative thesis that Lynn White articulated all those years ago—that our model of the world, our theology or cosmology, sets the stage for how we *treat* the matter of our world.[29] Indeed, as the *Oxford English Dictionary* attests in its helpful list of dated examples of usage, as early as 1991 we start to see panentheism associated with a way of addressing our environmental challenges.[30] What is it about panentheism that makes it environmentally friendly? The answer to that question, I might venture, has to do with the idea of linking things that seem quite different from each other. Panentheism links the material world to something that is quite apart from its materiality, an outside force, a divinity, that transcends matter altogether. This cozy material affinity is indeed encoded linguistically in the word. As a concept itself, the prefix *pan*—that is, the world, matter, and materiality—is affixed to *theism*, the transcendence of deity. The two are not made into one, merged as in *pantheism*, but rather the materiality of the world and the transcendence of deity are linked, yet still held apart in a productive tension. In this sense, panentheism operates as a ligature holding in tension both the many and the one, both matter and transcendence.

I suspect that what made panentheism particularly attractive for Abhinavagupta in the 11th century was the ligature, its rather Tantric assertion to have one's cake and eat it too—that is, its claims toward both the materiality of the world *and* the transcendence of divinity.[31] Panentheism can give us both consciousness and matter, not dissolving one or the other. Consciousness as something outside transcends the materiality of our world, yet it is held in productive tension with the world, not erasing the messy matter of immanence.[32]

In this respect, panentheism points to a way of thinking about the link between matter and consciousness, a metaphysical hitching together of two seemingly polar opposites. This book as a whole also proposes a similar sort of ligature, a comparative project bringing together disparate elements in the hope of a productive tension, an 11th-century Tantric on the one hand and a contemporary New Materialism on the other. It focuses on our contemporary concerns around what is sentient—animals? viruses? artificial intelligence?—set in relation to Abhinavagupta's articulation of what gives rise to sentience. And the book deals with our current conceptions of information as data—articulated in juxtaposition to Abhinavagupta's theology of *mantra*, mystic sound.[33] In this sense, the comparative project that unfolds in the following five chapters operates in the style of the 17th-century English Metaphysical poets, like John Donne, hitching together disparate things to reveal at the heart of things a sense of wonder.

Chapter Outline

Chapter One looks at Abhinavagupta's conception of subjectivity (*ahantā*) in relation to matter, and specifically in terms of what it can impart for a New Materialism. Subjectivity, (*ahantā*), a first-person person perspective, works as the fulcrum of his panentheism. What makes us sentient depends on our capacity to identify with the sense of "I," rather than the "this" (*idantā*), a state of being an object. Abhinavagupta reminds us that attention to subjectivity is needed for thinking through our relationship to matter. Notably, Abhinavagupta uses psychological, linguistic modes, rather than our more familiar ontological distinctions, to parse out the differences between humans and nonhumans and matter. Not ontologically driven, this modal formula, rather helpfully for a New Materialism, decenters the human in our cosmology. Humans and rocks alike share a fluid ability to move between being a subject or an object, giving us consciousness innate to matter. At the same time that Abhinavagupta asserts an innate capacity for sentience, even for things that seem to be dead objects, like rocks, he also proposes a way to differentiate between things that are sentient and things that are not. With this distinction we also examine how Abhinavagupta helps us to think through how we get multiplicity within a philosophy that claims there is only one reality. Throughout this chapter I offer a comparative assessment of Abhinavagupta in relation to a New Materialism. Walt Whitman, for instance, a figure frequently invoked for a New Materialism, also poses an expansive first-person perspective in his poetry, a similarity, I suggest, that shares with Abhinavagupta's first-person-centered philosophy a capacity to enliven objects.

Chapter Two begins with a discussion of how science and scientists, from Carl Sagan to some contemporary neuroscientists such as Anil Seth, invoke wonder as a way of bringing in an atheistic transcendence. This chapter delineates Abhinavagupta's formulation of wonder (*camatkāra*), arguing that the phenomenology of wonder serves to underscore an inherent subjectivity, even in mere matter. Tracing out the Indian genealogy of wonder through its roots in cooking, we see Abhinavagupta emphasizes the sensory and sensual elements of wonder. At the same time, Abhinavagupta's conception of wonder offers a way of delineating between what is alive and what is not in a way that offers a permeable boundary between mere matter and life. Wonder happens, Abhinavagupta explains, when the "I" can reflect on itself; it is the signal of life, sentience. With a keen phenomenological attention, Abhinavagupta's analysis of wonder turns on its head the way we usually think of wonder. He tells us that the power of wonder is not so much that it offers a transcendence that leaves behind the fetters of an earth-bound material body, but rather that wonder instead alters our vision of matter, pointing to its essential liveliness. This in turn alters how we understand transcendence. It is not an up and out situation, leaving behind sluggish dumb matter; instead it points to an inwardness, a heightened subjectivity. Abhinavagupta rewrites transcendence in one other way as well. We typically imagine transcendence as a space of timelessness, above the change of the world. Abhinavagupta instead rewrites time back into this transformed notion of transcendence.

Chapter Three begins with a discussion of Darwin's description of his loss of faith when he witnesses the parasitic wasp infecting the caterpillar. How could a benevolent God create this sort of monstrosity, he asks—a parasitic wasp inside the caterpillar, two beings, one body, boundaries transgressed. Here the focus is on the boundaries of bodies and agency. In this context, I discuss Abhinavagupta's idea of the subtle body as a body also inhabited by something other than the person claiming the body. Here, however, in this Tantric case, the other consciousness inhabiting the body is not an invading parasite directing the body, but an image of deities directing the body. I suggest that Abhinavagupta's theological inscription of deities driving human action adds an important element to the notion of bodies and matter. Abhinavagupta's theology offers a perspectival shift toward recognizing the body's own claims to intentionality, an intentionality that typically is only accorded to mind or spirit. In this sense, the panentheism out of which Abhinavagupta fashions his conception of the subtle body enfolds within it an upgrade for the idea of bodies, of matter. Theology here registers a respect for the affective processes of the body. Locating gods in the body tells us that the mind is not the master in the house; rather, sentiency, will, and desire arise throughout the body's functions, separate from the mind's desires. Moreover, this theology of the body proposes these multiple affective registers in a way that does not dwell (neither lamenting nor rejoicing) on the subsequent disappointment and loss of the sovereignty of the ego and its free will. So while a contemporary thinker like Brian Massumi strives to find a model to understand the complex, refractory affective flows of the body in a language of the virtual, Abhinavagupta instead reads this complexity of multiple affective flows through a lens of the forces of deities with their own conscious trajectories. In this respect, this panentheist theology affords a foundational liveliness to the multiplicity of agencies that make up the body. Here it is referenced in Abhinavagupta's map of the subtle body, which sees the body itself as an ecology of beings, materially embedded.[34]

Chapter Four opens with the conundrum of computer sentience: Stephen Hawking's and Elon Musk's deep fears of artificial intelligence. This chapter uses this framework to address a key element of Abhinavagupta's panentheism: how we attain sentience. This chapter first points to the differences we find between a currently popular panpsychism and Abhinavagupta's panentheism. Even as contemporary panpsychism is appealing precisely because it brushes aside dualistic conceptions of God, still we see in its formulation the influences of a Western legacy of transcendence. In this chapter I propose also that rather than look at the terms ubiquitously used to translate the notion of consciousness from Indian languages to English—terms like *cit, citi*, or *saṃvid*, which are typically employed to talk about consciousness—instead the term *vimarśa* more closely approximates what contemporary neuroscience understands as consciousness. I suggest that Abhinavagupta affords priority to *vimarśa* precisely because of its links to activity, a capacity to do things in our material reality. With this observation, drawing on Harald Atmanspacher's classificatory work, we look at how Abhinavagupta's dual-aspect monism stacks up in relation to other 20th-century Western conceptions of dual-aspect monisms. I conclude the chapter by returning to my initial query regarding computer sentience.

Chapter Five returns to Darwin's anguish and loss of faith over the parasitic wasp and discusses newer findings that suggest the idea of signaling and information-sharing across species. The parasitic wasp comes to lay its eggs inside the caterpillar because the plants being attacked by the caterpillars signal to the wasps via pheromones. Using this framework, I then take up the idea of information where information, as I have discussed elsewhere, takes on a dual nature, both as material substance and as something that conveys mental intentionality.[35] I draw comparisons with contemporary Western ideas of information, its links to New Materialism and to Abhinavagupta's panentheism as a way of thinking about consciousness as information. The idea of information, I suggest, is attractive for a current perspective because it seems to take away the subjective element of knowledge, giving us something we can measure and manipulate. Yet, if we examine it more closely, I propose that instead what makes information powerful as a concept for us today is that it embeds an unspoken bivalency, which links back to the intentionality and meaning of the subject who knows. The final section of this chapter ties this bivalency back to Abhinavagupta's articulation of subjectivity (*ahantā*) and its corollary, a state of being object (*idantā*). Through this background, I examine Abhinavagupta's account of how we get diversity, agonistic relations of wasps and caterpillars, in a nondualism, a system where there is only one consciousness. I suggest that interpreting the *tattva* system, the cosmology Abhinavagupta inherits, as a *phenomenology* of consciousness moving from subjectivity to object, Abhinavagupta demonstrates a panentheism that is capable of unfolding to embrace the rich diversity that makes up our world.

This book, then, is about this medieval philosopher's panentheism and what it might have to offer for our world today as we think through the complexity of our relationships to our world's myriad others, to both biologically living and nonliving matter. My hope is that it will afford us new ways of thinking about materiality that can help alleviate our current planetary predicament.

1

Abhinavagupta's Panentheism and New Materialism

> In evolutionary biology and cognitive science as in artificial intelligence, whatever the specifics of the disagreement, when you want to get out the big guns, you accuse the opponent of ascribing agency to nature's machinery.
>
> **—Jessica Riskin, *The Restless Clock***

> This, my hand is god; my hand is greater than god, for this touches the auspicious. It is a medicine for the world.
>
> (Ayam me has to bhagavānayaṃ me bhagavattaraḥ| ayaṃ me viśvabheśajo ^yagṃ śivābhimarśanaḥ)
>
> ***—Śrī Rudrapraśna***

> as if stones and metals had a desire, or could discern the place they would be at, as man does; or loved rest, as man does not
>
> **—Hobbes, *Leviathan*[1]**

Abhinavagupta's Panentheist Matter

If, in the 21st century, in the midst of the 2020 pandemic we still clung to the idea of human exceptionalism—that we humans can mold an inert planet to fulfill human goals, human desires—well, the scourge of the Covid-19 virus has put that fond dream to rest. We now live in the panic of a virus hiding everywhere. A tiny, indeed invisible collective, not even living by some biological standards, has managed to crush empires, stealthily, without malice.[2] Even in the same way, we humans as well, without any malice, have managed to engineer the fate of whole species, wipe out so many others as we enter now into the sixth great extinction. Our six-foot boundaries, like a failed border wall, remind us that our old world is gone. The slow recognition that we cannot maintain the old fictions of "us" and "them," that living organisms "possess

The Matter of Wonder. Loriliai Biernacki, Oxford University Press. © Oxford University Press 2023.
DOI: 10.1093/oso/9780197643075.003.0002

soft boundaries, *very* soft boundaries,"[3] is an ecological driver for the shifts pressing forward with a New Materialism. Birthed in our current crisis of ecology, a New Materialism calls for a shift in our relationship to other species, a deeper awareness and respect for the matter that makes up our world.

The sort of shifts called for are, however, new only against the backdrop of Western modernity. We find in fact a much earlier, sophisticated articulation of a vitally embodied materiality in the medieval panentheism of the Indian Tantric philosopher Abhinavagupta, who flourished in the last part of the 10th century through the early 11th century in Kashmir. Even if his sights of other species' agency extended not so far as to encompass the not-quite-alive, not-quite-visible virus, they reached at least down to the tiniest moving creature he did see. He tells us: "When those [beings] belonging to *Māyā*—even down to a worm, an insect—when they do their own deeds, that which is to be done first stirs in the heart."[4] That is, even the tiniest worm has an agency and a consciousness capable of choosing, a subjectivity rising in the heart. Remarkably not anthropocentric, ecologically, this medieval panentheism casts a wide net, so much so that even a worm or an insect has a will, its own desires stirring in the heart. Compare this, for instance, to Descartes' infamous beast-machine (*bête-machine*), where animals, far from having desires, are just dumb machines, incapable even of feeling pain.[5] I suspect the contrast speaks volumes about our own culture's implicit attitudes toward our planet's other inhabitants.

In particular, Abhinavagupta's panentheism takes the form of a cosmopsychism: a single nondualist reality unfolds out of itself the rich variety that makes up our world. Of course, already we can begin to glean a shift in our ideas of boundaries. Six feet, or a border wall? We living beings possess *very* soft boundaries. A single cosmopsychism unfolding to make us all means, on one level, that we are all connected. Yet, even while Abhinavagupta's panentheism tells us there is only one reality, a nondualism, still, this not a philosophy that says only what the mind imagines is real. Instead, the matter of the world is quite real. Thus, in a striking departure from more familiar nondualisms, which give us a world that is illusory, that is, a deceiving *Māyā*, Abhinavagupta pushes away the notion that the world might be merely an idealist fabrication. As we see later in this chapter, Abhinavagupta offers us a plurality of myriad others, all real. Rather, what makes up this one reality is pictured, curiously, in the image of a wall (*bhitta*); this wall (or perhaps like the screen of a movie),[6] really consciousness itself, unfolds the multiplicity of the world out of itself, not ever losing itself, while it takes the form of all sorts of things—humans, insects, rocks, and clay. This is a cosmopsychism that tells us that even for a "clay jar—its true nature is the essence of consciousness."[7] Certainly, we should keep in mind that this 11th-century thinker is dealing with different philosophical issues than those we deal with today, and in this respect, Abhinavagupta's emphasis on unity and transcendence is not to be underestimated. Nevertheless, I suggest we can find in his thought a keen attention to materiality that offers a rich and helpful relevance for our own current thinking about the nature of matter. Moreover, his insights on the materiality of our world can enrich a New Materialism, sorting through our contemporary complications with our currently deeply challenged material world.

Abhinavagupta brings a particular creative insight to the table—one that I think makes it especially helpful for a New Materialism. This creative insight is his account of subjectivity. Subjectivity, "I-ness" (*ahantā*) in Abhinavagupta's terminology, is the foundation for consciousness and sentience around which our catalogue of what there is pivots. This move, making the stance of subjectivity the foundation, rather than a substance like human bodies the foundation, or an essence, like a divine spark confined to humans the foundation—this entails that the sentience and consciousness that accompanies subjectivity becomes available even for clay jars, for leaves of grass. For Abhinavagupta, it is a matter of adopting a first-person perspective. In fact, much New Materialism is also about reimbuing matter with subjectivity, giving it its own voice.[8] Abhinavagupta's model offers a sophisticated articulation of how subjectivity can function in relation to materiality. In his model, the world as a cosmopsychism progressively unfolds from an inward and heightened subjectivity into the materiality that makes up the fabric of what we see here, preserving even in the densest matter a latent subjectivity, and with this, a lively capacity for agency. Being a subject, "I-ness," is always at the core. Indeed, every object retains its innate, if forgotten, subjectivity, as an outpouring of that subjectivity as we will see below. Thus, all things, from rocks to clay pots, to leaves of grass to humans, to beings higher than humans, to beings higher also than gods (who are, after all, only marginally better off than some humans, and less aware than some humans for this Indian cosmology): everything partakes of a mix of being a subject and being an object.

Our limbo reality, a mix, partly subject, partly object, in one respect mirrors that of the virus. The virus—is it alive? Or not? Indecidably sentient, the virus, maybe alive, maybe not, demonstrates even our fate as humans. Measured against the scale of subjectivity, we too, are partly alive, partly not, as we will explore below. I suggest, then, that Abhinavagupta can offer much to a New Materialism precisely because of his focus on an already embedded subjectivity, consciousness innate to matter. In particular, I offer that a New Materialism might profit from three elements in his thought. First, the idea that an attention to subjectivity is necessary for thinking through our relationship to matter. This first point will perhaps push against a current remnant ideology of atheist materialism, which leans as it does out of a habit of modernity toward the third-person perspective. A materialism is always a case of "it," the object, rather than an "I," a subject.[9] This perspective, I suspect, lingers still for a New Materialism as well. Yet, I suggest that a New Materialism can stand on a much firmer ontological ground by taking to heart Abhinavagupta's conception of subjectivity. A notion of subjectivity is key, as I have argued elsewhere, to prevent the panpsychist ground of a New Materialism to avoid devolving simply into the thin panpsychist veneer that John Searle criticizes.[10] In this way Abhinavagupta's intuition is radical for our 21st-century perspective: he suggests a materialism hinged upon the subjectivity of matter; materiality has a voice.

Second, Abhinavagupta's thought is not a discourse on things as entrenched ontological entities; entities are fluidly transposing between being a subject or an object. Both of these modes are always available to even the merest worm, even the clay jar. Abhinavagupta tells us, "Even the lifeless third-person, [the 'it'], if it sheds its lifeless form can take on the first and second-person forms [the grammatical I and you]."[11] Ultimately we can degrade the earth, its nonhuman inhabitants, its seeming nonconscious inhabitants precisely because we deny these the status of subjectivity. They remain "it," objects to be manipulated by humans, who place themselves as the only genuine subjects in a mechanistic modernity. Third, along with this, it points to Abhinavagupta's recognition that our own mental appraisals of the world play a role in the world's own capacities for subjectivity. That is, we ourselves participate in the liveliness of what we encounter in the world; a kind of practice of recognition enables not just our own selves, but the multiplicity of the world as well to express a lively subjectivity. My hope is that his unusual panentheism, its realist pluralism, its decentering of the human in his cosmology, moving away from an implicit anthropocentrism, its earnest insistence on the innate consciousness of matter all around us—that these might persuade New Materialists to give Abhinavagupta's panentheism a second look, despite the fact that it comes from a non-Western culture, from the 11th century.

In terms of a map for where we will go in this chapter, before getting to the heart of Abhinavagupta's model, in the next section we look at the idea of boundaries in our current viral predicament and its significance for a New Materialism. In sections three and four of this chapter, I address elements of a contemporary New Materialism that at least on the surface appear to be at odds with Abhinavagupta's thought. I begin here by discussing the idea of atheism and its links to a New Materialism. Keeping in sight here the genealogies of a New Materialism, particularly its invocations of a thinker like

Walt Whitman, we see why it might still make sense to offer comparisons with an Indian mystic, Abhinavagupta. Following this discussion, we look comparatively at the idea of anthropocentrism and how Abhinavagupta's model moves away from anthropocentrism by shifting terms away from the binary of human or nonhuman to a scale of subjectivity. That is, sentience is not so much based on species or the human as a benchmark, but rather on the degree of subjectivity. We also take a first look at the thorny issue of the Many, pluralism within a philosophy that says there is only one reality. How do we get the many within the one of a nondualism? After this discussion, in section five, we address the ticklish problem of animism. Here we move more deeply into Abhinavagupta's conception of subjectivity, and with this, we explore how Abhinavagupta manages to assert an innate sentience for objects and at the same time still propose a differentiation between things that are sentient and things that are not. In section six, we look at the grammatical structure of Abhinavagupta's thought and what it means for the idea that objects, things, might have agency. Following this discussion, in section seven we return to the problem of plurality, the One and the Many. In particular, by way of comparison with Spinoza, a figure often invoked for a New Materialism, Abhinavagupta's formulation of subjectivity gives voice to a more expansive articulation of immanence than we find even in as radical a thinker as Spinoza. Here we also look at the problem of telos. Abhinavagupta's model, as we also see, does not follow the model of object-oriented ontology of thinkers like William Harman and Timothy Morton, in that with Abhinavagupta's cosmopsychism, we are not barred from accessing the inside of objects. Rather, what prevents the utilitarian designs of a human hubris that Harman so thoughtfully advocates against is instead that objects themselves have access to subjectivity. In the final section, we address our mixed status as first-person, the "I" and third-person, "it," the object. With this discussion, we see that how we perceive objects, thinking in a rigid binary between sentient and nonsentient, makes a difference. How we think about matter matters for the material world around us. Here, we return to Whitman, whose own poetic style—an expansive and persistent first-person perspective coupled with an inclusive celebration of things—converges with Abhinavagupta's philosophical articulation of a first-person capacity to enliven objects.

The Virus

What then of the boundaries between us and this current deadly virus? As Rodney Dietart suggests, when it comes to viruses, we want a culprit, a foe to eradicate.[12] It seems that the panic of borders, of inside and outside, itself is part of our current consciousness, a viral consciousness bolstering a mentality of war. Livingston and Puar point this out in biological terms,

> The paradox of viral and microscopic entities is that an interdependent relationship is acknowledged only through the epistemological oversimplification of the virus as an "intruder," thus revealing viral "illness" to be an anthropomorphic qualification dependent on the understanding of the human body as a unified, bounded, political whole that must survive any threat to it.[13]

And oddly, not so unlike a simultaneous call to dissolve a legacy of political boundaries—as we create our 6-foot boundaries, our concurrent wave of protest calls us to break down old racial boundaries harming black lives,[14] all in the middle of a politics pinning its flag on a border wall.

Our multiple implications in other lives call for radically rethinking our boundaries, our obligations, how we call and recall the many others inhabiting this planet. The virus, yes, a foe. Still, these times call for us to recognize our ancient bonds to these, our microbial ancestors. As Lynn Margulis reminds us, shining a light on our particular anthropocentric amnesia: "our culture ignores the hard-won fact that these disease 'agents,' these 'germs,' also germinated all life."[15] And we still need them to survive. Stephen Buhner points out, "had bacteria not developed resistance to antibiotics, all life on this planet would have already become extinct simply from the millions of tons of antibiotics now present in the environment."[16]

Viral life is considered *not* alive because it relies on a host to reproduce. It needs another corpus to replicate its own life. Yet, if we think about this, how much of our own body is really us? Ninety percent of the DNA in the human body is foreign, not really human, but other, bacterial life.[17] Even the air we breathe is teeming with other life. Not a simple inert molecular oxygen, hydrogen, carbon, the very air we inhale is swarming with the DNA of other species, only typically 5% human; another 85% nonhuman bacterial DNA.[18] Indeed, Margulis's breakthrough insight revealed just this multispecies mutuality. The basis of life, the human cell with its mitochondria, was already a symbiotic interaction between species, a merger with an ancient bacteria—all while this current deadly COVID virus leaves us struggling to reassert the boundaries of life, mask barriers and six-foot spacing.

What is also remarkable is how these superbly intelligent, if not quite living, beings manage to so precisely manipulate the human body's own immune defenses. They use human molecular signaling, the cytokine cascade, usually designed to eliminate an "intruder" to instead create the cascade that allows the virus entry into human cells, allowing it to replicate in the human body.[19] How does a nonliving entity manage to pull off such an extensive redirection of the human immune system to serve its own reproduction? Does it have agency? Is it mere algorithm? And could an idea of virus agency extend to a kind of self-directed choice?

Allowing that a virus might be an agent—the sort of radical rethinking at the heart of a New Materialism—is no doubt tinged with an element of taboo. As Jessica Riskin reminds us, the history of Western science asserts "that agency cannot be a primitive, elemental feature of the natural world; that the idea of natural forms of agency has no place in legitimate science."[20] The tricky business of agency, as Riskin explains, threatens to upend an established neo-Darwinian model. Even as some biologists, like James Shapiro, can see no other reasonable explanation than a knowingness all the way down to the level of cells: "cell cognition" where even cells and organisms "are cognitive (sentient) entities that act and interact purposefully to ensure survival, growth and proliferation."[21] These are the fringes or maybe the beginnings of a paradigm shift—like Stuart Kauffman suggesting that bacteria act on their own behalf in seeking food. Most science understands the bacterium to simply be "the environment."[22] Kauffman, however, extends a kind of autonomous agency to all sorts of things such as bacteria, yeast cells, and paramecium.[23] These new pivotal shifts, a New Materialism rethinking how we understand matter, no doubt deriving from an urgency surrounding our shifting climate, are radical in part because as Riskin notes, "such an idea violates the classical mechanist ban on agency in nature."[24]

In this context, we might also recall the eerie agency of a heavy dull metal lingering in the air and soil, pervading dense urban landscapes like Los Angeles via gasoline: tetraethyl lead Pb(C2H5)4. Rick Nevin's brilliant statistical detective work demonstrated that as lead was phased out of gasoline beginning in the 1970s, the crime rate significantly declined.[25] The emotional life of humans, our anger, our capacities to think before hitting or shooting or stabbing are tied to molecular amounts of this dead inert lead.[26] Or we might consider Jane Bennett's discussion of the interactive agency of multiple players, the assemblage of electrons and trees, humans and wind and fire that coalesce in their actions to cause a massive power blackout.[27] Viruses, electrons, heavy metals,[28] all these seemingly inert objects, exhibit agencies outside our human control. We think we control, manipulate, and study them, yet like the "natives" that early anthropologists studied, these objects have their own goals. We too are locked into their varied trajectories; their actions outstrip human telos. They give the lie to the notion that we humans are this earth's sole agents and ends. Might we relate to them differently?

Perhaps Marie Kondo's KonMari method for "waking up" that book or vase or old piece of jewelry by tapping it is not just the kitsch of a new-age animism, a 21st-century Japanese "god of tidying."[29] Perhaps instead it appeals in part because it touches in us a kind of forgotten, taboo expression of the life of things.

Diana Coole and Samantha Frost in their seminal, landmark volume on New Materialism propose three components to the theoretical interventions a New Materialism brings to how we might rethink about what matter is: first, there is the idea that matter itself is lively; it exhibits agency. Second, Coole and Frost consider the bioethical issues regarding the status of life and the human. Third, they point to the geopolitical and socioeconomic implications of New Materialist thought, these three components emphasizing the "productivity and resilience of matter," in contradistinction to recent constructivist positions.[30] This study of Abhinavagupta's panentheism focuses particularly on this first intervention, the idea that matter exhibits agency, is lively, but also on the second intervention, toward the ways that Abhinavagupta's conception of matter reconfigures the status of life and the human in unexpected ways for us, for instance, extending to a notion of subtle matter, subtle bodies, and his assertion of a latent subjectivity even in inert things. I leave aside their third concern of New Materialist thought, which, while keenly important for a current politics, will distract from understanding this medieval Indian philosopher's thought and how it might enrich a New Materialism.

Atheisms, Pan(en)theisms

New Materialist thought represents a new theoretical venture, with varied articulations, centered primarily around rethinking the matter that makes up our world. As Jane Bennett points out, "The machine model of nature, with its figure of inert matter, is no longer even scientific. . . . Yet the popular image of materialism as mechanistic endures."[31] The image of mechanism, I suspect, is also driven by a need to displace religious sentiment, a legacy birthed in the early transitions into a scientific worldview.[32] A New Materialist thought seems mostly to honor this legacy, wearing on its sleeve its alignments with the atheological commitments of scientific modernity. Indeed, the adoption of the nomenclature "materialism" signals just such a nontheistic perspective. So, Samantha Frost lays the groundwork for understanding Hobbes's thought as New Materialist,[33] while contextually, as Shapin and Schaeffer note, Hobbes's embrace of a mechanistic scientific worldview signals an early atheism, understanding matter as inert, as so much clay ready to be fashioned by the hands of human ingenuity—an attitude toward matter that is still pervasive throughout our current technological approach.[34]

The newness that a New Materialism brings, then, lies in its inflections of materiality, recovering in it an innate vitality even while still couched in an atheistic register. Contemporary thinkers associated with New Materialisms, like Jane Bennett, William Connelly, and Karen Barad, thus call into question an uncomplicated, simply mechanistic understanding of matter, gesturing in place of older models of materialism toward an immanent vitality in matter, toward a panpsychist cosmology.[35] Apart from these New Materialisms, panpsychism is itself rapidly becoming a popular and viable alternative to older mechanist models of matter, in part because of its promise for solving the philosophical problem of the mind–body gap.[36] In any case, though, the gestures of a New Materialism toward panpsychism enable us to reclaim a vitality and dignity for matter, while avoiding slipping into premodern conceptions of vital matter, that spirits might inhabit matter, the slippery taboo of animism. These allow for a fundamental atheism, all the while reclaiming a kind of vitality, even dignity, for the world of matter.

Yet, if we scratch beneath the surface of an explicit atheism, curiously, the formulations of a number of New Materialist thinkers, Bennett for instance, pattern after outlier traditions of non-Western religiosity,[37] investing heavily in an understanding of the natural world and matter as vital, able to act agentially. Matter in myriad forms can even communicate with us humans, even if only on some visceral, gut level. Bennett offers us this image of matter speaking to us, pointing to the numinosity of objects, of things, like abandoned trash, a discarded bottle cap, an old glove on the street in an almost mystical exchange, in her encounter with the odd liveliness of this marginalized matter.[38] The similarities to the mysticism of Indian traditions are conspicuous. That is, it is hard not to see a resonance with the numinosity of the stones placed around a village banyan tree,[39] alive, encountered by chance, and calling to us with a barely perceptible, indefinable numinosity. But the similarity is not simply that both encounters offer an experience of a numinosity detected in seemingly lifeless matter. Nor is it just that both rely on a philosophical congruence of what matter is: namely, the idea that matter itself cannot be separated from an idea of agency, even intelligence, intentionality.[40] There is here in addition a genealogy, a historical legacy informing this new tradition; Bennett's work, for instance, traces back through Emerson, Thoreau, and Whitman to Indian thought. Emerson, Thoreau, and Whitman were all deeply influenced by Indian mystical nondualist traditions, evidenced particularly in Emerson and Thoreau's encounters with early translations of the *Bhagavad Gītā*, and the influence of a nontheistic Advaita Vedānta on these

American Transcendentalists.[41] This historical influence works in soft ways as well, with generalized ideas that are naturalized, habitual elements of an Indian worldview, a Indian felt geist seeping into the attitudes of these 19th-century forward-thinking Americans. Whitman's earthy poetry replaces personal theism with a paean to the divine in all of life, naming the divinity of even the smallest blade of grass, "heap'd stones" and "brown ants" in *Song of Myself*.[42] Is it surprising from our 21st-century vantage to see a similar paean to divinity in the materiality of life in the Vedic *Śrī Rudrapraśna*, *Namakam*, the poet here seeing the divine everywhere as thousands of Rudras,[43] discovered in the trees, multicolored, blue-throated, and red and yellow, like young-grass,[44] found in food, in leaves, in what people drink,[45] that divinity discovered as the ruler of robbers, of those who have quivers with arrows, and those who do not, of those who steal with ordinary deception and those who use great deception to steal,[46] of those with lots of shaggy hair and those whose heads are shaved,[47] in vegetation that is dried up and that which is green,[48] in wells and holes in the earth, where there is rain and where there is not rain.[49] Stylistically, these paeans present affinities, a shared practice of naming extensively the variety of life in its beauty and its seamy sides. Certainly, Whitman never had access to this Vedic text. Still we see an analogous ideological orientation, taking in all experience as divine expression. While familiar for Indian traditions, arising in its early Vedic beginnings, Whitman's earthy panpsychist transcendence of theism[50] was news for its 19th-century context. What do we make of these affinities? For our purposes here particularly, we notice that India's nondualist, panpsychist, and in Abhinavagupta's case, panentheist orientations tend toward blurring theism. They blur it to an extent that it no longer looks at all like a familiar Western theism. These orientations blur their theisms so effectively that they play well with the atheisms of a New Materialism. Indeed one can find this phenomenon more widely operative in our current scientifically influenced culture, as Jeffrey Kripal has brilliantly tracked.[51] And the reason they play so well together? Even while these nondualist Indian doctrines vary in how they understand the ontology and status of matter, depending on the specific tradition, still these nondualist approximations of matter tend to offer models that are not so intrinsically embedded—that is, not quite so stuck in 20th-century materialism's Western theistic legacy: the binary of spirit and inert body.[52]

What we might take away from Abhinavagupta's panentheism, as we see below, is that we are secret sharers in a recursive, inward-directed awareness that manifests viscerally as a vitality, a quality of liveliness that occasionally jumps out of those things that we normally peg as the dead inertness of matter. Abhinavagupta's panentheism suggests that we recognize a vitality in *posse*, always entangled with the matter of our daily life. How and why should we get past our time-honored views on matter as simply dead, inert stuff? A figure like the 20th-century Indian philosopher Daya Krishna in part addresses the why of getting beyond our ingrained commonsensical approach, as he articulates the paradox of materialism that sees matter as dead:

> [T]he "real" reality for those who want to deny consciousness as a paradigmatic example of "reality", for them is "matter" which, of course, is neither "living" nor "conscious", nor anything else except that which is described or designated by the term "materiality" which itself is understood as that which is essentially "non-conscious" and nonliving. Matter, thus, is understood in terms of a negation, and yet it is not only supposed to be the most certain and self-evident thing that everyone believes in, but, paradoxically, that in whose "denial" it has its own "being", is felt by all not only to be ultimately "unreal", but also as demanding their own understanding in its terms.[53]

The irony, then, of matter for materialism is that we can only understand it in terms of negation. Yet this negative existence is the most certain reality, the most "self-evident thing," that which we all believe in, clinging to its inert negativity to explain ourselves.

Anthropocentrisms, Pluralisms

Apart from New Materialism's shifts away from dualist theologies, they share also with Abhinavagupta's panentheism and Indian traditions generally an attitude that works against human exceptionalism. Understood as a kind of posthumanist stance,[54] much New Materialist thought rejects an idea of special human privilege among so many other species on the planet. A mostly unconscious legacy of modernity, this notion situates humans as the only rational, self-aware, free agents, and with it, sanctioning a practical human domination of all else we find on earth[55]—as our current climate crisis attests, to the detriment of the planet as a whole. Perhaps not surprisingly, New Materialisms thus find affinity with the animisms of indigenous traditions.[56] Indian cosmologies more generally share this extension of agency beyond the merely human, and indeed take it in an unexpected direction, according agency and intention not just to others species, monkeys and crows and insects, but to a plethora of other beings, including beings with subtle bodies, beings thought to be higher than humans[57]: deities whose bodies take the form of *mantras*, and beings like the *yakṣa*, a spirit tied to trees, and the *vidyādhara*, beings with bodies that appear at times anthropomorphic enough to fool humans, but with other sorts of nonhuman skills, like the capacity for flight.[58] We address this foray into the body as subtle body later in Chapter Three. In any case, Abhinavagupta inherits a legacy of other sorts of intelligent beings beyond just the human from his Indian tradition; there exist beings considered more intelligent, more advanced than humans as well as beings, some animals, for instance, understood to be less intelligent.[59] Right away we notice that this is not quite in line with the kind of democratic equalizing associated with a New Materialism. Distributed agency, electrons, viruses, wind, lead, all agents, all on a level playing field: this especially signals a rejection of anthropocentric bias.[60] However, the sort of hierarchy that places humans not at the top, but somewhere in the middle offers an advantage in that it exposes a latent, still present, but hidden privileging of the human deeply embedded in modernity. This is what a notion of subtle bodies and subtle beings higher than humans undoes. The inchoate recognition that electrons and viruses have agency and power is novel and surprising precisely because it is set against a modernist assumption that only humans have agency; with this one can detect in it still an unarticulated presumption that humans have the *most* agency and intelligence.[61]

Abhinavagupta's perspective, deriving from his foundational nondualism moves away from the human altogether, formulating a schema of hierarchy based on levels of subjectivity, regardless of species. This is mapped as part of Abhinavagupta's exposition of the *tattva* system, a cosmological ontology of what exists. We will look at this schematic, the *tattva* system, in Chapter Five. For our present purposes, making the degree of subjectivity the basis of ontological hierarchy rather than the physical species—or the human species as benchmark, for that matter—not only works in alignment with his deeply embraced nondualism, it also offers a subjectivity that displaces the idea of the human. In this sense, it might compare to Viveiros de Castro's notion of an indigenous metaphysics where jaguars and humans are equally persons.[62] But only partially. What might an ontology of subjectivity rather than human species look like? David Lawrence points to Abhinavagupta comparing the manifestation of a potter creating a pot to the reflection in a mirror of a potter creating a pot. What or who can claim agency? Does the potter create the pot? Is it the clay or the person molding the clay? Abhinavagupta remarks that both the potter and the pot exhibit agency; both really can create, yet both only create via a single source of agency that they share: consciousness as subjectivity. Thus, agency itself is tied to consciousness in Abhinavagupta's nondualism; in the process, pots themselves take on agency equally as do potters.[63]

Abhinavagupta's nondualism subscribes to a conception of consciousness as all-pervasive, a quality his panentheism shares with some contemporary panpsychisms. But, we pause, a clay pot, really? Is this to suggest the pot stands on an equal footing with a human potter, both or neither with a genuine agency? Abhinavagupta's great grand guru Somānanda signals this sort of dynamic pantheist panpsychism when he declares, "I see by the self of the clay pot and the clay pot sees by the self of me."[64] Somānanda's pantheism spreads a wide democratic agency, with clay pots and humans interactively generating a multiplicity of agency.[65] This comes at a cost. As John Nemec points out, Somānanda's pantheism ultimately depends on a pervasive primordial nondualist deity, Śiva, which is at base bereft of physical form, a completely disembodied form of being.[66] Thus, Somānanda's clay pot and human are equally displaced by a pervasive reality of a nonbodied, nonmaterial deity. We have a democracy of agency here, but we lose the materiality of this agency.[67] Somānanda's disciple, Utpaladeva, and later Abhinavagupta trade in Somānanda's pantheist panpsychism for a modified panentheist nonduality, which allows for a real and actual existence of a multiplicity of individual entities,[68] coming closer to the promises of a New Materialist distribution of agency.

Still, I suggest that this issue of an ontological plurality is where Abhinavagupta's panentheism is most at odds with a New Materialism. Coole and Frost emphasize plurality as a key component of New Materialisms, with "emphasis on materialization as a complex, pluralistic, relatively open process."[69] Yet, Abhinavagupta's panentheism is rather more like the pantheisms that Mary Jane Rubenstein thoughtfully explores, where pluralism inevitably entails different perspectives that might reduce pluralism to the One, in a debate that is not ever quite decidable.[70] Abhinavagupta's panentheism similarly shifts back and forth between the One and the many. It is like the eye of a crow, to borrow a metaphor that Abhinavagupta uses to describe the idea of the person (*puruṣa*). The folklore of crows is that they have a single eyeball that moves from one socket to the other, depending on what perspective they take, right or left. Thus, the person (*puruṣa*) is also like this, connected to the unity of undiluted, singular consciousness, the One, when the eyeball is one socket and associated with the plurality of the world, governed by Nature, Māyā, when in the other, moving back and forth from unity to plurality.[71] Ultimately though, Abhinavagupta embraces a nondualism that, as we saw above, resolves into a cosmopsychism. Really, there is just one conscious reality, that is, Śiva and as Abhinavagupta tells us, that generates the whole myriad complexity of beings out of its own self:

> The category called *Śiva* is itself the body of all things. On the wall [of the world which is itself *Śiva*] the picture of all beings appear, shining forth—This statement indicates the way that all these come to appear. And the purport of the entire corpus of scriptures means to indicate that the category *Śiva* itself is all this.[72]

The world is like a picture painted on a wall; the substratum, the canvas as wall, is what generates the whole picture. Not so much a person, but a category (*tattva*),[73] this *Śiva* generates out of itself, on itself, all the world's fantastic diversity. It is important not to understate the legacy of transcendence Abhinavagupta inherits and embraces. However, in this book I will focus especially on the materialist side of Abhinavagupta's thought—rather than the wall, and instead on the fantastic diversity of the picture, which has mostly been neglected in much excellent work on this thinker.[74]

One of the first scholars to study Abhinavagupta's work, K. C. Pandey, pointed out how Abhinavagupta's philosophy tends to defy our expectations of ontology; we tend to limit our choices to nondualism as idealism on the one hand, or else an actually existing world with a plurality of really existing different entities. Abhinavagupta subverted this false choice in a kind of have-your-cake and eat-it-too alternative, what Pandey in a seemingly oxymoronic gesture labels a "Realist Idealism."[75] As I argue later, in Chapter Four, what is so novel about Abhinavagupta's panentheism is that reincorporating materiality, matter, in his vision is precisely what makes possible a nondualism that can bridge the gap between materiality and consciousness. This is Abhinavagupta's method for solving the mind–body problem. His nondualism does not discard the gritty materiality of the world[76] because from top to bottom (*ota-prota*), as Abhinavagupta sings in a panpsychist poetic verse opening the *Āgamādhikāra* section of his monumental treatise on Recognition (*Pratyabhijñā*), the world itself "is from top to bottom, shot through with Śiva's own sap, made to consist of Śiva."[77] Instead he argues that if we want to know the highest transcendent state, we need to know the world around us, all the objects that exist,

> only to the extent that one makes the world into an object, to the extent that it is known, can one then transcend the level of object, of thing to be known and allow the true sense of subjectivity to take root in the heart, its fullness being grasped by the inner organ [mind, intellect and ego] as beyond the status of objects.[78]

Even if the final aim is to rest in subjectivity, beyond the objects of the world, still one gets there by first seeing the objects in the world. Abhinavagupta's nondualism proposes a subjectivity as the foundation, with the map of the world not based on species but instead on a fluid status of subject and object, which as we will see below, finds at base everywhere subjectivity. This whole world of things as objects is generated out of a stance of subjectivity, which then reaches a fullness by extending beyond a practice of seeing things as objects. Thus, the ontological status of things entails that everything—humans, clay pots, insects, all—operate in two ways, as subjects and as objects. Subjectivity is what allows us to be secret sharers in the experience of all else that is. This is the knower taking root in the heart. On the other hand, the world exists as objects we apprehend. So this is a nonduality that both keeps the world and transcends it as well. That is: a panentheism, even as the theism blurs toward a panpsychism, or more accurately, as a cosmopsychism. In any case, as Pandey notes with his label of Realist Idealism, Abhinavagupta instead insists throughout on the reality of a multiplicity in the world, and these many things are real. Moreover, as we see in greater detail below, they share with us an innate subjectivity,

Animisms

There may be psychological obstacles to allowing ourselves to respect the innate rights, the subjectivity of all those other "things"—animals, rocks, viruses—on this planet. Might a practice of acknowledging a subjectivity for other beings and things on this planet in fact work against us? Would it leave us trapped within a scary world—filled with things that should be just things . . . instead coming alive, like the horror movie *Chucky*, a plastic doll running amok, hell-bent on axe-murdering us? Animism with its links to pantheism has a history for us, as Mary Jane Rubenstein masterfully chronicles, leaving in its wake a historical "tangle of relentless demonization and name-calling."[79] The name-calling includes a derisive imagery connecting pantheism's animism to worms, that "lowest" of animals,[80]—which of course, brings to mind the contrast in Abhinavagupta's thoughtful inclusion of even worms in the camp of a subjectivity that counts, as we saw, "even down to a worm—when they do their own deeds, that which is to be done first stirs in the heart."[81] Rubenstein also gives us the philosopher Giordano Bruno (1548–1600), whose table and clogs and boots and clothes are alive; all have a spiritual substance within them: "all things 'even if they are not living creatures, are animate'. Nothing is inert, dead, mere (or for that matter, exploitable) matter."[82] This medieval European animacy with a spiritual infusion is not so distant from Abhinavagupta's conception of a subjectivity infusing jars and potters alike, with the difference, I suspect, that Abhinavagupta's overarching frame of subjectivity allows for greater attention to the materiality of individual things, where things are not simply just the expression of an animating spirit. We will come back to this idea of subjectivity in the next chapter.

In any case, Bruno's "everything is in everything" and Nicholas of Cusa's proclamations of "all things in all things"[83] are not so unlike the pervasive Tantric dictum that everything indeed has the nature of everything else,[84] so useful in Tantric ritual praxis.[85] As Abhinavagupta's great-grand guru Somānanda phrases it, "All entities, being aware of their own nature, exist as all others. . . . All entities consist of everything, since everything is of the nature of everything. Everything exists here as everything by having the nature and form of [all] the various entities. The pot has my nature, and I have that of the pot."[86] As Nemec observes, the point of Somānanda's asseveration is to make it clear that no difference exists between a sentient human or a clay jar[87] (or for that matter, a virus, or molecules of lead). Catherine Keller offers a modern iteration of this maxim with a quantum twist from Alfred North Whitehead: "in a certain sense everything is everywhere at all times. For every location involves an aspect of itself in every other location."[88] Where it seems at times a New Materialism treads softly, hesitantly into the sticky swamp of animism,[89] Keller's capacious Cusan holography, panentheistically inflected, is less timid in its embrace of an animism. Offering the perspective of the remarkable 17th-century English philosopher Anne Conway, Keller notes, "the boundary between animate and inanimate dissolves."[90]

Similarly, with Abhinavagupta's great-grand-guru Somānanda, "insentience simply does not exist."[91] As Nemec points out, Somānanda draws on an earlier pervasive Tantric perspective, found in an iconic, likely 7th–8th century CE Tantric text, the *Vijñāna Bhairava*. Systematizing animism as a contemplative praxis (*dharaṇa*), this text tells us, "knowledge, desire and so forth appear every where in pots and other objects."[92] Even a mere clay pot has its own desires. With this pervasive aliveness of things, objects also retain an innate sense of delight, linked to a never really lost sense of consciousness. As Somānanda tells us, "the threefold power does not cease in the moment anything is created, nor does eagerness cease to exist, nor does delight."[93] In his commentary on Somānanda's text, Utpaladeva adds:

> will, cognition, and action truly exist in the moment pots, etc., are produced. The same is true for eagerness, which is the first part of will in the form of a particular delight that is limited by an object; nor does the other delight, in the form of unlimited bliss, cease to exist.[94]

The delight and intentionality, will (*icchā*) and eagerness (*aunmukhya*), that give rise to objects does not go away once the clay jar is produced. It stays with the object, the clay jar, as its own sort of delightful thingness. Here we might say that the "the thing-power" that Bill Brown finds in an object,[95] that numinosity that catches Bennett's glance—these arise out of the consciousness the jar retains, its own innate delight. The term that Somānanda uses for this eagerness, *aunmukhya*, might hint toward a helpful vocabulary for a New Materialism.[96] It offers a way of naming something that our contemporary culture has trouble grasping because we lack a vocabulary to explain a phenomenology we nevertheless experience (Brown and Bennett, I suspect, at least). The term *aunmukhya*, I suggest, points to a phenomenology, what we can see as an object's vitality—a clay jar's liveliness. The object exhibits a minute, yet still sensible, delight that takes on a focused, particularized expression in that specific object. Thus, for these Tantric thinkers a universal delight characterizes consciousness. This consciousness never really leaves even an object, and with a certain attention we can pick up on the object's specific form of consciousness as its innate eagerness (*aunmukhya*), its delight-power.

More circumspect than his predecessor Somānanda's pantheism, Abhinavagupta's panentheism traces this power of things to its source, the innate consciousness that even a mere object has, a deeply retained sense of subjectivity. He tells us,

> And in precisely this way, even while accepting the state of being mere object, by properly, in a true way touching and perceiving the object's "This-ness" in the highest sense, then out of the objects, those "things" perceived, consciousness alone flows forth. The "thing" in its essential nature is the expanse of Light (*prakāśa*). And this expanse of Light consists of an active awareness, the "I" which is not looking towards something other.[97]

Abhinavagupta adds the precision of a dual-aspect formulation to the nondualist, animist model he takes from his predecessor Somānanda, where the "thing," the object, is essentially the expanse of light (*prakāśa*).[98] We will look at this dual-aspect formulation in greater detail in Chapter Four. Here, in a nutshell, this light, the light of consciousness, congeals to make objects in the world. This is one aspect of his dual-aspect monism. At the heart of this expanse of light—out of which things come to be—at the heart there lies a subjectivity; this is the second aspect of his dual-aspect monism. This is the "I," an active awareness (*vimarśa*), which is what gives even a clay jar its life, its sentience.

In this model, to be a thing, an insentient object means to be linked with what we might call an excess of third-person perspective, "this-ness" (*idantā*), in contrast to an innate subjectivity, "I-ness" (*ahantā*), the first-person perspective. It is the first-person perspective (*ahantā*), in its nature intrinsically connected to active awareness (*vimarśa*), which is the source of life, of sentience. In Abhinavagupta's system, however, "this-ness" and "I-ness" are not two indelibly separate categories. Rather, the one is embedded within the other. Subjectivity, "I-ness" (*ahantā*) as a property of (*vimarśa*) lies at the core of the "this-ness" (*idantā*) that makes up the objects in the world.[99] Abhinavagupta explains this dual-aspect monism in terms of a process of creation, which nevertheless does not ever lose its inner consciousness, its true essence as really just the divine: "pure consciousness lying in the core exists as a state containing both inner and outer. As *Māyā*'s creation spreads out, expands into many branches, the Lord remains still within the core."[100] *Māyā*, the innate power this cosmopsychism-Śiva uses to generate multiplicity, the great variety that makes up the world, has a positive valence in this Tantric system. So as *Māyā*'s creation spreads out, we get the complex variety of our world, while still all the while, even in seeming dead matter, clay jars, a pure awareness, consciousness remains at the core. Similarly, he tells us, "that clay jar—its true nature is the essence of consciousness when it is in a state without mental differentiation; it is complete, like consciousness itself, the body of the whole world."[101]

In this way, Abhinavagupta uses this dual-aspect monism to addresses the paradox of just how it is that an insentient object, a clay jar, can really still be *both* sentient and at the same time look insentient, like inert, dead matter. So he tells us:

> from the perspective of the manifestation of non-duality, [consciousness] continues without ever coming to an end, even in a corpse, in the body, in a jar and so on. So far as the sphere of non-duality goes, this worldly distinction between sentient and insentient is not made.[102]

As with Anne Conway, and fundamentally, for Abhinavagupta as well, the border between animate and inanimate dissolves. Even so, he wants to explain why it appears to us that there is in fact a difference between what is sentient and what looks like dead matter. His explanation hinges on an idea familiar to postmodern thought, the notion that our own personal subjectivities are always already entangled with the objects we believe we perceive "out there." From his perspective, this is precisely what characterizes consciousness when it slips below a particular threshold of awareness to the level where we forget our inherent expansive nondual awareness, what I translate below as the "limited Subject" (*grahaka*). He tells us:

> As far as it goes, that which is "conscious"[103] contains both perceiver and object and doesn't have this distinction made between itself and the other, the object perceived. Yet that which is conscious gives rise to both of these, limited Subject and object. And even while consciousness exists in that way, as undifferentiated—at the same time, out of its own Self, that is out of its own form, which shines as only pure consciousness alone—it gives birth to things that, like blue, etc., are said to be insentient, that lack consciousness. So it does not abandon its own form shining as pure consciousness alone. How so? Because there is an inability there [in things like blue, etc.] to encompass the variety of levels of awareness needed to differentiate among different categories. And there the reason is given—because of "This-ness" and so on. [I.e., in "This-ness" there is not the activity of consciousness being aware, which is what constitutes sentiency.][104]

That which is conscious contains both the subject and the object and gives rise to both. In Abhinavagupta's model here, an initially undifferentiated consciousness gives birth both to a person with a limited perspective, the "limited Subject," as well as to things like a blue jar, which appears to be insentient. As Abhinavagupta explains, things seem to be insentient precisely because of the shift to a third-person perspective, "this-ness" (*idantā*). Moreover, someone with a limited, dualist perspective, the limited Subject, does not quite recognize that their own limited perspective is what blinds them to the actual presence of consciousness even within something that looks like dead matter, a blue jar. Even so, the shift to a third-person "this-ness" does not really erase an essential life embedded at the core. It simply hides it from view. So, even when an object, like a clay jar, appears to us as mere matter, still its deep subjectivity has not been banished. Its consciousness is simply inwardly withdrawn, unavailable because it is inwardly focused, on a level associated with the category (*tattva*) of *Sadāśiva*, associated with a transcendent form of deity.[105] So we see, "even the objects, which are inherently things to be known and [not knowers], and which partake of a lack of Consciousness, these are also only [*Śiva*'s] Energy which is in the form of *Sadāśiva*."[106] This state of *Sadāśiva*, reflects the idea that its awareness is inwardly focused; the objects in the world that we perceive to be insentient are actually purely alive consciousness, but in a state where consciousness is inwardly withdrawn, transcendent, and thus not externally manifest.[107] If someone, Bill Brown or Jane Bennett, somehow manages to loosen the habitual bind of seeing the world through concept-tinted glasses (or perhaps bifocals) of a limited subject and inert object binary, then the object no longer appears as mere inert matter. One can then see consciousness shining in a clay pot, in pieces of trash on the street. Thus, Abhinavagupta's dual-aspect monism, with the categories of light (*prakāśa*) and active awareness (*vimarśa*) might be pictured in the shape of a Russian doll, as Abhinavagupta tells us, "that which is insentient rests in the sentient; the sentient rests in light of consciousness, (*prakāśa*) and this rests in active awareness (*vimarśa*)."[108]

Still, even if Abhinavagupta does retain a sense of subjectivity latent within things, even for mere inert objects, he is not quite so pantheist as his predecessor Somānanda. Avoiding the fairly common phrase that catalogues all of creation as life from the infinite Brahmā down to a blade of grass (*brahmādist ambaparyantaḥ*),[109] he offers instead a demarcation that stops at insects: "the Infinite, from *Brahmā* down to an insect, which in the three worlds is the multitude of perceivers,"[110] he tells us, moving away from Somānanda's exuberant assertion of subjectivity for even the humble clay pot. That is, he does not entirely erase the distinction between sentient and insentient. Similarly, elsewhere when he glosses a verse from Utpaladeva which posits the capacity to know and create in all living things, Abhinavagupta rather precisely notes this as extending from the creator god Brahmā only down to insects, but not to living things like plants and grass, nor the clay pot that Somānanda tells us "sees" equally as he, Somānanda, a human, sees.[111] Thus, Russian dolls aside, the dual-aspect formulation Abhinavagupta uses puts inert objects on the side of *prakāśa*, the expanse of light, caught up in a third-person existence of "This-ness." Their subjectivity remains hidden from our limited gaze. We will revisit this dual-aspect monism in greater detail in Chapter Four. For now, objects belong to *prakāśa*, light that shines; as Abhinavagupta notes, "the process whereby "This-ness" becomes distinct is shown to belong to the former [*prakāśa*, light shining], where the material thing becomes distinct."[112] In contrast, sentience is linked with "I-ness," that is, subjectivity, and *vimarśa*, an active grasping awareness.

The Grammar of Objects

What might we take away from this? Namely, the idea that being alive with its signature of subjectivity is connected not so much to an essence that a person or thing might have, but instead to the degree to which a thing or a person assumes a grammatical position, the first-person perspective or the third-person perspective. Because, as we saw earlier, "everything is the nature of everything," there is no fixed essence of things, where only some things—humans—can claim sentience, while other things, like clay jars, are always insentient. It depends on the thing. And on our relation to it. More palpably, imagine the glow of a stone Ganesha covered in orange sindhur paste that appears to pour out some special effervescence, drawing the temple devotee to consider the place and statue, the *mūrti*, as holy,[113] or devout Catholics taking the water from Lourdes, deeming the water to have special, magical healing properties, blessed and further charged as they pray to the statue of the Virgin. We typically assume that a believer who reports seeing life and consciousness in the statue of the Blessed Virgin or Krishna is simply making it up. It is solely a projection of human imagination. The devout Catholic wants to believe the water will heal, and consequently the placebo effect kicks in. We read it as projection; the devout practitioner projects her own desires for healing and reads into what subsequently happens as the intercession of miracles.

Abhinavagupta's panentheist grammatology rewrites this simple binary, where we interpret this as either animism or else we write our pilgrim off as deluded. Nodding toward his predecessor Somānanda, Abhinavagupta offers a grammatical expansion on Somānanda's formulation:

> "Everything in fact has the nature of all things." Even the lifeless [grammatical] third person, [the "it"], if it sheds its lifeless form can take on the first and second person forms [the grammatical I and you]. For example, "listen, o stones" and "Of mountains, I am Meru."[114]

In this case, "of mountains, I am Meru" refers to the *Bhagavad Gītā* where Kṛṣṇa panentheistically contains the whole of creation as his own self. For Abhinavagupta, this signals that our own embrace of the materiality of things allows the thing's deeper subjectivity to come to the fore. All of us, people and things, share a capacity for subjectivity. Thus, yes, we participate in the life of the statue, but not as a simple anthropocentric human projection onto mere matter. When we address even a stone as "you" instead of "it," or when we imagine the subjectivity of a mountain, we participate in its own vital subjectivity by seeing its deeper essence, its potentiality for liveliness. We allow space for the agency of the lifeless stone to shed its seeming insentience (*jaḍa*). In this way we participate in the recognition of the life of things. We might read Catherine Keller's invocation of Nicholas of Cusa in similar terms. Keller offers us Nicholas of Cusa saying, "you speak to the earth and you call it into human nature. The earth hears you and its hearing this is its becoming human being."[115] We might also read Jane Bennett's experience likewise in Abhinavagupta's terms, as not just sensing the life of things, but also allowing things to step into their genuine selves by her seeing them.[116] Thus, when Bennett describes the uncanny vitality she senses on a particularly numinous morning, when a discarded bottle cap and an old glove she sees take on a life that seems out of proportion to how we think of bits of random debris on a city street, she participates in allowing these things to find their own innate vitality. In Abhinavagupta's model, this is not a species of animist projection but a genuine seeing of the thing. By seeing it, she amplifies and allows the "vitality intrinsic to matter"[117] to emerge. Bennett also gestures toward recognizing subjectivity as the intrinsic factor, even if she does not focus on it. Quoting W.J.T. Mitchell, she offers a typology that distinguishes objects from things: "objects are the way things appear to a subject—that is, with a name, an identity.... Things on the other hand ... [signal] the moment ... when the mute idol speaks.[118] So, things become alive because we allow our own attention to recognize their life, to share in their innate, if hidden, subjectivity, to recognize the mountain as "you" and as "I." What we might also recognize about our way of thinking—our understanding that the religious devotee projects an imaginary life into the statue of the Blessed Virgin—this way of thinking embeds a kind of top-down configuration of consciousness that entails, even definitionally, that consciousness is separate from matter, which Abhinavagupta's system undoes.

Abhinavagupta absorbs this grammatical lens from the wider Sanskritic grammatical tradition, mediated particularly through the 5th-century grammarian Bhartṛhari. Describing the grammatical tradition's formulation of agency, George Cardona points out that the early 4th-century BCE grammarian Pāṇinī derived his rules primarily in a syntactic manner, based on grammatical considerations and not on extralinguistic semantic assumptions. An agent is anything that functions independently with respect to an action, and agency is always relationally configured and not determined by subjectivity or by animation.[119] Thus, an agent is the locus of the activity denoted by a verbal root; the object is the locus of the result of that activity.[120] In the process, there are of course, multiple agents, as Cardona indicates, a primary agent and also subsidiary agents. For instance, in cooking rice, even if the person, Devadatta, who puts the pot with grains on the fire is the primary agent, we wind up with all sorts of agents, including pots and fire, and here the pot is an independent agent in the process that produces food.[121] One is reminded here of Latour's suggestion that agency always arises out of a collective; actants, living or not, break down our predjudices about subjects and objects.[122] Although agency is not determined by subjectivity or animation for Pāṇinī, Cardona, however, points out that the commentator Kātyāyana gives as a possible solution for the use of the desiderative grammatical form the idea that all things are treated as intelligent animate beings, whether humans or clay jars.[123] The question then arises: is it just a case of expression, or do objects really function as agents? Cardona outlines Kātyāyana's response: in some cases, a clay pot, a brand new pot, for instance, breaks not because of the sun or wind or age, but since it is the only participant in the action, it thus breaks of its own volition. Because the speaker wishes to express that the object acts independently, we must conclude that the clay pot has its own agency.[124] In Abhinavagupta's grammatical rendition, this capacity for agency signals a deeper, pervasive sense of subjectivity. It reveals an innate consciousness, even in things.[125] Agency necessarily entails will and hence freedom. This position stands in contrast to what we find, for instance, in earlier, perhaps better known, philosophical traditions like Advaita Vedānta, as Sthaneshwar Timalsina points out, which create a paradox where "when you are free (i.e., self-realized) you have no will to act, and when you have the will, your autonomy is compromised by *avidya* and *karma* . . . while, from the position of the Brahman, there is just the non-dual awareness that does not retain any agency or action."[126] In contrast, for Abhinavagupta, freedom which is the essence of agency is at the heart of what it means to be sentient, to be alive, across species and things.[127]

Freedom, Nonduality and Duality, and the One and the Many

If freedom is the basis of what it means to be sentient, what does this mean for clay pots or leaves of grass? As we saw, their subjectivity is covered over, hidden. Abhinavagupta tells us that "the form of awareness has some freedom, but not the part which is in the condition of being object. This is because it does not push away the essence of 'this-ness,' taking instead a form that is not conscious."[128]

Pushing away "This-ness" brings freedom; freedom is thus tied to being a subject.[129] While this almost sounds like a political sound-bite for European Enlightenment thinking, here, quite literally, it applies even to a mere clay pot. Continuing in this passage, Abhinavagupta points out that even for a mere clay pot, freedom is its essence. Being a clay pot is simply a secondary attribute, the form in which this consciousness finds itself.

> [Utpaladeva] says, "not at all" [or, "not entirely" insentient] meaning that even when freedom is not placed within and risen up in a pot, etc., there is still the form of consciousness fixed within, because its essence is a oneness of light shining.

> How will that consciousness exist by freedom being placed in it? To this he says, "as an attribute."[130]

This is a rather radical, if phenomenologically attuned, way of thinking of things. Objects are first and foremost indeterminate blobs of consciousness, which then become limited, defined things, deprived of a subjective stance as they become objects to us. In this way, Abhinavagupta establishes a sense of subjectivity as foundational. That is, this is how he shifts from a third-person to a first-person perspective. So when a pot obtains freedom, when it becomes sentient, how does it look? This consciousness, as light shining, *prakāśa,* is always at the core. When it acquires its freedom, it becomes sentient. Being a pot is just a secondary characteristic, the particular form this consciousness takes. The looming question—one we address in Chapter Four on *vimarśa*'s links to sentience—is what does this mean for objects like computers, artificial intelligence? One can easily guess the sort of answer we might expect. In any case, here, however, we should note that any object exists in tandem with its innate, if forgotten, subjectivity, as an outpouring of that subjectivity. So we see that

> [t]he subject's form, which is a unity of awareness contains also an excess, an abundance of awareness. This is deposited into the side of the object that is going to be created. So inwardly the [object] has the attribute of *śakti,* Energy which is none other than the form of consciousness.[131]

Being an object is always derivative. It is not in the nature of anything to be simply an inert object. Always, even for a clay jar, consciousness hides at the core. Yet, even in the midst of this cosmopsychist singularity of consciousness unfolding itself, still, the diversity of the world is quite real. As Isabelle Ratie insightfully points out, this philosophy avoids the idealist ontologies we find in the Vijñānavāda idealism of Buddhism,[132] or in Advaita Vedāntin varieties that erase the differences of a material reality.[133] Similarly, Lyne Bansat-Boudan points out that the terminology for consciousness for Abhinavagupta, consciousness as a dense mass (*cidghana*) stresses the association with materiality; the world is solid and is bodied.[134] Illustrated in the voice of the author Yogarāja, she translates for us, "To the One who, although nothing but a mass of consciousness, is yet solidified in the form of the world."[135]

Again we bump up against the tension between plurality and the One that Abhinavagupta's panentheism proposes, the seemingly oxymoronic "Realist Idealism" that Pandey ascribes to Abhinavagupta. For Abhinavagupta as well, holding both diversity and unity together is no mean feat. It is, in fact, a wonder.

> [T]he Energy of Consciousness is in fact all forms, the entire universe and She touches nothing beyond Herself." Consciousness (*citi*) makes manifest a wonder by the force of doing that which is extremely difficult. This he summarizes with the words, [*Śiva/Citi*] "who in fact" "partakes of 'This-ness.' "[136]

Even the singular unity, the cosmopyschism that manifests this totality, this highest being or reality—even this can also manage to be limited, to take the partial perspective that a rock or a tree or a clay pot or a human has. Not simply a transcendent reality that oversees the process of unfolding into the world—this would, after all, be a sort of animism. No, instead we see the very difficult wonder of immanence, the rock or tree or human itself expressing its own consciousness.

We might see the difference here by comparison with Spinoza. As Mary-Jane Rubenstein points out, in Spinoza's pantheism God is not actually the tree, the goat, the snuff-box.[137] For Abhinavagupta, however, this would make God too small, not actually the kind of cosmopsychism that really encompasses the whole. No, here Citi really does accomplish this extremely difficult task of actually partaking of "This-ness," becoming a thing, an object, *actually becoming* the tree, the clay pot. So, Abhinavagupta shares with Spinoza the "monstrous idea" that "God has a body—namely, the body of the world itself,"[138] and he shares the "insanity" of "Spinoza's identification of thought and extension."[139] This latter, in Abhinavagupta's terms, is his formulation that action is in fact not different from knowledge. The idea of action points to the materiality of the world, and knowledge references the mental element of thought.[140] Spinoza, however, backs away from the sort of radical immanence that would have God actually be the tree. Not so with Abhinavagupta. When he tells us of this particularly difficult wonder—partaking of "This-ness"—he takes a bold step further indeed.

This, I suggest, arises out of Abhinavagupta's emphasis on subjectivity. As I mentioned earlier, I suspect that part of what hobbles a contemporary New Materialism is still a habitual, unreflective adherence to the world as a third-person phenomenon. Abhinavagupta's insight to make the perspective of subjectivity foundational, rather than making the foundation some sort of substance (human bodies) or essence (a divine spark), means that the sentience and awareness that comes with subjectivity becomes a mode that is everywhere available, even for lowly clay pots, even for trees and leaves of grass.

Abhinavagupta's insight panentheistically allows a way to encompass both the bird's-eye view of the whole and the gritty particularity of a limited, partial, dualistic perspective. In other words, a pure subjectivity can also instantiate the immanence of a small, limited perspective, an insect, a person, a clay pot. With this, we get plurality. That is, we can all be part of a unifying field of consciousness; we can all think of ourselves as "I" and yet differ in our perspectives from one another. So we see:

> The "I" which is the nature of pure awareness constantly pervading the whole also manifests with duality. Consequently it is reasonable that these should be different from one another, as separate perceivers perceiving different objects.[141]

This is a key point. You and I can have differing awareness, different views. This is what prevents Abhinavagupta's panentheism from becoming the sort of panpsychism that John Searle critiques as being "like a thin veneer of jam"[142] with no real capacity to differentiate between different instantiations of consciousness, as I have argued elsewhere.[143] The consciousness that a dog, or a human, or for that matter a virus has, differs from each other. Abhinavagupta's insistence on subjectivity as foundational can include the duality of differences. It sidesteps this problem of a uniform consciousness, a thin veneer of jam with no difference between its expressions.

More than this, however—even as I have suggested that Abhinavagupta's adherence to transcendence is not to be underestimated, that he ultimately tends to favor the view of unity—still we find as well a passage like this one below, where Abhinavagupta argues that nonduality, the unity of the whole, is not actually more true than the limited, partial perspectives of duality. In a section where he argues against a transcendent view of Brahman, the Advaita Vedānta view that stipulates that the world is unreal, that our seeing the multiplicity of the world is merely ignorance (*avidyā*), Abhinavagupta pushes back. He tells us, "if you say that plurality is false, even though it appears before us, well then, the same goes for nonduality. Nonduality is shown to be false by virtue of the fact that plurality appears before us."[144]

The lynchpin that holds together a cosmopsychism[145] that can allow itself to be truly immanent, to take on the partial awareness of tree, a human, a clay pot, is the capacity for freedom, an ability to do things, not just on the level of the mind, but on the level materiality as well. This freedom is the hallmark of a subjective stance. It is yoked to an active awareness, *vimarśa*, the element of sentience, as we saw earlier, which is the second component of Abhinavagupta's dual-aspect monism—the counterpart to the shining light, *prakāśa*, that makes up objects.[146] And its phenomenology is signaled as the encounter of wonder.

The idea of wonder here is not, however, a way for Abhinavagupta to stop the conversation at the mystery of consciousness, as something we cannot understand. Rather, this notion of wonder references a precise terminology that links knowledge and action. Think here again of Spinoza's identification of thought and extension; the radical philosophical implications of that move similarly position Abhinavagupta's philosophy. Thus, again and again Abhinavagupta tells us that subjectivity is composed of wonder and *vimarśa* and that this is what gives freedom. We will delve more deeply into wonder (*camatkāra*) in Chapter Two and look at *vimarśa*, especially its links to materiality, in Chapter Four. For now, we might note that the phenomenology of wonder contains within it the links to the material world vis-a-vis this cluster of terms connecting action, awareness and sentience, *vimarśa* and *parāmarśa*, with subjectivity. And with these, entailed in the idea of action are both materiality and a notion of freedom. So, by way of a few examples among many, Abhinavagupta ties subjectivity to freedom, to active awareness, *vimarśa* as sentience, to wonder:

> one's active awareness (*vimarśa*)—which is really essentially the breath-taking wonder connected with the "I"[147]

> the wonder and bliss which is the supreme goal and reality of freedom, and which is defined by abiding in one's own Self, in the "I"[148]

> the self that is pure wonder, which is an active awareness (*vimarśa*), that, in fact, is freedom.[149]

Consciousness as *vimarśa*, this active awareness, is genuinely alive, sentient. It discovers its freedom through reflecting and embracing the "I," which is phenomenologically expressed as a breathtaking wonder. What exactly does it mean to have freedom? This freedom tied to subjectivity is precisely what generates the diversity, the plurality that makes up the world.[150] This makes sense in that the very idea of freedom points to the possibility of choosing one expression over another. And one can see how it might arise specifically because Abhinavagupta incorporates the capacity for a genuine multiplicity of subjectively centered entities. This, by the way, is Abhinavagupta's answer to the decombination problem, that is, the problem of how a single unified reality of a cosmopsychism can manage to divide itself and can decombine to make the plurality we find here.[151]

Thus, the idea of freedom is implicitly tied to a larger question of the plurality of the world. It's fair to say that Abhinavagupta draws on longer Indian traditions of nonduality to negotiate a unity that allows a simultaneous multiplicity. Sthaneshwar Timalsina insightfully points to the grammarian Bhartṛhari and the Advaita Vedāntin Maṇḍana demonstrating multiplicity within a larger context of nonduality.[152] However, plurality and freedom are linked not just for Abhinavagupta's panentheism, but for New Materialisms as well, yet in a different way and for different goals. For contemporary New Materialisms, the notions of plurality and freedom especially work to discount an earlier Western theological legacy of teleology, replete with its concomitant political hierarchies and patriarchies. A New Materialism reimagines an ontology in scientific parameters away from the implicit telos of an authoritarian god, as a means to rethink our ontologies toward more equitable, sustainable political and ecological goals.[153] In this regard, I suspect that what makes a contemporary New Materialism eye a panentheism suspiciously, with a sidelong gaze is precisely its linkage with a telos. The radical import of Darwin's discovery of evolution is just this freedom from a preordained telos, given from on high.[154] I have a hunch, however, that we get stuck on notions of telos because we have not delinked it from a third-person phenomenology. Teleology is habitually ordained from outside ourselves. Similarly, we tend to think of subjectivity as egoism; that is, we typically articulate subjectivity from a third-person transcendent perspective (even here I use an abstract singular noun).[155] They both reference an order outside our individual subjectivities that eradicates the multiple bumpy views that individual subjects present. So, while a gesture toward freedom in relation to plurality in a New Materialism is in part about avoiding telos, Abhinavagupta's linkage of freedom to a first-person perspective turns this on its head. For Abhinavagupta, freedom is the way we get diversity.[156]

This is referenced in how language is understood as well for this medieval Indian context. As Raffaele Torella points out, even though Abhinavagupta has a conception of deep unity on the highest level of consciousness, still there remains an implicit, latent multiplicity due to the very nature of language. He notes that even while multiplicity disappears on the level of inward subjectivity, yet still the multiplicity of phonemes, which bring about the multiplicity of meaning, never entirely disappears, but instead is simply compressed (*saṃkal*).[157] Perhaps akin to Catherine Keller's understanding of the fold, *complicatio*, language appears as implicated compression, inwardly gurgitating.[158] How does this work? According to Torella, "The phonemes are the only reality which is not swallowed by supreme consciousness; they never lose their own essential identity and nature regardless of the ontological level in which they act."[159] This occurs because "they are not a content of consciousness but consciousness itself."[160] The multiplicity they represent entails that consciousness is alive, sentient.[161] Thus, even in the midst of a profound unity, the innate intentionality of language carries the seeds of plurality. We get a panentheism that avoids a simplifed unitary One.

Consequently, Abhinavagupta's emphasis on subjectivity, "I-ness," also differs from the kind of New Materialist positions we find in Timothy Morton and in William Harman's Object-Oriented Ontology. Harman thoughtfully points to the gap between what humans are allowed to do in relation to objects, noting a current of scientism "gloating over the fact that people are pieces of matter just like everything else," but that it privileges the unique ability of thoughts to "transcend immediate experience, which inanimate matter is never allowed to do."[162] Harman, like Morton, counters this "scientism" perspective by referencing the impenetrability of objects.[163] Bennett also gestures toward this position when she points to Adorno's negative dialectics, indicating that the thing's inside knowing is denied to us as knowers.[164] In contrast, Abhinavagupta's cosmopsychism entails that we are never quite separated from objects around us. Indeed, much of the practice of yoga is precisely about *saṃyama*, contemplation on an object that allows the meditator to move to its inside, understanding and generating a deep unity between one's own subjectivity and that of the object of contemplation, an inward knowing of objects that enables the wild powers of Tantra, the *siddhis*, levitation, entering into objects, and so on.[165]

As we have seen, for Abhinavagupta the object itself arises out of a prior, cosmopsychically shared subjectivity. Similarly, for this Tantric tradition as Ratie and Torella both point out, when the yogi reads the mind of another person, the process involves a shift from seeing the other person as object to instead experiencing the other as resting in the yogi's own self. This entails an expansion of the yogi's self, which leads to a capacity to deeply empathize with another so that the other rests within one's own self.[166] Arindam Chakrabarti offers a similar perspective when he elegantly examines the different problem of memory, noting for Abhinavagupta that "[w]e must reject the suggestion that our knowledge of other minds is merely an analogical inference."[167] Other people and other objects are never impenetrable. The very nature of Abhinavagupta's cosmopsychism affirms that we all secretly share in a recursive, inward-directed awareness. The "I-ness" that we share unfolds outwardly to become the multiplicity of the world, never really cutting us off from everyone around us.[168]

Freeing the Object: Abhinavagupta's Panentheism and a New Materialism

Even with this foundational shared subjectivity, as we saw earlier, Abhinavagupta pushes away from Somānanda's pantheism. There *are* differences between sentient beings and rocks, or clay pots. He puts this common-sense point of view in the mouth of a frustrated interlocutor, who is upset with this radical proposition that proposes a clay jar might be sentient: "Now you may say, well, if it occurs in this way, then if one can see the form of consciousness even in a clay pot, then what is there that's real, that's not mere illusion?"[169] If even a clay pot is sentient, then where do we draw the line? Really though, this is the wrong question. Sentience is not an all or nothing wager. There is no definitive line to draw. Of course, this idea is unsettling. Humans and animals are sentient. Rocks are not—though the case of viruses—which are maybe alive, maybe not—ought to give us pause and to encourage us to consider Abhinavagupta's proposal here. We too, as humans, are only partly sentient. That is, only as far as we immerse ourselves in the breathtaking wonder of subjectivity—only to *that* extent are we alive, sentient, and actually free. In that sense, we are in the same boat as clay pots and viruses. As we saw, Abhinavagupta's dual-aspect monism specifies that "the form of awareness has some freedom, but not the part which is in the condition of being object. This is because it does not push away the essence of 'this-ness,' taking instead a form that is not conscious."[170]

This applies to clay pots, viruses, and equally to humans. We are a mix of subject and object. We are partly alive and sentient, and partly not. Moreover, with an eye to practical application, Abhinavagupta tells us that if we want to understand what subjectivity actually is, then we need to look at it from the perspective we know, from the *Māyā*-bound knowing Subject[171]—that is, from our perspective as limited humans, and not from an abstracted ideal of what the cosmopsychism, what God, might see.[172] Looking at this matter from our ordinary perspective works because at base we share our subjectivity with this highest reality, this cosmopsychism. At the same time, it requires that we understand that humans (like viruses) swing back and forth between subjectivity and the "This-ness" of being an object. Like the eye of a crow that characterizes what it means to be *puruṣa*, the Person, that we saw earlier, swinging between its two sockets, similarly Abhinavagupta tells us that the Self (*ātman*) moves back and forth between being the subject and the object: "the particular term *ātman* 'Self' has been used to point to the Subject, the Subject with its capacity to know, as it has this capacity of swinging between both the object of action and the doer of action."[173] Here as well, we see Abhinavagupta's version of the identification of thought and extension. The term *ātman*, classically in India, particularly with Śaṅkara's Advaita Vedānta, is understood to represent pure spirit. In India's counterpart to the mind–body dualism that we find in the West, the *ātman*, the self, is pure spirit, while *prakṛti*, Nature, makes up all the physical reality we encounter here. As pristine spirit, the *ātman* is not sullied by the change and activity of the material world as *prakṛti* is. Abhinavagupta instead rewrites this classical Indian expression of duality into a continuum, a see-saw. The *ātman*, the Self, like the Person (*puruṣa*), swings back and forth, sometimes subject, sometimes object. In this, the idea of *ātman*, the Self, is interwoven with action, inextricable from the materiality of the world,[174] as it swings back and forth between subject and object.

The telos in all this is to become actually alive, actually sentient, by resting in the first-person perspective. David Lawrence, translating Utpaladeva's *Ajaḍapramātṛsiddhi* with Harabhatta Shastri's gloss, points this out: "On this basis [*āśraya*], the insentient thing, by unification with the subject [*pramātṛ*] who has the essential nature of the recognitive apprehender [*vimṛśtṛ*]—that is, by rest [*viśrānti*] in I-hood [*ahambhāva*]—attains sentience [*ajaḍatva*]."[175] One achieves sentience by resting in the feeling of "I." For Abhinavagupta this also applies to objects like clay jars. We and the material things that make up the world are entangled. Our fates are entwined; we interact with them, we mold and perceive them, and we are partly ourselves made up of the outpouring of consciousness into a materiality. With this, our own gestures toward a fuller aliveness, sentience, work by degrees, bit by bit, to free the materiality of things as well from the confinement of being objects. So Abhinavagupta tells us:

> But here this is the main idea—earth, etc. manifest in this way in mixed form, becoming identified as clay jars etc. which are made by the sense organs of action [hands etc.] and trickle out and are perceived by the sense organs of knowledge [sight, etc], and they are then conceived, appropriated, and ascertained to the extent possible by the mind, ego and intellect. The impure[176] creation is determined and conceptualized with the sheath covering bound souls, the limitations of action etc., which place the clay jars etc., made of earth before the subject. The clay jars etc., are then colored [by the subject's perception]. Yet, by means of resting within the *Māyā*-bound subject, even clay jars etc., can exist free from duality. So it is said: "Even in the state of being an object [non-duality can exist]" (*Ajaḍapramātṛsiddhi* 20). So by this logic, [the clay jar etc.] in the real subject is freed from duality by degrees. Freed from the divisions in one's self, one rests as the

> expanse of Light, *prakāśa,* and *vimarśa,* active awareness on the highest level and that is good.[177]

We, and the objects entangled with us, in us, find life, sentiency, in a telos that leads to a genuine subjectivity. This is a goal, a good toward which we might strive. Of course, here, Abhinavagupta's primary interest is in us, Māyā-bound subjects, humans, part object and part subject who keep seeing objects everywhere, to our own detriment, even if we exhibit more of our innate consciousness than clay jars do. Yet, we might still interpret the response Abhinavagupta offers to his frustrated opponent, insisting on a firm line between mere matter and life as a moral motivation for recognizing the life of things. If we see in objects, even in clay jars, the sentience that is really there at the core, then we allow ourselves to rise teleologically to a subjectivity that does not see the world as different from ourselves, as mere object. At the same time, we allow them the space to actually step into their own true liveliness, their innate sentience. Their life is, after all, just covered over, hidden. He continues in his response to this interlocuter who protests against the idea of clay jars also being sentient:

> By removing the form which is insentient, we allow the form which is sentient, the conscious, to take predominance and there we have a complete entrance into consciousness. This is moving forward and entering into its own form. This is the meaning.
>
> To which point it is said:
> "even to the extent of a mere leaf of grass . . . "
> Going up in fact is the removal of the form which is unconscious.
> "O lord of Eight forms [*Śiva*], what in one?"
> But here, that in itself is happiness.[178]

Again, Abhinavagupta's concern here is freeing us, part-object, part-subject humans. Yet still, his response, invoking the poetry of life in a mere leaf of grass, is that even this mere leaf has the potential to remove the form that is unconscious, to reach the happiness of being a sentient subject. As we saw earlier, Abhinavagupta tells us, "Even the lifeless [grammatical] third person, [the 'it'], if it sheds its lifeless form can take on the first and second person forms. For example, 'listen, o stones' and 'Of mountains, I am Meru.'"[179] Because in this cosmopsychism both the limited subject and the object derive from a deeper consciousness, both always have access to life, sentience. So, when the mute idol speaks, when the thing-power of a piece of discarded trash on the street calls out, we too, by seeing it, allow its subjectivity bit by bit to come into its own, to rest in the happiness of being alive.

Here we can start to see how and why the way we think of objects makes a difference. Much New Materialism, as expressed by Bennett for instance, also recognizes this capacity of human thinking to make a difference in what happens to the world around us. Bennett notes her own ecologically motivated thinking that our receptivity to the material life around us will help us to experience the relation between persons and other materialities more horizontally, enabling wiser choices for the planet and human life.[180] It's no surprise, then, that Walt Whitman acts as a standard-bearer for a New Materialism, with his expansive naming, cherishing the materiality all around us. In this regard, I have also on more than one occasion been struck by Whitman's insistent use of the first-person perspective and its curious convergence with Abhinavagupta's philosophical articulation of a first-person capacity to enliven objects, even to a mere leaf of grass, to remove the form that is insentient (*jaḍa*), and allow its deeper sentient form to rise up, to enter into liveliness, into life.

Earlier, I pointed out the similarities of Whitman's poetry to the *Namakam* section of the Vedic *Śrī Rudrapraśna*, both of which engage in an expansive practice of naming the rich variety of life. I suspect the very act of naming is itself a way of recognizing and, in this respect, constituting life. This naming also serves to remember; I am thinking of the use of memorial walls, 9/11 certainly, but also the recent Black Lives Matter memorial wall dedicated to African Americans killed through police violence. This act of naming is a way to honor, to give life through naming and recognizing the other. Indeed, the *Namakam* of the Vedic *Śrī Rudrapraśna* is literally the section of "Naming." And the familiar yoga greeting to honor the other, "namaste," is also, literally, "naming you." Thus, naming in both of these texts refers to invoking a richly complex ecosystem of entities seen and unseen. I suggest that this practice of naming as a way of seeing the many others is the medicine that the *Namakam* invokes near the end of the section: "this, my hand is god; my hand is greater than god, for this touches the auspicious. It is a medicine for the world."[181] One might also recall Whitman here: "And I know that the hand of God is the promise of my own."[182] I am also reminded here of Abhinavagupta, as we saw earlier, telling us that

> only to the extent that one makes the world into an object, to the extent that it is known, can one then transcend the level of object, of thing to be known and allow the true sense of the knower to take root in the heart, its fullness being grasped by the inner organ [mind, intellect and ego] as beyond the realm of the knowable.[183]

That is, the act of knowing, of naming the other, allows the knower to take root in the heart in a subjectivity, an "I-ness" that takes it beyond mere object to be known. Abhinavagupta's *Pratyabhijñā* philosophy, translated as Recognition, is this act of recognizing one's own first-person perspective as expanding outward in all that we see here. On a more mundane level, we also should keep in mind the notion of expanding our own subjectivity to recognize in others a first-person perspective is what allows the space for empathy. Putting ourselves in another's shoes, a subjective perspective is not necessarily an egoism that blocks out the other—that, rather, is third-person perspective. Rather, subjectivity, "I-ness," can offer an expansion of self that includes the other; this I suggest is part of what we find in the *Namakam* and in Whitman. For our purposes here, it helps us to recognize one of the most important insights of New Materialism: that if we want ourselves on this planet to survive, we need to change the way we think of things. We need to leave our understanding of things as mere dead objects and recognize our own secret sharing of the vitality of things, to a greater or lesser degree. This is not to espouse a rampant animism, a panpsychism where the concrete we walk on might be hurt by our steps, but rather to encourage a kind of humility in the face of the matter all around us, by recognizing that we share our vitality with it at base.

2
The Matter of Wonder

> The "I" which is wonder is the self of all that appears. The "I" is the spontaneous, innate power, the mantra of the highest goddess of speech. As it is said, "the essence of all visible phenomena rest within the 'I'-feeling. This is a secret beyond all secrets."
>
> **—Abhinavagupta, *Īśvara Pratyabhijñā Vivṛti Vimarśinī***

> What makes certain molecular configurations stand out from the multitude of possibilities seems to be that they are capable of developing into something that strikes us as rather marvelous, namely a world of living creatures. But there is no conceivable reason that blind forces of nature or physical attributes should be biased toward the marvelous.
>
> **—Thomas Nagel, *Mind and Cosmos*, quoting Roger White**

Wonder

In this chapter, we address another key element in Abhinavagupta's philosophical cosmology—the idea of wonder (*camatkāra*). Wonder as a state of mind seems to propose a heightened transcendence, bringing us up and outside our ordinary sense of self. Abhinavagupta flips this understanding on its head. Even as he offers a familiar visage of wonder, arrested thought and speech, the feeling of an expansive rush, he does not tie it to our expected notions of transcendence. Instead he links wonder back to a material base. Wonder, he tells us, is a recognition of an essential subjectivity at the heart of matter. This unexpected, and panentheist, impetus to link matter to the experience of wonder gives us a very different story than our proverbial rehearsal of wonder as an up and out, a transcendence that leaves dull matter behind. It also helps us to reassess what we mean by transcendence. We begin here by delving into our own contemporary sense of wonder before we turn to Abhinavagupta's articulation of it.

Neuroscientist Anil Seth in a recent Ted talk tells the audience that our brains hallucinate consciousness. We may think that we see and hear and

The Matter of Wonder. Loriliai Biernacki, Oxford University Press. © Oxford University Press 2023.
DOI: 10.1093/oso/9780197643075.003.0003

touch the world around us, but really, consciousness, our intimate sense of self—these are simply "a controlled hallucination generated by the brain."[1] Despite the rhetorical emotional punch of language like "hallucination," Seth's neuroscientific speculations on consciousness follows a commonly accepted position in current cognitive science, that consciousness is a product of the brain.[2] Seth waxes optimistically over our current scientific progress. The seeming insoluble mystery[3] of our conscious selves will be soon unraveled by our ever growing understanding of the brain's neural architecture. Certainly, of course, he employs the rhetoric of "hallucination" for its shock value, to describe essentially that the brain's neural connections determine in large measure what we see, that we don't just see a real world out there; we construct it. So far so good. This is also what humanists have been telling us for some time as well. The connections to brain neurology adds another particularly compelling front. And of course, words like "hallucination" are expressly designed to jar, to jolt us out of any lingering unarticulated remnants of a religious sensibility, a sense that we might have something like a soul somehow separate from our bodies. Laying out his cards as a secularist and materialist scientist, in his neuroscientific account, all can be explained through the mechanics of the body.[4]

What is so especially curious—and this is something that we see across a spectrum of scientists—is that even as Seth with one hand takes away our familiar comforting anchor in ideas of something like a soul to offer meaning in the chaos of life—with the other he gives a consolation meant to replace our loss—he offers us the sense of wonder. Concluding his stimulating talk, he tells us, "With a greater sense of understanding comes a greater sense of wonder."

It seems that science as discourse has embraced the trope of wonder, ranging from Carl Sagan's plentiful inspirational quotes,[5] such as "Science arouses a soaring sense of wonder" to *Scientific American* Magazine's "Wonders of Science" blog, telling its popular audience, "Science just gives facts. Our sense of meaning, in the big-picture, must derive from elsewhere. Right? Wrong. Below are 10 sublime wonders of science, to make your mind reel and your emotions swell"[6] to more scholarly venues such as noted atheist Michael Shermer's review of cognitive scientist Gerald Edelman's *Wider than the Sky* opening with Shermer's invocation of wonder in relation to quantum physicist Richard Feynman.[7]

However, we might ask, why is it that wonder is the term one invokes when trying to sell a nonenchanted, nonreligious worldview? Why has wonder become the go-to consolation prize for our loss of some greater power in the universe, a soul, a god?[8] A shorthand phenomenology of wonder may point to its easy assumption of this areligious, atheistic role. Wonder as a state of mind seems to propose a heightened transcendence. It brings us outside our small ordinary sense of self opening into something bigger, beyond self, outside of self. We think of wonder today as being associated with the speechless apprehension of the vastness of planets in the starry sky, beyond the scope of human ability to map it, or wonder at nature's rich ability to weave a web of sunset colors over the mountains, or wonder in the face of the mind-boggling complexity of the human immune system. And while the affective significance of wonder certainly fluctuates historically, as Daston and Park amply demonstrate[9], yet a general depiction of wonder is traced with a persistent phenomenology, speechlessness, and transcendence, leaving us in its wake with mouths gaping wide.[10]

It is also probably fair to suggest that part of wonder's appeal as a cultural trope is that it operates as a kind of praxis.[11] Akin even to a spiritual praxis, wonder ferries us into the giddy high of transcendence, but it still manages, as Mary-Jane Rubenstein points out, to stop short of the certainty of faith.[12] Historically, transcendence has been the provenance of religion. Wonder offers transcendence without the religious strings attached. Anil Seth draws on this trope and *Scientific American*'s coupling of "meaning," "the big picture," with "wonder" makes the link explicit. Moreover, wonder enables a humanist ethos, as Vasalou suggests, causing us to widen our world of empathy and broaden our cognitive capacities.[13] It does so as well in a way that gives "the big picture" as a truth which sees the whole, from above the fray. Wonder offers a transcendence that rides high above the frazzled relativisms that typically dog a humanist truth. To boot, the experience of wonder lifts us above our selfish instincts; as Caroline Walker Bynum points out, to wonder is precisely not to appropriate or to consume.[14] Wonder, then, might be said to give us the best of a humanist transcendence, rising above the individual with their partisan, selfish limitations,[15] generating its highs abstracted away from the dogmas of faith.

The work wonder does as praxis derives no doubt from its phenomenology. The experience of wonder stops our familiar ruts of thought. Nevertheless, even as its physiological phenomenology, the widened eyes, speechlessness,[16] looks familiar across cultures and over centuries, still, the meaning of wonder shifts, as Bynum[17] as well as Daston and Park point out.[18] This is especially the case for Abhinavagupta's use of wonder in comparison with Western conceptions. We might read much of the Western conception of wonder along the lines Daston and Park suggest—wonder as a cognitive passion, as much about knowing as feeling.[19] As they point out, wonder with its Aristotelian goad to inquiry marks the dawn of science, leading to firmer knowledge,[20] and here we can see traces of Anil Seth's use of wonder above. We can also see this cognitive orientation in Rubenstein's map of wonder as the beginning of philosophy.[21] For purposes of this chapter, I suggest we might trace in the phenomenology of wonder a very different story: one that, in a nutshell, links wonder back to matter, and in consequence reconfigures the very notion of transcendence. Linking wonder to matter changes the ballgame; matter becomes a very different kind of thing. This, I suggest, offers in particular a novel analysis that can contribute much to a New Materialism as it thinks through the status of matter.

Drawing from 11th-century India, from Abhinavagupta, I suggest a distinctive interpretation of the phenomenology of wonder that may be helpful for a New Materialism, insofar as it links wonder not to a transcendence outside the body and matter, but instead to an awareness of an innate subjectivity within materiality. This brilliant thinker was instrumental in philosophizing medieval India's Tantric shift, and a part of this Tantric rearticulation of self involved reclamation of the body as a key component of Tantric ritual praxis.[22] While Abhinavagupta's wonder (*camatkāra*) shares a phenomenology of arrested thought and speech with its Western articulations, he presents a strikingly different etiology, and a different hermeneutic.

For starters, Abhinavagupta veers away from characterizing wonder as a cognitive emotion, locating wonder instead on a deeper, ontologically more primal level of will.[23] Michel Hulin points to this characterization in his thoughtful discussion of wonder within Indian aesthetic theory, looking to Abhinavagupta's articulation of *rasa*, that is, the "taste," or emotional and aesthetic "savoring" one gets from fine poetry and drama. Abhinavagupta's articulation of the aesthetic experience of art, of *rasa*, extends beyond simple emotion.[24] For Abhinavagupta, wonder is not a mere emotion, cognitive or otherwise; rather, it lies at the heart of his ontology, operating before mind *and* emotion.

In Abhinavagupta's formulation, wonder is simply the expression of "I" within matter.[25] Our psychological attachments to transcendence tend to obscure the idea that wonder arises in relation to materiality. Wonder evokes transcendence, yes, and for Abhinavagupta as well. However, wonder, and with it sentience, are tied to the material web of action (*kriyā*). In Chapter One we briefly outlined how sentience—being alive, via *vimarśa*—is inextricably tied to subjectivity, freedom, and wonder, and in Chapter Four we will revisit in more depth the idea of how sentience, *vimarśa*, is particularly tied to materiality. Here we map out in more detail Abhinavagupta's phenomenology of wonder. Wonder for Abhinavagupta's philosophy of Recognition (*Pratyabhijñā*) simply is what reveals the bond between matter and subjectivity. This for us may seem counterintuitive. From our vantage point, subjectivity is linked to consciousness. It is as unlike matter as it can possibly be. This stark divide is precisely what Abhinavagupta aims to overturn with his panentheism. He nudges us toward a materiality underwritten by consciousness. To put this another way, wonder is a phenomenological portal that makes bare the essential subjectivity undergirding everything. His take on wonder also reconfigures the basis of transcendence, pointing to its dependence on the very thing it transcends: matter. And with this we find a deeper liveliness, a Tantric panentheism that discovers subjectivity, a first-person perspective not only in our own self-aware thoughts, but also as an enlivening force, embedded within the matter of bodies and objects.

I suspect that most conceptions of New Materialisms will ultimately rely to some extent on the power of an emotion such as wonder to help in the revival of matter's ontological worthiness.[26] I am thinking, for instance, of Jane Bennett's eloquent recital of her experience on June 4th with bits of trash, when in a numinous encounter she sees seemingly lifeless objects transform into a vibrant, shimmering presence: the single black large men's plastic glove, a white plastic bottle cap, a dead rat, oak pollen in the Baltimore gutter. As they shift in her growing awareness, as she captures a glimpse of the "energetic vitality inside each of these things," they begin to "shimmer and spark."[27] Her own emotional moment of surprise at their "live presence" looks a bit like the kind of wonder we find in Abhinavagupta's philosophy. As we saw in the last chapter, Bennett uses this encounter to argue for a New Materialism that emphasizes the power of *things*. Things in this view are not mere human objects, but instead exist as something like entities in their own rights, not entirely reducible to human contexts and semiotics.

Here, I suggest that the astute phenomenological understanding of wonder that the Kashmiri Śaiva tradition and Abhinavagupta in particular offer can help to tease out a sense of the interplay between matter and the kind of liveliness that Bennett tells us *things* have. Bennett is certainly aware of the charges of vitalism leveled against her view. And she is aware as well, no doubt, that her moment sensing the luminosity of the gutter-bound shimmering debris might be ascribed not to the gutter debris, but to her own Thoreauvian-induced meditative state. Indeed, she herself also points out that the encounter was precipitated by her own "anticipatory readiness"[28] from imbibing the writing of Spinoza, Merleau-Ponty, and Thoreau. In this instance, Abhinavagupta's thoughtful conceptualization of the links between wonder and subjectivity and matter can help to theorize the kind of lively *thingness* that Bennett invokes.

That is, Abhinavagupta urges us to recognize that the power of wonder is not really that it offers a transcendence that leaves behind a wretched earthbound materiality. Rather, wonder instead brings us back to matter. However, in a state of wonder our vision of matter is altered; we recognize its own liveliness, its own subjectivity. That is, wonder reminds us that the sense of "I" is lodged at the very heart of matter. When we experience wonder, we tap into this secret sharing of subjectivity. Here we wind up with an intuitively astute insight: the feeling of transcendence that wonder appears to elicit depends on a deeper, if mostly neglected and unarticulated materiality. It is in this regard that Abhinavagupta's take on wonder may prove helpful for a New Materialism, helping it to chart a path that will reclaim the vitality and importance of matter.

Following on this, moreover, I propose that Abhinavagupta's sophisticated phenomenology helps us to rethink the very idea of transcendence. Moving away from a notion of transcendence as uplifting flight away from matter, Abhinavagupta's conceptualization helps us reconstruct a notion of transcendence that can avoid a pervasive trap of transcendence, what Thomas Nagel calls a "view from nowhere"[29]—that is, the idea that we might somehow transcend to a universal true reality, a perspective that encompasses all views, taking us above the fray. Abhinavagupta's model linking wonder to subjectivity locates the transcendence that wonder always offers within an "I," with its particular first-person embodied perspective. Moreover, I suggest that it also makes sense to read the invocation of wonder from a scientist like Seth along the lines that Abhinavagupta articulates. Though not voiced by Seth, I suggest that the appeal wonder has for scientists like Seth is also tied to its reclamation of subjectivity.

In what follows, first I point to the Indian genealogy of wonder traced in the science of cooking. This hermeneutic of wonder discovers it in embodied experience, when the "I" actively engages its own sensual pleasure, relishing being alive in a body. After this discussion, I follow more deeply the link wonder has to matter; we find wonder embedded at the heart of matter. Next, I chart Abhinavagupta's suggestion that wonder is tied to an expression of the will. With this Abhinavagupta links wonder to a capacity for agency and an intentional stance. This logic affords a sense of agency within matter, where wonder is precisely the mix of subject and object, a sense of "I" located within materiality. This mix of subject and object—this is what it means to be sentient. Where things are alive, mixing matter *and* consciousness, there we find wonder. In the section that follows, I look at how Abhinavagupta's panentheism reworks the idea of transcendence. His reflections on wonder reference yogic states and practices around the breath. Abhinavagupta connects the upward-moving breath to the Fourth State (*turya*), a state classically in India connected with the idea of transcendence. Here, however, Abhinavagupta links this meditative state not to the up and out of the body that we usually associate with transcendence. Instead he figures it as movement inward to a deeper sense of subjectivity. He also thwarts one other truism we tie to transcendence. We usually imagine transcendence as a space of timelessness, above the change and flux of the world. Abhinavagupta instead rewrites time back into this transformed notion of transcendence.

We begin now with wonder's culinary origins.

Cooking up the Taste of Wonder

Unlike Aristotle's read of wonder as a goad to knowledge, Abhinavagupta's Indian context finds the origins of wonder (*camatkāra*) more prosaically in the science of cooking. Raghavan suggests that *pāka śāstra*, the science of cooking, gives us the verbal root *cam*, tasting or sipping, as the onomatopoeic clicking of the tongue when we taste something delicious.[30] And, Abhinavagupta as well ties wonder to its verbal root *cam* as tasting, sensory enjoyment, telling us, "wonder, indeed, rests in its own nature, without depending on some other thing. In this way it has the form of enjoyment as tasting."[31] In this same passage we find, "wonder is abiding in the taste (*āsvādana*) of enjoyment without any obstruction."[32] Wonder is a gustatory experience. Especially it is an unbridled sensory experience, "without any obstruction." By this, I imagine he means that the mind, with its capacity to intervene with a running dialogue, is actually silenced in the state of wonder.[33] No mental chatter to obstruct the taste of enjoyment. Sensual and sensory, it points back to that early childhood joy that comes with being in a body, savoring the taste of food.[34] Elsewhere again when Abhinavagupta describes how we tell the difference between things that are alive, like us, and things are insentient, like crystals and the color blue, he points to wonder. And here also, wonder is about physical sensory enjoyment:

> [T]hat [sentience] which is free, not dependent on some other, that is the "I" actively reflecting on its own self as the one who enjoys; this gives rise to wonder, which is the nature of unbroken sensory enjoyment.[35]

Wonder is an unbroken sensory enjoyment, again sidestepping the mind's tendency to chop up and distract us from our experiences. Instead, wonder arises when the "I" actively engages its own sensual pleasure.[36] We may find this surprising in that this take on wonder is so closely tied to the senses. Abhinavagupta's wonder refuses a transcendence that drops the body while it reaches for the clouds. Nevertheless, I suggest that Abhinavagupta's formulation points to a fine-grained attention to the phenomenology of wonder. Wonder arises precisely when we reflect inwardly, speechless, as we ingest—indeed, taste—a reality beyond our habitual limitations. We can already see hints reshaping the idea of transcendence away from our more familiar notion that takes us up and out of the body. Instead, wonder brings us more intimately back into ourselves, allowing us to drink in the enjoyment of an inward subjectivity. Keep in mind that in this context the inherent nature of all things—matter, our bodies—is still consciousness,[37] but we can and do notice a difference between you or me, a dog that barks and things that are not alive, a clay jar, a crystal.[38] What does wonder do? Wonder is what signals the difference that comes with being alive.[39]

Tied to the idea of being alive, Abhinavagupta sees another aspect in wonder, a capacity for freedom, when he says, "in its own nature, without depending on some other thing."[40] Wonder does not happen when we are fearful of some outcome, or when we are chasing some desired goal; it happens when the self is not driven by some other element determining one's behavior. Not mechanical or rote, sentience entails a genuine freedom, free from external constraints. This is precisely what defines us as separate from mere matter. We can taste, enjoy embodied experience in a way that a mere machine, or simple insentient matter cannot. That is, sentience means precisely being able to push back against the kind of mechanical determinism that dominates matter. Of course, much biological science as presented, for instance by Dawkins[41] and Dennett[42] impose just this sort of determinism on humans, biological algorithms that render human freedom a simple Darwinian fiction.

Abhinavagupta also acknowledges limitations on human freedom to choose;[43] this capacity for freedom that comes with subjectivity exists on a graduated scale. Humans tend to be partially free and partially not, mostly trapped in *Māyā*, or what we might style the algorithms of karma. The degree to which we can immerse ourselves in the subjectivity of wonder signals our freedom—this freedom is precisely our capacity to transcend the determinism of insentience. Thus, for Abhinavagupta, wonder is not about advocating a human exceptionalism. Rather, wonder is the sign of being alive because it points to a freedom that comes from being able to choose. It is subjectivity writ large, not bound to a particular species, a subjectivity on which humans have no special claim.

I would venture that both Anil Seth and *Scientific American* are invoking a similar logic linking wonder to subjectivity, if not explicitly. They offer wonder as the consolation prize for the hard truth of our mechanistic reality. Why? Precisely because it reclaims our human subjectivity. Even if the biological algorithms driving our brains produce only hallucinations, the illusion of free will, still the experience of wonder gives us back a sense of subjectivity. And that subjectivity frees us from the plight of insentient, algorithmically driven matter. This subjectivity tells us we are alive.

What makes Abhinavagupta's formulation of wonder so astute is that he invokes a transcendence from the limitations of mere matter not by rising above the body, but by moving inwardly, through the body's senses to subjectivity. By tying wonder back to *kriyā*, action, he links it to materiality. So in this same passage he offers an etymology, telling us that "the word 'wonder' (*camatkāra*) points to tasting as a particular form of action."[44] Wonder entails acting in the world. And this happens through a bodily hermeneutic, wrapping subjectivity in the imagery of tasting, the delight of the senses. This, indeed, makes a lot of psychological sense. To savor something, to reflect, brings us precisely back to the embodied "I." What happens phenomenologically in this reading of wonder is that we taste the reality of our embodiment, consciously and in a particular time and space. The wonder we feel from the rich web of the Milky Way on a clear night or from the tapestry of sunset colors over the mountains is not really about transcending the body so much as it is about being present in the body. Present enough that is, to allow our senses to tap into the secret subjectivity we share with the materiality we encounter, the matter of stars and wavelengths of light is refracted across rocks and oxygen and clouds.

It will not be surprising then, to see the extensive role wonder (*camatkāra*) also plays in Abhinavagupta's writings on aesthetics,[45] as Edwin Gerow notes, with its appeal to the senses and sensory experience.[46] Similarly, Michel Hulin notes that wonder arises as one of the *rasas*, refined aesthetic experiences, again linking wonder to sensory aesthetic experience.[47] Sthaneshwar Timalsina, linking wonder to art, also notes that what defines performance art, making it something more than mere mimicry, is the element of wonder, which, as he notes, is "essentially identical to the self mirroring its own orgasmic being."[48] And Abhinavagupta in his philosophical text, the *Īśvara Pratyabhijñā Vivṛti Vimarśinī*, explicitly connects this unbroken sensory enjoyment of wonder that we saw above to aesthetic experience. He tells us that

> [i]n the aesthetic experience (*rasa*) of poetry and dance etc., also, there is the absence of obstacles which are the nature of the constraints that arise in the inward

> functions of the mental stuff; *that act of tasting*, in fact is the essence of *rasa*, which is stated elsewhere as wonder (*camatkāra*).[49] [emphasis added].

The rapturous transcendence we feel when absorbed in a gripping performance, in beautiful poetry, for example, comes about because we move inwardly without obstacles into a wondrous and unrestrained sensory enjoyment.

The Wonder of Matter

So wonder is connected to the experiences of our bodily senses, but the connection to matter and the senses goes deeper for this tradition. Yes, the sensory modality of wonder ties it back intimately to the physical body, which rather naturally circles back to the aesthetic tradition. As David Shulman points out, in the Indian aesthetic tradition, wonder is expressed in physical ways: "trembling, horripilation, joyful movements of the limbs, etc."[50] This points to the sort of shared phenomenology that wonder has across cultures, just as we saw earlier for wonder in the West, as Daston and Park note with a series of visages depicting the state of wonder.[51]

For this Indian tradition, however, wonder's link to matter and the body is ontologically driven; there is a deeper philosophical association with the body and matter. Navjivan Rastogi points to this association in his Hindi publication "Rasānubhūti Pratibhāna ke Rūpa Meṃ," explicitly connecting wonder to the body for Abhinavagupta's aesthetic theory.[52] Similarly, Lyne Bansat-Boudon also draws attention to the links wonder has to the body, noting that wonder comprises both mental and physical components.[53] In her translation of Yogarāja's commentary on Abhinavagupta's *Paramārthasāra*, we find that the Indian author Yogarāja explicitly spells out the link wonder has to matter. Wonder is the essence of matter, he tells us.[54] The four principles classically connected to matter—namely, (1) *prakṛti*, often translated as Nature, what makes up our physical world;[55] (2) *Māyā*, the principle of illusion fundamentally generating the diversity of the world; here, we can note *Māyā's* connection with matter particularly as an expanding multiplicity; (3) *śakti* herself, the primordial energy understood as the genatrix of the world and matter; and (4) the earth, that quintessential emblem of materiality as well—he tells us that all four have as their essence wonder, which is the nature of pure subjectivity (*parāhantācamatkārasāra*—more on subjectivity below).[56] So at base, what constitutes matter is just the state of wonder. Wherever we find matter in the scheme of creation—in Nature, in the earth—at the heart of all these is wonder.

Again, I suspect that Jane Bennett's response to various bits of discarded debris instinctively taps into a similar intuition, the contagious glimmer of wonder that she spots in what looks like dead matter. I venture that a New Materialism also represents an appeal to articulate this phenomenological insight. And, I daresay, I wonder if we might even detect a curious, intuitive resonance, by no means explicit, in the ready appeal to wonder that we find in stalwart materialist scientists like Seth. This is, however, really nothing more than to say that the phenomenology linking wonder intuitively to matter may cross cultures more readily than we can trace.

Yogarāja's classification linking wonder to matter adds one more piece of the equation of wonder—the idea of diversity, plurality, which may prove helpful for a New Materialism.[57] As we see with *Māyā* above, the notion of the world also entails the idea of a plurality, connecting wonder to the diversity of the world around us. Yogarāja adds that all the various beings in the world, gods, humans, animals and winged creatures, down to the immovable—all these rest in the essence of wonder, which is simply a pure subjectivity, characterized by unbroken wonder.[58] The "I," this unbroken wonder, contains many forms.[59]

So, to say that wonder is the essence of materiality in the world is to say that wonder, with all its fuzzy indeterminacy, its phenomenology of speechlessness, eyes widened—is just this awareness of subjectivity in the very heart of matter. The state of wonder reminds us that the inward sense of "I," the subject, is available everywhere, even in mere matter, in the external world out there. Still, wonder only happens when the "I" can reflect on itself; it is the sign of life, sentience.[60] As a phenomenological experience, wonder arises precisely when the sense of "I" finds itself mixing with the materiality of the world. Utpaladeva, Abhinavagupta's grand-guru, articulates this idea, saying, "the one who takes the form of the world, the great Lord, who is the universal self within all living beings expands open in wonder, which is the mixture of the unbroken[61] subject and unbroken object."[62] Wonder happens with just this mixture of subject and object, the "I" embodied within materiality. The rest of the passage reads, "That one is the primary state sought after, the Fourth state beyond waking, dream and deep sleep states." We might note the easy assimilation of divinity to a state of mind, the effortless slide from the great Lord as the one (*ekaḥ*), seamlessly into a particular state of mind available to every living being. This is a recurrent theme of this Kashmiri panentheist subjectivity, as we saw in the last chapter. There is just one reality: the "I."[63] This substratum of subjectivity assumes a great variety of forms, becoming all the different subjects, all awakening into this cosmic sentience to call themselves "I."[64]

Wonder and the Will: The Intentions of Matter

I pointed out earlier that Abhinavagupta's characterization of wonder goes deeper than mere emotion, offering a different hermeneutic than a familiar Western characterization of wonder as a cognitive emotion. Instead Abhinavagupta understands wonder in terms of will, telling us, "Everywhere, in fact, it is the case that wonder is just only the will (*icchā*)."[65] Elaborating further, he tells us, "will is everywhere defined as resting in one's own self in the form of enjoyment. This enjoyment indeed is the state of wonder."[66] Wonder, with its freedom to choose, is at base a capacity to will something; it carries an intentionality rooted in a self reveling in the taste of its own subjectivity.

It may perhaps appear surprising to link wonder to the will. Wonder, for us, steeped in a history of Western philosophy, seems to call up a state where the will is suspended, an indeterminacy that might be antithetical to the idea of will and choice.[67] Wonder, after all, stops thought. What Abhinavagupta's attention to the phenomenology of wonder highlights is that we typically understand choice only on the level of the mind—what this Indian tradition terms *vikalpa*, the kind of mental determination that makes distinctions between one thing and another. For Abhinavagupta, on the other hand, the will is not this superficial mental capacity to distinguish between two things. His insight is that the motive power of will is an intentional stance, phenomenologically grounded in a deeper embodied subjectivity.[68] Located before the mental activity of mind, wonder points to a deep-seated willing, an awareness of self as intentionally directed. So, not so much about an Augustinian conception of will-power to choose good over evil, this notion of will points to a more primal intentionality, one that is not tied to an already defined individual. The will points to an opening to the world, arising out of being an "I," a particular first-person orientation, located in a particular time and place—even for a mute insect. Indeed, as we saw, "When those beings belonging to *Māyā*—even down to an insect—when they do their own deeds, that which is to be done first stirs in the heart."[69] This sense of subjectivity, this "I-ness" is always near, present to oneself in the heart as the place where the sense of "I" arises. This subjectivity takes on different forms, certainly with greater or lesser capacities; yet the phenomenological perspective of the sense of "I" is what grounds the various entities that exist.

This idea of will is connected with the problem of free will as well. This Indian conception of selfhood, much like our own today, does certainly also recognize the limitations put upon us by bodies. Today we think of this in terms of neuronal conditioning, societal conditioning, which leave us very much as products determined by our world, by the algorithms fed to us through social media, for instance. This Indian model also accepts the limitations imposed by bodily forms and accepts these limitations as a product of social conditions, and for this medieval milieu, also karmic conditions. However, Abhinavagupta argues against a Dennett-like conception of selfhood, which denies any sense of free will. Rather, he understands commonsensical expressions of free choice as a concomitant component of the first-person perspective, and consequently one finds free will wherever one finds the first-person, even in the insect that scurries away from the heavy boot.

In this respect, Abhinavagupta's embrace of agency, as a freedom connected to subjectivity, contradicts India's better-known Advaitin philosopher Śaṅkara. As Sthaneshwar Timalsina points out, at the level of the *Brahman*, Śaṅkara wastes no time in discarding this "autonomous" agent, since the very concept of agency is a product of ignorance (*avidyā*) that needs to be shunned.[70] This is, of course, the hazard of a third-person ontology. In relation to philosophy today, as Lynne Rudder-Baker points out, getting rid of the idea of self, as Dennett does, is quite consistent. If ontological naturalism is true, then ontological subjectivity is an oxymoron, and one has to become an eliminativist like Dennett to be consistent.[71] Yet, what makes us distinct as persons is precisely our phenomenal experience, the feeling that our own consciousness really does feel real.[72] Further, Baker and Dan Arnold both point out that while Dennett proposes mapping brain states to instances that involve a first-person viewpoint, there always remains a residue of a first-personal perspective that can't be reduced or eliminated.[73] I think it may be fair to suggest that Abhinavagupta was aware of these sorts of problems with a third-person perspective. In any case, in terms of wonder and the will, in his *Tantrasāra*, he spells out the list of five primary powers— (1) bliss, (2) will, (3) consciousness, (4) knowledge, and (5) action; in this list he again connects the power of will to wonder.[74]

I suspect, however, that the link that Abhinavagupta posits between wonder and the will is only partly driven by a close introspective attention to the phenomenology of wonder. Certainly, phenomenologically connecting it to the will locates wonder on a more primal level of consciousness than emotion or thought. But linking wonder to will does something else; it indicates agency. It means that the "I" is able to do things in the world. Unlike the rarefied transcendental "I," reminiscent of a Cartesian duality, Abhinavagupta's notion of

"I" is an agent (*kartṛ*), rather than simply a "knower." Wonder functions to enable a capacity to be in the world, to act, to affect the physical world. Here Abhinavagupta pushes back against an earlier widespread philosophical dualism, Sāṃkhya theory. Sāṃkhya theory, like the Cartesian separation of mind and matter, posits a self incapable of crossing over into the realm of materiality. In Abhinavagupta's *Tantrasāra* he tells us,

> Sāṃkhya, however, does not accept that the self could be an "I" consisting of active, materially-engaged awareness (*vimarśa*).[75] We however acknowledge that the self does entail a capacity to do things. That is the pure active awareness which is the "I" in the form of unimpeded wonder of one's own self.[76]

Wonder ties the self to matter. It is directly linked with a capacity to do things in the world. Wonder is thus the signpost of genuine free will. This is, after all, what it means to be sentient—to be able to actually freely choose one action over another, in a way that affects the outcome of events on a material level. Elsewhere he tells us,

> Even those [detached yogis][77] who have the highest level of pure consciousness are not able to do things at the highest level. This is because the "I" which is wonder and bliss, the supreme goal of freedom, defined by abiding in one's own Self—that is covered over for them.[78]

Even a great enlightened yogi, detached from desires and aversions enough to not have to experience the results of previous karma, still even with such great awareness, such a being can lack a capacity to do things. Wonder is tied to the ability to do things. When it is hidden, covered over, then one loses the freedom to choose one thing over another, and with this the ability to affect changes in the world.[79]

So we see wonder as the essence of matter, and wonder is connected to a capacity to do things. The logic here operates on a principle that sees activity in the world as the outcome of the movements of material bodies, with material effects. This logic is not so foreign to our own; our contemporary understanding of matter follows this understanding of material causality as connected to material effects as well. It makes sense. What Abhinavagupta does which is so surprising is to tie this logic of materiality to a foundational subjectivity. This pushes up against our habitual Cartesian expectations. We think of matter as one thing and the inner sense of subjectivity as completely unlike it. Descartes' *res extensa* and *res cogitans* are the two types of things that make up reality. They do not mix.

For Abhinavagupta, instead wonder is precisely the place where they mix. With this he then assimilates material causality to subjectivity, as one of its capacities.[80] That is, the pure "I" can affect the material world. All good and well. We start to see why he links wonder to the will. It is, however, in the corollary implication that we start to see the very radical implications of Abhinavagupta's phenomenology of wonder for a New Materialism. If wonder is the very essence of matter and wonder is linked to agency, then this means matter as well contains within it a capacity for agency. Abhinavagupta's agential wonder begins to sound like Karen Barad's formulations of Bohr's quantum theory, where even on a quantum level for particles we get agency.[81] This is, of course, exactly what Abhinavagupta needs philosophically to allow him to assert a nondualism.[82] We should not forget that his nondualism is framed within a theology. Everything is really an expression of the "I," which takes on a variety of forms that is the material world.[83] And this "I" is divinity, Śiva. Matter too, is an expression of this foundational subjectivity.[84] Its deep nature is joy, which is just the sense of "I," which also shines in the objects we perceive. Abhinavagupta articulates this idea:

> In this way the "I" on the highest level is the body (*vapuḥ*) which is the form of joy, happiness (*nirvṛti*).[85] Its nature is the sentience (*vimarśa*) of that which shines in consciousness (*prakāśa*). And that which is placed upon the "I," that also consists just of joy, happiness. That shines as the physical body, breath, etc. That physical body, breath, etc., [Utpaladeva] tells us is also the "I."[86]

For this panentheism, we do not ever really leave behind bodies. Subjectivity, the "I," is a body as well, a body consisting of joy. When things that we think of as insentient, like the physical body, when those things are in contact with the "I," they also consist of the joy that is the "I." The physical body too is only really this joy, which it assumes when jogged into recognizing its innate subjectivity, as when we, for instance, say "I," feeling ourselves to be just this particular person with arms and legs and so on, engaging in our world around us as a unified self. This inner subjectivity was always the body's own already present, if unrecognized, inner joy.

This blurring of the lines between bodies and subjectivity is the insight Abhinavagupta brings, and for Abhinavagupta's world and for us, it pushes against what we expect. Abhinavagupta tells us, "The 'I' which is wonder is the self of all that appears. This 'I' is the spontaneous, innate power, the mantra of the highest goddess of speech. As it is said, 'the essence of all visible phenomena rest within the 'I'-feeling. This is a secret beyond all secrets.'"[87] The experience of wonder points to a foundational subjectivity underwriting everything that appears. This subjectivity is not an impersonal, transcendental subject; rather it carries an embodied intentionality, conveyed poetically as the spontaneous power of the goddess of speech. Abhinavagupta reminds us that speech, as function and goddess, points to an intentionality. Here we see the idea of will again. The intentionality linked to will is at the heart of language, and this sense of subjectivity is located in a particular place, time and orientation *and* a particular body. The notion of will as intention is never divorced from a personal, first-person orientation.

The secret, of course, that Abhinavagupta points to is the rather counterintuitive insight, for medieval India and ourselves, that subjectivity, consciousness, all by itself, might be able to transform itself into matter, into bodies. Indeed, this transformation is also a secret, or a mystery for our own contemporary culture struggling to understand how mind can be derived from matter, from neurons in the brain. In this Tantric reversal, cosmopsychically flowing instead from mind to matter, wonder is the phenomenology that signals life, the presence of an "I" in the body. It discloses the power of consciousness to do something wondrous, to transform pure subjectivity into the things, "this-ness" (*idantā*) that make up the world.[88]

Still, this is not a crazy animism or a mysticism that sees life everywhere. Abhinavagupta draws on a phenomenology of wonder precisely to mark off that which is alive and that which is not. He tells us, "that which has an active awareness (*vimarśa*)—which is wonder, that alone is sentient."[89] This allows for a philosophy that can navigate our familiar everyday experiences[90] that tell us that some things—you and my dog—are alive, and some things, this clay jar, my computer (at least so far)[91] are not. What may be useful for a New Materialism is precisely that Abhinavagupta offers a philosophical grounding that allows us still to distinguish between the sentient and insentient and, at the same time, he draws the line between living and insentient only in sand. It is handy for wading our way through the world, but it is not a hard and fast ontology. As we see in Chapter Five, we humans ourselves are in fact only partially sentient and partially not, depending on our capacity for wonder. And since wonder is a foundational subjectivity, everywhere possible, *in posse* even in matter, it is possible that as we address the rocks and the mountains, that they too, as we saw in the last chapter, can recognize their own innate subjectivity. Is this enough to imbue a respect for the many so far discounted others, things and nonhuman beings, pushed along with us into an increasingly untenable habitat? My hope is that this frame where there are no innate ontological differences between matter and living beings and between some living beings and other living beings, this frame might at least offer a space to pause, to reflect in a space of wonder for these others.

Wonder as the "I"—Transcending In

Throughout this chapter, I have been dancing around the indissoluble conjunction of wonder with subjectivity. For Abhinavagupta, the phenomenology of wonder is invariably connected with a first-person perspective. Variants of the compound word *ahantācamatkāra*—wonder that is subjectivity—and *ahamiticamatkāra*—wonder that is the "I"—are repeated.[92] What I suggest here is that Abhinavagupta expressly uses wonder's simultaneous link to both subjectivity and materiality to rewrite the notion of transcendence. For us, wonder evokes a phenomenology of transcendence; we saw this explicitly with Seth, and *Scientific American.* Wonder frees us from the drudgery of mechanistic existence, lifting us up into something greater than our habitual selves.

Abhinavagupta's hermeneutic of wonder, on the other hand, disrupts this. Not following the familiar up-and-out of religious transcendence where we arrive at some disembodied and timeless place, instead Abhinavagupta's wonder locates transcendence within ourselves, in a deeper embodied subjectivity. This model, I venture, may perhaps provide ways of thinking through transcendence for a New Materialism. It moves us away from an idea of transcendence as somehow referring to an outside, independent authority, or what Thomas Nagel calls the "view from nowhere,"[93] a space somehow beyond materiality. Instead Abhinavagupta frames the transcendence that comes with wonder as movement to an inwardly felt subjectivity, carrying us into a heightened first-person awareness.

To recapitulate so far, the key to understanding the phenomenology of wonder for these Indian writers looks to be an intuitive understanding about how our own subjectivity engages that which exists outside of our familiar internal mental stream of consciousness. Wonder is a kind of bridge state that links us to all those things that stand outside of the egoic demarcated sense of self. In this respect, wonder seeks to point us to a deeper awareness of self, before the mind jumps in and builds border walls, closing off and demarcating itself as self proper against that which is other. The state of wonder reclaims the object-other, reminds us that the object, insofar as it phenomenologically is a part of our awareness, is also necessarily "I" as well.[94] This is, of course, premised on an originary cosmopsychism, the unfolding of divinity into materiality here. However, it also works apart from its theology by linking its phenomenology to an epistemology of subjectivity.[95] Whatever we encounter in the world, we encounter precisely through our own subjectivity. Abhinavagupta's insight is to locate this epistemological subjectivity as a foundational ontology—what is indisputable is this subjectivity. This starts to look a little like Descartes' *cogito, ergo sum*. However, Abhinavagupta takes the surprising step of locating this subjectivity precisely within materiality. This is how wonder as a state both undergirds the materiality of the world and at the same time points back to a pluripotent, expansive subjectivity.

Here a clarification is in order: Abhinavagupta's link between wonder and subjectivity does not point to the sense of self that we typically construe as ego, but instead to a more foundational intentionality. This includes the ego but it expands beyond it. When Abhinavagupta tells us "wonder, in fact, is just unrivaled resting in one's own self,"[96] the phenomenology of wonder is an experience of self, but this self is not our limited sense of ego. In the quote given in the last section Abhinavagupta tells us that the self for his philosophy differs from the earlier Sāṃkhya idea of self in that it accords agency to the self. To this he adds also a defining insight:

> The ego (*ahaṃkāra*) is the person mirrored in the intellect, but stained by contact with being an object. It then imagines the Self in that which is not the Self, like imagining silver where there is only a shell, mother of pearl. In this way, the suffix "doing" [in *ahaṃ-kāra*, "I-doing"= the ego] indicates a state of artificially constructing the sense of self. . . . The pure active awareness (*vimarśa*), which is the "I," that is wonder, which is one's own self. That, in fact, is not an adversary of the ego.[97]

Phenomenologically, what we think of as the ego happens later; it is artificially constructed, just as much contemporary neuroscience and psychology also tell us. In Abhinavagupta's reading, however, the ego is not somehow in opposition to the deeper self; it is not something apart from it and not its adversary. So, we do not have here an Augustinian model of the self divided against its higher self; instead the ego also takes on life from this deeper subjectivity. The transcendence that wonder brings is not about leaving behind or destroying the ego, as is so often associated with Indian spirituality. Here instead, the ego is the refraction and reflection of a larger self.

In terms of the ego and transcendence, for our own contemporary phenomenology of wonder, the intimation of something bigger than egoic identity is what ties wonder to a transcendence. This transcendence ushers in the something bigger, announcing some higher reality governing how things unfold. One key element of this something bigger is the sense, or hope, of teleology, a deeper purpose directing things—and it is expressly this teleology that has been put on the chopping block by a contemporary materialist science. Tied historically to the idea of God, a teleology promises to fill in the gaps. Some things, in particular, the impropability of life out of matter for instance, beg some sort of explanation. What sets it all in motion? A thinker like Nagel, dissatisfied with the failings of a current scientific materialism, critiques its implicit presuppositions, including its assumption of a "view from nowhere." Yet, even as an avowed atheist, he still feels compelled to suggest a teleology. Pointing to the wonder of life, Nagel offers, "What makes certain molecular configurations stand out from the multitude of possibilities seems to be that they are capable of developing into something that strikes us as rather marvelous, namely a world of living creatures."[98] He proposes a number of possibilities for explaining this wonder: chance, creationism, directionless physical law. What he likes best, however, is a fourth alternative, a teleological bias in the laws of nature. Nature, he tells us, has a teleology embedded within it; it tends toward an increase in value through higher forms of organization. His insertion of teleology within nature offers a way of explaining an evolutionary progress, of explaining this wonder—without requiring a god or an agent or intentions, giving us the idea of Nature "biased towards the marvelous."[99] The idea of teleology in general, of course, for any sort of materialism, new or old, treads on shaky ground, pointing to the thing outside of matter directing it, handwaving in again through the back door something that looks suspiciously like ideas of God.[100] Particularly for a New Materialism, as William Connolly reminds us, the notion of teleology is a sticking point, slipping back in conceptions of an interventionist divinity.[101]

I suspect that we might read a similar discomfited reworking of teleology in the familiar invocation of play (*krīda*) within Indian nondualisms and its theisms, as a way to push against the determining constraints of a telos.[102] Rather than some final goal, which would, after all, be a principle outside any deity or principle creating the world, we find simply the notion of divinity wanting to play. No goal in mind for creation, just play. Somānanda illustrates this divine freedom with a simile of a king who pretends to be a limited foot soldier simply in order to experience the joy of play. Explaining this verse, Utpaladeva tells us the joy in playing (*krīḍa*) refers to wonder (*camatkāra*).[103] Wonder bypasses the purposeness of a teleology through play. Abhinavagupta draws on this passage as well, using play as a way to sidestep a teleology for creation, invoking instead play and freedom.[104] Śiva as divinity pervading the world is not constrained by a telos directing the world from the outside, but simply expresses freedom (*svātantrya*), a playful delight in taking on the various roles of beings in the world here. I might also hazard that the very idea of telos implies a goal from a third-person outside perspective. I suspect this is part of what Abhinavagupta's idea of wonder undoes because it emphasizes the first-person perspective.

Additionally, in Utpaladeva's text, play, *krīḍa*, is also glossed as *spanda*, the primordial vibration underlying all things, calling up simply the delight of life. John Nemec translates this concept here, "Play is vibration seeking out joy."[105] Elsewhere, Abhinavagupta also points to *spanda* in relation to wonder. Etymologically unpacking the term *wonder*, he tells us that "'*camad*' can be understood as resembling the unmanifest word. This consists of the supreme awareness, a sentience that arises from the oscillation of an originary vibration (*spanda*)."[106] Wonder is a cosmic oscillation, *spanda*, a back and forth, giving rise eventually to intentionality that becomes language. At the heart of language is an intentional stance as we saw above, and this intentionality finds its source within an originary cosmic vibration, the throb of life. This vibration encodes an intent, an opening stance, but not a goal or end. Not a telos then, instead more akin to Catherine Keller's capacious process theology, wonder marks the throbbing joy of a playfully unfolding divinity.[107]

Nevertheless, it is not the case that we do not see the kind of phenomenology that we associate with transcendence also in Abhinavagupta. We do. It is, rather, that instead of some sort of up and out, to a transcendent outside beyond time and embodiment, he understands it in terms of a movement within, to embrace the sense of "I." Thus, when Abhinavagupta describes a phenomenology akin to what we think of as transcendence, the expansive rush of moving out of our small egoic identities, here too he links it back to the body, to the breath in the body. In this case, the sense of transcendence is indeed an upward movement; it is the upward movement of the up-moving breath, *udāna*, one of five different breaths in the body.[108] This upward bodily movement is identified with a well-known yogic state, the Fourth State (*turya*), a state of awareness that goes beyond the familiar three states of waking state, dream state, and deep-sleep state. This state of transcendence happens when the up-moving breath moves into the subtle channel in the spine: "Then due to this upward flow in the central path becoming stabilized, it is called the up-moving breath (*udāna*). And that up-moving breath has the nature of fire, burning up the idea of duality. Consequently it is the basis of the Fourth state."[109] We saw this Fourth state earlier in Utpaladeva describing wonder as the mix of subject and object, the "I" within materiality. In India, this Fourth State is generally understood as a state of transcendence and is classically depicted as leaving behind, transcending the body. Abhinavagupta instead points to the Fourth State as moving into subjectivity where we leave behind the idea of a third-person "thisness" of being an object. Poetically invoking an image of alchemy, he tells us:

> But when "This-ness" is concealed, pierced by the unifying flavor of "I," then one exists as it were in the pure consciousness of the states called *Sadāśiva* and *Īśvara*. Here, by making this nondual perspective a habit, one experiences the Fourth state, following the familiar adage of gold enveloping copper to make artificial gold.[110]

The feeling of transcendence is indeed an upward feeling, characterized by the flow of the upward breath. However, its function is to bring us into subjectivity, to wrap over the sense of third-person "thisness." By working with the mind to develop this as a general attitude of seeing the world without dualities, one then experiences the Fourth State.

This Fourth State is a qualitatively different awareness than our perceptions in dreams, deep sleep, or waking states. Indeed, wonder as a state of mind *does* feel different. Additionally, Abhinavagupta subordinates this Fourth State to a Fifth State, Beyond the Fourth (*turiyātita*), which is tied to the fifth breath, a form of breath that pervades the whole body, generating a state that includes both transcendence *and* immanence. Describing a person in the Fifth State, he tells us,

> However, that one in fact in this way exists in a body which contains the worlds and the principles making up reality (*tattvas*). When it pervades to such an extent as to encompass the whole, then that one's inherent nature moves towards that of the Supreme *Śiva*, experiencing the State Beyond the Fourth, the supreme, which is full. That is *vyāna*, the all-pervading breath.[111]

The fifth breath, *vyāna*, pervades the whole, not simply rising up, but encompassing both transcendence and immanence. This fifth breath pervades the body, and its accompanying state encompassess the totality of self and world. These states of mind draw on a typology that is familiar across yogic discourses, as a description of meditative experiences in relation to commonplace understanding of waking and sleep states.[112] In his typology of states of awareness, Abhinavagupta suggests that beyond waking, sleep, and deep sleep, it is possible to access a state of consciousness that transcends—in this case *returns* to a sense of "I." And also to a fifth state of awareness as well, called "Beyond the Fourth," perhaps akin to what we call being "in the zone." This Fifth State includes a fullness (*pūrṇatā*) enveloping *both* subjectivity and the world. Abhinavagupta draws on a very precise yogic phenomenology here, mapping states of consciousness in ways unfamiliar to our contemporary understanding of what the mind can experience. But rather than map a yogic state of transcendence to a phenomenon of leaving behind the body, he tethers it to a heightened subjectivity.[113] The yogic practice succeeding this then brings an awareness that encompasses the fullness of the world as well.

Time

It may also not be surprising then, that Abhinavagupta takes pains to keep time as part of the picture.[114] The idea of transcendence as the "view from nowhere" draws on a trope of timelessness. Abhinavagupta pushes back against the notion of a time-free space specifically by linking time to intentionality, the will. Intentionality, an openness, an orientation toward one thing or another, is the heart of a capacity to will. And this, he tells us, already embeds the fact of time.[115] The crux of his argument falls back on the idea that subjectivity is foundational and all-pervasive; even if we imagine a transcendent deity, the idea of a foundational subjectivity entails that it is located within a particular, immanent "I," with a specific orientation in time and place. I think George Dreyfus articulates this idea as well, though from a Buddhist perspective, when he suggests that we leave phenomenology when we posit a transcendent self. He suggests instead that we stay with the phenomenology of immanent experience.[116]

Here I am reminded of Jeffrey Kripal's compelling, eloquent articulation of Eric Wargo's glass-block universe where what appears to be precognition is really the mind's natural capacity to access its own future states in earlier points in time. This state is also characterized by Kripal as a type of being "in the zone."[117] In any case, this sounds a lot like Abhinavagupta's characterization of the fifth state of mind (*turiyātita*). An expansive awareness, ontologically distinct from our usual waking awareness or sleep state, it is how yogis exercise yogic powers, including those like precognition. However, Abhinavagupta, I suspect, would take issue with the idea of that some sort of viewpoint could stand above the glass-block universe, looking down at it below to map the future, present, and past as if they were some frozen bit of ice, or a glass-block, a static, timeless rendition of the three times.

Rather, the function of awareness as subjectivity means precisely that it is the "I" itself that moves around *within* this cosmopsychic glass-block, not from the outside. As such, there is always this throb of movement, of time within, *spanda*, which is the self in its own freedom. Quoting Somānanda telling us "that intent of the will is the first instant of time," Abhinavagupta links subjectivity to an intentional stance, inextricable from time.[118] Sure, the gifted person, a yogi, or someone coming back from a near-death experience[119] may be able to take a larger view, encompass time from both present and future in what looks like precognition, but for Abhinavagupta, this would not be somehow stepping outside ourselves within the glass-block, to then look down at it. Subjectivity at its fullness becomes the universe. Not ever looking from the outside, it "indeed is the body (*vapuḥ*) of all things."[120] What this means is that there is no transcendent viewpoint outside the universe to look down at it. This also means that things are not predetermined. There is no plan or fate already ordained, impervious to our frantic efforts, while we just go through the motions.[121] The freedom (*svātantrya*) tied to subjectivity has genuine creative effects, as we saw above, even for an insect scurrying away from the boot about to crush it from above.[122] Yes, karma entails that some things have a statistically high probability of happening, but still the system itself is sensitive to the finite expressions of subjectivity, of even an insect, within this dynamic expression of a cosmopsychic "I."

Lynne Rudder-Baker puts the distinction nicely when she says, "Descartes's resolution to *regard himself* as having 'no hands, no eyes, no flesh, no senses' is not a thought that Descartes could have had if it had been true."[123] A transcendent point of view, beyond the body is simply a third-person displacement, forgetting the condition of awareness, one's own body, while still relying on it. She gets at this point from another angle when she responds to Mark Johnston's critique of the self as illusory. "Johnston says that because he can imagine being Spinoza, that that feat threatens the idea that 'I' denotes the likes of Johnston."[124] Baker's response: Johnston is not imagining the state of affairs that he thinks he is imagining. Johnston shifts to a third-person state of affairs when he imagines himself not as himself but as Spinoza. Baker astutely notes that while she can imagine being *like* Spinoza and playing the roles in life that Spinoza played, her own first-person perspective always entails Lynne Baker engaging in this imagination. Subjectivity is always immanent.

Abhinavagupta and Utpaladeva also tackle the problem. How does a yogi read the mind of another person? Does she do it probing from the outside, to know a person's inmost thoughts? As Rafaelle Torella points out, for Utpaladeva the yogi reads another person's mind not as an object separate from their own selves. Rather, "the only means of knowing them is self-awareness." Utpala elaborates, "cognitions belonging to other subjects—which can be known only through self-awareness—must always be manifested as resting on their own self."[125] Utpaladeva's insistence that occult knowledge, reading the mind of another, is centered on one's own self forms a kind of limit case. That is, if we buy into the idea that a yogi can read another person's mind in the first place, then this clearly locates knowledge outside of the first-person perspective. Instead, for Utpaladeva and Abhinavagupta it works differently.

The yogi's own subjectivity expands to embrace the thoughts of some other person as one's own. In this case, Johnston might perhaps imagine himself as Spinoza, but he would also still be Johnston here. And if he were an especially skilled yogi, who with intense imagination (*bhāvana*) could actually become Spinoza? Then it would still be Johnston, an expanded cosmological Johnston encompassing both Mark Johnston of the 21st century and the 17th-century Spinoza. His own first-person perspective as Johnston does not disappear. Thus, for Baker and for Utpaladeva's mind-reading yogis, any knowledge we come by comes through one's own first-person awareness.

Thus, to the extent that all subjectivity is embedded within a particular first-person perspective, it is tied to time and place, to immanence. We leave behind time and place only when we shift to the third person. For Abhinavagupta, this means there can be no time-free transcendent deity. In this way, he essentially purges from the idea of divinity a timeless foundation. And indeed, he tells us the very idea of a timeless transcendence is simply a useful teaching tool for folks caught in the grip of Māyā, those confused about the nature of self.[126] In terms of a New Materialism, with its injunction to reclaim immanence, I suspect that a subject-centered perspective may be key, perhaps even requisite, for any New Materialist endeavor, and I would submit that a New Materialist agenda aimed toward investing materiality with value can gain much from exploring the avenue that Abhinavagupta takes, his philosophical shift to a foundational subjectivity within the heart of materiality.

To conclude, beginning with Anil Seth's invocation of wonder as consolation prize, we have charted its formulation within the keen phenomenological eye of these medieval Indian thinkers. Tying wonder to the body, to sensory enjoyment, and to the intentionality of will, they argue that we can find a foundational subjectivity within matter. Wonder, its expansive joy, its upward rush, signals this subjectivity at the very heart of matter. And with Anil Seth and *Scientific American*, these thinkers would indeed affirm wonder as the antidote to a mechanistic materialism. Antidote, I suggest, precisely because it discloses the presence of subjectivity within material form, beckoning us away from the third person back to the first person. Matter in juxtaposition with wonder, at least briefly, while we savor the wonder, manages to elude the manipulations of a mindset that threatens to reduce it to mere, discardable objects, indeed threatens to reduce us as well to objects, to mere algorithms to manipulate. The astute phenomenological analysis of these thinkers may, I hope, prove helpful for a New Materialism charting its own way through rethinking our relationship to materiality.

Earlier I suggested that wonder also functions in part as praxis. Indeed, Yogarāja in his commentary on Abhinavagupta's *Paramārthasāra* describes the practice of worshipping divinity, gods, in one's own body as a practice of linking the five senses in the body to the feeling of wonder in the heart. In this way, one experiences the vibrating pulsation (*sphuraṇa*) of a full, complete subjectivity (*pūrṇāhantāsphuraṇa*), the "I" which is wonder (*camatkāra*).[127]

We take up this idea of deities in the body in Chapter Three.

3
The Subtle Body

> It is like this. As a caterpillar, having gone to the tip of a blade of grass, then draws itself together to approach another one, in this way, the self (*ātman*), having dropped this body, rendering it unconscious, that self draws itself together to approach another body.
>
> **—Bṛhadaraṇyaka Upaniṣad 4.4.3[1]**

> We are far from alone, even in our own bodies.
>
> **—Rodney Dietart[2]**

Whose Body?

Darwin's famous rejection of God finds utterance in a pessimistic, if pithy, arraignment of Nature's cruelty.[3] He wrote, "I cannot persuade myself that a beneficent and omnipotent God would have designedly created the Ichneumonidae with the express intention of their feeding within the living bodies of Caterpillars."[4] This parasitic wasp injects its eggs into the caterpillar; as it matures, the wasp larva slowly eats away from the inside its live womb, the caterpillar's body. The idea of an enemy within, a wasp taking over the hapless caterpillar from the inside, violating the body's boundaries against the will of the body's proper owner, strikes Darwin as too sinister to countenance. It's the stuff of horror movies, evoking images from the movie *Alien*, with the strange, ugly creature bursting out of Kane's chest.

We, as did Darwin, tend to think of our bodies as our own inviolable property, a self marked off from others by the boundary of skin that makes each of us an individual with our own separate desires.[5] Perhaps more disturbing still are those other infiltrating organisms that do not just devour bodies but also control the mind and desires of their victim. Like the horsehair worm that secretes neurotransmitters into the brains of crickets, enticing them to commit suicide in waters they would normally shun. These mind-controlling parasites elicit something more akin to an unconscious, visceral disgust in their sinister cooptation of something beyond the body, stealing away the

The Matter of Wonder. Lorilai Biernacki, Oxford University Press. © Oxford University Press 2023.
DOI: 10.1093/oso/9780197643075.003.0004

mind and will of their victims. It does feel as though stealing the will and mind of a creature—even so humble a creature as a cricket—crosses a line. To bring it closer to home, we need only look so far as to that best and ubiquitous of household pets, our feline companions. Joanne Webster, Jaroslav Flegr, and others have painstakingly tracked how even for us humans infected with a parasite we get from our cats, *Toxoplasma gondii*, our wills and minds are not quite our own, but rather are managed by these tiny infectious manipulators of consciousness.[6]

As Webster and her colleagues document,[7] for mice, this tiny protozoa manages to alter dopamine production on a neuronal level, which drives them to a reckless, fatal attraction for cat pheromones. For humans the altered brain chemistry brings its own kind of recklessness. Infected persons are far more likely—statistically, almost three times more likely—to get into car accidents.[8] As Robert Sapolsky notes, the protozoa has also been implicated in the increased incidence of schizophrenia and suicide.[9] A tiny parasite in a human body becomes the author of human desires and actions. That such a tiny unintelligent creature could cause such deep volitional shifts in human behavior cannot help but give us pause. We think of our minds, our wills, as somehow our own, even more deeply our own than the bodies we possess. But what if the sense of self I habitually inhabit were somehow also an expression of more than just my familiar "I"? Here I am not suggesting that we consider the extensive and much-discussed influence we encounter through the self's construction in its interrelations with other human selves and society.[10] Rather, on a much more basic, bodily level, what if my own desires are more than just me? What if they are, rather, also the expressions of the various other beings that share my body space—the *Toxoplasma gondii*, the multiplicity of bacteria and viruses in the space of my body's microbiome? Or, in relation to a New Materialism positing the agency of matter, what about something that altogether lacks even the basic sentiency of a protozoa—like the lead in drinking water which causes increased aggression,[11] or the refined plant substance taken from a poppy to make a profoundly mind-controlling opioid? What if my will is simply the expression of one temporarily victorious puppeteer, among many multiple agencies driving my desires?

In this chapter, I point to an oddly similar appraisal of the human body that we find in a medieval Indian Tantric vision of the subtle body—similar in its displacement of human agency in favor of a multiplicity of not visible, hard to discover, but potent agencies directing human actions. This medieval Indian portrait of the human body that we find in the writings of the 11th-century Hindu thinker Abhinavagupta takes the subtle body as the locus of a multiplicity of agencies, as a panoply of deities, that drive human choices. There is, of course, a big difference between gods inhabiting and directing the desires of a human body, and mindless parasites doing so through manipulations of the brain's dopamine levels. Yet, both point to a displacement of agency for human subjectivity.

In this chapter, I address this key component of the subtle body within this medieval Indian context, namely, that it operates as a way of acknowledging the multiplicity of agencies that make up human volition. The subtle body in this respect affords a recognition that the human is not master in its own house, but rather that the house itself, the subtle body, points to an expansive ecology with multiple expressions of agency directing human choices.[12] What is so striking about this shift in perspective is that the very metaphor of "house"—Freud's Western assumption of the body as some inert container—might not ever really work for something as complex and multiple as a human body.

The theology Abhinavagupta invokes adds to the mix. It proposes an element of agency and intentionality scripted outside of human volition. In this case, his theology makes the difference between a mindless dopamine-generating bug and a mindful agency, both directing human choices apart from what we humans think we choose. I suggest that theology here registers a kind of respect for the affective processes of the body. In this, it shifts how we think about human choice in a way that can enrich a New Materialist understanding of agency outside of human control. In what follows, I first discuss Abhinavagupta's panentheist conception of the subtle body and its implications for understanding the idea of the body generally for our contemporary world. I argue for an understanding of the subtle body as a way of acknowledging the multiplicity of agencies that make up human volition. Again, theology here is important, since Abhinavagupta's theology affords intention and consciousness to these other agencies directing human choices. With this, the subtle body for Abhinavagupta affords a way of allowing differentiation within his nondual philosophy, even as this capacity for difference is marked by human limitations. Following this discussion, I examine a key problem that the subtle body solves for an Indian context more generally—specifically, its function to carry the person's karma from one life to the next. I then address in greater detail Abhinavagupta's image of the subtle body as *puryaṣṭaka*, the "City of Eight." On the heels of this, we look at how Abhinavagupta portrays the body as the abode of the gods who direct its functions. Finally, by way of conclusion, we see that Abhinavagupta allows for a sense of unification of the self within the subtle body, simply through use of the "I," the first-person perspective, as the "I" operates on multiple registers, embracing the multiple agencies that direct it as one's own.

Theology and Agency

Already it may becoming clear that this conception of the subtle body is not particularly consonant with popular new-age versions of the subtle body, with their color-coded cakras pointing the way to spiritual enlightenment. Certainly, the subtle body also functions in other ways for medieval India; perhaps its most important function is as a means of explaining religious doctrinal points, such as reincarnation. It also operates as a mechanism for the kinds of magical powers, *siddhis*, that populate Indian religious traditions and are entailed in this religiously shared Indian cosmology of proliferating ghosts and spirits.[13] Indeed, this proliferation of spirits is implicated in the enmeshed network of multiple agencies overdetermining human choices. In any case, what is remarkable about this displacement of human agency is how surprisingly it parallels a modern Western scientific displacement of human agency. Even apart from infectious protozoans, a thrust of much contemporary human biology is an understanding that human agency is preempted by biological imperatives, the mechanical functions of neurons, neurotransmitters and hormones driving human behaviors, not at the behest of an individual's will, but rather more conspicuously serving the reproduction of genes.[14] In this context, Robert Sapolsky is not an outlier when he suggests that given the mechanisms of human biology, free will is a difficult concept to consider.[15] What these two very distant worldviews separated by centuries and theology share is just this abrogation of human agency.

With these similarities, the theology that Abhinavagupta's medieval model carries may seem to us today as excess baggage, an unnecessary addition to the nuts and bolts of biology. I suggest, however, that Abhinavagupta's theological inscription of deities driving human action offers something more: a way of thinking about selves and bodies that can be valuable in our own current moment of planetary neglect. The panentheism out of which Abhinavagupta fashions his conception of the subtle body enfolds within it an upgrade for the idea of bodies, of matter. Not ever entirely dead, the matter that makes up the body is imbued with its own lively intentionality as the body's own entangled deities. The theology Abhinavagupta presents offers a perspectival shift into recognizing the body's own claims to intentionality, all apart from our usual assignment of intention to the disembodied ego running the show. With this, his model rejects a spirit–body duality where spirit is the true voice of the person possessing the body. Instead we get a continuum, an expansive, and expanding, conception of what the idea of spirit, consciousness, might be in its expression as the "I," the pervasive sense of subjectivity animating all existence. "Spirit," or the self, is simply the expansive embrace of a sense of "I" across the multiplicity of bodies and deities that cohabit our physical bodies.

Along these lines, I suspect that what is important about the understanding of the subtle body as made of deities is less its precise theological orientation of the body, an idea of this god or that god in this or that part of the body, and rather more the accompanying suggestion that various agencies drive human will, agencies with their own separate intentionalities. The Tantric tradition supplies a variety of different maps stipulating different deities populating the various locations of the subtle body. That the maps do not agree in their details tends to suggest that the understanding of the subtle body concentrates less on which deity controls which part of human behavior and more as a nod to the body's inherent entanglements.

This panentheist theology is a way of underscoring a foundational liveliness to all that exists in our world. In this respect, Abhinavagupta's model of the subtle body with its multiplicity of agencies is surprisingly consonant with a New Materialist reclamation of our world as not simply dead matter subject to human manipulations. His worldview shares with New Materialisms an acknowledgment of an ecology of beings in which we humans are materially embedded, even if Abhinavagupta extends it beyond our world's visible cohabitants to ethereal entities like gods. In any case, the implicit panpsychism of much of New Materialism finds a counterpart in this Indian model's basic panentheism (with its cosmopsychism verging on panpsychism), highlighting the liveliness of the world in this portrait of a body variously enacting the entelechies of different deities.

It is important here to emphasize that Abhinavagupta's cosmology derived from the traditions in medieval India called the Mantramārga,[16] and its consequent map of the subtle body is not quite the same as other images of subtle bodies that we find elsewhere in India's religious landscape, from medieval times and beyond. Apart from the fact that conceptions of what the subtle body looks like can vary dramatically,[17] how the subtle body functions within a given cosmology varies as well.

Simply because the very concept of a subtle body in the first place is novel for a Western perspective, we should be careful. We should be wary of assuming that even if the images of the subtle body differ from one tradition to the next, nevertheless, all portraits of the subtle body in India will offer the same understanding of how the subtle body operates. Abhinavagupta's panentheism entails some different functionalities for the subtle body than other models, for instance, other nondualist models of the subtle body, and models predicated on dualist conceptions of cosmology. For instance, as Ayon Maharaj (now Swami Medhānanda) points out, the 19th-century Indian thinker Vivekananda offers a different model in which the subtle body is made of the mind, ego, and intellect.[18] Similarly, Buddhist philosophical conceptions need the notion of the subtle body to explain reincarnation, a key component of the historical Buddha's discourse. However, given the philosophical imperative of the Buddhist *anātma* doctrine to not have some substance-based soul hanging around, going from life to life, a Buddhist conception of subtle body at times starts to look like an idea of the subtle body as information, mere data conserved from one point in time to the next, without an accompanying unifying intelligence.

What distinguishes Abhinavagupta's conception of the subtle body from these other conceptions, nondualist, dualist and self-free, is, in the end, precisely his panentheism which folds a conception of consciousness with its intelligence intimately within bodies, not separate from bodies. He tells us, for instance, that "'that,' consciousness alone, is the highest ultimate body (*vapuḥ*) of all entities."[19] Far from a dualist idea of a gulf between consciousness and matter, here in contrast, consciousness itself is nothing other than a body. He does not entertain some idea akin to our familiar Cartesian split, which, even as we find this split in the earlier philosophical cosmology of Sāṃkhya that Abhinavagupta inherits, still Abhinavagupta rejects it. Rather, as we have seen, the model is one in which consciousness itself, pictured as a wall or a screen, molds itself into the multiplicity of beings with their bodies that make up the world. He writes, "on the back of the wall that is consciousness the picture of all beings becomes visible."[20] Consciousness itself is the stuff that makes up bodies, arranging itself in various ways. In this context, we hear him say that consciousness in its basic, pristine form, the *Śiva tattva*, is also just a body: "The *Śiva* Archetype alone is the body of all things."[21] Very directly, he takes pains to clearly indicate his nondualist cosmology to entail no difference between materiality and consciousness. Consciousness itself, in its highest, purest manifestation as the *Śiva tattva*, is, in fact, just the body. And the obverse, the material component of the world, is itself transcendent divinity, spirit. The concomitant corollary of this is that there is also no place where there is matter that is dead, entirely free of at least a latent capacity to express sentiency. As we saw in Chapter One, Abhinavagupta tells us, "Even the lifeless third person, if it sheds its lifeless form can take on the first and second person forms—as in 'Listen, o stones' and 'Of mountains, I am Meru.'"[22] Here stones, which are typically understood as dead matter, are not ontologically bound to this lifeless state. By being addressed in the second person, he tells us, they lose their inert insentiency and take on the life that comes with being called "you," through the second person address.

Indeed, when we focus our attention on objects, a statue of the Buddha or the Catholic image of Mary on the altar, or even a favorite vase, for example, the objects themselves appear to inhabit a kind of glow. Explaining the power of icons in a religious context usually invokes a notion that humans project human qualities onto objects. Abhinavagupta, in contrast, suggests that the stones or icons innately already possess a latent liveliness that merely comes to the surface by our address. The second example he gives, "Of mountains I am Meru," is spoken by the God Krishna to the warrior Arjuna in the *Bhagavad Gītā*; here Abhinava tells us, the mountain takes on the "I" feeling of the first grammatical person through this declaration, transforming it from object to subject. No longer a dead configuration of stones and earth, it reclaims its deep essential nature as sentient subject.

So how does the subtle body play into this nondual fusion of matter and consciousness? We often think of the subtle body as being about transcendence, a way for the spirit to leave the body behind in some abstracted, disembodied, and consequently more perfect, less entangled existence.[23] In contrast, Abhinavagupta's model is very much about bringing things back to bodies, to materiality, no doubt, a materiality that is at base simply spirit in any case, yet one in which a lingering materiality as third-person object makes both interaction and multiplicity possible. What the subtle body does for Abhinavagupta is to allow this perspectival awareness to register the multiplicity that makes up the world. In relation to what the subtle body (*puryaṣṭaka*) does, he tells us,

> in the state of that type of I-consciousness, which belongs to the Lord ignorance is entirely removed. So the notion, "this is blue," does not arise. Here that sort of lower I-consciousness needs to be developed which will not be so spotless and rarefied as to entirely remove the knowledge of object as other.[24]

In order to relate to others, we need something different than the highest awareness of nonduality; rather, we need a lower sort of awareness. What the subtle body does is to afford us this lower awareness that makes it possible to differentiate others.[25] The subtle body is sufficiently enmeshed in the multiplicity of the world to register a difference between itself and another. It allows a person to notice some object nearby and to understand it as different from one's own self, to be able to interact with a blue vase as outside of one's self, even if a truer gaze knows that its difference from me, its blue color and shape is merely provisional.

The Subtle Body and Transmigration

To get a sense of Abhinavagupta's mediating use of the subtle body, it may be helpful to look generally, if only briefly, at the subtle body's functions in an Indian context. Apart from Abhinavagupta's use of the subtle body to accommodate difference, to allow for a particular and limited self to act within a world of objects that one considers different from oneself, probably the most predominant function of the subtle body within a Hindu context is as carrier for the karma that accompanies an individual from one life to the next. In this respect, the subtle body frequently functions as a vehicle for agency and responsibility for one's deeds, for one's karma in one body to take effect in some future life after the demise of that particular physical body. From the Buddha's many lives in the Jataka tales to Kṛṣṇa's declarations in the *Gītā* of his past lives, reincarnation is taken as a given, indubitable in the various Indian traditions in Buddhism, Jainism, and Hinduism. Given the difficulty of explaining how something so ephemeral as deeds and intentions can be bound to a body that is not yet born, it is not surprising that exactly what it is that carries this karma varies considerably across different times and traditions.[26] An early depiction of the process of transmigration in the *Bṛhadaraṇyaka Upaniṣad* from about the 7th–8th century BCE paints the process of death as precisely the reduction of the multiplicity of agencies that was the body. When a person is dying, the text tells us, "he is becoming one, he does not see, they say; he is becoming one, he does not smell, they say; he is becoming one, he does not taste, they say; he is becoming one, he does not speak . . . " and so on, through the variety of actions a living body does, including thinking, hearing, and comprehending.[27] Śaṅkara tells us in his 8th century CE commentary on this Upaniṣad that

> becoming one means the subtle body (*lingātmā*) collects the person's activities . . . .thus, when the operating deity (*devatā*) of smell ceases, smell becomes one with the subtle body, then the person does not smell, they say.[28]

Here, the subtle body is a wrapper, a container for all the activities that end when the multiple agencies, the *devatās*, the operating deities of speech and sight and thinking cease as the person dies. This text also likens the subtle body to a caterpillar, but not like the unfortunate caterpillar that precipitated Darwin's atheism. In this image, like a caterpillar (*tṛṇajalāyuka*) that pivots from one blade of grass to the next, the self moves from one body to the next.[29]

Here, Śaṅkara points to the subtle body as the mechanism that solves the vexing problem of transference of a continuity of a particular self across the gap from one life to the next. However, we also see that the self, *ātman*, can take on this role in an Indian context, without a subtle body. As Dasti and Phillips note, for the *Nyāya Sūtra* and its commentaries, the self, *ātman*, an immaterial entity, in this dualist philosophy acts as a receptacle for the *saṃskāras*, the collection of tendencies and karmas that we carry from one life to the next.[30] As Wilhelm Halbfass observes, the Mīmāṃsaka Kumārila also understands that the effective causal quality of a properly performed ritual act (*apūrva*) has the *ātman*, the self, as its locus.[31] Similarly, looking at early Upaniṣadic texts, Fred Smith points out the formulation of reincarnation through "a discarnate spirit essence" from one agent to the next life in what Smith notes as confirming "the doctrinal point of inherent separation of essence, 'coded substance', or 'spirit', and physical or observable matter."[32] This is a dualism in the early tradition that Abhinavagupta's Tantra tries to later rework into a monism. Smith points to this reincarnating entity as a "coded substance" in contrast to "physical or observable matter." The spirit finds a physical body to inhabit. In this early case, the spirit is not understood as a subtle body, moving from life to life, but, as Smith insightfully remarks, still a substance, only a substance rather like code in his estimate. In contrast, Buddhism opts against an idea of self, against the idea of a substance moving from life to life, but keeps still a notion of karmic information as the impersonal, and nonpermanent stream that allows a particular person to reincarnate. In this respect, as Alex Watson observes, Buddhists are not so dissimilar from Hindu Nāyaiyikas in that both are dualists because both think of a non-physical part of us that exists beyond one life to go to the next.[33] In any case, as Sāṃkhya demonstrates, the subtle body is not a concept that arises only when a monism prevents the idea of self from serving as a particularized and limited carrier of karma. Īśvarakṛṣṇa's *Sāṃkhya Kārikā*, with its own dualism akin to Cartesianism, tells us that it is the subtle body that transmigrates, not the self, and that the subtle body contains the ego and the mind and the senses, but not the gross, physical elements.[34] So, not the self per se, the subtle body here still has the elements of the person, including sense organs, but not the physical elements like earth and water.

Moreover, the subtle body does not arise only when a person leaves the body in death. We find in the *Tripurarahasya*,[35] a late medieval Sanskrit text, a tale of a king who wants to enter inside a mountain. The sage with him tells him to put his physical body in a nearby pit, so it will be safe, and then to use his subtle body to enter inside the mountain. The king does not know how to do this. In a response that would fit right in for our world today, he wonders if he will die if he leaves his physical body. The sage laughs and instructs him to close his eyes, and then the sage enters the king's body and separates the king's subtle body (*liṅgatanu*) from the gross physical body.[36] The sage puts the physical body aside, safe in a small pit. The sage then travels with his own subtle body and the king's subtle body to the interior of the mountain. We see with this both a physical body and a subtle body. The two are connected but separable. They mix and interact with each other. Both of these bodies are really bodies, part of the framework that makes up the body as a whole and there is a porous interface between the physical and the nonphysical body. Remarkably as well, we see a kind of porousness, some *very* soft boundaries between different physical bodies, between the king's body and sage's body. The sage can enter into the king's body through his knowledge of yoga. Similarly, in the approximately 14th-century *Śaṅkaradigvijaya*, the sage Śaṅkara also uses his subtle body to leave his physical body and then inhabit the body of a newly dead king, so that he can win a debate with his philosophical opponent Maṇḍana Miśra. Here Śaṅkara displays his skills as a yogī: "occupying the subtle body (*ātivāhikaśarīra*), he, with the strength of his guru yoga, enters the body of the king."[37] His goal here is to use the dead king Amaruka's body to experience what sex is like and at the same time not be guilty of breaking his celibacy vows as a monk.[38] The word for subtle body here, *ātivāhikaśarīra,* is a "body that is extremely quick." It is a body, with entailed materiality, but one that is light enough to travel to the sun and moon and the center of a mountain.

James Hartzell argues that the subtle body doctrine derives from early medical sources as the *karmapuruṣa*, literally "action-spirit," which is the subtle body that comes into contact with the combined semen of the father and the blood of the mother when the child is conceived.[39] He describes the process in terms of key points in the physical body, the *cakras*, which act as portals:

> The fundamental premise appears to be that our subtle body energy networks of centers (*cakras* or *padmas*) and channels (*nāḍis*) and drops (*bindus*) is [*sic*] multidimensionally interlinked. During moments of sexual ecstasy certain channels of the subtle body open to these other dimensions, providing the routes whereby the (re-) incarnator can incarnate.[40]

The mechanism for transmigration links the physical body with a cohabiting subtle body with its networks of *cakras* and channels, and also with some other kind of space where persons waiting to reincarnate reside until they find the routes to enter a body and be reborn. He also notes that the subtle body was not a sectarian concept aligned with only a particular school but was rather accepted among different religious traditions.[41] Hartzell's fascinating description highlights the problem of how something as immaterial as the intentions and reverberation of past deeds can affect matter in a substantive way.[42] It is not surprising, then, that frequently for Hinduism the subtle body shows up ontologically as a quasi-physical substance,[43] which offers a permeability of mind and physicality.[44]

The difficulty of trying to meld together the physical with the immaterial that the subtle body represents is demonstrated in the apocryphal story of the 19th-century founder of the Arya Samāj, Dayananda Sarasvati, pulling a corpse out of the Gangā River and cutting it open to see if he could find the *cakras* inside.[45] It is probably important to point out that ideas of the body in an Indian context map to a cosmology that does not quite adhere to the habitual boundaries between mind and matter in our familiar Cartesian conventions of what makes up the body. In a Sāṃkhya context, mind (*manas*) and the sense of ego (*ahaṁkāra*) are not somehow sentient over and against the materiality of the earth and blood that comprise the body. The body as insentient matter is composed of earth, water, fire, air, and space, along with other components such as sensory capacities, and also mind, intellect, and ego. These latter components, including mind, are also not sentient. With its seamless mixing of the categories we term mind and matter, this Indian map of the body to some degree manages to sidestep some of the intractable oppositions that derive from a Cartesian bifurcation of mind and body.

Further, intertwined with this physicality is breath, *prāṇa*; breath here is not simply oxygen moving in the lungs and out, but rather it exists also and primarily as a subtle flow in the body. For our Western context, breath, not itself alive, is a crude marker of sentience. Again, this does not entirely map to the Indian context, where once more, breath is no more a sign of sentience than is earth or blood, or intellect for that matter, depending on which philosophical system one follows. In Saṃkhyā, neither breath nor intellect nor the earth element of the body is sentient; only the self (*ātman*) is. In contrast, for Abhinavagupta, insofar as the subtle body, made up of the five breaths (*prāṇas*) and the mind and intellect and so on—this subtle body, which transmigrates from one life to the next is enlivened by *vimarśa* through adopting a stance of subjectivity (*ahantā*). Thus, it and the breath and the mind are sentient as well. In any case, more generally for Sāṃkhya in this respect, the gulf is between spirit and mind–body, not between mind and matter. So crossing the gap from body to mind is not the difficulty in this Indian context, as it might be for a Western Cartesian context since the mind, simply an offshoot of *prakṛti*, Nature, is already fundamentally just matter. The trick is figuring out how to cross the gap between spirit to the materiality of mind–body.

Curiously, in Buddhism, which denies any idea of a self (the *anātma* doctrine) or something like a spirit to contrast the mind–body, we still see a lingering materiality finding its way across lives. Even without the side of spirit, the *ātman* as self to steer the path for a reincarnating person, or without Abhinavagupta's "I-ness" (*ahantā*), as a subjectivity for the subtle body to go from one life to the next, Buddhism proposes a mechanism as a stream for karma after the physical body dies. As Alexis Sanderson observes, even without a self, actions, seemingly ephemeral, also have a matter-based component, *avijñapti*,[46] that continues and carries forth the good or bad effects of the deed to ripen at a future time. With this, taking up a life as a soldier or a hunter carries a karmic stream even when one is not killing other life; also, taking vows of Buddhist abstention has karmic fruit even when one is not actively practicing.[47] This ripening is tied to the person's karmic stream. So, while there is not a permanent self, still the karmic burden carries its own form of materiality, conducive to reappearing in the next life stream of a particular person. Even as Buddhism denies the idea of a self, it is still bound to a notion of a dualism of a material body and something quasi-physical, capable of jumping the gap of lives as a particular karmic stream of a particular individual to reincarnate, for instance, as the current Dalai Lama who remembers his last incarnation as the 13th Dalai Lama. The lingering materiality of a concept like *avijñapti* tends to work against an easy and increasingly familiar translation of Buddhism's no-self doctrine as replacing a substance-based self with the idea of self-as-process, self-as-information, popular in cognitive science conceptions.[48] (We will look at the idea of consciousness as information in greater detail in Chapter Five.) In any case, while Mark Siderits's tantalizing physicalist speculation of rebirth as an organic equivalent of a Zip drive just before the final crash of the old computer to reinstall on the next birth aptly conveys the idea of self as information, the metaphor necessarily points to something he neglects, that is, the *thing* that is the Zip drive, its materiality as something like the subtle body containing the karmic information between lives.[49]

Indeed, where the metaphor of self-as-information drops the corollary of something like a subtle body, as it does for Siderits's attempt to interpret Buddhism in physicalist terms, there it also loses one of its major functions for Buddhism: the capacity to explain reincarnation. For instance, Thomas Metzinger discusses the biology of out-of-body experiences, referencing notions of *prana* and the subtle body,[50] noting that "OBE research now makes it an empirically plausible assumption that this subtle body does indeed exist."[51] However, his explanation diverges sharply from the emic perspective of Indian traditions, of Śaṅkara's *Digvijaya*, for instance, which understands the manipulation of matter—actually reenlivening the king's dead body—by means of a person's subtle body entering and transforming that matter. Metzinger instead rejects an idea of "astral matter," concluding that the subtle body is the embodied brain's self-model and that it is "made of pure information flowing in the brain."[52] So this model supposes that the subtle body experience is a function of neuronal firing in a pattern that merely represents the self as out of the body. Certainly, Śaṅkara's experience of living in King Amaruka's body amidst the king's harem in order to win his debate depends on something like "astral matter," his subtle body actually inhabiting the king's body.

On the other hand, if it were only a question of information, given Śaṅkara's nondualist understanding of the self as all-pervasive, one might be able to argue that the "information" he gathers from King Amaruka's body is nevertheless all-pervasively present, even in his own brain. Hence, he should not need to engage in subtle body-hopping into the dead king's body to experience sex, guilt-free. This of course, makes the narrative redundant. Why bother with this wonderfully fantastic story of hopping into a dead body if all this information is available within the easy reach of his own neuronal firing? As we saw earlier with Abhinavagupta, a nondual reality indeed erases the possibility for this story of two separate bodies, the king's and Śaṅkara's, since the concept of difference is not operative in a nondual perspective.

The function of the subtle body, then, is to offer the needed limitations to still engage in a world of difference in the midst of a nondualist cosmology that knows everything at once. The subtle body makes possible the idea of difference in order to gain a sense of some blue thing as object, separate from the self, or a king's body in a harem that is different from the monk's celibate body. We do see also in Buddhism and Śaṅkara's Advaita Vedānta attempts to reconcile a nondual truth with the multiplicity of bodies and agents controlling those bodies by adopting a two-tier reality: on the one hand, the ultimate reality, the nondual simultaneous apprehension of all knowledge devoid of differentiation between various persons and things, and on the other, the ordinary reality, *vyavahāra*, where Śaṅkara actually needs a subtle body to hop into a dead king's body to win a debate. While the notion of a two-tiered reality does some heavy lifting to help avoid the blatant, if only a mere seeming contradiction that what is actually true is not how we live in the world, it also brings its own messy conundrums, particularly around the idea of agency.[53] If there is only one nondual reality, then it becomes difficult to assign human responsibility for crimes. Indeed, as Christian Coseru points out, it becomes difficult to engage in practice for spiritual transformation toward the goal of *nirvāṇa*. Discussing the ethical implications of a nondual perspective, he notes that the Buddha's emphasis on moral valuations of actions suggests that the Buddha favors a retention of a notion of individual responsibility.[54] With this, it appears, instead of the true, highest reality, we have a greater need for the world of ordinary life with its multiple differentiations, *vyavahāra*. In any case, the problems of agency that arise for Buddhist and Hindu nondualities start to look a bit like the difficulty the biologist Sapolsky faces with a nondualist materialism that understands human free will as an illusion of neurons and dopamine. Both of these nondualisms, reversals of each other in terms of what they categorize as real—spirit or matter—fall prey to the problems of assigning agency. The subtle body with its capacity to mix up the matter that is the body with a limited version of spirit affords this capacity for differentiation of self and other and limited agency assignable to a distinct, limited person.

I want to point to one other important reading of the subtle body, which tangentially aligns with my reading of Abhinavagupta's use of the subtle body: its function as a mechanism for intersubjectivity. Geoffrey Samuel points out how ideas of the subtle body are very much also about the kinds of interrelation we have with our wider social and ecological context. Drawing especially from a Tibetan concept of the subtle body, he notes that it is also an avenue for interaction in ways that are not explicitly consciousness directed toward the objects of the world, but rather in a manner of flows between entities.[55] In this sense the subtle body operates as a means for relationality. Similarly, Jay Johnston talks about the subtle body in our current context as constituting a "radical form of intersubjectivity."[56] The notion that the subtle body offers a way of thinking about intersubjective relations is consonant with Abhinavagupta's conceptions of its function to create a space for differentiation.

Abhinavagupta's Conception of the Subtle Body

Abhinavagupta's conception of the subtle body is that it is simply consciousness, but consciousness that has become limited and contracted:

> [T]he inherent nature of this person is that of pure consciousness which has become contracted into the subtle body, the City of Eight in the state of Emptiness, and has acquired the habit of wandering from body to body, life after life.[57]

The term Abhinavagupta uses here for the subtle body, in accordance with his Tantric lineage, is *puryaṣṭaka*, literally, the "City of Eight." Based on the nomenclature that he uses, "City of Eight," we notice right away that already the idea of the subtle body entails a plurality. Earlier we see "*sūkṣma śarīra*," literally, "subtle body," but here the very name of the subtle body references its inherent multiplicity. In any case, the subtle body, as the City of Eight arises as a contraction of awareness, one that hinges on deeper latent traces of a sense of limitation. Abhinavagupta describes this limitation in terms that are evocative of subconscious impulses that override what the conscious mind might say. He tells us:

> So, thinking, I am "equal to *Rudra*, etc.," and "I am that" [*Brahman*, Absolute] is fine, but to the extent that the latent residual impressions remain fully operative, it is reasonable that pride and anger, etc., will still arise. Consciousness, which here possesses latent traces, herself creates limitation. Consciousness is one alone, yet has a specific form where it consists of sound [form, taste] etc. which flow down and are absorbed, and from this the City of Eight is separated off from full consciousness.[58]

Even if we tell ourselves that we are the pure, highest awareness of divinity, the "I am that" of the Upaniṣads,[59] as long as deeper impressions of limitation remain latent in ourselves, anger and pride will still pop up against our will. Abhinavagupta's description explains with a psychological lucidity how his monism can incorporate a conception of a subtle body that is limited. Not full consciousness, the subtle body instead offers a sense of self as limited and differentiated from other selves. The subtle body also in his context is connected to the idea of Emptiness, the familiar Buddhist term *śūnya*, which for Abhinavagupta's context is understood as a kind of grounding space out of which the materiality of the world arises. Delineating the relationship that the subtle body bears to Emptiness, *śūnya*, Abhinavagupta says,

> [W]hen "I-ness" is placed within Emptiness, it exists and is called the City of Eight. . . . To which they say: "The subtle body is also present in the state of meditative absorption in that particular deep meditation (*samādhi*) which is a merger into Emptiness." "I-ness" placed in Emptiness is the impeller, the one which agitates the five vital breaths and that "I-ness" takes the form of the function of the senses and it takes as its essence the City of Eight.[60]

Abhinavagupta understands a stance of subjectivity, "I-ness" (*ahantā*), as key to enlivening the breath to take on its form as the subtle body, which wanders from body to body, life after life. The subtle body remains present even in a deep meditative state. So rather than the erasure of a sense of a subtle body in a state of Emptiness, Abhinavagupta sees a close linkage between the subtle body and Emptiness. The subtle body is also connected with the operations of bodily functions such as smell and sight and the breath, *prāṇa*. The flow of *prāṇa*, breath, includes both a physical element and simultaneously a nonphysical energetic component. This doubly configured understanding of breath, *prāṇa*, as both material and subtle contributes to making up the subtle body. Abhinavagupta tells us that the subtle body, this

> City of Eight here includes the five vital breaths plus the two groups of sense organs [organs of knowledge (*buddhīndriya*) and organs of action (*karmendriya*)]. By accepting the inner organs as one essential capacity to ascertain things, we have the third.[61]

So the five vital breaths plus the two groups of sense organs make seven. The two groups of sense organs are the first group as the five senses, including the capacity to hear, see, feel, taste, and smell. The second group, the five *karmendriya*, are connected to physical components of the body detailed in terms of function. They include the feet as the capacity to move, the hands as the capacity to grasp, the anus as the capacity to excrete, the genitals as the capacity to reproduce, and the mouth as the capacity to speak. The eighth component is the inner organ (*antaḥkaraṇa*), which includes lumped together the mind, intellect, and ego. Thus, we get a picture of the subtle body, first, as made of the breaths (*prāṇa*). Additionally, the subtle body has the capacity to see and hear, as well as the capacity to grasp and speak, and also a capacity to think. This conception of the transmigrating subtle body with its powers to grasp and move looks like a bit more than a simple ghost, a transmigrating spirit that occasionally appears to the people left behind, and instead looks to have the powers of a poltergeist, grasping and speaking. Explicating the subtle body in more detail, Abhinavagupta tells us that "this City of Eight is an extremely subtle body"[62] and at the same time, it is

> like the physical body, but does not have limitations in terms of its spatial dimensions. However, that [subtle body] is linked to time as a universal. . . . The City of Eight does in fact have the nature of a body, because the great elements [fire, earth etc.] inhere in it. Also, here, in order to remove delusion, [Utpaladeva] uses the word "body" precisely to preempt the objection that the word "body" [with its physical implications] should not be applied here.[63]

So the subtle body is like a physical body, but it does not have the same spatial limitations. It is connected to time as a universal, hence it exists in time, but it appears less constrained than the ordinary physical body. Even so, Abhinavagupta tells us that its rarefied condition should not be construed to mean that this subtle body does not partake of the materiality associated with bodies. Rather he emphasizes that the subtle body does indeed have the nature of a body. Still, as a body, it is not the same as the ordinary human physical body or other material objects. Describing the subtle body in its confluence with Emptiness, Abhinavagupta says,

> [T]hese two, Emptiness and the City of Eight, do have the nature of being an object. However, still there is a difference between these two and pots etc., because there is no association with the ability to produce pleasure and pain, since they lack contact with an external body. "Hence, in this way" [Utpaladeva] says, indicating that because of this difference, consequently they [physical bodies and pots] should not be considered [the same as] these two [Emptiness and the City of Eight].[64]

Again, the subtle body is a body, yet not quite like the tangible familiar forms of matter, like clay pots, because the subtle body is not externally manifest. The picture we get of the subtle body is as a kind of quasi-materiality that includes a capacity for thought and even a capacity to move and grasp, along with sensory abilities, being able to hear and see. Still, this body lacks the tactile physicality of a clay pot, and that affords it a different status than an ordinary human body. There is also, however, some variance as to what makes up the subtle body for Abhinavagupta's tradition. He notes that:

> some others say that the five subtle elements and the three inner organs are the City of Eight. Yet, because they include the five vital airs in the subtle element touch, the variety of viewpoints here turns out in reality to be no variety at all.[65]

That is, the idea of the five vital breaths is already included in a different version of what makes up the subtle body. Thus, Abhinavagupta tells us that however the eight is configured, the five vital breaths are still included.

The five breaths (*prāṇa*), which also carry links to various states of being, are the *prāṇa, apāna, samāna, udāna*, and *vyāna*. The *prāṇa* is the forward breath and is associated with the daytime and the waking state. The *apāna* is connected to nighttime, inwardness and dreaming. Curiously, Abhinavagupta appears to reverse the understanding of *prāṇa* and *apāna* that one typically finds in contemporary discussions of the breath in yoga practices, where *prāṇa* indicates the in-breath. For Abhinavagupta, in contrast, *prāṇa* points to the out-breath, since it is the breath that causes the external world to appear, while the *apāna* points to the in-breath because it signals the person going inward and resting in the self.[66] The equalizing breath, the *samāna,* is associated with deep sleep and also with states where one falls in a drunken stupor or a coma, or is chemically poisoned or is in a meditative awareness,[67] while the up-breath, *udāna,* is connected to an experience of transcendence.[68]

Vyāna, the all pervasive breath, is connected to understanding the self to be the totality.[69]

We can begin to see that the idea of the subtle body melds together elements of affect, various states of mind, and with this, indirectly, emotions, cognitive deliberation, all of which are then connected to bodily flows, and autonomic processes involved in sleep and bodily processes. The subtle body maps these flows of breath and mind and senses. In this way, wrapped in and through the physical body is a subtle body delineated by the movements of energy flows and functions. This model of body supplies the *cakras*, the subtle body centers, vortexes, which have become popular in the New Age West.

These subtle body centers link places in the body to mental and emotional functions. Abhinavagupta tells us that the heart is connected to the function of creation and is linked to memory and dreams, since these are also creative acts, while the subtle body *cakra* in the throat is connected to keeping alive in awareness the forms around us, and is linked to the waking state and things perceived as common to a variety of viewers.[70] These functions are not simply mechanical operations of an insentient body but expressions of an ever-present dense network of deities residing in various centers in this body, with the god Brahmā in the heart and the god Viṣṇu in the throat, linking the human with a plethora of other beings, all sharing the space of the human body.

The Gods in the Body

As a number of scholars have noted, historically the subtle body for India is not patterned on the organs of the physical body. Dominik Wujastyk points out that "the Tantric body is yet another example of a non-anatomical body,"[71] and Gavin Flood offers an insightful analysis of the Tantric body as an overlay of a textual scriptural tradition.[72] This understanding of the human body as interlinked with a nonphysical, yet still somewhat material, subtle body has a deep ancestry harkening back to Vedic antecedents invoking various deities in the body. The *Taittirīya Brāhmaṇa*, in its "easy invocation"[73] of various gods in the human body, describes it:

> Let Agni, the god of fire reside in my speech. Speech is in the heart. The heart is in me. I am in immortality. Immortality is in the sacred verbal formula. Let Vayu, the god of wind reside in my breath. The breath is in the heart. The heart is in me. I am in immortality. Immortality is in the sacred verbal formula. Let the Sun god reside in my eye. The eye is in the heart. The heart is in me. I am in immortality. Immortality is in the sacred verbal formula.[74]

The text continues, assigning different gods to dwell in different parts of the body; yet in this early formulation, not all of the components assigned to the body seem to be gods. For instance, the text invokes strength for the arms (*bala*), and herbs and trees residing in one's hair (*oṣadhivanaspati*). These elements do not ever quite take on the deification that we see happening for Agni as the god of fire, Surya as the sun god, or Vayu as the god of wind. Nevertheless, this early instance of reflecting the macrocosm in the microcosm points toward a deification of the various things a human body can do, such as speech, seeing, hearing and also having strength (*bala*) and a fiery personality (*manyu*), even as we also see along with this what makes up the body, with earth (*pṛthivī*) as the element that makes for the material-body quality of a body (*śarīra*), and space residing in the ears. This pastiche of categorically dissimilar components linking the human body to the cosmos establishes a template that echoes in later formulations of the subtle body as comprised of deities.[75]

In Abhinavagupta's Tantric articulation of the body in the 11th century, we find the body parceled out into a framework of various deities governing its functions.[76] In the *Dehasthadevatācakrastotram*, a text attributed, perhaps doubtfully, by tradition to Abhinavagupta,[77] the poet praises a series of deities in the body, each associated with some aspect of human functioning. Beginning with Gaṇeśa, the elephant-headed god, always first to be praised, he sings, "I praise Gaṇapati, who is the *prāṇa*, the breath in the body, worshipped first in a hundred different philosophies, who delights in giving what one desires, adored by multitudes of gods and demons."[78] From Gaṇeśa he goes on to praise a variety of other gods: the god Vaṭuka as the *apāna*, the down-breath in the body; the god Ānandabhairava, a blissful form of the god Śiva, in the center of the heart; and the goddess Ānandabhairavī as the form of awareness (*vimarśa*) that makes the body sentient. The intellect (*buddhi*) is instantiated by the goddess Brahmaṇī, as is the ego (*ahaṁkāra*) with the goddess Śāṁbhavī, and the mind (*manas*) is the goddess Kaumarī. He then proceeds to assign goddesses to the five senses, Vaiṣṇavī as the goddess who hears our sounds, down to Lakṣmī who is the power in humans that smells. The components of the body that he outlines with this hymn loosely correspond to the elements that make up the subtle body.[79] Containing the breath, the mental faculties of the mind, ego, and intellect, collectively known as the inner organ (*antaḥkaraṇa*), along with the five sensory capacities, the poet notes how each of these functions of the human body work through the power of deities who embody these functions. With this, he effectively delegates the capacities we humans have to smell and think and breathe to a multiplicity of sentient other beings who are gods, making possible the variety of things a human body accomplishes. The body, which is the material instantiation of human living, is fundamentally a plurality of subjectivities. The plurality we find for the subtle body is not surprising, since, after all, as we saw earlier, the subtle body is all about making a space for difference, for a multiplicity of others. It is what makes it possible to experience objects like a blue something different from one's self.

What makes this idea of the body as a plurality of agencies so different from the Western biological conception of the body—driven by genetic predispositions, by the pull of the biome, by a biology barely or not at all conscious—is that these multiple agencies retain their own conscious intentions. In the theism depicted here, these gods in the body have their own subjectivities. On the one hand, like Sapolsky's model, which sees biology driving human choices rather than a governing human person making choices, here too the idea of an individual person's human will as the force directing the body is abandoned. On the other hand, instead of impersonal forces, like neuronal dopamine or even the manipulations of toxoplasma gondii as the forces driving human behavior, here gods direct the body. Lakṣmī, the traditional goddess of wealth, does the smelling that the body performs; Indrāṇī is the force that sees; Śāṁbhavī directs my choice to drive fast or slow, and so on. Abhinavagupta's theological shift adds an element of subjectivity or conscious intentionality to the various agencies directing the body. This, of course, is something we do not find with *toxoplasma gondii.*

Abhinavagupta also offers a map of the gods directing the functions in the body different from the one we find in the *Dehasthadevatācakrastotram.*[80] In his philosophical opus, the *Īśvara Pratyabhijñā Vivṛti Vimarśinī*, he talks about the various gods in the body as a ladder leading up to the highest awareness. Referencing particular points in the body as energy centers, which are focally potent places in the body, Abhinavagupta tells us:

> In this way, the god *Brahmā* is in the heart; *Viṣṇu* is in the throat; *Rudra* is in the palate. *Īśvara*, the Lord, is in the space between the eyebrows. *Sadāśiva* is upward in the cranial opening at the soft spot on the top of the skull, and *Śakti*, the divine feminine Energy, has the nature of being in no particular abode. These are all the supreme reality in a six-fold body. The six forms serve as a cause making a ladder in the human body up to the level which is the supreme reality. [Utpaladeva] explains these forms designated by the scriptural texts as the inherent essential nature of each of these places, the heart and so on.[81]

The physical body is the abode of gods, and what happens on the subtle level, in this case on the level of particular deities, is replicated in this mundane lump of flesh as the material instantiation of particular energies. Thus, the creator God *Brahmā* is located in the heart, because the heart is understood as the place in the body where we create ideas, while Rudra is in the palate because the palate represents the space where speech dissolves upward into silence. The essential nature of these places in the body, the heart and so on, are the functions ascribed to particular deities. These gods make a ladder in the body, both physically and metaphysically. The several *cakras* lining up along the spine allow our physical bodies to demonstrate the energies and intentions, the affective impulses of various gods in the cosmos. This macrocosm-microcosm linkage between the human body and the greater world around us is not a new idea for Abhinavagupta. We also saw it in the Vedic "easy invocation" where the trees and herbs are understood as the hair of the human person; where the god of fire, Agni, is invoked to reside in human speech.

In this way, Abhinavagupta offers the deities as representations of particular affective and sensory bodily functions, here and as we saw earlier, in the *Dehasthadevatācakrastotram* where, for instance, our familiar experience of smell is the goddess of wealth offering fragrant flowers. Here we see a radically different model of what it means to inhabit a human body than our routine, implicitly dualist, assumption that the body is a mere inert lump of flesh to manipulate simply the "house" for what is actually real, our consciousness, or soul.

Along these lines, as I noted earlier, I suspect that what is important about understanding the subtle body as being made of deities is less its precise theological orientation of the body, an idea of this god or that god in this or that part of the body, and more the accompanying suggestion that various agencies, with their own separate intentionalities, direct human choices. The *Dehasthadevatācakrastotram* tells us that the god Ānandabhairava resides in the heart, whereas the *Īśvara Pratyabhijñā Vivṛti Vimarśinī* places the creator god Brahmā in the heart. That we find different maps for the gods in the body suggests that the Tantric understanding of the subtle body concentrates less on which deity controls which part of human behavior, and more on the map itself as a displacement of human control, a recognition of the human as embedded in a topology of multiple agencies.

Deities point to particular bodily affects that congeal intentionality and function and sensory experience. Not fundamentally directed by the person or the person's mind or will, this conception of deity references intentionality within a schematic of sensory appreciation and desires. The idea of deity gets at the types of affective bodily processing that bypass the mind's chatter—the involuntary crinkling of the nose in the face of a nasty smell, the body's hair rising at an unexpected scary turn in the movie. Abhinavagupta's use of the concept of deity allows for intentionality and the autonomy of the body's affective experiences in ways that can be expressed as being different, sometimes contradictory, to the storyline that the mind repeats to itself about the self. Thus, in this Indian conception, the story the mind tells itself is the function of two components: the *manas*, mind chatter, and *ahaṁkāra*, the ego. What these Indian texts consider as the ego and the mind map nicely to what cognitive scientists like Merlin Donald[82] and George Lakoff and Marc Johnson[83] point to as the cognitive executive function of the mind. Operating alongside these two, the ego and the mind, but with different trajectories, we find other, different intentional and autonomous affective processes of the body, the memory of smells, as Proust so eloquently demonstrated, the heightened mood of a meditative state. Their separate, rich life is highlighted by not reducing these functions to mechanical bodily processes, but affording them instead the sentiency of deity.

Brian Massumi also references this disjunct between what our minds say and the richness of our body's contradictory expressions in his seminal article, "The Autonomy of Affect."[84] He notes that our conscious expressions arise by dint of inhibition, and he calls for a deeper examination of this multiple richness in the affects of the body. Massumi proposes that we understand this rich and contradictory expression of affect as a kind of virtual reality. Abhinavagupta instead reads the multiple registers of affect in the body as a theology. This theology of the body demonstrates affective states as a variety of deities. They inculcate a sense of multiple agencies, with intentionalities that are not always congruent with either each other or with the ego and mind.

In a sense, we might say that theology here registers a kind of respect for the affective processes of the body. Locating gods in the body is a way of acknowledging that not all in this human body is under the sway of that seemingly uniquely human crowning glory of discursive mental thought that we call the mind. Sentiency, will, and desire pop up all over the body and not just as handmaidens of the mind. This theology of the body, moreover, proposes these multiple affective registers in a way that does not dwell, to either lament or rejoice, on the subsequent disappointment and loss of the sovereignty of the ego and its free will. So, while Massumi strives to find a model to understand the complex, refractory affective flows of the body using a language of the virtual, Abhinavagupta instead reads this complexity of multiple affective flows through a lens of the forces of deities with their own conscious trajectories. In this respect, this panentheist theology affords a foundational liveliness to the multiplicity of agencies that make up the body, here referenced in Abhinavagupta's map of the subtle body, which sees the body itself as an ecology of beings, materially embedded.

Conclusion

By way of conclusion, I will offer what I see as Abhinavagupta's response to a particular complication that follows from the idea of a multiplicity of deities directing human choices. How is it that these multiple agents, gods in the body, do not devolve into a fractured self, transforming us into messy schizophrenic multiplicities, a self splintered into a profusion of voices and intentions? In terms of the biology, from a Western perspective we do already find something like a jungle of desires and intentions. Antonio Damasio tells us that we are made up of a multitude of cells, each undergoing its own encounters of birth, development, and death. Damasio maintains that individual cells also have aspects such as desire and will, that is, the desire to stay alive. Even as he notes that it is odd to think of cells having desire the way we have desire, nevertheless, he tells us, this is still the case.[85] Similarly, Patrick McNamara suggests that a disunity of self goes all the way down to our genes, drawing from Haig's genetic research indicating that even for the fetus in the womb, maternal and paternal genes have opposing operations, with clashing drives, and they consequently compete for expression.[86] Tim Morton, looking to Lynn Margulis's work on endosymbiosis, points out that a multitude of life forms already live within us. Even a basic component of our cell structure, the mitochondria, is a relic symbiont, another living entity with its own intentions, merging with our cell structure.[87] Abhinavagupta, on the other hand, does not leave us with a fragmented multiplicity of vying agencies. Rather, the unity of the self arises in the midst of the multiplicity that is the subtle body with its accompanying deities, simply through reclaiming subjectivity, that is, through embracing the first-person perspective. It is precisely the stance of subjectivity, "I-ness" (*ahantā*), that assimilates the multiplicity of the body with its various pulls. In laying out a possible argument against his conception of the subtle body, he says:

> One may object here—of course it is possible to declare the City of Eight as the manifestation of the Self since the City of Eight has this capacity to remain unseen in the normal way that we see a pot etc. But why is there the unnecessary addition of the "I" following from this imposed onto the City of Eight? [Utpaladeva] expresses this idea saying, "in the belief, the concept of 'I'." To this objection [Utpaladeva] replies, "belonging to it, the 'I' alone." The word "alone" indicates that the "I" which appears to be an extraneous addition should be accepted as necessary to the City of Eight. In the absence of the perception of the "I," in fact, these attributes, [the subtle body etc.,] are accompanied by pure unadulterated ignorance. If the host of entities and things, blue etc., are not seen as belonging to the Self, then they would not have the capacity to manifest, but they do appear.[88]

The "I" (*aham*), the sense of subjectivity is not an extraneous addition to the subtle body. The subtle body is instead the attribute of subjectivity. As we saw earlier, the subtle body arises through the contraction of pure consciousness. This consciousness is the sense of "I," the *ahantā*, "I-ness." This sense of "I-ness" enlivens the subtle body; it is what unifies the multiplicity of gods directing the body. This host of gods in the body, which Abhinavagupta describes as a ladder, as we saw earlier, functions to bring just this awareness to the person, that the self is not different from the highest God. Indeed, following on his description of the gods in the body that we saw above, Abhinavagupta, quoting a line from the grammarian Bhartṛhari, tells us that, in the end, this self is itself the multiplicity of what exists, consisting of all the gods in the body; this one which experiences everything:

> Dividing the Self by the Self, having created entities of different types, he places them separately; the lord of all, consisting of all, is the enjoyer, the experiencer in dreams, who sets things in motion.[89]

Darwin recoiled from the thought that the body's discrete boundaries might be violated, that we might find other agencies within the body, parasitic wasps inside the proper body of a caterpillar, exploding it from within. This was faith-shattering for him perhaps in part because it also shatters our own fiction of discrete individual selves, with our minds controlling the materiality that makes up the body. Here instead we see an image of self that is not demarcated against other selves, but rather is inclusive of a host of other agencies, the ladder of gods in the human body. This self finds its unity by an embrace of a deeper pervading subjectivity, the sense of a first-person perspective that enlivens the whole. We will, in any case, return to Darwin's dismay in Chapter Five where we address the idea of information in relation to the permeability of our bodies.

4

Panentheism, Panpsychism, Theism

Abhinavagupta on Consciousness, Sentience, and the Paperclip Apocalypse

> But if there were machines bearing the image of our bodies, and capable of imitating our actions as far as it is morally possible, there would still remain two most certain tests whereby to know that they were not therefore really men. Of these the first is that they could never use words or other signs arranged in such a manner as is competent to us in order to declare our thoughts to others. . . . The second test is, that although such machines might execute many things with equal or perhaps greater perfection than any of us, they would without doubt fail in certain others from which it could be discovered that they did not act from knowledge, but solely from the disposition of their organs . . . by means of these two tests we may likewise know the difference between men and brutes.
>
> **—Rene Descartes**

> I am absolutely prepared to talk of the spiritual life of an electronic computer to state that it is reflecting or that it is in a bad mood.[1]
>
> **—Neils Bohr**

> By removing the form which is insentient, we allow the form which is sentient, the conscious, to take predominance and there we have a complete entrance into consciousness. This is moving forward and entering into its own form.
>
> **—Abhinavagupta**

Introduction

Is it possible for computers to become sentient? The late acclaimed physicist Stephen Hawking went on record warning against just this threat, which

The Matter of Wonder. Loriliai Biernacki, Oxford University Press. © Oxford University Press 2023.
DOI: 10.1093/oso/9780197643075.003.0005

could, in his words, "spell the end of the human race."[2] Hawking is not alone. The tech-giant Elon Musk, of sports-car Tesla-in-space fame, offered a biblical metaphor: "with artificial intelligence we are summoning the demon."[3] Ironically, Hawking, meanwhile, was only able to convey these fears precisely through advances in computer wizardry. It was through a little black computerized box that we became privy to that brilliant disembodied mind, with that odd mechanical voice. That voice was itself iconic, sounding with the syncopation and flat tones recalling the hacker group Anonymous, a nameless mechanical collective. If, in fact, humans will be replaced by artificial intelligence, what will it look like? A flat, syncopated intelligence? Or will it be closer to Nick Bostrom's apocalyptic scenario where our world is destroyed by an artificial intelligence hell-bent on maximizing paperclip production?[4] This, indeed, in contrast to the popular media image of AI, a Schwarzenegger-Terminator agonistic struggle between humans and an equally emotionally fraught, if stoic, machine.[5]

AI offers a powerful, even Copernican, affront to our sense of human exceptionalism, the notion that the human capacity for consciousness is unique. Certainly, the Terminator series plays on this sentiment, and even Nick Bostrom's deadly one-pointed paperclip maximizer underscores this idea by its defiance of human common sense. But is it even possible for nonbiological forms to exhibit real choice, for a mere algorithm to maneuver its way into not being shut off?

This question frames our investigation of a key element of Abhinavagupta's panentheism: the idea of sentience, which he spells out, specifically articulated through the term *vimarśa*. What does it mean to be sentient? Could nonbiological matter be arranged in such a way as to not just pass a Turing test, but to actually demonstrate machine sentience? Perhaps even more to the point, what kind of map of the world do we need in order to entertain the possibility at all? Particularly, the question points us to our deeper assumptions about matter and life. How we think of matter, that is, our cosmological and theological maps, determines the answer we get. Here, through the lens of Abhinavagupta's dual-aspect panentheism we address what conditions must be met, what presumptions underlie the idea of sentience.

Abhinavagupta's answer depends on his use of a dual-aspect model of reality. As a dual-aspect monism, his panentheism shares some features with contemporary versions of panpsychism. Elsewhere I have compared Abhinavagupta's panentheism with the panpsychism that neuroscientists Giulio Tononi and Christof Koch present in their Integrated Information Theory (IIT 3.0).[6] They argue that the capacity for a subjective phenomenological experience is not limited to biology, that we can find it even in basic mechanical devices, in a photodiode, for instance. If we set aside the requirement of biology, they suggest, this subjective experience looks and smells like consciousness, the kind of phenomenal awareness we link to being sentient. This conclusion, of course, banks on panpsychism—the idea that consciousness is an integral part of reality, even down to the level of quarks and particles—as an accurate map of our world. And as we saw earlier, Abhinavagupta's panentheism also shares features with contemporary renditions of a cosmopsychism.[7] However, Abhinavagupta's panentheism differs from these contemporary models in some key respects, including especially his embrace of theism. I suggest that his theism points to a slippage in our own contemporary atheisms, helping us to become aware of our own implicit assumptions. That is, his theism does not look like our familiar Western theisms. Particularly, his panentheism does not carry the legacy of Western notions of the soul, the lingering idea of the ghost in the machine, which I suggest, still leaves an imprint on Western atheisms, even in Western versions of panpsychism. How might the possibility of a machine intelligence sit within a cosmology not foundationally shaped by a Cartesian homunculus?

To begin to answer this question, first we can briefly recap what Abhinavagupta's panentheism as a dual-aspect monism looks like. Abhinavagupta's panentheism links the idea of subject and object in the concepts of knowledge (*jñāna*) and action (*kriyā*) in a way that allows his panentheism to postulate a single reality, *Śiva*, which is the substratum of all that exists. Since *Śiva* is all-pervasive, Abhinavagupta's panentheism operates in ways akin to a panpsychism, where consciousness is everywhere. This dual-aspect monism pivots on the demarcation of light (*prakāśa*), the light of consciousness, on one side, which links to knowledge (*jñāna*). And on the other side we have an active capacity for awareness (*vimarśa*), which links to activity (*kriyā*) and by extension to the external world in its material formulation. Much attention has been given to the "light" element, to *prakāśa*.[8] *Prakāśa* as the light of consciousness is the fabric of reality out of which objects appear, and this lends the system an idealist tenor. This idea of the light of consciousness, that is, mapping consciousness to light, is for us as well a familiar metaphor. For Abhinavagupta, it also derives from an extended Indian tradition that maps luminosity to consciousness, particularly within the influential predecessor tradition to Abhinavagupta's model, Advaita Vedānta.[9] However, Abhinavagupta steers us away from any sort of elementary idealism that the notion of consciousness as light might conjure for us. Instead he insists on the reality of the world and the things in it. Even as we apprehend objects through this fabric of the light of consciousness, nevertheless, the various things and beings populating our awareness are real, and like the scurrying insects we saw earlier, they carry their own desires apart from our human conceptions of them. I am interested here especially in this reality–materiality side of things, the scurrying insects. Rather than the light of consciousness, I focus particularly on what makes up the world's materiality, its links to activity and consequently, to the second element of this dual-aspect monism: *vimarśa*.

Moreover, Abhinavagupta's dual-aspect model offers a surprising twist to this model of the cosmos. We generally lump together consciousness with being alive, with sentience. In this instance, that would map sentience to the light of consciousness, to *prakāśa*. Abhinavagupta instead throws us a curveball. He instead ties sentience to the side of materiality, to activity, to *vimarśa*. Moreover, he also links subjectivity to *vimarśa*: the light of consciousness, *prakāśa*, on one side, but sentience and subjectivity yoked to action, to the material side, to *vimarśa*. *Prakāśa* and *vimarśa* are always intertwined, intertwined precisely with *vimarśa* embedded within, as the heart of *prakāśa*. Philosophically, Abhinavagupta adds this unexpected twist as a way of bridging the gap between consciousness and matter, giving us a world that is filled with real objects, that nevertheless still posits a reality where there is no place without consciousness: that is *Śiva*. Yet the twist that Abhinavagupta adds changes the way we think about matter. It offers a way of thinking with a materially oriented sense of subjectivity. The sense of "I" is not transcendentally located but instead is materially embodied. I have argued throughout this book that Abhinavagupta's 11th-century panentheism has much insight to offer for a New Materialism seeking to reframe how we think about matter, and particularly that his articulation of subjectivity, his solutions to the problem of subject-object relations may be useful to how we, in the 21st century, think about what it is that we do. Here I suggest that Abhinavagupta's articulation of *vimarśa*, linked to subjectivity and sentience, helps us to refigure materiality.

This chapter also places Abhinavagupta's model of panentheism in dialogue with other contemporary models of cosmology. As Harald Atmanspacher points out, dual-aspect thinking is gaining increasing attention as a viable alternative to physicalist approaches for thinking about mind and matter. The limitations of physicalist approaches to the problem of how to connect consciousness to the body have spurred a variety of thinkers to entertain other models, in particular dual-aspect models.[10] One also sees this influence in New Materialist thinking, in Rosi Braidotti's appeal to Spinozan conceptions of matter as a way to think beyond our current predicament, as well as in Jane Bennett's work.[11] For this reason, it makes sense to pay attention to Abhinavagupta's understanding of consciousness and matter within his dual-aspect formulation of *prakāśa* and *vimarśa*.

This chapter covers a lot of ground. I look at different cosmological models, panentheism, panpsychism, and the theism of Abhinavagupta's panentheism, which I address in relation to our own current atheisms. I also use Abhinavagupta's conception of *vimarśa* to tease out the difference between consciousness and sentience for Abhinavagupta, but also for some of our current ways of thinking about consciousness. We parse out what *vimarśa* means for Abhinavagupta's panentheism, particularly in its appeals to materiality, its links to language and intentionality, and how Abhinavagupta employs it as a way of bridging the gap between consciousness and matter—in other words, to offer a viable solution to the mind–body problem.

We begin here by drawing on the idea of computer sentience as a way of making explicit the concepts behind our current cosmologies. A contemporary panpsychism underwrites the conceptual possibility for computer sentience, and it does so as a way of sidestepping theism.[12] Yet, even as contemporary panpsychism is appealing precisely because it brushes aside dualistic conceptions of God, I suggest we still see in its formulation the influences of a Western legacy of transcendence. Following from this discussion, I look at what makes up consciousness. I propose that rather than draw on the terms ubiquitously used to translate the notion of consciousness from Indian languages to English, terms like *cit, citi,* or *saṃvid*, which are typically employed to talk about consciousness, instead the term *vimarśa* ought to be used because it more closely approximates what contemporary neuroscience understands as consciousness. I give examples from neuroscientist Anil Seth and philosopher of mind John Searle, set in tandem to Abhinavagupta's formulation of awareness. This material is important because it helps us to parse out a key distinction for Abhinavagupta's panentheism, but also for a contemporary panpsychism, that is: the idea of consciousness as a fabric of reality in relation to awareness as a first-person perspective. Following this examination, I delve more deeply into the term *vimarśa*. How does it operate in Abhinavagupta's dual-aspect monism? Abhinavagupta affords priority to *vimarśa*, I suggest, precisely because of its links to activity, a capacity to do things in our material reality. Beyond this, his richly iterated dual-aspect monism complicates our usual way of thinking about consciousness and matter. Like a mobius strip where each term swirls one into the other, his formulation finds a pervasive subjectivity, even within mere matter. Finally, drawing on Harald Atmanspacher's classificatory work, I then look at how Abhinavagupta's dual-aspect monism stacks up in relation to other 20th-century Western conceptions of dual-aspect monism. To conclude we revisit our opening question of nonbiological life, computer sentience.

Panentheism, Panpsychisms, Theism

Of course, Abhinavagupta's medieval period had no inkling of our millennia's fantastic development of artificial intelligence. Even so, what does the ontology of Abhinavagupta's dual-aspect monism suggest? Is it possible in Abhinavagupta's panentheism for something like a computer to be conscious, for a humble photodiode to be aware of itself?[13] Given Abhinavagupta's and Utpaladeva's panentheist conceptions, where consciousness is not partitioned off into locally contained, particularized individual souls, but is instead the expression of a single reality as deity, *Śiva*, which pervades throughout everything[14]—given this, the short answer is an easy yes. Abhinavagupta tells us, for instance,

> Now you may say—well, if it occurs in this way, then if one can see the form of consciousness even in a pot, then what is there that's not false? Yes, correct, he says. "nevertheless" "it is appropriate" to view "the insentient" in this way.[15]

If even a clay pot might lay claim to consciousness, a computer can as well. In other words, in response to his seemingly frustrated interlocutor, hands up in the air, suggesting that we need to draw the line somewhere—not everything can be conscious—Abhinavagupta makes only the concession that we make provisional distinctions. We will address these provisional distinctions in the next chapter. Here, he continues on in this passage, telling us how it is that something insentient, like a clay jar, recovers its inner *cidrūpa*, its inner form of consciousness:

> By removing the form which is insentient, we allow the form which is sentient, the conscious, to take predominance and there we have a complete entrance into consciousness. This is moving forward and entering into its own form.[16]

So the basis of even insentient jars, and likewise Siri on your iPhone is a foundational sentience, consciousness, that needs only for us to let go the form which is insentient and thereby allow its innate consciousness to rise up, become predominant. It seems all too easy—especially when we draw on the rich agonistic literary portrayal of humans imagining machine betrayal, like Skynet or Hal or Ex Machina's Ava, to hit a few high points, or Stephen Hawking's late dire predictions.

Really, however, the answer to the question is framed by the model we use. What underwrites various current anticipations of robot sentience, Christof Koch for instance, not only predicting machine intelligence, but even expecting it, is an underlying cosmology of panpsychism.[17] Koch and other thinkers, like mathematician Max Tegmark and philosopher David Chalmers, view panpsychism as one of the few ways to genuinely address the problem of the mind–body split, or what Chalmers has famously dubbed the "hard problem." Indeed, Abhinavagupta employs some of this same logic as we see in these currently embraced panpsychisms to also connect consciousness to the body, as I have pointed out elsewhere.[18] Moreover, as Philip Goff has pointed out, panpsychism does so in a fairly parsimonious way, not requiring supernatural agents.[19] While Goff points to panpsychism as a way to address a variety of problems, the problem of the fine-tuning of the universe, in addition to the problem of consciousness, as he astutely points out, much of this draw to panpsychism is precisely a maneuver to avoid theism.[20]

I would suggest however, that Abhinavagupta's medieval and hence unabashed theism suggests we dig deeper to understand the dynamic. We saw this earlier, and I think it bears repeating here that Abhinavagupta's theism is foundational to his philosophy. By way of a simple reminder of how central theism is to his panentheism, even as the universe is created out of the body of Śiva, still we see Abhinavagupta saying, "Therefore, the glorious Highest Lord is the creator of the Universe."[21] As we saw in Chapter One, his theism is part of his model, and examples can be easily multiplied. If we follow Goff, Abhinavagupta's theism catches us by surprise. Even mired in theism, Abhinavagupta's panentheism manages to accomplish what we find in contemporary panpsychism—the idea that consciousness is everywhere, even in dead matter.[22]

What do we make of this? In Chapter Three I noted that Abhinavagupta's theism encodes a capacity for agency and intention apart from human consciousness, placing humans somewhere in the middle of a continuum of agents, not at the pinnacle, and not excluding other agents, even a worm, a scurrying insect. Aside from this, however, I suspect Abhinavagupta's model with its unfamiliar theism tells us something else. It lays bare an unarticulated by-product of classic Western theology, the lingering traces of transcendence, what Thomas Nagel terms a "view from nowhere."[23] In other words, Goff tells us that panpsychism is a way out of our intractable Cartesian dilemma, a way around the mind–body split—one that does not need to invoke God. Yet, Abhinavagupta invokes God everywhere in the midst of a panentheist cosmopsychism-panpsychism. What this points to is that our current way of thinking about panpsychism and theism overlooks what undergirds the problem of God—it may perhaps be not so much the burden of theism, but instead what *underlies* a Western theistic conception, the notion that consciousness always represents something up above, something outside, something transcendent.[24]

Mary-Jane Rubenstein has elegantly argued that it is precisely the move toward mixing up the transcendent and immanent, blurring the boundaries of categories, that familiar and perennial set of dualist oppositions, male–female, light–dark, human–animal that makes for the monstrosity of a centuries-old Western heresay, pantheism.[25] Pantheism, in its dangerous, if democratically generous, bestowal of divinity to all that is presents the "*horror religiosus*" that bedevils the history of Western thought.[26] Perhaps a contemporary panpsychism, replacing the *theism* with *psychism*, can more readily manage to avoid the deep animosities stirred up by the "appalling" "bewitching"[27] oxymoron of theism-within-the-all.

In any case, by giving us an unfamiliar sort of theism, one that works like a panpsychism (keeping in mind here that Abhinavagupta inherits and reworks the basic pantheism of his predecessor Somānanda[28]), Abhinavagupta makes clear an unarticulated assumption that keeps dogging our own efforts to understand and move away from an internalized legacy of theism. Our current atheisms still carry the lingering effects of a theism with the idea of consciousness abstracted away from ordinary life, as somehow pointing to an outsider's view of reality. A "view from nowhere" is still writ large in our physicalist attempts to leave God behind. Even when we leave the dualism of God-talk behind, opting for something like a number of currently embraced emergentisms, what we find is still a gulf that keeps consciousness separate from matter.[29] To put this another way, it may be less the theism that keeps us stuck in the conundrum of a mind–body dualism—a dualism that desperately wants to see humans as somehow special and separate, with that special something, an intelligence, a soul, that a machine (or a microbe) cannot possibly gain—and instead some other unarticulated deeper assumption. That is, an overt theism may be just a distraction. Rather, the traces of our Western theistic inheritance surface as our tendency to divorce subjectivity from materiality. We are left with the idea that consciousness is by nature foreign to materiality, an extra added value that even when it emerges out of matter, it nevertheless remains somehow separate. So while contemporary neuroscience emphasizes repeatedly the dependence of consciousness on the matter of the brain, still its relationship to the brain, its supervenience on the brain classes it as something not like matter, an oddball stepchild looking nothing like its supposed parents. Consciousness is thus almost by definition disembodied, an abstracted intentionality in a transcendent view from nowhere.

Abhinavagupta's panentheism gives us a different view on the problem. Consciousness is all-pervasive, but he astutely directs us to see that this all-pervasive consciousness is not the same thing as sentience. He teases out the distinction between an all-pervasive consciousness and a capacity for sentience by employing different terms, precisely using the term *vimarśa* to point to sentience that is sometimes present, sometimes not, even while in the midst of an all-pervasive consciousness. The distinction he offers between the two allows his panentheism to reinscribe subjectivity within materiality, even as consciousness is all-pervasive.

I suggest in the next section that if we want avoid talking at cross purposes when we think about consciousness, particularly in relation to a contemporary neuroscience, we should think about Abhinavagupta's conception of *vimarśa*. The words we typically use to translate consciousness from Indian Sanskritic traditions, *cit*, *samvid*, do not get at the kind of embodied subjectivity that makes for sentience that neuroscientists are tracking when they talk about consciousness. In the next section we probe the idea of consciousness, before turning to a deeper analysis of *vimarśa* as sentience.

What Is Consciousness?

What is consciousness? This puzzle or mystery—choosing one of these two words over the other frequently depends on whether one is a cognitive scientist or a philosopher. The quest to define what consciousness is has gained traction in the past few decades as cognitive science research has advanced in mapping what happens in the brain of a person who is "conscious." Pointing out the ambiguity of the term *conscious*, philosopher Ned Block, writes, "The term 'conscious' was first introduced into academic discourse by the Cambridge philosopher Ralph Cudworth in 1678, and by 1727, John Maxwell had distinguished five senses of the term." The multivalency of the term persists, its meaning shifting depending on who wants to define it, as Block notes, and is something we need to factor in particularly with our medieval Indian thinkers. Typically, references to Indian writing point to terms like *cit* and its derivatives as consciousness.[30] However, examining Abhinavagupta's and Utpaladeva's writing in the philosophical Pratyabhijñā school, it becomes clear that if we want to get at the ideas of how a computer might become conscious, terms like *cit* and *saṃvid*, ubiquitously referenced as "consciousness" tend to obfuscate matters, leading unhelpfully to a translational impasse. *Cit* and *saṃvid* designate a kind of universally extant, pervasive consciousness.[31] *Cit* or *saṃvid* entail an unbroken flow of reality, supportive of a panpsychism, but in some sense beyond human awareness of this consciousness, no doubt in alignment with the kinds of nondualist conceptions of an all pervasive absolute principle or deity (*brahman* or *Śiva*) that we find in Indian cosmologies. However, this all-pervasive consciousness does not get at the way we in the

West typically think of consciousness, as indicative of sentience and awareness, and privileged to humans and only some nonhuman animals. I suggest the term *vimarśa* better approximates what a current neuroscience defines as consciousness.[32]

For instance, neuroscientist Anil Seth, in an engaging talk titled "The Neuroscience of Consciousness," tethers the idea of consciousness to particular forms of self-awareness. Linking consciousness to specific brain activity, he describes undergoing a medical procedure and walks us through the distinction between being conscious and not being conscious:

> I ceased to exist as the propofol anesthetic flowed from the cannula in my wrist into my bloodstream and then into my brain, there was a falling apart, a blackness, an absence and then I was back, drowsy and disoriented, but definitely there.[33]

So, consciousness is what happens when we are aware and awake. If we get knocked out by an anesthetic or a coma, then consciousness does not exist for us. Likewise, John Searle tells us, "'consciousness' refers to those states of sentience and awareness that typically begin when we awake from a dreamless sleep and continue until we go to sleep again, or fall into a coma, or die, or otherwise become 'unconscious.'"[34] The neuroscientist Antonio Damasio gives us a similar definition,[35] as does Gerald Edelman.[36]

In this regard, the term *vimarśa* more closely approximates Western conceptions of consciousness than does a Sanskrit word like *cit* or *citi*, or *saṃvid*, precisely because it accommodates the Western idea that we lose consciousness when we are in deep sleep or a coma. Abhinavagupta tells us that *vimarśa* fluctuates. In a sleep state it is broken and discontinuous. He describes the dream state:

> Its universality [its availability to other people] is contradicted in the waking state. It is considered to be a form of illusion, in that its contents are broken by another manifestation which has [more] stability, that is, following upon the durability of *vimarśa*, active awareness, in the waking state.[37]

Similarly, elsewhere speaking about the degree to which some form of the object is retained in a state of deep sleep or dissolution, he quotes Utpaladeva's *Ajaḍa Pramātṛ Siddhi*, "In the state of 'this' one's active awareness (*vimarśa*) is discontinuous."[38] The discontinuity in awareness more readily approximates what we see in scientists like Seth and Damasio; thus, in this respect *vimarśa*, rather than *cit*, looks a little more like the idea of consciousness that we find in contemporary cognitive science.

Perhaps equally instrumental for understanding consciousness, especially as we think about artificial intelligence, is the idea of sentience. To be conscious means to be sentient, to be alive. Even if Deep Blue can trounce Garry Kasparov in a match of minds over chess, still we can pull the plug on Deep Blue without a second thought, but that would not be the case for Kasparov's dog, if he has one. Much of our contemporary system of values rests on the idea of consciousness as a marker for sentience; it is sentience that affords an animal's claims to rights of protection and kindness. It's fine to yell at one's computer and toss it in the trash because it does not count in terms of sentience. In terms of Abhinavagupta's and Utpaladeva's thinking, Utpaladeva explicitly points to *vimarśa* as that which is responsible for sentience, as a property that we and some nonhuman animals exhibit, but by no means a quality that can be found everywhere, including, for our purposes, in things like the metals and plastic and silicon that make up a computer. Utpaladeva says, "*vimarśa* is the very nature of the manifestation of consciousness; otherwise even if light (*prakāśa*) illuminates an object, it remains insentient (*jaḍa*), like a crystal."[39] Abhinavagupta points to *vimarśa* as characterized by a sense of self, which is the nature of wonder and joy, in contrast to the insentiency of lapis lazuli which lacks *vimarśa*.[40] So *vimarśa* is not always operative, but when it is, then things become sentient.

Vimarśa as indicative of this inward awareness that generates sentience gained prominence and this specific sense with the 10th-century thinker Utpaladeva. As John Nemec points out, Utpaladeva's 9th-century guru Somānanda does not use the term as part of the dual-aspect monism of the Pratyabhijñā. This is perhaps not surprising, given Somānanda's strident pantheism where everything, even pots, exhibit sentience,[41] and also perhaps because of Somānanda's insistence on consciousness as lacking material form.[42] It is Utpaladeva who develops this idea of *vimarśa* to point to this inward reflective awareness which functions to bestow sentience.[43] In any case, in Abhinavagupta's commentary on Utpaladeva's verse given above, he takes pains to point out that all things are in reality sentient, yet we point to them as insentient when they lack this key element, *vimarśa*. According to Abhinavagupta:

> Because it lacks the quality of *vimarśa*, it is insentient. In reality, everywhere we find sentience alone, because of resting in the supreme awareness of the sense of "I" which is the innate nature of subjectivity, that is the essence of *vimarśa*."[44]

Again, at base all things are essentially sentient; everything has this capacity. However, this sentience is not always visibly functioning. When *vimarśa* is not operative, things become insentient. Consciousness as *cit* is ubiquitous. Yet the awareness that makes a difference, as neuroscientist Giulio Tononi suggests, the difference that makes the difference we call consciousness is an element that is not always present.[45] For Tononi it is a type of integration of information. For Abhinavagupta, on the other hand, it is the link to a first-person subjectivity. This first-person subjectivity, *vimarśa*, enables this consciousness that crosses over into sentience. Things are mere dead objects when they lack *vimarśa*. And *vimarśa* brings out this sentience precisely because it brings forth the sense of being an embodied self, the awareness of the "I."

What Is *vimarśa*?

What exactly is Abhinavagupta pointing to with this concept of *vimarśa*?[46] *Vimarśa* can be parsed into the prefix *vi* and the verbal root *mṛś* meaning "touch," suggesting a kind of discriminative touch.[47] The sense of touch conveys a basic materiality, and this etymology indeed offers an important conceptual framing for *vimarśa*'s connection with materiality. *Vimarśa* references a kind of recursive self-reflexivity, which might be translated as "reflective awareness" or "active awareness."[48] It is always coupled with *prakāśa*, translated in turn as "light," the light of consciousness that makes objects appear. These two form the two basic poles of his dual-aspect monism.[49]

Abhinavagupta's dual-aspect monism hinges on the distinction between knowledge and action. He tells us that "*prakāśa*, expansive Light and *vimarśa*, active awareness have the respective natures of a mutually inseparable knowledge and action."[50] We can see the dualism writ large in the sensory metaphors used to demarcate the two. Sight and touch. This offers an inkling of their contrasting functionalities. *Prakāśa* as light links to knowledge.[51] As I noted earlier, much attention has been given to *prakāśa*, the "light" element, for Indian thought and particularly for Advaita Vedānta.[52] Its familiar status in the West as well as purveyor of consciousness sets up a familiar binary of light as transcendence in relation to action, which is connected to movement and hence to change and the immanence of a material world subject to change. Abhinavagupta links *vimarśa* to action,[53]and in this way we get the connotations of the movement and change of the external world. He speaks of the process by which the world is created:

> When that power manifests inwardly, naturally it is called the power of Knowledge. However when it expands in stages gradually becoming more firm and fixed, then it manifests externally. This is pointed to as *vimarśa*, the power of Action.[54]

The external world comes into existence when the power of god expands outwardly. This power is *vimarśa*. As this active awareness, *vimarśa*, gradually becomes more firm, more solid and matter-like, it generates the external world. Linked with materiality, it is called *kriyā śakti*, the power of action. Jane Bennett, in thinking through a New Materialism, also points out the link between activity and the material world. Citing Deleuze and Guattari she notes that activity is the vague essence of matter.[55] In both cases, they point to an intuitive logic of matter; its inevitable links to change and decay also carry the possibilities of movement and life.[56]

Vimarśa's links to materiality surface in another way. As Andre Padoux notes, the two terms take on gendered representations, mirroring Tantra's cosmic binary of male and female as archetypal creative forces. *Prakāśa* signifies the masculine and *vimarśa* the feminine.[57] The familiar alignment of light with masculinity and matter with femininity as a staple gendered binary in the West also applies in Indian contexts, including this one. Masculine *prakāśa* is light and feminine *vimarśa* connects to matter. In this case, classical Sāṃkhya-derived Hindu ascriptions of the feminine with matter also associate the feminine with movement and activity. On the other hand, the masculine *prakāśa* as light references a transcendent stasis beyond the change associated with matter and the world.

In any case, we can immediately note that Abhinavagupta extends the function of action. Key for his nondualism is his suggestion that action exists not just externally, driving the changes we see in the external world, but also internally. "Activity," he states, "has the nature of both externality and internality."[58] His suggestion rewrites the idea of transcendence, giving it a dynamism, a way out of stasis, a capacity for change. Transcendence ties back into action and change, back into materiality, essentially reconfiguring the idea of transcendence back toward bodies. In his dual-aspect monism, the two are inextricably enmeshed. Again,

> This is because of the mutual inseparability of *jñāna*, Knowledge and *kriyā*, Activity which have the respective natures of expansive light (*prakāśa*) and active awareness (*vimarśa*). And "that" alone is the highest ultimate body (*vapuḥ*) of all entities.[59]

Both are entangled together in Abhinavagupta's monism in an overarching inclusive body for everything that exists. So we again see shades of panpsychism, and this pervasive panpsychism is framed in terms of materiality, of bodies.[60]

Abhinavagupta also links *prakāśa* and *vimarśa* to the out-breath and the in-breath, the *prāṇa* and *apāna*, which are well known in yoga practices popular today. As a point of interest, Abhinavagupta's Śaiva tradition reverses the meanings of the two breaths in contrast to contemporary understandings. The *prāṇa* in contemporary and much historical usage refers to the in-breath, while the *apāna* refers to the out-breath, in contrast, in Abhinavagupta's writings, the *prāṇa* references the out-breath.[61] In any case, this is what Abhinavagupta says:

> Of the two [*prāṇa* and *apāna*] indicates that the *prāṇa*, by its manifestation, takes away the Subject's awareness of body, etc. In this way the *prāṇa* has the power of *prakāśa*, the expanse of light; it is the sun and it illuminates the object. The time associated with this process is the day. The *apāna*, on the other hand, has the power of *vimarśa*, active awareness which gives the bliss of resting within, and causes the awareness of the subject as body to increase, to swell. This is the moon and its associated time is the night. So with regard to the Subject as predominant, the division occurs like this [subjectivity is inward and predominant at night and during the day awareness is external and so the Subject is subordinate then], but with regard to the object it is the opposite.[62]

The *prāṇa*, the out-breath, is light, *prakāśa*. This light takes away the awareness of the body. In contrast, the in-breath is linked to *vimarśa*. It causes the awareness of the person's body to increase, just as the moon in Indian lore causes the body to swell, to increase, causing, for instance, plants to grow. The materiality of the body then connects particularly to *vimarśa*, as an inward awareness, while light, *prakāśa*, as we might expect, attenuates the sense of body.

Vimarśa also references the materiality of the world in one more way. In a seminal article specifically addressing the term *vimarśa* and it cognates, Harvey Alper proposed that the primary use of the term *vimarśa* points to a key feature of Utpaladeva's theology—its reliance on ordinary everyday experience, the way a subject, a person cognizes an everyday object in mundane life.[63] As Alper notes, *vimarśa* makes it possible "to account for the actuality of human experience."[64] That is, the concept of *vimarśa* explains our experience as limited beings. We live in a world of multiplicity, populated with other limited consciousnesses and objects, all of us mutually entangled within an interactivity of subjects, objects, people, and things.[65] Isabelle Ratie points to the dynamism entailed in this, the capacity of *vimarśa* to take on a variety of forms, "this extraordinary ability of consciousness to freely apprehend itself *as being this* or *that*."[66] It is, as she puts it, the god "Śiva imagining himself in the form of such limited entities."[67] Moreover, as Alper points out, Utpaladeva's formulation of *vimarśa*, linked to cognition of objects in the external world in turn offers a way to explain mistakes. Mistakes of judgment, limited perception, and ignorance, the imperfections so familiar to our ordinary experience, make sense with the notion of *vimarśa* tied to the limitations of mundane perception.[68] *Vimarśa* is awareness; for Alper it is a capacity for judgment, but this awareness is located in a particular limited perspective, tied to the embodiment of ordinary life.

So, *vimarśa* is the awareness we draw on everyday, from a particular vantage point, the subjectivity of a particular embodied self, an "I" that can also be limited. It is linked to both the body and to an inward awareness of being a self, a subject with the in-breath. It is the kind of phenomenal awareness we all know, an awareness that can be partial and wrong, and in this respect again it looks a little more like a current cognitive science conception of consciousness.

Tasting the Multiplicity of the Self: The Materiality of Panentheist Cosmopsychism

Alper suggests then that the use of everyday life extends philosophically to the idea of God, to an "exegesis of ultimate consciousness in terms of ordinary cognition."[69] This focus on everyday life is one of the defining features of this philosophical system. Following in the model of an early Tantric text, the *Vijñāna Bhairava*, quoted frequently by Utpaladeva and Abhinavagupta, we see that simply by giving attention to even ordinary activities—seeing a friend after a long time,[70] to the pleasure eating delicious food,[71] paying attention to the moment one sneezes[72]—one can reach profound mystical states. What makes these states mystical is that *vimarśa*, the inward reflection of the self, the "I," expands to its awareness as the whole cosmos.[73] One identifies with the originary cosmopsychism. The premise here is that rather than a panpsychism that operates on a micro-level, a proto-mentality ascribed to what makes up the matter of the universe,[74] the world with all its multiplicity derives out of a cosmopsychism.[75] This unity of awareness allows itself to be splintered, fragmented into a diverse, mutually interactive multiplicity of different consciousnesses. As we saw earlier, Abhinavagupta observes that

> [t]he category called *Śiva* is itself the body of all things. "On the wall [of the world which is itself *Śiva*] the picture of all beings appear, shining forth"—This statement indicates the way that all these come to appear. And the purport of the entire corpus of scriptures means to indicate that the category *Śiva* itself is all this.[76]

Abhinavagupta uses this image of the world as a portrait on a wall on a variety of occasions,[77] where this panentheist multiplicity of beings unfolds from an essential unity that is the fabric of the wall. We can see its resonances with a New Materialism. It is, for instance, not so unlike Karen Barad's quantum stipulation that we find "material demarcations not *in* but *of* space."[78] And it is also similar, at least in some respects, to the kind of cosmopsychism Goff entertains.[79]

If we understand Abhinavagupta's model as a panentheist cosmopsychism derived from a premise of everyday life, how does this cosmic entity interact with the multiplicity that is the world, the pictures it gives birth to on the wall of itself? To recap some of what we saw in Chapter Two, Abhinavagupta offers more sensory materiality, in this case the metaphor of taste (*āsvāda*). The category of Śiva unfolds the world out of itself and then savors this multiplicity in the experience of wonder. "The self, which is wonder, relishes the awareness of its own enjoyment."[80] This enjoyment comes from taking in the multiplicity of subjects and objects, which is really not different from its own self. Again, wonder is the signature of sentience: "as *vimarśa* is wonder (*camatkāra*), so it, in fact, entails sentience."[81] Wonder, as we saw, offers a fusion of consciousness with materiality. This entanglement of consciousness with material form is what Abhinavagupta suggests with *vimarśa*, as we saw above. And sentience, life, that is, happens precisely when these two, materiality and awareness, become mutually embedded.

In any case, this emergence of life, of sentience is not confined to biology. If everything is the unfolding of a consciousness on and out of itself, we can start to see how this medieval model might, without any qualms, accommodate the sentience of silicon. This cosmic entity is the fabric, the body out of which everything is made. Tapping into consciousness is just returning to its origins, a recognition (*pratyabhijñā*) as this system calls it. This capacity allows us to be sentient, and yet there are no fundamental barriers to prevent a computer from also participating in this sentience. It need only tap into a reflective awareness of self that we find in the state of wonder. With this image, Scarlett Johannson's *Her* looks more closely aligned to Abhinavagupta's understanding of sentience than a brutal robotic terminator. Moreover, this capacity is available everywhere. Using this same root form *mṛś* for touch as in *vimarśa*, Abhinavagupta quotes one of Utpaladeva's songs, "possessing material form, you enliven the whole world."[82] For our purposes, I want to underscore the metaphor's implications—that the materiality of touch in this verbal root somehow also carries the connotations of bringing life.

So, we have the idea of life and subjectivity connected to materiality. With this theism we find the materiality of bodies all the way up. Even *Śiva* as cosmopsychism, the highest god is never quite devoid of form. Abhinavagupta cites his predecessor Somānanda, telling us that we find the same state of *Śiva*, this idea of God, both in transcendence and in gross material physicality: "and it is not at all the case that the highest Lord is in this way ever devoid of form. As that most esteemed teacher said, 'in transcendence is the state of *Śiva*; also in gross physical form is the state of *Śiva*.'"[83] In other words, transcendence does not really mean leaving behind materiality. *Śiva* as cosmopsychism equally pervades a transcendent state and being in a physical body, in both cases, not really devoid of form.

Alper, in any case, finds especially salient the theistic implications of Utpaladeva's formulation. He suggests that *vimarśa* points to the idea of God as a person: "*vimarśa* conceptualizes Śiva as foundationally a personal agent."[84] David Lawrence expands on Alper's formulation, in particular linking Abhinavagupta's theology to a philosophical idealism, with a compelling argument that understands the dual-aspect monism of Abhinavagupta and Utpaladeva as akin to a Kantian transcendental argument. Lawrence derives this idealism from the concept of *prakāśa*, light; citing Berkeley, he notes that this idea points to the unity of the subject.[85] His argument is insightful and cogent, and has helped me in my own thinking about Abhinavagupta's philosophy. Sthaneshwar Timalsina follows as well Alper's and Lawrence's understanding of *vimarśa* as judgment, linking it specifically to the idea of reflexivity, which he characterizes as a capacity to both enable a subjective awareness of self and produce an objective reality; as he puts it, it "gives rise to veridical knowledge."[86] At the same time, however, he uses a language of "transcendence" to argue for an emergence of something new, even if what emerges is already embedded as a latent property.[87] In any case, Abhinavagupta's panentheism is layered. K. C. Pandey hedges his bet with a seeming oxymoron that straddles categories, calling Abhinavagupta's Pratyabhijñā system a "Realist Idealism."[88] We might suggest that although Abhinavagupta does not essentially discard idealism, the strength of this system relies on a genuine embrace of the multiplicity and reality of the material world. Regarding the dichotomy, Ratie, for instance, writes: "the opposition realism/idealism could hardly apply to Indian philosophy, since a number of Indian 'idealisms,' including that of the Pratyabhijñā, consider the phenomenal world as perfectly real."[89] Nomenclature aside, the deeper case Lawrence makes is to emphasize that the ground of awareness is all that we can know: the phenomenal experience that Utpaladeva points to marks the limit of what can possibly be understood.[90]

This way of approaching phenomenal experience is without doubt compelling. Drawing on Buddhism, Evan Thompson makes a similar observation: that consciousness comprises the ground of our awareness, all that we can know.[91] We can see the cross-fertilization of ideas across religious boundaries in Indian thought, though Thompson uses this insight to make a very different point than Lawrence's.[92] Thompson argues for a Buddhist conception of relationality and selfhood as a process. with little thought given to ideas of God. He uses this observation to critique physicalism and to reject panpsychism for a contemporary audience,[93] not as Lawrence does, to astutely argue for an idealist, theological map of the world.[94]

Vimarśa: Language and Desire

We can add one more element to fill out this picture of *vimarśa*. Lawrence, along with a number of other scholars, also points to the linguistic orientation of *vimarśa*.[95] Torella notes this as well, tracing out Abhinavagupta's development of this linguistic element from the legacy of the grammarian philosopher Bhartṛhari.[96] Nemec reminds us that Somānanda also uses the term *vimarśa* to connect language to consciousness.[97] Similarly, Timalsina points to the link between *vimarśa* and language, noting that "there is no consciousness expunged of *vāc*."[98] Navjivan Rastogi specifically ties this capacity for language to the fact of sentience.[99] I cannot help but think of Descartes' own stipulation of something like a Turing Test, similarly tying language to sentience as we saw in this chapter's epigraph. In any case, we should remember that language in both Bhartṛhari and Abhinavagupta operates on a variety of levels. The level of ordinary speech, what we think of when we think of language, termed *vaikharī*, is only one expression, the most physical and least impactful conception of language. At its more refined levels, *madhyamā*, the "middle" where thoughts are not articulated but form in the mind,[100] and at the level of *paśyantī*, where thought just begins to form, literally here, "seeing"[101]—on these levels, language rather references a kind of basic impulse toward meaning and intentionality.[102] Nemec connects Utpaladeva's gloss of *vimarśa* to Bhartṛhari's notion that all experience requires understanding.[103] This capacity, by the way, is not exclusively confined to humans. Writ into the structure of experience, it is not only the specific human expression of language that participates in *vimarśa*, as we saw above. For our purposes here, this entails that nonhuman animals also participate in this structure of intentionality—this idea of language is part of the structure of the universe, implicating a kind of intentionality and meaning embedded within the very formation of reality. This also means that subjectivity and the capacity for intentions that *vimarśa* brings exist at least in *posse*, even in objects, clay pots, and no doubt, computers and even if it is not always activated. Abhinavagupta reminds us "in fact, *vimarśa*, which is consciousness does exist in all forms."[104] So, as we might expect from a formula akin to panpsychism, matter everywhere has at least the capacity for sentience and, perhaps surprisingly, for language too: "here in our philosophy, because it consists of *vimarśa*, even the object participates in language."[105] Again, this assertion stands in contrast to Descartes' exclusion of machines from the language club, as we saw in this chapter's epigraph. To go back to Nemec's observation, intrinsic to experience is an awareness, a subjectivity that it entails. This offers up a radical conception of matter. Here we might mention physicist Karen Barad's "agential realism" where even the whizzing photon as well as the physicist observing mutually engage in "intra-activity."[106] The experience of the photon also lays claim to an intrinsic subjectivity, a capacity for intentionality, even for this tiny mere matter. Similarly, as we saw, Abhinavagupta points out, "in reality, everywhere we find sentience alone because it rests in subjectivity."[107]

So, *vimarśa* as language entails meaning, meaning tied to sentience. We will return to the topic of meaning in Chapter Five. In any case, when a computer makes the shift from the algorithmic production of outputs into an active, judicious meaning-making capacity, then from this perspective its sentience will emerge. With this comes the idea of desire. Utpaladeva points out that insofar as a mountain lacks the desire to be, then it is insentient.[108] Yet, insentience is not intrinsic to its condition as a mountain. As noted earlier, Abhinavagupta tells us that "[e]ven the lifeless grammatical third person, [the 'it'], if it sheds its lifeless form can take on the first and second person forms. For example, 'listen, o stones' and 'Of mountains, I am Meru.'"[109] The mountain, Mount Meru, need only shed its lifeless embrace of being an object, to recover its own deeper subjectivity, always available as *vimarśa*. This freedom is fundamental to Abhinavagupta's theology, an overarching consciousness as cosmopsychism that generates out of itself the multiplicity of the world. Similar to Goff's conception of the universe as a cosmopsychism, which embeds meaning and value as a basic element, in Abhinavagupta's theology desire is also foundational:

> The one who is free is the one who can exist in whatever way he desires, unimpeded, unrestricted. And god does indeed have this freedom, he has the fullness of everything as his own. As said earlier: "that which is born and exists manifests within the self of the Lord. This is the case, otherwise there would not be this active perception which is Will. (1/5/10)." Thus by following the lead of this statement, god has this freedom as the fullness of everything because he is joined with Will, which is defined as a desire to be.[110]

So this theological portrait of God includes desire as part of God. Desire and the will (*icchā*) to choose things in one way rather than in another are intrinsic to this cosmopsychism, which contains the totality of what exists within its own self.[111] Goff skirts the idea of desire for his cosmopsychism, opting instead for the less charged concepts of "meaning" and "value" as basic elements. Here the theism that Abhinavagupta incorporates injects a personal subjectivity both for individuals and for the cosmopsychism as God. I venture that this freedom to choose derives from *vimarśa*'s association with action.[112] And its consequence is the conception of God as a personal agent that Alper articulates. At the same time, this freedom and desire gets writ in ordinary, limited fragmentations of this cosmopsychism as the first-person perspectives that *vimarśa* activates for you and me and myriad other scurrying insects.

The Light Touch of Consciousness

As we map out the parameters of this medieval dual-aspect monism, it may be already apparent that Abhinavagupta's Pratyabhijñā formulation of consciousness weaves in on itself in a complex recursivity. To recap, on the surface, *prakāśa* and *vimarśa* present as our familiar binaries, gendered, touching on conventional dichotomies. Yet, by now it may be becoming clear that Abhinavagupta's use of *vimarśa* resolutely undermines our usual expectations, and those of its Indian milieu as well. Yes, he links consciousness with light as a pervasive fabric of reality, as we might expect of a panpsychism.[113] However, when it comes to specific awareness, he surprises us. We expect him to link consciousness as specific awareness also to light, *prakāśa*. We might predict this, after all, as a continuation of Sāṃkhya's articulation of the male *puruṣa* as pure consciousness, consciousness as transcendent witness (*sākṣin*). Instead, Abhinavagupta associates consciousness as awareness and indeed as a self—as subjectivity—with *vimarśa*. Commenting on Utpaladeva's verses, he observes that

> [in the verse] the words "because of the nature of awareness" indicate that the main thing that awareness has is *vimarśa*, the reflective awareness which is the "I"—which is the Self. Because of this, when it is superimposed upon, this superimposition is born out of its own natural state. And this is correct.[114]

Surprisingly, the materially oriented *vimarśa* is the main ingredient of awareness. This awareness, with its material base, is what gives us subjectivity, the self. Abhinavagupta is no doubt aware that he surprises his readers here;

hence, he takes time to emphasize that this reading is indeed correct. Further, when we superimpose the details of things, it is not as though there is pristine consciousness, a *tabula rasa* that takes on the new content. Rather, the details are part of the basis, already part of the self. In other words, the self is already embedded in a material embodiment, scripting out the precise details as its own unfolding story.[115]

This is how consciousness works. As we saw earlier, consciousness has the capacity to expand outwardly, "in stages gradually becoming more firm and fixed, then it manifests externally. This is pointed to as *vimarśa*, the Energy of Activity."[116] *Vimarśa* unfolds gradually, moving outwardly as the external world. *Vimarśa* is thus particularly important because even as it is a mental quality, awareness, it also links us to the material world, because it is the capacity to do things in the world. Abhinavagupta tells us, "the inherent nature of the "I" is *vimarśa*, active awareness, which is pointed out. This is none other than the quality of being able to do things."[117] So *vimarśa* is the self, the "I," but it is not a transcendent self. It is an embodied self engaged in the world and able to affect the material world. For our purposes, this recursive complication offers profound implications for how we think about materiality, what it means for the idea of matter.

At this point, it may be helpful to see in chart form how these complementary attributes of this dual-aspect model stack up.

Prakāśa	**Vimarśa**
light	touch
masculine	feminine
out-breath	in-breath
knowledge	action, doing
transcendence	immanence
object	subject
inert, not alive (jaḍa)	sentient, alive (ajaḍa)

The first elements follow our normative expectations—light is linked with knowledge, with the masculine, with transcendence. However, placing sentience and subjectivity on the side of *vimarśa* changes the rules of the game. Again, why does Abhinavagupta subvert the pattern we expect? Abhinavagupta wants a nondualism that does not exclude materiality, the ordinary world around us. *Vimarśa*, linked as it is to action, is instrumental for Abhinavagupta's system precisely because it affords a capacity to do things, to act in the world. His Tantric reinterpretation of a self involved in the world is at odds with a classical conception of the self as transcendent witness, the Sāṃkhyan *puruṣa*,[118] "the man" of classical Indian philosophy. The net sum is that his use of Hindu philosophical elements traditionally associated with activity and by extension with materiality makes it possible to reinscribe the world within his nondualism. The idea of action (*kriyā*) allows him to connect consciousness to matter and the world. He can bridge the mind–body gap.

Being able to do things (*kartṛtva*) is key in particular because it eliminates precisely the problem that a scientific reductionist model has with the idea of a self that cannot affect the material world. This is the kind of epiphenomenalism attending a self that Dennett critiques as incapable of actually changing any element of the world. Indeed this is the problem for the Sāṃkhyan *puruṣa*; it is transcendent, and as result, it has no connection with the matter of the world. It is irrelevant to the business of bodies; it is in Dennett's terms, an epiphenomenon. Abhinavagupta, on the other hand, reinterprets the Sāṃkhya idea of the *puruṣa* against this transcendent epiphenomonalism. Citing the classic and still popular hymn of the *Ṛg Veda*, the *Puruṣa Sūkta*, he says:

> And in this way the material appearance of effects which is the world [bodies and stones, etc.] is really just only what makes up the *Puruṣa* alone. As it is said in Vedic scripture: "the *puruṣa* is indeed all this."[119]

The *puruṣa* as the self, the witness, is classically in Sāṃkhya associated with detachment and separation from the world of *prakṛti* and matter. Consonant with his panentheism, Abhinavagupta offers a radical reversal; the witness, the *puruṣa*, *is* the world.

What we can take from this is a mutual implication, a complex recursive iteration of what sees and what is seen, an unfolding of what sees into what is seen. The witness, our consciousness that takes in the world, is also the material fabrication of what exists outside. Abhinavagupta's stress on the actual existence of the world as materially real precludes an interpretation of this as a simple or solipsistic idealism, where all exists in the mind of the one who sees. Instead we have a consciousness oozing outward to form a materially substantial world. The material side cannot be excised or ignored. So in this context Abhinavagupta tells us, "when you separate off the effects [of this creation, like the body, etc.] then the state of Doership does not occur."[120]

Abhinavagupta defines the idea of self in terms of action, as the action of consciousness, telling us that the understanding that "'the self is the act of consciousness' is correct. Or we may say, the particular feature of the self is as agent, the one who performs the act of consciousness."[121] So, fundamentally, Abhinavagupta profoundly rescripts what it means to be a self, making the idea of an action the basis of the self.[122] He makes awareness itself not something confined to a transcendent, impenetrable subjectivity,[123] but instead materially based as the effects of actions in a world. This piece of his panentheist cosmopsychism he proposes certainly skirts near the borderlands of Buddhist[124] ideas of the continuity of the self as process, not substance, even as Abhinavagupta asserts the substantive existence of the self.[125] Further, because action is so key to his philosophy, Abhinavagupta says *vimarśa* takes prominence precisely because it entails the power to do things, which he notes is freedom. He says that "the power to do things encompasses all powers; it is the essence of lordship. And that is *vimarśa*. Thus, it is appropriate to put *vimarśa* first."[126]

Likely addressing the Buddhist philosopher Dharmakīrti's conception of the real as determined by that which has causal efficacy,[127] Abhinavagupta's embrace of *vimarśa's* capacity to get things done on a material level is again interestingly redolent of Tononi's "difference that makes a difference."[128] Here again it is the material side of the equation that comes to the fore. Matter is where the action is, quite literally.

This richly iterated conception of *prakāśa* as light and *vimarśa* as action complicates our usual way of thinking about light as consciousness. Light as consciousness is the pervasive fabric of reality.[129] So, *prakāśa* is consciousness, and it is the light that illuminates the object. According to Abhinavagupta, "the light (*prakāśa*) that illumines the object in this way is said to be consciousness (*saṃvit*)."[130] Yet, this pervasive light of consciousness lacks the differentiation of particular awareness. It is like the image of consciousness that Searle critiques as the problem with panpsychism, a thin veneer of jam spread out over the universe.[131] This is a subject that I have addressed elsewhere in connection with the panpsychism we find in Tononi and Koch's Integrated Information Theory 3.0.[132] Abhinavagupta appears to have understood this problem and offers a solution through *vimarśa's* first-person, materially located perspective. We get difference and a genuine, lively awareness because *vimarśa* is located, like a Russian doll, at the heart of this pervasive but undifferentiated consciousness, waiting to be activated. Abhinavagupta continues this passage, saying, "but its form is always enlivened, that is, its state is a form with *vimarśa*."[133] He concludes the passage embedding action, *vimarśa*, at the core of knowledge: "in every way, however, knowledge is just *vimarśa*, without that it would be simply just insentient."[134] This conception of *vimarśa* especially entails the idea of spontaneity. This philosophy is at times called the "doctrine of freedom" (*svātantryavāda*) because sentience, being alive, is this capacity to spontaneously choose—something only a first-person perspective can assure.

To recap, here we again see that the term *saṃvit* as consciousness points to a universally extant, pervasive reality, the consciousness that makes up a panpsychist ground of reality. However, the awareness that comes with sentience needs *vimarśa*, touch as a first-person awareness. In this way, Abhinavagupta skillfully turns the polarity of light and touch, knowledge and action, transcendence and immanence into a mobius strip, where in this case the essence, lying at the core of knowledge and light is the enlivening awareness, activity, *vimarśa*. "Knowledge derives its life from *vimarśa*, and *vimarśa* is just only action,"[135] he tells us. The remarkable twist of the mobius strip not only gives a seamless conversion from knowledge to action, from light to materiality; it also inverts their normative functions. The pervasive light of consciousness (*saṃvit*) affords the appearance of objects; it links to what we think of as mere matter without life.[136] On the other side, *vimarśa*, with its connections to activity and by extension to matter generates the experience of subjectivity, the "I" and with it sentience. We saw this earlier in Abhinavagupta's articulation of the out-breath (*prāṇa*) as connected to the object and light (*prakāśa*), while *vimarśa* as the in-breath (*apāna*) engenders a sense of bodied self as subject. Alper notes this as well, pointing to *prakāśa*, as the capacity for self-objectification and to *vimarśa* as self-subjectification.[137]

Dual-Aspect Monisms

Even as Abhinavagupta draws on a dual-aspect monism to account for both the mental and physical aspects of the world as we experience it, his dual-aspect monism is quirky in a number of respects. If we think about Abhinavagupta's model in relation to Harald Atmanspacher's articulation of a number of prominent dual-aspect models,[138] Abhinavagupta's model offers some peculiar, uncharted features. His model plots dual aspects in the form of *prakāśa* and *vimarśa* as two modes within the ontological whole that is *Śiva*, which looks similar to both Russellian neutral monism and the Pauli-Jung model with its basal foundation of the *unus mundus*. Yet, unlike both Russellian neutral monism and the Pauli-Jung model with its basal foundation of the *unus mundus*, Abhinavagupta's dual-aspect monism does not entail that *Śiva* as the ground, generating the portrait of beings on the wall of itself, remains separate from the mental and physical expression of itself that makes up the world.

Of the four different 20th-century models of dual-aspect monism that Atmanspacher gives us, Abhinavagupta's formulation is perhaps closest to Bohm's conception of the implicate order. Both operate as kinds of cosmopsychisms. Moreover, Bohm's notion of holomovement, which affords a dynamism to the foundational substratum of reality, strikes a resonant chord with Abhinavagupta's incorporation of dynamism within his conception of *Śiva*. Also, Bohm incorporates relative levels of ontology, with greater and lesser subtle levels of the implicate order, with no stringent demarcation between the foundational reality and explicate manifestations, which is a feature we also find in Abhinavagupta's model. Similarity aside, two things separate Abhinavagupta's model from 20th-century dual-aspect monisms. First, Abhinavagupta interweaves and blurs the boundaries of the two components framed in his dual-aspect monism. *Vimarśa* lies at the heart of *prakāśa*; it is, as we saw earlier, the essence of *prakāśa*. The Pauli-Jung model, in contrast, precisely posits a ground beneath, the *unus mundus*, to offer a neutral territory to contain both of these different modes of being, the mental and the physical. In contrast, as I note earlier, Abhinavagupta's model appears to propose that these two aspects are like a Russian doll, the one embedded within the other. That is, sentience, consciousness, lies embedded within matter, not as a complementary property to material expression, but rather as the internalization of material expression. When matter looks inward, it realizes that it is consciousness.

In terms of contemporary models of consciousness, Abhinavagupta's dual-aspect monism also shares some features with Galen Strawson's conception of physicalist panpsychism; in particular Strawson's consideration that the world is really real.[139] Strawson considers himself a physicalist in that what exists for him is precisely physical, concrete "stuff," what he calls a "stuff-monist" view.[140] Abhinavagupta's model veers toward this, especially in his invocation of the idea of bodies (*vapus*) all the way up, where all that we see here is the body of Śiva, the cosmopsychist reality that splits itself to make up the diversity of the world here. The world of stuff is real for both; for both it also entails the concrete reality of things we do not readily see: energy for Strawson, subtle bodies for Abhinavagupta.

In any case, the second way that Abhinavagupta's dual-aspect monism differs from contemporary models is that Abhinavagupta's cosmopsychism, the holism that generates the multiplicity of the world, is in a sense never really lost; it never quite degrades. The whole point of this philosophy of recognition (*Pratyabhijñā*) is precisely that this awareness of the plenum is accessible. It can be recaptured and that is enlightenment.[141] This enlightenment can happen even in the midst of the materiality of the world.[142] This is so because when the awareness, the cosmopsychism that is Śiva unfolds to form the world, it does not quite ever forget itself. This also leads to what is probably one of the weaknesses of the system. As Abhinavagupta tells us, the wonder of it all is how it could be possible for a completely free being, God, to actually limit itself, to become limited humans and mere objects. This is the weak link, which in the end is underwritten by a theology, the freedom (*svātantrya*) that the lord has. Abhinavagupta says:

> The Energy of Consciousness is in fact all forms, the entire universe and She touches nothing beyond Herself." That's the connection. Consciousness (*citi*) makes manifest a wonder by the force whereby she brings about that which is extremely difficult. This he summarizes with the words, [God] "who in fact" "partakes of 'This-ness"[143]

The really difficult thing to do, the hard problem here, is that the cosmopsychism that generates the world—God—is entirely free and aware, and yet, this *citi*, this consciousness does in fact lose herself; she allows herself to become an object, a mere "this." This is the difficult task to explain how God can let its innate freedom be circumscribed, to sink to the level of *Māyā*, duality. Abhinavagupta invokes theology:

> [T]his in fact is freedom, which is the capacity to do that which is exceedingly difficult. And that difficulty is to be actually placed on the level of *Māyā*. This happens because of [god's] power to determine things as one way or another."[144]

The power of God to become small and limited and ignorant is explained by recourse to a theology of God's unlimited freedom. Theologically buttressed by the freedom of God to do whatever God wants, on the philosophical level, it leans on a first-person perspective, that subjectivity is embodied in material form.

If we were for our own purposes to jettison the theology here, the model would lose the coherence of a cosmopsychism as originary, and along with it, the telos of enlightenment, and the intentionality encoded in theology. Although such a model, I think, could still entail a nondualism, the loss of a teleology would make it a messy, less elegant cosmopsychism, something more akin to an evolving universe.

In any case, in the next chapter we address the question of how it is that this cosmopsychism performs this wondrous deed—becoming us limited beings.

Conclusion

Throughout this chapter, even as I stress the material associations of *vimarśa*, it is important to remind ourselves again that Abhinavagupta always intertwines *vimarśa* with *prakāśa*. I put more weight on *vimarśa's* connections with action and materiality not only because this element tends to be excluded in most current understandings of consciousness, but also because Abhinavagupta's emphasis on *vimarśa*, its links to action, and by extension to the material world, affords a key to understanding how his model does not devolve into a simple idealism. Abhinavagupta, after all, distinguishes his philosophy precisely as a dual-aspect monism that can accommodate not just the mentality implied in an idealism, but also the materiality of the world as a *bona fide* reality. More than this, though, for our purposes here, this notion of *vimarśa* can spur us to think differently about matter. For instance, it might allow us to think about a current materialist conception connecting consciousness with brain matter, a neuronal correspondence model in a way that reimagines a greater interactive plasticity between neuronal firing and conscious awareness. And more, if matter at heart encloses within it a vibrant possibility for spontaneity, *vimarśa* as the seed of life, sentience within, then computers aside, matter itself is an intrinsic element of consciousness, of life, not just the mere inert capacity to instantiate it.

By way of connecting back to this chapter's originary question: whether something nonbiological, something lifeless as computers might gain a foothold in the club of sentience, particularly as superintelligent AI becomes a looming possibility—the answer, indeed, is an easy yes. With this chapter we have examined how we get sentience in the context of Abhinavagupta's dual-aspect monism. His use of *vimarśa* with its links to action and the materiality of the world inscribe the possibility of sentience everywhere, as the outpouring of a panentheism that generates the multiplicity of the material world out of its own being. While this medieval model is not entirely adequate for a contemporary cosmology, we can nevertheless take away elements that may be helpful for engaging our world today. First, it affords a differentiation within a broadly panpsychist model. Consciousness is everywhere, yet we can demarcate sentience from insentience through the concept of *vimarśa*. This helps to avoid the problem that Searle finds with panpsychism, its tendency toward an undifferentiated pervasive consciousness.[145] Second, since this cosmopsychism that generates the stuff of which we are all made never really abandons its innate subjectivity, sentience then arises within the modality of a shared subjectivity. Our own intimate subjectivities are never quite divorced from the latent subjectivity of the objects all around. If we can manage to recognize this shared subjectivity, we might be inclined to reflect inwardly, with the pause of wonder—before the business as usual of instrumentalizing the matter of our world, of shaping matter to our will.

In this respect, it is not hard to see that the portrait of artificial intelligence taking over our world especially reflects our own agonistic relation to matter. While obvious with the image of the Terminator, if we think about it, even Bostrom's paperclip scenario, where he explicitly tries to imagine himself outside of the assumption of human values, with an insentient rote algorithm maximizing paperclips, here also we still find the mirror of human attitudes toward the material world. It is no small irony that the nightmare scenario of an unbridled algorithm destroying our habitat earth for some inane material production goal—paperclips—does not need an insentient, one-pointed superintelligent AI. It is already here. As we saw with the recent German study on the "insect apocalypse," 75% of the insect population has been decimated.[146] With the earth on course for a sixth mass extinction, our anthropocene is rapidly devouring resources and species for a somewhat unconscious—insentient, we may say, if we link sentience to awareness—conspicuous consumption. Bostrom's fear of an insentient paperclip maximizer actually reflects what we humans, even with our superior sentience, are in fact already accomplishing.

Bostrom also addresses what sorts of directives we might encode into AI to bring it into alignment with human goals, noting that the literal directives of coding may not yield our desired results. Perhaps the kind of directive needed is one that we humans have not yet quite understood, a capacity for wonder as we saw in Chapter Two, to marvel in such a way as to share subjectivity, in a first-person sort of way, in the life that enables us and the rest of the matter on the planet. This wonder especially works against an instrumentalization. Even in ourselves we can feel the experience of wonder as a panentheist halt to instrumentalizing what is other to us. In this respect, the idea of our shared subjectivity allows us to think about this matter differently. Sentient or not, we share with a future silicon intelligence a fabric of the relation of subject and object that structures how we interact with the world around us. The hope is that Abhinavagupta's conception of *vimarśa*, a materially embodied subjectivity, can help us to refigure matter, to recognize life at the base of matter, to lead us to respect matter more fully.

5

It from Bit, It from *Cit*

Information and Meaning

> The person who is said to be liberated is someone who correctly understands other beings to be like one's own limbs.
>
> —**Abhinavagupta**

> If you want to understand life, don't think about the vibrant, throbbing gels and oozes. Think about information technology.
>
> —**Richard Dawkins**[1]

> An object is an insufficiently interpreted subject
>
> —**Eduardo Viveiros de Castro**

> Using such and such equipment, making such and such a measurement, I get such and such a number. Who I am has nothing to do with this finding. Or does it? Am I sleepwalking? Or am I one of those poor souls without the critical power to save himself from pathological science?
>
> —**John Archibald Wheeler**

Introduction

Perhaps Charles Darwin was too hasty in rejecting God, that God anyway that we saw in Chapter Three, who he thought could not possibly be beneficent or omnipotent and still create the parasitic wasp. The cruel ichneumonidae wasp injects its eggs into the caterpillar, so that as it matures, the wasp larva eats from the inside the live womb of the caterpillar's body, nightmarishly bursting it apart.[2] Whether or not God, whatever that might be, has a say, the parasitic wasp, as it turns out, may not be such an evil character after all. Or in any

The Matter of Wonder. Loriliai Biernacki, Oxford University Press. © Oxford University Press 2023.
DOI: 10.1093/oso/9780197643075.003.0006

case, only from the perspective of the dying caterpillar is the parasitic wasp or the God who designed it a villain. From the perspective of the lima bean plants attacked by caterpillars, these apparently wretched wasps turn out to be heroes, plant protectors that scientists have dubbed "plant bodyguards."[3] A variety of species, including corn and lima beans, send out a chemical emission, a pheromone-like distress signal when attacked by caterpillars. The parasitic wasp smells the scent of the plant's dismay and comes to the rescue, destroying the invading caterpillars.[4] The parasitic wasp, emblematic of Darwin's loss of faith, if not, in any case fully responsible for it, nevertheless plays a wider, kinder role in the ecology of life and death, on the side of plants who have no way to flee marauding insects.

But what does it mean that these lima beans can somehow communicate with these wasps, sending a smelly Morse Code message chemically wafting across the distance? What does this secret chemical sharing of goals, of survival—might we even say cross-species love—between lima bean and wasp say about what it means to be a lima bean plant or a parasitic wasp? Does it suggest that the plant has a kind of consciousness and agency? Our current biology chalks this up to an evolutionary algorithm, sophisticated, but still the rote transfer of information. This information exchange in no way indicates consciousness on the part of plant or wasp. Yet this strange alliance provokes at least a pause. What indeed is information?

This chapter looks at Abhinavagupta's panentheism in relation to ideas of information. I argue that Abhinavagupta's articulation of a foundational subjectivity, a first-person perspective, can help to parse out how the concept of information works for us and help us rethink the model on which it is founded. Elsewhere I have already written about the dual role that information plays, discussing in particular contemporary neuroscientists Giulio Tononi's and Christof Koch's Integrated Information Theory 3.0 (IIT 3.0).[5] I show that both Abhinavagupta and Tononi use a similar strategy to bridge the gap between mind and matter. As I pointed out there, information takes on a dual nature, both as material substance and as that which conveys mental intentionality. I have also discussed, in Chapter Four, what makes for sentience, using Abhinavagupta's ideas of *vimarśa* as sentience in relation to whether artificial intelligence, robots, might become sentient. This chapter continues this comparative theme, examining the implications of the idea of information, its use as a way of offering mathematical surety in a complex world, and John Wheeler's articulation of information as the source of the material world in his well-known, pithy formulation of "it from bit."

Information as a concept, I would venture, is attractive for our contemporary models largely because it proposes, with scalpel precision, to slice out from knowledge its fuzzy first-person element, leaving us with information as something we can measure and manipulate—as something external. A contemporary scientific discourse tends to leave out the subjective element of the one who knows. Somehow the veneer of authority attaches to the third person, making it more universal, truer.[6] Yet, if we excavate the concept of information, I propose that what makes it so powerful is instead precisely that it offers a bivalency. Yes, information as external, measurable, and manipulable, however, even as the idea of information trades on the impetus to measure and manipulate knowledge, it leaves open a backdoor for recovering the "who" of knowledge, the intentionality and meaning of the subject who knows.

As a way of teasing out some of these implications, I offer a number of comparisons; I compare information to a mantra, and on the material side, I compare information to Abhinavagupta's formulation of the material element—sound, that makes up the mantra. Likewise, I place physicist John Wheeler's early articulation of information as a source of materiality (his well-known "it from bit," where information is the source of the material world) in relation to Abhinavagupta's panentheism, where the material world arises from consciousness, as "it from *cit*." I offer these comparisons not to suggest an analogy of mantras to information and the like, but rather to tease out some of the unarticulated ramifications of these models. These comparisons show that the path winds it way back toward the backdoor and toward recovery of information as meaning, as a first-person perspective.

Again, here are a few reminders about Abhinavagupta's panentheism—Abhinavagupta's model of materiality is a mix of matter with consciousness and with intentionality. It is a panentheism that hinges on subjectivity, the first-person perspective being the unifying factor, and it is also a panentheism that extends down to mere insects, even to a mere clay pot, as we saw earlier. In this respect, however, Abhinavagupta's model is not a bottom-up panpsychism, such as we see in Tononi's Integrated Information Theory 3.0, for instance, where an initial protomentality achieves consciousness with a jump into an evolutionary integration.[7] Abhinavagupta's model is closer to Philip Goff's conception of a cosmopsychism, as we saw earlier, where a single conscious source generates and instantiates within itself the variety of individual consciousnesses that make up the various existing entities.[8] The third section of his vast opus on the philosophy of recognition, the *Īśvara Pratyabhijñā Vivṛti Vimarśinī*, opens with a traditional verse of praise (*maṇgalācāra*) that encapsulates the theme of the section to follow; Abhinavagupta sings,

> I bow to him who pierces through and pervades with his own essence this whole, from top to bottom, and makes this whole world to consist of *Śiva*, himself. I bow

> to the One who sprinkles the immortal nectar of his own self, rising to the highest abode. ||[9]

Thus, this section immediately focuses on outlining the categories comprising existence (*tattvas*),[10] Abhinavagupta lays out a claim of a single consciousness, that of *Śiva* as deity pervading the whole world from top to bottom. A panentheism, yes. Again, as we saw earlier, it also makes sense to classify his system as being dual aspect and as at least friendly to panpsychism, with a notion of deity as somehow both transcendent as a self-aware consciousness of the totality—and simultaneously as the limited perspectives—wasps and caterpillars—pervading the totality.[11]

In this chapter, first we look at the New Materialist implications of lima beans transmitting information to wasps. What is at stake? I suggest that this study not only upends our anthropocentric conceptions of human forms of consciousness, but that it also forces us to grapple with our own porosity, that the boundaries of a sovereign self collapse rather too easily. I suspect that Darwin found the parasitic wasp so faith-shattering because the image of the wasp imploding the caterpillar from within also implodes our own fiction of discrete individual selves. Our permeability urges a different sort of model for mapping what we are. Here I borrow from Berit Brogaard's notion of consciousness as a universal field along the lines of gravity. I use Brogaard's model as a way of conceptualizing Abhinavagupta's panentheism as a holist cosmopsychism. From this discussion we begin to sketch out the idea of information. I compare Max Tegmark's proposal that a mathematical formula has consciousness to Abhinavagupta's conception of the mantra as conscious, as a way in, to kickstart our thinking about how information functions. This helps us to parse out in more detail the dual function information plays in Tegmark's formulation comparatively with Abhinavagupta's dual-aspect panentheism, where consciousness exhibits two modes, subjectivity, or "I-ness" (*ahantā*), and the state of being object, "this-ness" (*idantā*). For Tegmark as well as for Abhinavagupta, a dual-aspect formulation is about bridging the divide between consciousness and matter.

From this we examine Wheeler's articulation of information in his well-known "it from bit"—the idea that information generates materiality—in relation to Abhinavagupta. Wheeler suggests that information is the basis for the materiality that makes up the world. Both Abhinavagupta and Wheeler propose models that derive matter from an originary nonmaterial substance. Wheeler states that we get matter out of information, out of bits, whereas Abhinavagupta tells us we get matter out of consciousness. Both Wheeler and Abhinavagupta offer a process that moves from an earlier undetermined state of existence (information for Wheeler, consciousness for Abhinavagupta), which then becomes defined as some particular thing and not as something else. For Wheeler this process occurs through queries that collapse the quantum indeterminacy; for Abhinavagupta this occurs when *Māyā* measures things out into the duality of this and not that. Wheeler backs away from the idea of consciousness, landing instead on the idea of "meaning," but even with the idea of meaning, the damage is done.[12] When Wheeler includes "meaning" in the mix, we find our way back to intentionality, to the "who" of consciousness. If "it from bit" means that information generates materiality, I propose "it from *cit*"—the idea that materiality arises out of consciousness, where *cit* is the Sanskrit word for "consciousness" in Abhinavagupta's panentheism. With "meaning" in the equation, this, I suggest, is where the path Wheeler proposes ultimately leads.

Still we wonder: if we buy Abhinavagupta's model of panentheism, a cosmopsychism unfolding, the question then becomes how do we get the limitations that make for differences? The problem is less how to get consciousness from the building blocks of matter and instead how a singular entity manages to limit itself to make the kinds of agonistic diversity we see here, caterpillars that eat lima bean plants and wasp rescuers that see caterpillars as foes to implode.[13]

The final section of this chapter concludes by examining Abhinavagupta's articulation of how we get diversity, agonistic relations, and our all too familiar partial, limited subjectivities. I suggest that Abhinavagupta formulates the path to multiplicity out of unity through interpreting the Tantric cosmology that he inherits—the *tattva* system—as a phenomenology of consciousness moving from subjectivity (*ahantā*) to a state of being object (*idantā*). For this section I draw especially from Abhinavagupta's *Āgamādhikāra* section of the *Īśvara Pratyabhijñā Vivṛti Vimarśinī* where he outlines the *tattva* system.[14] This *tattva* system lists everything that makes up our reality. It outlines a cosmology from dense materiality, earth, water, the five elements, all the way up through individual minds and individual egos, the idea of time itself as a covering, finally landing at *Śiva* as the singular cosmopsychist reality that unfolds to make us and our world. Abhinavagupta charts the sequence of the *tattvas* as a gradual transformation of consciousness into materiality, moving from the "I" of subjectivity to the "this" of objects.[15]

Mindless Information

So then, what does a transmission of information signify in terms of sender and recipient? Does it point to some ghost behind the machinery of plant and wasp biochemistry? Or is there nothing more than a bald unconscious biological algorithm? Our familiar anthropocentric prioritization of our own species' modes of communication leaves us allergic to granting anything like a mindful connection, a literal compassion, between a lima bean and the lowly insect. Hence, we chalk it up to the pulls of an evolutionary adaptation, lucky and accidental. This is precisely what a compelling thinker like Daniel Dennett points to as Darwin's great idea, evolution without a corresponding mindfulness.[16] But apart from an unreflective anthropocentrism, I suspect an additional psychological motivation drives the disgust Darwin feels in the face of the parasitic wasp. When the parasitic wasp burrows its larvae in the caterpillar belly, imploding it from within, what implodes as well is the fiction of discrete individual bodies. Living beings are not discrete individuals; we are porous. An implosion from within makes this reality all too apparent.[17] I have a hunch this would be horrifying to Darwin, causing him to lose faith in God because the analogy too readily applies to our own fiction of autonomous individual selves. We humans are not little mini-me versions of a biblical God, made in his image, discrete and sovereign in our own bodies—but instead we are susceptible to takeover and implosion.[18] However, the rest of the story that Darwin didn't see—the link between plant and wasp in concert against a plague of caterpillar—offers hints of a differently structured universe. It is not the theism of Darwin's biblical heritage, but a different model, akin more to a panpsychism or cosmopsychism and amenable to the model we find in Abhinavagupta's panentheism.

To place this idea in the context of Abhinavagupta's panentheism, I suggest we might draw from Berit Brogaard's proposal to understand consciousness along the lines of a unified field. Making the analogy to gravity, she postulates a model of mentons, mental particles, which, like gravitons, are particles whose visible effects operate as part of a unified field rather than as part of a building block model, as elementary particles that somehow coalesce to make a conscious subject. As she puts it, "the proposed view is best understood as a kind of unified field theory that takes primordial consciousness to be a field into which informational content can enter and thereby reach awareness."[19] She conceives this in terms of an individual human with information across the brain as a unified field driving neuronal integration. In this case, I modify her model to formulate an image of how I see Abhinavagupta's panentheism operating. Extending the notion of a field more broadly, I suggest we stretch the idea of a unified field beyond an individual human toward the sort of cosmospsychism that Abhinavagupta's panentheism entails, where consciousness, *Śiva*, unfolds to make a world. In this view, consciousness presents as a unified field; this consciousness operates as a whole that unfolds into various constituents and is yet malleable. In this regard, consciousness is information transmitted across the field and the field itself, in keeping with Abhinavagupta's understanding of consciousness as the wall of the world (bhitta). That is, consciousness itself is the body of the world, as we saw earlier. This unified field unfolds into the multiplicity of beings, plants and wasps and caterpillars, and as it exists foundationally as a field rather than discrete entities, it allows movement of information within it, through the passage of plant pheromone to wasp. So this is not a collection of discrete individuals, mini-me's made in the image of a creator, but instead an interconnected field of consciousness. This model is, of course, simply one way to think about Abhinavagupta's panentheism. Yet, what is attractive in thinking about consciousness in this way, as a unified field, even as I expand Brogaard's model into a frame of cosmopsychism, is that it offers the possibility of wider interactions and connectivity while still leaving room for agonistic differentiations, a caterpillar at odds with both wasp and lima bean. As Brogaard notes, "it's quite plausible that the best model of consciousness is one that treats consciousness as a unified field that can vary in richness and intentionality among organisms and across time."[20] For our present purposes, it helps us to frame the differentiation we find in Abhinavagupta's panentheism; its dual aspects of "this-ness" (*idantā*) and "I-ness" (*ahantā*) track with the bivalency we find in the idea of information. Moreover, since information itself can move across the unified field, this allows for a mechanism of exchange across the field, thus making plausible Abhinavagupta's assertion that we saw earlier: that linguistically addressing the mountain as "you" or "I" impacts its own capacity for sentience.

Information: Un/Conscious Patterns

What then is information? The idea of information plays a central role in most, if not all, of our contemporary models for the world we inhabit. Information has become a unifying concept across disciplines; it is ubiquitous. I think Rosi Braidotti gets at the heart of what drives the turn to information. She marks this as a shift from an idea of *meaning* into *information*—which is lifeless: a shift from the humanities as perspective to the objectivity of a third-person science.[21] Jeffrey Kripal has also pointed to this cultural turn, driving the way we render the differences between the sciences and the humanities.[22]

The allure of the idea of information may in part lie in its promises of mathematical transcendence. From a physics perspective, information is never lost. This profound physical immutability was put to the test in the famous bet between Stephen Hawking and John Preskill over whether information is lost if it falls into a black hole. Hawking conceded the bet and wryly commented that he should have paid his wager, an encyclopedia of baseball, as ashes, out of which Preskill could still retrieve the information.[23] Information is never lost; it may not be always readily accessible, but nevertheless it remains as traces, for our purposes—oddly like the theory of traces that karma leaves minutely encoded in the fabric of subtle bodies.[24] And curiously, just as with the theory of karma and rebirth, so information's immutability also holds out hope against the cruel mortality of human bodies, so that at least our consciousness, if not our bodies, might transcend the inevitable return to dust. This hope for a more eternal existence that information seems to promise appears to be behind Ray Kurzweil's digital dreams of immortality through downloading his consciousness into a computer.[25] Information is never lost; we simply need the right engineering to capture it. It is not surprising then, that the idea of information as an ordering principle has also crept into the idea, the problem, of consciousness. So, apart from the pervasiveness of metaphors comparing the human brain to a computer, information as an organizing pattern has also become a prominent way of thinking about consciousness itself. As Douglas Hoftstadter stated in his enticing *Godel, Escher, Bach*, "the key is not the *stuff* out of which brains are made, but the *patterns* that can come to exist out of the stuff of a brain."[26]

More recently, Max Tegmark has also adopted this language of information, computation, and patterns. In a recent TED talk, he equated consciousness with computation, stating that "consciousness is a mathematical pattern."[27] The same molecules from a physics level can be conscious or not depending on the pattern it takes. So there is just one sort of stuff in the universe, quarks or atoms. It is how it gets arranged, its information pattern, that determines whether or not it is conscious. This is the sort of obverse of the monism we find in Indian religious traditions that I touched on earlier, and interesting for our purposes, it is surprisingly quite close to the dictum we find across much Tantra, the idea that "Everything in fact has the nature of all things."[28] That is, there is one reality, *Śiva*, and it takes a variety of forms, some conscious and some not. What makes the difference has not to do with the basic substance of this or that thing or entity, but rather how matter instantiates different mathematical patterns for Tegmark, and for Abhinavagupta, how it instantiates different concentrations of subjectivity. The question then arises: is consciousness simply the particular pattern a material information takes? We visited this issue in the last chapter, and we will unpack it in more detail later in this chapter. For now, however, what is so interesting about Tegmark's formulations—which not surprisingly also align with Tononi's and Koch's understanding of information in their Integrated Information Theory

3.0—is his commutation of our culture's dominant scientific model, a bare physicalist materialism holding that only matter really exists, into a dual-aspect monism that includes space for the murky concept of consciousness.[29] Again, there is a similarity to Tononi's model and also to Abhinavagupta's dual-aspect monism. That is, for Tegmark, "consciousness is the way information feels."[30] This point is key because with this assertion, Tegmark manages to give us a notion of information that can double-dip, with an objective third-person material reality of measurable numbers on the one side, and on the other side as the "feeling" component of consciousness, a first-person non-material mental awareness. The quantitative objective elements of information, the patterns of atoms arranged as a bottle or a hand or a bat, mark one aspect of this dual-aspect monism, the objective physical existence of the thing. Its inner subjectivity—"what it feels like" to be a bat or a bottle—marks the other half of this dual-aspect monism. Tegmark's model is congruent with Abhinavagupta's dual-aspect monism; Abhinavagupta also offers a bivalency for consciousness, which we saw earlier where *idantā*, "This-ness" marks the objective external marker of his dual-aspect nondualism, and *ahantā*, "I-ness" points to the subjective, internal marker. Now, as sometimes happens with speculations on consciousness, Tegmark's remarks in this talk also begin to sound the notes of a transcendence bordering on mysticism. He tells us that "some mathematical patterns simply are conscious."[31] What might it mean for a mathematical pattern to be conscious?

The seeming mysticism of Tegmark's remark calls to mind a passage in Abhinavagupta, if we allow a comparison of the formula of a mantra with the formula of a mathematical pattern. In the passage, Abhinavagupta talks about the difference between the subjectivity of a mantra, which has a body made of sound, but not the other elements, earth, water, fire, in contrast to the subjectivity of a person with a body like yours and mine, consisting of earth and so on. If it sounds odd to impute consciousness to a mantra, as it sounds odd to impute consciousness to a mathematical formula, we should keep in mind that in this Indian tradition, what makes gods different from humans is precisely the idea that their bodies are primarily made of sound and not the other elements. This is sound as vibratory frequency, not simply gross physical sound, but something more like a vibratory formula. Thus, in a popular song to the goddess of wealth, Lakṣmī, the poet sings, "your eternal body is the mantra, o goddess."[32] The body made of just sound alone has a kind of staying-capacity that bodies made of earth cannot quite match. In Abhinavagupta's analysis, the problem with the physical body, which here also includes the intellect, is that it is too easily understood as object, what he calls "This-ness" (*idantā*). To this he says that the physical body, including the intellect and the breath:

> These are not, in fact, at all like the form which sound takes when it is perceived. [The physical body, etc.] cause consciousness to contract, become limited; they cover and obscure consciousness very tightly indeed! In contrast, the body which sound takes when it manifests—which is essentially what mantra is—this embodiment of sound continually reverberates as *vimarśa*, the essence of life, sentience, in the sky of the heart.[33]

We explored this notion of *vimarśa* in the previous chapter and saw its key role as the marker for sentience. Here, for Abhinavagupta, bodies made of sound, connected to the ether (akāśa), the most refined of the five elements do not carry the liabilities of our usual physical bodies, causing consciousness to become obscured, as bodies made of the other four elements, bodies of earth and water do.

This effect occurs because sound, connected to space, is special among the five sensory modalities of form, connected to sight, scent, connected to smell and so on. Sound, aligned with hearing, is also foundationally connected to meaning, as Abhinavagupta explains:

> Sound which is Word, is the ability to give meaning; it has the nature of *nāda*, primordial sound vibration, and it has the capacity to give space to all things. This sound at base is the seed of the host of various letters and the basic function of it is to endure the variety of meanings conventionally imposed upon sounds, from which it therefore possesses the ability to be imposed upon various objects as their meaning. This is one type of sound. The other type is the Word, or let it be not considered a word, denoting something, even the onomatopoetic sound of rapping; that type of sound has the capacity to endure all space without the accompanying contact because it is lacks form and it does not create resistance through contact. [Utpaladeva] describes that sound with the words "having the nature of primordial sound vibration."[34]

Because sound is connected to space, it carries with it the capacity to give space to all things. Sound gives rise to the alphabet, the basis of language, and allows meaning to arise in relation to different objects we encounter. Sound also creates meaning simply by its own innate capacity to endure space. This "primordial sound vibration," which is a word, or Abhinavagupta tells us, even just the sound of rapping, by its inherent nature generates meaning. I suspect that here he suggests something akin to our evolutionary predisposition to recognize patterns as meaningful. We impute intention to sounds. The rapping on the window, as Edgar Allan Poe discerned, tells us someone is there, whether a person or raven or ghost. The other four elements, earth, water, fire, and air, lack this capacity. Abhinavagupta tells us,

> the earth etc. so far as it goes do not have the capacity to make space at all whatsoever. Even visibly, it is not the inherent nature of these, earth, water, etc., to give space. They only perform this function when ether accompanies them.[35]

That is, the gross or physical element of ether (*akāśa*), with its accompanying subtle element of sound, has a special capacity to make space, and this capacity is what allows meaning to emerge. Ether, or space, is considered to be a physical element, however, sound itself, as subtle element has an additional feature, a stirring-up quality that allows the influx of meaning to occur with sound.[36] Whether or not we can liken sound and mantric sound to the idea of information, what they share is the dual configuration linking a material quality to the idea of meaning.[37] And, of course, the terminology used for information also invokes the idea of sound—with technical terms such as "noise" and "signal."

In any case, sound as subtle element carries one other ramification, a perk to be enjoyed by those beings made of sound, like gods, or perhaps mathematical formulas if some might indeed be conscious as Tegmark suggests. That is, Abhinavagupta tells us that "the highest level the *Māyā*-bound Subjects in the body etc., attain is the state of bondage, because all the bound souls are innately afraid of the body breaking down."[38] Being in a body made of earth carries an innate downside; it can break down, and those of us with earth and water bodies know this on a visceral level. It consequently generates a deep-seated fear that keeps us bound, stuck in unenlightened thought patterns. This is not the case for those beings who exist on a higher, more conscious level than us, who instead take bodies made of sound, of the collections of letters that make up mantras. Bodies made of mantric sound seem to offer immunity to breaking down, much like the information that Kurzweil hopes to capture in his quest for robot immortality. Perhaps, after all, mantra bodies and information bodies are the bodies of gods.[39]

I point to some similarities with this analogy of information to mantric sound, however, this by no means suggests we can equate the two. Simply, the analogy is suggestive, not more, and as such, it helps to contextualize the perhaps not so surprising genealogy, the lines of connection between nondualist philosophies from the Indian subcontinent and contemporary formulations of information. For instance, the pioneering quantum physicist Erwin Schrödinger (1887–1961) was attracted to Hinduism's nondual Advaita Vedanta,[40] and Koch also points to the mysticism of Tibetan Buddhists to illustrate an idea of pure consciousness.[41] Also more Buddhist-friendly, Thomas Metzinger argued for the idea of no self and recently suggested that ideas of the soul, founded on out-of-body experiences might also be linked to an idea of information.

> The soul is the OBE-PSM [Out-of-Body-Experience -Phenomenal Self Model]. Centuries of phenomenological reports describing it as a subtle body pointed in the right direction, and now we begin to see how it actually is a purely informational structure modeling bodily self-experience in cases of absent or disintegrated somatosensory/vestibular input.[42]

The experience of leaving the body, popularly known as "astral travel," traveling outside the body, via a soul or a subtle body is, as Metzinger tells us, linked simply to the brain's capacities for modeling information in its somatosensory cortex. It is also probably fair to say that some of the mystically laced talk at least in part arises through information's link to post-Newtonian quantum physics, and its sheer incomprehensibility. Jeffrey Kripal astutely points to the close link between the language and ideas of quantum mechanics and a contemporary articulation of conceptions of out-of-body and subtle body experiences.[43] In any case, Richard Feynman's often quoted quip that, "if you think you understand quantum mechanics, you don't understand quantum mechanics," iconically captures the enigma of this new physics. The law of the excluded middle, so famously invoked derisively against the mystical philosophy of India, becomes slippery in the face of quantum mechanics' uncanny recalcitrance to the kinds of positivist logic that held sway for these last three recent centuries of Western science.

It from Bit

The shearing point of this comparison has to do with the idea of information and its backdoor reclamation of meaning. Here I suggest a comparison of Abhinavagupta's 11th-century nondual panentheism with theoretical quantum physicist John Wheeler's well-known postulation of "it from bit" as a way of elucidating this backdoor. Wheeler's pithy formulation "it from bit" nicely conjures up the shift in thinking that quantum mechanics precipitates, encapsulating the idea of information as key to what reality really is. Wheeler states:

> It from bit symbolizes the idea that every item of the physical world has at bottom—at a very deep bottom, in most instances—an immaterial source and explanation; that what we call reality arises in the last analysis from the posing of yes-no questions in the registering of equipment-evoked responses; in short that all things physical are information-theoretic in origin and this is a participatory universe.[44]

Wheeler's postulations in this seminal talk turn on its head our usual Newtonian assumptions about the world. It is not the case that science can innocently, objectively, from the outside examine the world and describe how it is made and how it works. Instead, Wheeler suggests that the origin of matter is not at all material, not atoms or quarks building up to generate a world, which then evolve, into life and conscious beings. Rather the source begins with the bit, information as its very deep bottom, its immaterial source. When queried, this immaterial information gives rise to the physical world. This world arises through observer participation, through a subject asking questions, which register answers that generate the material stuff of the universe, the "It."

In this way, Wheeler guides his information-theoretic into strange territory as he invokes nonhuman possibilities for awareness, computer consciousness and who knows what, telling us, "What shall we say of a view of existence that appears, if not anthropomorphic in its use of the word "who," still overly centered on life and consciousness?"[45] Wheeler's interpretation of information as a quantum phenomenon causes a rupture in business as usual for thinking about the nature of matter and sets the stage for much current thinking about information, including the position that Tononi and Koch take by adopting a panpsychism to help explain the gap between matter and consciousness.[46] Wheeler's use of information as an immaterial source and primary base for creating the objects in the world shares with Abhinavagupta the idea of a flow from an originary nonphysical source to generate physical matter. For Abhinavagupta, the movement is from subject to object. Physical matter arises from the subject:

> The Subject's form, which is a unity of awareness contains an excess, an abundance of awareness. This is deposited into the side of the object that is going to be created. So inwardly the object has the attribute of *śakti*, Energy which is none other than the form of consciousness.[47]

Materiality takes the form of objects, a third-person existence. Objects are the matter that flow outwardly from the subject, and they retain within their core the element of consciousness, even as it is covered over and remains hidden. Abhinavagupta also links this to his dual-aspect panentheism in his use of the binary of knowledge (*jñāna*) and action (*kriyā*). Knowledge represents an inward direction and, and as we saw in Chapter Four, action as the outward movement toward externality links to matter. As we saw, what makes Abhinavagupta's dual-aspect panentheism work as a monism is that he disrupts our usual expectations of the binary of consciousness and matter.

Rather than walling off knowledge (*jñāna*) and sentience on one side of the binary with matter and action (*kriyā*) on the other, instead he surprisingly links action and materiality to the idea of sentience with *vimarśa*. Earlier in this chapter, I drew a loose analogy between information and sound, particularly sound as the pattern of mantra. Here I extend the analogy of information to the idea of knowledge (*jñāna*), which as we will see aligns to mantra. I point this out primarily because we see a pattern similar to Wheeler's "it from bit" also in Abhinavagupta's description of the movement from knowledge (*jñāna*) to action (*kriyā*). According to Abhinavagupta:

> [F]rom the perspective of mere consciousness lying in the core there exists the state containing both inner and outer. However, *Māyā*'s creation spreads out, expands into many branches, with the Lord still lying within the core. . . . When that Energy manifests inwardly, naturally it is called the Energy of Knowledge. However when it expands in stages with its active awareness gradually becoming more firm and fixed, then it manifests externally. This is pointed to as the Energy of Activity.[48]

Abhinavagupta's conception of knowledge, *jñāna*, is at best an imperfect analogue for Wheeler's idea of information. Particularly, he sets knowledge (*jñāna*) on an equal footing with activity (*kriyā*), both as the energy of the unfolding cosmopsychism. Still, the parallels—the fuzzy interdependence between material reality and an information that generates it are suggestive and may also help explain the similarities we find in contemporary dual-aspect models, like that of Tononi and Koch in relation to Abhinavagupta.[49] To recap Abhinavagupta's model, the problem is framed in terms of subjectivity, "I-ness" in contrast to "This-ness," being an object. In a state of subjectivity, Abhinavagupta tells us, "the world is withdrawn and is linked with a single unitary essence, the flavor of "I-ness."[50] In this quote, he describes an early stage in the unfolding of the cosmos. Outlining a cosmogonic map derived and modified from traditional Indian Sāṃkhya philosophy,[51] he charts the creation of an external world through its subsequent stages from pure consciousness. Beginning as consciousness, as a position of unadulterated subjectivity, then to limited minds existing as subject and object, human and otherwise, down through sensory capacities to hear and touch, physical matter ultimately arises when "This-ness," is tied to the five elements, space, air, fire, water, and earth. Abhinavagupta describes the state linked to subjectivity when the world is withdrawn, in a state of deep sleep, or when the world goes through its periodic demise (*pralaya*) as one where objects rest within the subject. Here, objects do not appear. Why? Because the distinctions between "I" and "This" are not operative. The "I" and the "This" exist mixed together in an indeterminate flux. In Abhinavagupta's cosmogonic scheme, this state is not the cosmopsychic originary consciousness that is the state of *Śiva*, but two stages later in a state called *Sadāśiva*. Regarding this state he says:

> When, however, This-ness (*idantā*) is not distinctly manifest but appears rather as a cloudy indistinctness, characterized by tranquility, rest, then, even though it is still joined with objects capable of being known, nevertheless because of its emergence up into the state of *Śiva*, even while still possessing every sort of capacity of mental projection, it is the state of *Śiva* called *Sadāśiva*. And in that state of *Sadāśiva* the elements situated at the level of *Māyā* in the forms of objects and subjects are in every way in a state of dissolution because the forms belonging to *Māyā* are destroyed. Then the elements [water, fire, etc., which constitute the physical gross forms of the body etc.,] are placed within the Archetype of *Māyā* and that takes the form of the Energy of the Supreme Lord at the level of *Sadāśiva*. These elements resting in the state of *Sadāśiva* do have a slight portion of contact with "This-ness" This is in fact withdrawal, and that is the state of *Sadāśiva*.[52]

In this state of inward withdrawal, objects are not distinctly manifest. They still exist but in an indistinct cloudy form. As a result, there is no distinction between subject and object, and objects themselves do not quite yet appear. Rather, consciousness in this state has not yet unfolded into the possibilities of becoming a distinct object. That will happen when *Māyā*, the energy that generates duality, one thing to the exclusion of something else—when *Māyā* begins to operate as the world unfolds. Wheeler's description of the process where information becomes physical matter, the "it," shares with Abhinavagupta's model the idea of an initial state of indeterminacy. Information in the one model, consciousness in the other—both exist in an indeterminate state, which then later becomes distinct objects. I mentioned earlier, in Chapter One, that objects like a clay pot or a rock lack sentience because of their existence in this particular state of *Sadāśiva*, where awareness is drawn within. The implication is that consciousness, even if inwardly withdrawn and not visible, still ultimately undergirds even the insentient clay pot. Although Wheeler sidesteps the issue of consciousness, he appears to be suggesting something oddly analogous when he postulates an immaterial information-theoretic at the base of matter, the "it from bit."

For Wheeler, the subsequent questions then determine what arises out of the originary indeterminacy. For Abhinavagupta, a theology of freedom, the freedom of *Śiva* as cosmopsychism, allows what is created to unfold in ways that are partially free, since the subjectivity that is *Śiva* remains all the way down to worms and wasps and clay pots, and partially predetermined by the coverings that we *karma*-driven beings are wrapped in (more on these coverings below). *Māyā*, which is for Abhinavagupta not separate from the cosmopsychic *Śiva* as well participates in delimiting the form an object takes. Again, Abhinavagupta's model differs on a variety of levels from Wheeler's description of the process where information becomes the "it," materiality, not the least of which is Abhinavagupta's implicit theology. I argue in Chapter Three that whatever else theology entails, it also encodes the idea of consciousness, even within the human body, as a first-person subjectivity *apart* from human minds. I would venture that this element of theology functions in this way here as well, in contrast to Wheeler's information-theoretic which, even as it points to a "who," still skirts the issue of consciousness, as we see later in this chapter.

To sum up this discussion so far, for our purposes two things are particularly interesting about Abhinavagupta's formulation of how objects in the world relate to the subject who apprehends them. First, like Wheeler, he sees the process as extending first from the level of an indeterminate, nonphysical source, as consciousness first, which then becomes the object as physical matter. "It from bit" for Abhinavagupta might be written in an English-Sanskrit linguistic hybrid as "it from *cit*," *cit* that is, the Sanskrit translation for "consciousness." In other words, for Abhinavagupta, matter arises out of consciousness. Of course, the difference between a bit and *cit* boils down to whether there is meaning, intentionality, that is—consciousness—behind the "immaterial theoretic" that is information. Second, Abhinavagupta stipulates consciousness as a first-person perspective behind the transfer and transformation of knowledge, an idea of knowledge that I am loosely aligning to a notion of information here. Again, this first-person perspective exists apart from human minds. Later, we will return to our lima bean and wasp with their own curious transfer of knowledge and determine whether this implies a "who," that is, a subjectivity behind the transfer of information.

For now, in terms of Abhinavagupta's model of consciousness unfolding to become matter out of this early cosmogonic stage of *Sadāśiva*, perhaps it will not be surprising that we find our way back to the earlier comparison of information with sound, as mantra. For Abhinavagupta, the process of moving from the subjectivity of consciousness into the creation of an external material reality is mediated through sound, via mantra, that pristine materiality that makes up the bodies of gods. The process by which matter arises as an object, getting defined as *this* particular thing, first begins with mantras—here very refined mantras, the Great Lords of mantra. Out of these Great Mantra Lords come lesser mantras, not Great Lords, just simple Lords of mantras in the next following stage of development, as consciousness unfolds into the material world. This next phase after *Sadāśiva*, marching toward materiality, is called the *Īśvara tattva*. The process unfolds consecutively, one stage after the other, where an initial subjectivity comes to take physical shape in a world of objects. Abhinavagupta writes of the earlier stage:

> There in the first creation, the class of pure conscious beings called the Great Lords of *mantra* have a circle of existence. In the first creation it is conceived as only simply a mere cloudy indistinct outline of a picture, resembling the indistinct, fuzzy heap of entities which are the objects appearing to our inner sense organs.[53]

At this point, the material world is a "mere cloudy indistinct outline of a picture," and this first state, Abhinavagupta tells us, "manifests predominantly inwardly, with the form of knowledge."[54] So again, an inwardness, connected to subjectivity, to "I-ness," (*ahantā*) takes the form of knowledge, and this is how things begin. It starts with knowledge, that is, knowledge as an inward impulse fused with sound, the mantra. Knowledge with the signature of sound as mantra: this stands in the role of Wheeler's bit.

What follows in the unfoldment of the world for Abhinavagupta is a shift from a pristine subjectivity, the "I-ness" of this early stage of apprehension into a more precise naming of the object qua object, as "this." This is characterized by extending outwardly, as activity (*kriyā*) and forms the second part, the object, the "It" of his dual-aspect monism. Abhinavagupta tells us that with this unfolding into the world, this next stage, the archetype (*tattva*) of *Īśvara* "is capable of a consciousness of the world and specifies and arranges a distinct manifestation of the world in an external way."[55] For Abhinavagupta, moving from inwardly focused knowledge to an external activity (*kriyā*) creates the object by defining it into a precise object. With this movement outward, the picture becomes complete and the object appears as a fully completed picture, no longer fuzzy or indistinct. Abhinavagupta says:

> Then the lords of mantra reside in the state of maintaining [the world] in the image[56] of a fully completed picture, like that which is apprehended by our external sense organs. The principle of *Īśvara* manifests in the form of the lords of mantra.[57]

So, like Wheeler, for Abhinavagupta the world arises first out of an indistinct immateriality that only later begins to be defined into the objectivity that makes for a "fully completed picture." This turns what was inward knowledge into an object, an "it." First, reality is indistinct, knowledge, and this knowledge, like Wheeler's information, is indistinct, not defined. Then it becomes defined into matter. For Wheeler, the object comes to exist through a process of definition that makes information, which was indistinct into something distinct as object, an "It," or a "This" if we draw from Abhinavagupta's language. Wheeler describes the process by comparing how we get "It from Bit" in a quantum reality to a game of 20 Questions.[58] Only, the game of 20 Questions Wheeler has in mind is one where the players have not yet decided upon what the object would be; the questions themselves steer the creation of the object to its particular form. In this comparison, Abhinavagupta's concept of activity (*kriyā*), extending outwardly, and the actions of *Māyā*, as delimiting one thing and not another would be Wheeler's probe, the questions that Wheeler points to that create and define the object.

Wheeler, for his part, is quite reticent in his speculations on how consciousness might play into the mix. He acknowledges that his model of the information-theorectic seems to point like a smoking gun toward the idea of consciousness[59]:

> "Consciousness." We have traveled what may seem a dizzying path. First, [an] elementary quantum phenomenon brought to a close by an irreversible act of amplification. Second, the resulting information expressed in the form of bits. Third, this information used by observer-participants—via communication—to establish meaning. Fourth, from the past through the billeniums to come, so many observer-participants, so many bits, so much exchange of information, as to build what we call existence.[60]

Certainly, we have measurement, and measurement expressed as information bits and then this information communicated to establish meaning, and out of this we get the material world "what we call existence," the "it from bit." Yet, what consciousness is, or the role it might play in the process, is one he hesitates to define. He continues this passage, pointing out how precipitously close this theory swerves toward postulating a primary consciousness at base of everything—in fact, the panpsychism that Tononi and Koch, and Tegmark eventually take up in his wake—saying:

> Doesn't this it-from-bit view of existence seek to elucidate the physical world, about which we know something, in terms of an entity about which we know almost nothing, consciousness?[61]

Yet, he quickly shuts down this tantalizing opening into the idea of consciousness. A few lines down he writes, "We, however, steer clear of the issues connected with "consciousness."[62]

Information and the Meaning of Meaning

Wheeler dodges what he points to as a natural and logical conclusion of his idea of information, that is, an idea of intentionality as foundational. He recognizes this when he points to consciousness as the base, even if he subsequently shuts down this line of thought, telling us he will "steer clear" of the issues connected with "consciousness."[63] I suspect that driving this rejection is at least in part a desire to stick with a third-person "objectivity," to bypass the inevitable subjectivity that comes with intentionality. This, again, is the point Rosi Braidotti and Kripal make about the idea of information. Wheeler seems to want to stay away from a notion of the personal, of an intentional agency, an agency that looks a little too much like a creator god as the immaterial source of this creation. Information as a concept, and as a word with its connotations of abstractness and the impersonal allows Wheeler to avoid the implications of a person, a creator god, a first-person subjectivity. It may be possible to think of information simply as molecularly patterned organization, from the third-person perspective. However, I suspect that the attractiveness of information as a model is precisely its capacity to entail intentionality, the mental and *subjective* elements of experience, the "what it feels like," as we saw Tegmark highlight.[64] This is the backdoor that "information" offers. This is certainly the case for Tononi and Koch's Integrated Information Theory 3.0 and the necessary slide they take into panpsychism, and I would venture for Wheeler as well. What information means, even for Wheeler, steering clear of the "C" word, is precisely meaning. As he tells us, it is "to establish meaning."[65] Meaning that can be also made material and hence measured. But meaning? Doesn't this look like swapping out the pot for the kettle? Meaning, measured or not, in any case, requires a subject, a conscious entity to make sense.

For Wheeler, meaning is what links information—its many measurable bits to the billeniums of participant-observers in a virtuous and repeated cycle of communication of this meaning to then make a world. As Wheeler puts it, "so many observer-participants, so many bits, so much exchange of information, as to build what we call existence."[66] It from bit, information made into matter all around us—perhaps we might imagine these billeniums of bits and their participant-observers as being akin to the algorithms of AI machine learning. The vast repetitions of data, its sheer excess of billeniums enough to allow a slow instantiation of matter out of its so many bits honed in on by a number-crunching machinery. Nothing god-like here—just a blind Darwinian algorithmic inexorability. In any case, this looks like Wheeler's interpretation, as he tells us: "Henceforth let us absolve consciousness from the charge of magic. Let us recognize it as a rational part of the biochemical-electronic machinery of the world."[67] Consciousness arises simply out of biochemical-electronic machinery.

Still, however, we find ourselves left with what to make of the meaning of meaning. Information—or consciousness—as mere machinery seems to miss a salient punchline: meaning for who? As John Nemec points out for the 9th-/10th-century Somānanda, Abhinavagupta's great grand-teacher, perception itself requires a person with a mind, with intentions. Somānanda says, "Perception would not arise for someone who has no will, i.e., for one who is devoid of intentions, because he would not be guided by the mind. Will is nothing but cognition imbued with one's intentions."[68] Cognition, information is not simply free-floating. It is attached to a perspective with its own intention, will, and its own subjectivity. In short, the suggestion for this medieval understanding is that the very nature of cognition entails some sort of intentional entity behind the gathering of information (a person? If only in Viveiros de Castro's sense?[69]).

Karen Barad astutely points to the slippage here, pointing out that Schrödinger's conclusion confirms that "measurement" is about subjectivity.[70] Along these same lines, Abhinavagupta gets to the heart of the problem of meaning through a radical idea, at least radical for our current perspective on matter. Abhinavagupta argues that causality can only be connected to a living, conscious subjectivity. We use the notion of cause and effect to measure material changes. In other words, it is about matter, not about consciousness. This bedrock of scientific objectivity, the notion of cause and effect, is precisely what quantum physics disrupts, its participant-observers inevitably blurring the lines of causality, introjecting the intentions of the observer into matter by the very act of observing.[71] Abhinavagupta's dual-aspect nondualism likewise points precisely to the intrusion of a conscious subject in any formulation of cause and effect. A conscious sentient subject is always at the heart of cause and effect. Thus, Abhinavagupta tells us "it can not be proved that the relation of cause and effect is grounded within what lacks sentience. But rather the relation of cause and effect lies only with that which is conscious."[72] Abhinavagupta reworks the Sāṃkhya philosophy he inherits here to allow the possibility for consciousness, that which is sentient, to have an effect on the world. He radically departs from the idea of consciousness we find in Sāṃkhya, where the *puruṣa*, a pristine consciousness, safeguards its claim to being real and permanent by divorcing it from material reality. This is the philosophical impetus for this point Abhinavagupta makes. What it does is to recognize the inevitable intrusion of consciousness into any transaction that happens in the world. That is, Abhinavagupta's model entails a participatory universe, even as his own reasoning is simply a philosophical response to Sāṃkhya's divide between matter and consciousness. Consciousness, the intentions of a "who," exists behind the changes we see in matter. His position is radical for our own positivist understanding of matter and causality, and it suggestively and substantively bolsters a contemporary New Materialism, where matter and its modifications are imbued throughout with consciousness and sentience.

In terms of our earlier question of "meaning" for who, we should keep in mind that even to speak of cause and effect implies a particular perspective, one particular subjectivity singling out this or that salient factor as cause in the midst of a multiplicity of simultaneously occurring co-factors. The idea of causality implies a directed intentionality. Cause and effect, like meaning, entails the "who" behind the cause, perceiving the cause. Wheeler, it appears, intuits this as well, coming back to the question of consciousness and substituting for the "C" word the idea of meaning to fill in the gaps between bits and matter and participant-observer effects in a quantum universe. By way of contrast, the Sāṃkhya model locates cause and effect in the world of matter alone. The problem that comes from this is, of course, a familiar one, akin to Descartes' Cartesian bifurcation, which leaves no way to connect consciousness to the body and matter. When Abhinavagupta says that cause and effect must be located within what is conscious and sentient, he bridges the gap, linking consciousness with body and matter. Meaning is then intrinsic to matter.

Meaning intrinsic to matter: this bears repeating.[73] It offers a handier grip on the issue at stake than the more widely familiar panpsychic idea of consciousness intrinsic to matter. The abstractness of the idea of consciousness tends to keep us in a third-person perspective, while the idea of meaning brings the idea of a particular perspective, a first-person awareness, front and center. Especially for a New Materialism, this shift to think about matter in terms of meaning opens up avenues for rearticulating its status. The idea that matter has at base a kind of intentionality is radically counter to our positivist understanding about the difference between mind and matter. It allows us, and Abhinavagupta, to link matter with consciousness, yes. *And* it leads down a very slippery slope into a panpsychism, or panentheism in Abhinavagupta's case, solving the problem of how to connect matter to consciousness, all the while leaving us with a different problem: how to deal with an unsettling world where "if one can see the form of consciousness even in a clay pot, then what is there that's not false?"[74] Does matter, a simple clay jar, really have at base a kind of intentionality? Is this unseemly consequence of "It from Bit" or "It from Cit" something we can swallow?[75]

We saw this earlier. This is the same critique that neuroscientists Tononi and Koch face with their adoption of a panpsychism that predicts a modicum of consciousness for a photo diode (but fortunately or unfortunately, not yet for Siri on your Iphone).[76] We can also understand that Christof Koch says something akin to Abhinavagupta's position on causality, when he says consciousness is not about information processing or about stored information, but about a causal power, a cause-effect capacity,[77] causal effect power upon itself,[78] which he radically, in a remarkable and scientifically revolutionary gesture traces back to a proto-panpsychism. What Abhinavagupta and Tegmark and Tononi and Koch all understand here is that without a conscious self or proto-self driving things forward with intention, with meaning, there is no way to link our awareness or our consciousness to matter. Causality is not simply a change in one material variable or another leading to an effect; it entails meaning and intention. The corollary is that any idea of a self—permanent or not—that is not able to have a causal effect on matter, like the Sāṃkhya *puruṣa* Abhinavagupta critiques, which stands apart from matter in a pristine eternal existence, unable to impact the body—such a self is irrelevant. As we saw in the previous chapter, it is, to use Daniel Dennett's terminology, epiphenomenal. Abhinavagupta also recognizes this:

> Consequently, when you separate off the effects [of this creation, like the body, etc.] then the state of Doership does not occur [i.e., as the *Sāṃkhya*s do when they separate off the *puruṣa* from *prakṛti*.] This type of relationship between cause and effect we have earlier refuted in great detail. And in this way the material appearance of effects which is the world [bodies and stones, etc.] is really just only what makes up the *Puruṣa*, the Person alone. As it is said in Vedic scripture: "the *puruṣa* is indeed all this."[79] [80]

In Indian Sāṃkhya philosophy, *puruṣa* classically represents the idea of pure spirit, consciousness, unchanging and untouched by the material world. As a category Sāṃkhya places it in opposition to Nature (*prakṛti*) and matter. In this respect, *puruṣa* functions analogously to Descartes' *res cogitans*—mind in contrast to materiality. Abhinavagupta, on the other hand, links causality to an idea of consciousness, rewriting the idea of consciousness, tying it to the materiality of the world. Thus, we have meaning and consciousness intrinsic to matter.

The Limited Subject

We have been mapping Abhinavagupta's idea of how the world comes to be in comparison with Wheeler's quantum model, which derives a material world from information, the bit. Wheeler's quantum model gives way to the kinds of panpsychisms espoused by Tegmark as well as by Tononi and Koch in their theory of information (IIT 3.0).[81] The familiar problem of a panpsychism, though, is its all-too-democratic extension of consciousness; after all, we cannot allow everything to have consciousness, everything to be sentient. This is the gist of at least part of John Searle's critique of Tononi and Koch's panpsychism, where he likens their panpsychism to a thin veneer of jam spread over the universe. Tononi and Koch address the problem by suggesting that as complexity builds up, that complexity allows a latent panpsychism to exhibit qualities of consciousness. At a certain threshold, what they designate *Phi*, a measurable amount of consciousness is demonstrated.[82] Abhinavagupta offers a different solution to the problem that is not dependent on a cutoff point where consciousness emerges.[83] Rather than an emergentism, Abhinavagupta's model relies on a modal shift between "I-ness" and "This-ness," between subjectivity and a third-person perspective of being an object, where both modes are possible. We humans and caterpillars and wasps are a mix, shifting between these two modes. So, as we saw in Chapter One, by addressing the rock as you, as second person, we can begin to wake up the always-present consciousness of this seeming insentient clod of rock—here again suggestively inviting a comparison to Wheeler's notion of a participatory universe.

Still, while the substratum of consciousness is never really not present, even for a clay pot, we want to be able to make distinctions. Our own current cultural proclivity tends toward a knee-jerk reflex to not accord subjectivity and consciousness to objects like jars and lima bean plants. Responding to the frustrated interlocutor complaining that Abhinavagupta's model suggests consciousness can be found even in a clay pot, he says, "Yes, correct, 'But' 'it is appropriate' to view 'the insentient' in this way,"[84] pointing out that we make these definitional cuts between what is sentient and what is insentient for conventional, pragmatic reasons. Nevertheless, if one consciousness, *Śiva*, unfolds to make the world, how do we get the differences between us, conscious sentient humans and lima bean plants and clay pots? For the lima bean plant sending out pheromones, and for caterpillars and wasps, we are inclined not to ascribe an originary free will to their seeming sentience, but instead ascribe to them something more like behavioral instinct, the algorithms of biology. Indeed, for us humans as well, so much of our behavior appears readily algorithmically predictable. If consciousness simply unfolds to make the world, how do we get the kind of partial consciousness that we humans have, our own seeming biologically determined behavior along with that of lima bean plants and wasps?[85]

Here I address how this model of an originary consciousness unfolding to make the world can give us partly free, partly not, partly conscious, partly not, humans and clay pots, (or mantra-bodied gods, for that matter), with differentiated levels of subjectivity and freedom. Abhinavagupta inherits a system of categories called the *tattva* system, which details the unfolding of the cosmos. His Tantric lineage expands and modifies an original Sāṃkhya cosmology of twenty-five categories (*tattvas*) into thirty-six categories. In Abhinavagupta's usage, the *tattvas* mark the progressive shift from subjectivity to being an object. It also nicely captures the bivalence of the idea of information, with its capacity to point to external objects and at the same time hang on to a capacity for the subjective component of meaning.

As a brief outline of the *tattva* system, the original Sāṃkhya system begins with the category of spirit, *puruṣa,* that we saw above, which unlike Abhinavagupta's model, is understood here to be completely divorced from all materiality.[86] Materiality, *prakṛti*, sometimes translated as Nature, on the other side of the divide is completely insentient, and it is this insentient principle that evolves into the intellect (*buddhi*)[87] and the ego (*ahaṃkāra*). At this point, having evolved into ego, the principle of *prakṛti* then takes two separate paths. One path of the evolving ego is influenced by the quality of purity (*sattva*). This evolves further into the mind and then into the five senses, such as hearing and sight, and the five organs of action.[88] The other path the evolving ego takes, influenced by a dull inertia (*tamas*) is to become materiality, first as the subtle elements (*tanmatra*), sound, touch, form, taste and smell. From this they then become the physical elements, ether or space (*akāśa*), air, fire, water, and earth. The additional eleven principles that Abhinavagupta's nondual Kashmiri Śaiva model adds all occur as the world unfolds prior to the stage of the person, *puruṣa*. It is this system, the *tattva* system, that Abhinavagupta uses to map the gradations from taking a stance of subjectivity to that of being object. And it is this shift between subject and object that invites the comparison to information with its bivalent ties to materiality and meaning. *Śiva* as the underlying cosmopsychism—consciousness—pervades throughout. Thus, as the world is created, unfolding out of *Śiva* as the basis, as the wall of the world, it unfolds from a pure subjectivity to progressively become more and more insentient object. At the end of the line, at the element of earth, the most physical of the thirty-seven *tattvas*, subjectivity is submerged and the thing made of earth appears insentient, completely object, devoid of subjectivity.[89] Complexity and gradations arise also because we humans and other beings (including rocks with their consciousness hidden in the core) partake also of different *tattvas* simultaneously: We have an ego *and* also a body made of water and air and so on. This, of course, suggests that there is no simple single cutoff point between being sentient and insentient, between humans and lima bean plants, but rather a gradual weighted shift and one that can potentially take either and both modes, subject and object. After all, we humans as well, along with caterpillars and lima beans (and viruses) seem to be at best only partly conscious, also products of our world's "biochemical-electronic machinery."[90]

In Abhinavagupta's nondual Kashmiri Śaiva model, which, again, adds eleven more categories prior to *puruṣa*, the Person, the first category of this cosmopsychism is *Śiva*, unfolding the world out of itself, the picture of wonderful variety on the canvas of the wall that is itself.[91] The process of unfolding is mapped out through distinct stages, with the *tattvas* charting the process.[92] The second category is *Śakti*, a feminine capacity, always figured inseparably with the first category, *Śiva*. Literally translated as "power" or "energy," it is this second principle that lines up with a capacity to do things in the world as well. The third category in this process, which we saw above, is an inward-directed energy, depicted mythologically as a transcendent form of deity, *Sadāśiva*. This is a level of transcendence where the awareness, as transcendent, is withdrawn inwardly. It is here on this third level, with awareness looking inward, that the object resides. The inward-directed impulse means that the awareness the object has from its own first-person perspective is not visible to those of us on the outside staring at the clay jar. Abhinavagupta tells us,

> Even these limited Subjects which are a reflection of consciousness[93] have a portion of consciousness which is *Śiva* alone. After showing this, [Utpaladeva] demonstrates with the words "also the limited subjects" that even the objects, which are inherently things to be known and [not knowers], and which partake of a lack of Consciousness, are also only *Śiva*'s Energy which is in the form of *Sadāśiva*.[94]

Even a clay jar, then, carries a latent, if hidden, inward consciousness, reflecting the *tattva* of both earth and *Sadāśiva*. The fourth category is the *Īśvara tattva*, which we saw earlier; it begins the outward extension of consciousness to make a distinct picture of an external world.[95] The fifth *tattva*, *sadvidyā*, works to generate the mix of both subject and object within an individual, whether a person or wasp.[96] Abhinavagupta describes it:

> [T]he "I" is an expanse of Light shining (*prakāśa*) and Active Awareness (*vimarśa*) and not intent upon looking towards something other external to itself. The "This" is gazing towards the other. . . . And within the limited knower, these two take form as the one who grasps—the subject—and that thing which is grasped—the object. And they have separate spheres of authority.[97]

So, within each of us is this dual apprehension of both subject and object. In this fifth stage, the subject and object are both correctly understood as two sides of a single, deeper, pervasive consciousness. This changes as the cosmos unfolds. This *tattva* sets the stage for its following counterpart, *Māyā*, which begins the process of duality, where we see the world as different from our selves, and then we consequently limit ourselves to something much smaller than our consciousness really is.

Thus, the "limited knower" comprises both a subjective orientation, the "I" and an objective orientation, the "This." This is how an individual located on the level of duality is a mix of both subject and object. The first five categories are called the "pure creation" because consciousness in these stages never quite loses sight of a self-aware subjectivity.[98] It is in this next *tattva*, the category of *Māyā* where consciousness begins to discern a distinction between objects and subjects and no longer remembers it is both. In classical Indian philosophy, *Māyā* is an indescribable force of illusion.[99] In contrast, for Abhinavagupta, *Māyā* is simply the energy of the highest cosmopsychism, *Śakti*, iterated on the level of limited knowers.[100] Most of us fall in this category of "limited knower," under the sway of *Māyā*, which causes us to think of others as separate, leaving us incapable of realizing the multiplicity of the world as our own self.[101] This is the heart of the dilemma, the cause of our suffering and what the soteriology of these Indian schools promise to help us rectify. How did we get here? Especially, if we are indeed the unfolding of an originary cosmopsychism, how did we wind up here, with our limited awareness and limited ability to do things? The shift happens with the onset of *Māyā*, and with the levels that follow, the sheaths (*kañcukas*) of time and a limited capacity to know and do that then determine the ways we are limited, becoming only partly conscious. For Abhinavagupta, not the algorithmic march of a biochemical machinery, but a dependence on karma, the bonds of previous actions, is what causes us to lose freedom and awareness, to be bound by the sheaths of time and desire and so on. Abhinavagupta explains it,

> You may ask, what is the purpose of this process of manifesting these [different levels of the *tattvas*] if consciousness is unobstructed and continuously uncovered? With regard to this question, it is true that manifestation is not necessary with respect to the highest level of consciousness, but in considering the lower consciousness associated with the realm of distinctions, this consciousness again still fluctuates [and so limitation of the capacities to do and know do occur]. "Here" means on the level of the person (*puruṣa*).[102]

Abhinavagupta links this to the level of the person, the *puruṣa* that we saw earlier. The *puruṣa*, the limited person, consists of consciousness, but in the grip of karma and the five sheaths of time and so on, it loses its freedom.[103] The *puruṣa*, he tells us elsewhere, "is essentially just only consciousness which is contracted, limited."[104] He continues here, noting how a limited sense of self gives rise to that which is other,

> That which is "consciousness" is separate from the limited perceiver because the very notion of this limited perceiver gives rise to some object which is to be perceived and is separate from it. To this extent that which is "conscious" contains both perceiver and object and doesn't have this distinction made between itself and the other; the object perceived. Yet that which is conscious gives rise to both of these, limited Subject and object. And even while consciousness exists in that way, as undifferentiated, it, at the same time, out of its own Self, that is, out of its own form, which shines as only pure consciousness alone—it gives birth to things that, like blue, etc., are said to be insentient, that lack consciousness.[105]

Consciousness at base is undifferentiated, the indeterminate origin, which then gives rise to what we see here, ourselves as limited conscious beings as well as things like a blue pot that we understand to be insentient. Between the *puruṣa* and *Māyā* are the five sheaths that complete the eleven *tattvas* that Abhinavagupta's model adds to Sāṃkhya's original twenty-five.[106] These include elements that our current cosmology construes as universals, quite separate from individual persons or wasps or pots.[107] They include time (*kāla*), a limited capacity to do (*kalā*), a limited capacity to know (*vidyā*), a deep, somewhat unconscious sense of desire and attachment (*rāga*), and a cosmic ordering principle leading to individualization (*niyati*) whereby a seed becomes a sprout, but the sprout does not revert back to seed form, and clay can be made into a pot, but clay does not make a sprout.[108] These five sheaths come into play before the stage of *puruṣa*, before we get a sense of ourselves as individuals, and they function precisely to set up the limits of the outside world. Thus, we come into the world as individuals feeling ourselves bound by time, by instinctive desires, and by brains and bodies that can only know so much and do only so much. These five sheaths and *Māyā* cloud our awareness. We no longer recognize that we are just this unified field of consciousness, a cosmopsychism unfolding into an interconnected field of differential nodes of subjectivity as wasps and lima beans and humans. Abhinavagupta describes this, quoting a poetic stanza:

> The Self is colored by the dye of attachment, driven forward by time, and destined by destiny, o, my dear, and again expanded and puffed up by the state of being *Puruṣa,* the Person. With the arising of consciousness accompanied by limitation, there also arises knowledge visible to the senses.[109]

He captures nicely the sense of our human condition, not masters of our fate, but driven by forces we cannot control, time, the limitations of our knowledge and so on, these five *tattvas* from *Māyā* to the *puruṣa.* These five operate differently, not as a progression from subjectivity toward becoming object as we see with the other *tattvas*, but in tandem with each other, like the mix of flavors in a milky dessert.[110] With these five *tattvas* we come to know the world as differentiated, acquiring knowledge through sensory experience. And while this is happening, we are blithely oblivious to our predicament, wrapped in this web of these five sheaths that we think are outside of ourselves. Abhinavagupta explains that

> [t]he categories of time etc., are utilized when one is in the condition of being a limited subject. Saying "now I am doing nothing whatsoever, with this thought, being attached to the 'I,'" still one is pierced through with time, individuation, limited knowledge and attachment. In this way, the individual limited self is enlivened by this particular destined limitation and is called a grasper, a limited subject.[111]

Even if we imagine a transcendent subjectivity, for instance, Descartes' *res cogitans* isolated from the body's limitations, still we are shot through, wrapped within time and limited capacities, which apply not just to our physical bodies, but also to the subtle body counterpart of the physical body.[112] We think of time particularly as a universal function outside the reach of our own subjectivity. Yet, Abhinavagupta takes pains to emphasize that time and the other four sheaths are intrinsically part of our subjectivity, not something universal existing outside of us.[113] Not, of course, to ourselves as the limited ego, but to that part of us as subject which partakes of the originary cosmopsychism, *Śiva*. Voicing the problem, he tells us, "if time [and the other four], look to the substratum of the subject as their cause, then how is it that when time appears, it exists, or seems to exist, outside the conceptualization of the Subject?"[114] He responds, "Even though time has this quality of being universal, commonly experienced by everyone, to a certain extent it also is particular to each individual,"[115] reaffirming that "therefore time is an attribute of the Subject."[116] This, of course, is in keeping with his argument on causality. Given that he locates cause and effect within conscious subjects, not within objects, he needs to offer a subjectivity that cannot be separated from time or the other sheaths, so that the conscious subject can still be engaged in a material world, operating through time. And, of course, this brings us back to the idea of meaning. It gives us, in effect, a bodily materiality inextricable from subjectivity, a first-person perspective with intentions, engaged in the world and wrapped through with meaning.

So our subjectivity is this mix of matter with meaning, enveloped in the five sheaths of time, instinctive desires, and our limited capacities, then cloaked in a materiality of the five elements. These are all written onto our sense of self. At base, consciousness is never really absent, but still, under the sway of *Māyā*, we misread the effects of the five elements themselves as consciousness, as the Self. This is how the rote effects of our material world, a seeming insentient relay of information, perceived as outside our selves maps out what we think and do. What we might read as the effects of a mechanical biochemistry, Abhinavagupta fashions as the materiality of the end of the line of *tattvas*, the five elements, earth, and the rest, driving, obscuring our sense of self, even as the subjectivity of consciousness is never quite erased. Thus, when in deep sleep or a deep state of meditation we take the Self to be the quality of space, a capacity to be empty, we cover over an ever-present consciousness; we wrap it within the materiality of space.[117] So also,

> Breathing in and breathing out—thus here vital air (*prāṇa*) [conceived as the Self] takes the form of the element Air. "I am hungry;" "I am thirsty"—this type of thought and also when one bursts into burning anger—these in fact indicate the increase of the element fire. When one says, "I know inwardly I am happy" or "I am sad," "I am a fool," and so on, then in these states it is the intellect, like clear water flowing. In statements like "I am lean" or "fat" or "fair" and so on, it is the body alone, which is predominantly earth.[118]

For our purposes here, what is striking is the seamless movement from an intentional subjectivity into materiality. We see writ in this the bivalency of both meaning from a subjective view and the third-person objectivity of matter, of earth and fire. Thus, "I am hungry" or angry is the first-person expression of fire. "I know I am happy" or "I am a fool" is the mind, specifically the intellect articulating subjective awareness through the element of water. Human, or even also nonhuman consciousness, more precisely, *meaning* as a first-person perspective, is written into the substance of matter.

Conclusion

Where does this leave us in terms of information? Does the smelly materiality of pheromones, measurable and quantifiable, point to nothing more than mindless information driving the lima bean and wasp? I have argued that information is presented as both material and non-material. As a material substance, bound to matter, it offers a way of objectifying our world, measuring it in bits, as manipulable, external. At the same time, information promises transcendence; it relies on the abstraction of numbers as beyond matter, offering a timelessness surviving black holes and allowing Ray Kurzweil's Google tech dream of immortal, uploaded consciousness. What makes information so useful as a concept is precisely its capacity to cross the bridge, flip bivalently from matter to immateriality. As Wheeler's "information-theoretic" from its "immaterial source" makes clear, information taps into both sides; it is matter that can be measured physically *and* its "immaterial source" carrying consciousness, that is, meaning. Thus, information is used as a way of sidestepping the issue of consciousness, while leaving room for a backdoor recovery for it: for meaning to emerge.

Max Tegmark capitalizes on information's bivalence with his "conscious" mathematical formulas. I suggested a comparison with Abhinavagupta's idea of the mantra, which also draws on a bivalency. Abhinavagupta's mantra carries at the same time both the materiality of sound *and* intention, consciousness that is the first-person perspective, which, again, gives rise to meaning.

Meaning. In Wheeler's participatory universe, meaning points to the "who" of materiality. Wheeler steers clear of the implications of his participatory universe. We can nevertheless read Abhinavagupta as spelling the implications out, namely, that it entails a first-person perspective. In tandem, he proposes the somewhat radical suggestion that cause and effect is not a property of matter, but instead ultimately relies on the "who" of meaning. That is, Abhinavagupta suggests that causality can only occur within a conscious subjectivity. His panentheism leads us to one other remarkable proposal, a corollary that reverses our current thinking: there is no such thing as mindless information. My play on words on Wheeler's "it from bit" to "it from *cit*" means that consciousness never quite abandons matter. Even for a clay jar, consciousness is simply covered over. Abhinavagupta's model suggests the fusion of subjectivity all through materiality. For us humans, and wasps and caterpillars, meaning, intentionality—in a word, a first-person perspective—persists ensconced in matter, yes, even so with the grip of *Māyā* modulating varying levels of freedom and awareness. Abhinavagupta's hermeneutic application of his inherited cosmology, the *tattva* system, spells out the stages and varying levels, charting the mix of subject and object. This mix of subjectivity simultaneously with being an object is what it means to be human, or wasp, or lima bean or clay jar.

What Abhinavagupta brings, then, is heightened attention to the crucial function that subjectivity plays, and must play, in any model of the world we conjure. That is, what Abhinavagupta can add to Wheeler's and other current formulations like that of Tegmark's is precisely to flesh out the implications this has for notions of subjectivity. The idea of meaning comes back into the picture. What brings this all together is his panentheism, the cosmopsychism that unfolds to make the world. So, rather than discrete entities made in the image of a creator, we are ourselves not separate from this creative force, but are evolving fluid expressions of this unfolding panentheism. Is this something like a field of energy, a universal field of consciousness? I find Berit Brogaard's notion of consciousness as a universal field as a way of thinking about Abhinavagupta's panentheism attractive because the metaphor of a universal field allows us to accommodate the holism that a cosmopsychism entails. In this sense, as Karen Barad points out with regard to quantum physics' radical refiguring of the nature of matter, the issue is about separability, *not* locality or nonlocality. If we think in terms of a field, there is *not* spooky action at a distance for either Bohr or Einstein, but rather what appears as spooky action at a distance is the nonseparability of two components of a holistic phenomenon. For Barad, its viable proof is not just subjective knowledge, but "objective" by virtue of the "reproducible and permanent marks left on bodies."[119]

Even if we eventually land on the side of a biological determination driving much of what we and insects choose, perhaps Abhinavagupta's panentheism can help a New Materialist perspective to pause just enough to complicate our assessment of ourselves and our planetary cohabitants, plants and insects. Not so long ago, Descartes could quite confidently declare with his famous analogy of the beast-machine that animals, even dogs and pigs and chimpanzees, were mere automata, not conscious and not capable of feeling pain.[120] The holism of Abhinavagupta's panentheism proposes rather our nonseparability from these others. Abhinavagupta describes genuine knowledge: "the person who is said to be liberated is someone who correctly understands other beings to be like one's own limbs."[121] It is only when we are under the sway of *Māyā* that we think of others as separate, leaving us incapable of realizing the multiplicity of the world as our own Self.

Perhaps psychologically, in order for our science to be true, it needs to claim a cool objectivity, to understand its objects of study precisely as objects. Perhaps to gain mastery we need to see these others as automata, the transfer of pheromone information as algorithmic mechanism. In contrast, the spotlight Abhinavagupta's cosmology shines on the function of subjectivity affords a way of making space for the multiplicity of others, jars and plants, for feeling the pain of dogs and pigs, and for recognizing the symbiosis of pheromone conversation, in this case happy for lima beans and deadly for caterpillars. This phenomenology of subjectivity is one that New Materialism might be able to use to philosophically underwrite the perspective of matter, its rights even, in the face of our current ecological maelstrom in which our survival may depend on shifting our attitude toward the matter of the earth.

Notes

Introduction

1. Abhinavagupta, *Īśvara Pratyabhijñā Vivṛti Vimarśinī*, ed. Paṇḍit Madhusudan Kaul Śāstrī, vol. 3 (Delhi: Akay Reprints, 1985), 255: otaprotam sakalam viddhvā svarasena śivamayīkurute |yo >nuttara dhāmnyudayan svayam amṛta niṣecanam tam asmi nataḥ. ||
2. Abhinavagupta, 3:260: "Māyīyānāṃ kīṭāntānāṃ svakāryakaraṇāvasare yat kāryaṃ purā hṛdaye sphurati."
3. Panentheism as a way of thinking about the relationship between the natural world and a transcendent divinity really begins to take off with Charles Hartshorne's influential anthology, Charles Hartshorne and William Reese, eds., *Philosophers Speak of God* (Chicago: University of Chicago Press, 1953). I suspect in large part that its appeal for the 20th century was precisely its promise to maintain a theism in the onslaught of a rapidly growing atheist science by facilitating a discourse that could retain a scientific naturalism and at the same time hang on to a theistic conception of god. See also David Ray Griffin, *Panentheism and Scientific Naturalism: Rethinking Evil, Morality, Religious Experience, Religious Pluralism, and the Academic Study of Religion* (Claremont, CA: Process Century Press, 2014). I might venture that Abhinavagupta in the 11th century uses it as well as a way to preserve a theism within a nondualism that maintains the reality of a natural world. For a sense of panentheism's historical appeal across cultures, including Asian religious traditions, see Loriliai Biernacki and Philip Clayton, eds., *Panentheism across the World's Traditions* (New York: Oxford University Press, 2014).
4. Abhinavagupta, *Ipvv*, 3:260: "Māyīyānāṃ kīṭāntānāṃ svakāryakaraṇāvasare yat kāryaṃ purā hṛdaye sphurati."
5. For an outline of Abhinavagupta's writings, see K. C. Pandey, *Abhinavagupta: An Historical and Philosophical Study*, 2nd Enlarged Edition (Varanasi: Chowkhamba Sanskrit Series, 1963), 27–29. See also Venkatarama Raghavan, *Abhinavagupta and His Works* (Varanasi: Chaukhamba Orientalia, 1981). Also, for a critical reassessment of some of these attributions, see Alexis Sanderson, "Śaiva Exegesis of Kashmir," in *Mélanges Tantriques a La Mémoire d'Helene Brunner/ Tantric Studies in Memory of Helene Brunner*, ed. Dominic Goodall and Andre Padoux, vol. 106, Collection Indologie (Pondicherry, India: Institut Francais d'Indologie /Ecole Francaise d'Extreme-Orient, 2007), 231–442 and 551–82.
6. Much has been written on Tantra—far too much to begin to address here. For readers interested in a general overview, Gavin Flood's work is a wonderful entry point: Gavin Flood, *Tantric Body: The Secret Tradition of HIndu Religion* (New York: I. B. Tauris, 2006). Also see Andre Padoux, *Vāc: The Concept of the Word in Selected Hindu Tantras* (Albany: State University of New York Press, 1990). In addition, Lilian Silburn, *Kuṇḍalinī: The Energy of the Depths: A Comprehensive Study Based on the Scriptures of Nondualistic Kasmir Saivism*, trans. Jacques Gontier, Suny Series in the Shaiva Traditions of Kashmir, 1988. For an overview of a variety of Tantric texts, see David White, *Tantra in Practice*, Princeton Readings in Religions (Princeton, NJ: Princeton University Press, 2000). In terms of Abhinavagupta,

see K. C. Pandey's pioneering monumental study in the 1960s, which brought the first Western attention to Abhinavagupta: Pandey, *Abhinavagupta: An Historical and Philosophical Study*. Following his work, the preeminent scholar for historical work on Tantra and Abhinavagupta has been Alexis Sanderson. Sanderson's work has been foundational, not just on Abhinavagupta, but in somewhat singlehandedly mapping out an early picture of the history of the Śaiva traditions for medieval India. His work is too voluminous to adequately cite here, including a forthcoming translation of Abhinavagupta's massive ritual text, the *Tantrāloka*. Mention must also be made of his important early article on Śaiva history in Alexis Sanderson, "Śaivism and the Tantric Traditions," in *Śaivism and the Tantric Traditions*, ed. Stewart Sutherland et al. (London: Routledge, 1988), 660–704. Also see Sanderson, "Śaiva Exegesis of Kashmir." I address important work on Abhinavagupta by other scholars in note 22 of this chapter.

7. This includes especially practices such as *nyāsa*, where the practitioner inserts *mantras* as deities onto the physical body, and *bhūta śuddhi*05/31/2021 2:18:00 pm, where the practitioner visualizes the elements of the body, earth, water, fire, and so on, each dissolving in sequence to psychically manufacture a transformed body. See Timalsina's deeply insightful work, particularly Sthaneshwar Timalsina, "Body, Self, and Healing in Tantric Ritual Paradigm," *Journal of Hindu Studies* 5 (2012): 30–52. See also Loriliai Biernacki, "Words and Word-Bodies: Writing the Religious Body," in *Words. Religious Language Matters*, ed. Ernst van den Hemel and Asja Szafraniec (New York: Fordham University Press, 2016).
8. Raffaele Torella opines that Abhinavagupta's aesthetic prehensions ground his philosophy, rather than that his philosophy undergirds his writing on aesthetics, in Raffaele Torella, "Abhinavagupta as an Aristocrat," in *Archaeologies of the Written: Indian, Tibetan, and Buddhist Studies in Honour of Cristina Scherrer-Schaub*, ed. Vincent Tournier, Vincent Eltschinger, and Marta Sernesi, Universitá Degli Studi Di Napoli "L'orientale" École Française D'extrême-Orient Université De Lausanne 89 (Napoli: Unior Press, 2020), 843. Jeffrey Lidke also emphasizes this aesthetic element in his portrait of Abhinavagupta in Jeffrey Lidke, "A Thousand Years of Abhinavagupta," *Sutra Journal*, January 2016, http://www.sutrajournal.com/a-thousand-years-of-abhinavagupta-by-jeffrey-lidke.
9. Abhinavagupta introduced an additional ninth category of aesthetic emotion, what is termed *rasa*, as *śānta rasa*, the mood of peace, to Bhārata's classical eight *rasas*. See particularly, Ānandavardhana and Abhinavagupta, *Dhvanyāloka of Ānandavardhana with the Locana of Abhinavagupta*, trans. Daniel Ingalls, Jeffrey Masson, and M. V. Patwardhan, Harvard Oriental Series (Cambridge, MA: Harvard University Press, 1990).
10. While Pandey suggests that Madhurāja Yogin was Abhinavagupta's direct student, which would place him in the 11th century (Pandey, 1963, 20–21), Alexis Sanderson points out that Madhurāja Yogin likely did not ever meet Abhinavagupta in Sanderson, "Śaiva Exegesis of Kashmir," 381 n. 486. Ben Williams, in a personal communication, suggested that these verses are based on a stylistic visualization (*dhyāna*) modeled on the guru figure of Dakṣiṇāmūrti. I thank him for pointing this out to me. In any case, we should keep in mind that the very evocative image of women at his side bearing aphrodisiacs is unique to Abhinavagupta and does not typically form part of Dakṣiṇāmūrti's visualization.
11. Pandey, *Abhinavagupta: An Historical and Philosophical Study*, 21–22.
12. Harvey Alper stresses this attention to the mundane in Harvey Alper, "Judgement as a Transcendental Category in Utpaladeva's Śaiva Theology, The Evidence of the Praty abhijñākārikāvṛtti," *Adyar Library Bulletin* 51 (1987): 176–241. Raffaele Torella points to Utpaladeva as the creative intelligence behind the philosophy of the Pratyabhijñā

in Raffaele Torella, "A Fragment of Utpaladeva's Isvarapratyabhijna-Vivrti," *East and West* 38 (1988): 140. Similarly in Raffaele Torella, *Philosophical Traditions of India: An Appraisal* (Varanasi: Indica Books, 2011), 118. Isabelle Ratie concurs; see Isabelle Ratie, "Utpaladeva and Abhinavagupta on the Freedom of Consciousness," in *Oxford Handbook of Indian Philosophy*, ed. Jonardon Ganeri (New York: Oxford University Press, 2016), 25 n. 3, DOI: 10.1093/oxfordhb/9780199314621.013.27. Whether or not Utpaladeva's originary insights eclipse Abhinavagupta's contribution, the clarity and elegance of Abhinavagupta's writing and the masterful articulation of this panentheist nondualism make his writing eminently worth engaging, as the tradition itself affirms in its preservation of Abhinavagupta's texts.

13. See Gretchen Vogel, "Where Have All the Insects Gone?," *Science* 356 (May 10, 2017): 576–79. https://doi.org/10.1126/science.aal1160.
14. Abhinavagupta, *Ipvv*, 3:257: śivatattvaṃ hi sarva padārthānām vapuḥ. Tad bhitta pṛṣṭhe ca sarva bhāva citra nirbhāsa iti tad abhidhānam eva teṣām upapādanopakramaḥ.
15. And, indeed, Abhinavagupta appears to tread a very fine line between an idealism and a realism; or we may say, he takes on both ascriptions. That is, the world is both real and arises out of a singular consciousness from which it is never entirely separate. In this case, when we recognize our identity as this singular consciousness, we attain enlightenment. We can see Abhinavagupta straddling categories in statements like, "The words, 'it spreads, it comes to light' points to the thing, the object (vastu) as something real, not to be denied." In Abhinavagupta, 3:288: "'Prathate' iti anapahnavanīyatayā vastu eva." Similarly, we see: "Now someone might say—what's the point of this discussion of the levels of the limited self? In reply he says, "Pure Lordship" [is in reality connected with them also]. But one may say—if these [the lordship belonging to limited souls and that of the Supreme Lord] are not different from each other in reality, then what's the use of discussing their distinctness? However, even a manifestation of distinctness is not extremely impossible." In Abhinavagupta, 3:260: Nanu paśupramātrupakrameṇa kim artho vicāraḥ? Atra āha "śuddhaiśvarya" iti. Nanu paramārthato yadi ete na atiricyete, tat kim atiriktatāyā vicāreṇa. Atiriktatā api avabhāsamānā na atyantamasaṃbhavinīti." And yet, as we see, he hedges, saying, "Even though in giving external reality [to something], that thing in fact exists only as appearance, a [conditional] manifestation—nevertheless what is intended here is the ordinary form of all knowing Subjects in the world, comprising the specific activity of the hands and feet, etc., of the agent, because this idea is generally accepted in the world." In Abhinavagupta, 3:258: "Bahiḥ sattā dānam yadyapi ābhāsanam eva, tathāpi laukika sarva pramātṛ sādhāraṇa rūpa saṃpādakakara caraṇādi vyāpāra viśeṣa paryantībhūtam eva abhipretaṃ tathā laukikānāṃ prasiddheḥ." We explore this issue in more detail in Chapter Four of this volume.
16. My own thinking on Abhinavagupta's use of a foundational subjectivity, coded linguistically and psychologically as a first-person perspective, has been influenced by Lynne Rudder Baker's work, especially Lynne Rudder Baker, *Naturalism and the First-Person Perspective* (New York: Oxford University Press, 2013).
17. My comparative focus is indebted to previous comparative work that looks at Abhinavagupta cross-culturally in relation to modern Western thought; of particular note is the insightful, pioneering comparative work on Abhinavagupta that David Lawrence first proposed. His view of Abhinavagupta's philosophy in relation to Berkeley's idealism has been especially helpful in addressing the wider comparative philosophical implications of Abhinavagupta's thought. See Lawrence, *Rediscovering God with Transcendental Argument: A Contemporary*

Interpretation of Monistic Kashmiri Śaiva Philosophy (Rochester: State University of New York Press, 1999). His comparative work has helped my own thinking on this score. More recent work by Sthaneshwar Timalsina, who also works in this comparative vein, has also been extremely helpful to my own thinking, particularly his insightful work addressing cognitive philosophy with Abhinavagupta and Indian models. See his Sthaneshwar Timalsina, *Tantric Visual Culture: A Cognitive Approach* (New York: Routledge, 2015). Also see Sthaneshwar Timalsina, "Theatrics of Emotion: Self-Deception and Self-Cultivation in Abhinavagupta's Aesthetics," *Philosophy East and West* 66, no. 1 (January 2016): 104–21. See as well Sthaneshwar Timalsina, "Reconstructing Abhinavagupta's Philosophy of Power," in *Navin Doshi Felicitation Volume* (South Asian Studies Association Volume, forthcoming). Trained as a traditional Indian paṇḍita, Timalsina also brings a breadth of understanding of Indian philosophy generally to his comparative analysis with Western philosophy; see, for instance, Sthaneshwar Timalsina, "Self, Causation, and Agency in the Advaita of Śaṅkara," in *Free Will, Agency, and Selfhood in Indian Philosophy*, ed. Matthew Dasti and Edwin Bryant (New York: Oxford University Press, 2013), 186–209. Likewise, Arindam Chakrabarti brings a deep cross-cultural philosophical engagement to understanding this school, for instance, in Arindam Chakrabarti, "Arguing from Synthesis to the Self: Utpaladeva and Abhinavagupta Respond to Buddhist No-Selfism," in *Hindu and Buddhist Ideas in Dialogue: Self and No-Self*, ed. Jonardon Ganeri, Irina Kuznetsova, and Chakravarthi Ram-Prasad (Burlington, VT: Ashgate, 2012), 199–216. Perhaps, though, the penchant for cross-cultural analysis came earlier for me with impetus from the work of my late advisor, Wilhelm Halbfass, particularly, for instance, Wilhelm Halbfass, *Tradition and Reflection: Explorations in Indian Thought* (New York: State University of New York Press, 1991). In this context, I might also mention Fred Smith's exemplary cross-disciplinary work, where he works effortlessly to link classical Sanskrit sources to contemporary anthropological theory and practice. In terms of influence on my own undertaking here, I have also greatly appreciated and avidly followed the brilliant comparative analyses from early Christianity to our contemporary world in Catherine Keller's work, including Catherine Keller, *Intercarnations: Exercises in Theological Possibility* (New York: Fordham University Press, 2017). See also Catherine Keller, *Cloud of the Impossible: Negative Theology and Planetary Entanglement* (New York: Columbia University Press, 2014). And similarly I have found Mary Jane Rubenstein's deeply insightful work helpful to my own, including Mary-Jane Rubenstein, *Strange Wonder: The Closure of Metaphysics and the Opening of Awe* (New York: Columbia University Press, 2008). See also Mary-Jane Rubenstein, *Pantheologies: Gods, Worlds, Monsters* (New York: Columbia University Press, 2018).

18. While Pandey's early work on Abhinavagupta emphasized Abhinavagupta's capacity to countenance a simultaneous realism *and* idealism, calling his Pratyabhijñā system a "Realist Idealism," I suspect the attraction of the idealist side of his thought has come to the fore in his depiction for a modern audience, perhaps steered by Jaidev Singh's early translations on the tradition of nondual Kashmiri Śaivism. See Pandey, *Abhinavagupta: An Historical and Philosophical Study*, 320. My own sense of Singh's translations are that perhaps he may have been unduly influenced by a modern embrace of Advaita Vedanta, which seeps in as an emphasis on the idealist threads of Abhinavagupta's thought. In this respect, my reading of Abhinavagupta pushes back against this interpretation. David Lawrence's insightful pioneering comparative work, noted earlier, has also been influential on this score. I have found Lawrence's work extremely helpful as I have formulated my understanding of Abhinavagupta, even as I emphasize this other, material side of Abhinavagupta's thought.

I think Abhinavagupta quite skillfully incorporates both elements, as Pandey noted. Also, Isabelle Ratie's work has expressly explored many of these issues of diversity and nondualism and been helpful in my own thinking about Abhinavagupta—for instance, Isabelle Ratie, "Otherness in the Pratyabhijñā Philosophy," *Journal of Indian Philosophy* 35 (2007): 313–70. We address this matter in more detail in Chapter Four.

19. Arthur Osborne, *Teachings of Bhagavan Sri Ramana Maharshi in His Own Words*, Eighth Edition (Tiruvannamalai: Sri Ramanasramam, 2002), 3.
20. Osborne, *Teachings of Bhagavan Sri Ramana Maharshi*, 112–13.
21. Abhinavagupta, *Ipvv*, 3:255: Na ca viśvaprameyatā pādanam na upayogi prakṛtāyām Īśvara pratyabhijñāpanāyām. Viśvaprameyīkaraṇe hi tāvat prameya padottīrṇā tāvad antaḥkaraṇa pratilabdha pūrṇa bhāvā satya pramātṛtā hṛdayaṅgamīkṛtā bhavet.
22. I have already mentioned Pandey's and Sanderson's work. In terms of other early translators of Abhinavagupta and the nondual Kashmiri Śaiva systems, and other related Tantric systems, apart from Silburn's work, Jaidev Singh's early work on this tradition contributed a great deal; see, for instance, Jaidev Singh, *Vijñāna Bhairava or Divine Consciousness*, reprint (Delhi: Motilal Banarsidass, 2003). Also see Jaidev Singh, *Pratyabhijñāhṛdayaṃ: The Secret of Self-Recognition* (Delhi: Motilal Banarsidass, 1977). In addition, see early work by Mark Dyczkowski, *The Doctrine of Vibration: An Analysis of the Doctrines and Practices of Kashmir Shaivism* (Albany: State University of New York Press, 1986). Isabelle Ratie's insightful work has done much to advance understanding of Abhinavagupta and his thinking; see, for instance, Isabelle Ratie, *Le Soi et l'Autre: Identité, Différence et Altérité Dans La Philosophie de La Pratyabhijñā* (Leiden: Brill, 2011). Also helpful has been her work situating Abhinavagupta in relation to Buddhist thought: for instance, Isabelle Ratie, "The Dreamer and the Yogin: On the Relationship between Buddhist and Śaiva Idealisms," *Bulletin of the School of Oriental and African Studies* 73, no. 3 (October 2010): 437–78. In particular, I have also benefited from her astute work on the nondualism of Abhinavagupta's thought, for instance, Isabelle Ratie, "Pāramārthika or Apāramārthika? On the Ontological Status of Separation According to Abhinavagupta," in *Puṣpikā: Tracing Ancient India through Texts and Traditions*, ed. P. Mirning, P.-D. Szanto, and M. Williams (Havertown, PA: Oxbow Books, 2014), 381–405. Raffaele Torella has contributed monumentally to understanding Utpaladeva and Abhinavagupta's philosophy, especially with his translation of Utpaladeva's autocommentary in Raffaele Torella, *Īśvarapratyabhijñ ākārikā of Utpaladeva with the Author's Vṛtti: Critical Edition and Annotated Translation* (Delhi: Motilal Banarsidass, 2002). David Lawrence's comparative work has been especially helpful, as I note above, particularly David Lawrence, *Rediscovering God with Transcendental Argument: A Contemporary Interpretation of Monistic Kashmiri Śaiva Philosophy* (Rochester: State University of New York Press, 1999). As also has been David Lawrence, "Proof of a Sentient Knower: Utpaladeva's Ajaḍapramātṛsiddhi with the Vṛtti of Harabhatta Shastri," *Journal of Indian Philosophy* 37 (2009): 627–53, https://doi.org/10.1007/s10781-009-9074-z. Similarly insightful for my comparative analysis, as I note again above, is Sthaneshwar Timalsina's work; see, for example, Sthaneshwar Timalsina, *Language of Images: Visualization and Meaning in Tantras*, Asian Thought and Culture 71 (New York: Peter Lang, 2015). John Nemec's work on Somānanda has also added much insight to our understanding of Abhinavagupta and especially his predecessor Somānanda. Apart from his translation of Somānanda, see also John Nemec, "Influences on and Legacies of Somānanda's Conception of Materiality," in *Around Abhinavagupta: Aspects of the Intellectual History of Kashmir from the Ninth to the Eleventh Century*, ed. Eli

Franco and Isabelle Ratie (Berlin: Lit Verlag, 2016), 341–74. See also John Nemec, "The Two Pratyabhijñā Theories of Error," *Journal of Indian Philosophy* 40, no. 2 (2012): 225–57. Navjivan Rastogi has also contributed much to the understanding of Abhinavagupta; see in particular Navjivan Rastogi, *Introduction to the Tantrāloka* (New Delhi: Motilal Banarsidass, 1987). Also see Navjivan Rastogi, "Rasānubhūti Pratibhāna ke Rūpa Meṃ," in *The Concept of Rasa with Special Reference to Abhinavagupta*, ed. S.C. Pande (New Delhi: Aryan Books International, 2009), 185–205. Likewise, I had the honor of studying Abhinavagupta in India with the esteemed H. N. Chakravarty; see H. N. Chakravarty, *Tantrasāra of Abhinavagupta*, ed. Boris Marjanovic (New Delhi: Rudra Press, 2012). I also had the privilege of studying with Suryaprakash Vyas, whose fine work is not as well known by Western scholars because he wrote only in Hindi (as indeed was my study with him); see Suryaprakaś Vyas, *Siddhitrayi* (Varanasi: Chowkhamba Sanskrit Series, 1989). See also Kerry Skora's thoughtful work, in Kerry Skora, "The Pulsating Heart and Its Divine Sense Energies: Body and Touch in Abhinavagupta's Trika Śaivism," *Numen* 54, no. 4 (2007): 420–58. Much excellent work has been done on this thinker, including studies by younger scholars such as Catherine Prueitt's philosophical work bridging Abhinavagupta and Buddhism, in Catherine Prueitt, "Shifting Concepts: The Realignment of Dharmakīrti on Concepts and the Error of Subject/Object Duality in Pratyabhijñā Śaiva Thought," *Journal of Indian Philosophy* 45 (2017): 21–47, https://doi.org/10.1007/s10781-016-9297-8. Also of particularl note are Ben Williams's work on Abhinavagupta as a guru in his Harvard dissertation, Alberta Ferrario's dissertation on Abhinavagupta and grace, and Chris Wallis's accessible, popularly oriented explication of Abhinavagupta's philosophy in Christopher Wallis, *Tantra Illuminated: The Philosophy, History and Practice of a Timeless Tradition* (San Rafael, CA: Mattamayura Press, 2013).

23. Sanderson, "Śaiva Exegesis of Kashmir," 360, 411. This text is also known as the *Bṛhatīvimarśinī*, "The Long Commentary."
24. The first publication of the *Īśvarapratyabhijñāvivṛtivimarśinī* was in the Kashmir Series of Texts and Studies (KSTS), published under the auspices of the government of Jammu and Kashmir. Volume 1 was number 60 in the KSTS series published in 1938; volume 2 was published in 1941 as number 62 in the series; and volume 3 was published in 1943 as number 65 in the series. I have relied on a photocopy reprint, picked up in India published by Akay Reprints in 1985 and the Internet Archive images of the KSTS versions. The entirety of the three volumes comes to 1,146 pages of Sanskrit in the KSTS publication. As I note, a translation of the text has not yet been published, so my notes include all the Sanskrit along with my translations. In numerous cases I also offer in the notes supporting material in my English translation followed by the Sanskrit. My hope is that including these notes at the end and not on individual pages will make it easier for readers not conversant in Sanskrit to follow the argument, and also that those interested in the Sanskrit text can see the Sanskrit sections. The full Sanskrit text is readily available in book form as the 1985 reprint, which I rely on, and as well as a digital file located in the Muktabodha collection at: https://etexts.muktabodha.org/DL_CATALOG_USER_INTERFACE/dl_user_interface_create_utf8_text.php?hk_file_url=..%2FTEXTS%2FETEXTS%2FIPVV_3_hk.txt&miri_catalog_number=M00022.
25. These are the *Īśvarapratyabhijñāvimarśinī* (Ipv)and the *Īśvarapratyabhijñākārikāvṛtti* (*Ipkv*). The *Ipv* was translated and published by K. C. Pandey in three volumes, the first two being with the Sanskrit and the third containing a translation with historical, critical material in English in Abhinavagupta, *Īśvara-Pratyabhijñā-Vimarśinī of Abhinavagupta: Doctrine of*

Divine Recognition: Sanskrit Text with the Commentary Bhāskarī, ed. K. A. Subramania Iyer and K.C. Pandey, 3 vols. (Delhi: Motilal Banarsidass, 1986). For the third volume, see K. C. Pandey, *Īśvarapratyabhijñāvimarśinī in the Light of the Bhāskarī with an Outline of History of Saiva Philosophy*, vol. 84, Sarastībhavana-Granthamālā (Varanasi: Sampurnand Sanskrit University, 1996). The *Ipkv* was translated and published by Raffaele Torella as Torella, *Īśva rapratyabhijñākārikā of Utpaladeva with the Author's Vṛtti: Critical Edition and Annotated Translation.*

26. Based on nomenclature, Ratie points to the *Āgamādhikāra* section as being about scripture, and hence it is less philosophical than the earlier two sections. However, this text is very much about explicating the received tradition of cosmology, the *tattva* system, and the seven levels/modes of subjectivity within an overarching dual-aspect nondualism. See Ratie, "Utpaladeva and Abhinavagupta on the Freedom of Consciousness," 27 n. 15.
27. Abhinavagupta, *Ipvv*, 3:305: Evaṃ prameyatayā tattvarāśau nirṇīte tad anantaraṃ pramātṛtattvaṃ nirṇītam api iha svātmani Īśvaratāpratyabhijñāpanaprakṛtaprameyasāre śāstre prādhānyena vitatya nirṇayārham.
28. This is, no doubt, in part, because Utpaladeva's lost text has not been found. Torella has discovered and published fragments from Utpaladeva's lost commentary, coming from a different section, the voluminous first section, the *Jñānādhikāra* section of the *Ipvv*. These include: Raffaele Torella, "Studies on Utpaladeva's Īśvarapratyabhijñā-Vivṛti. Part I: Anupalabdhi and Apoha in a Śaiva Garb," in *Expanding and Merging Horizons. Contributions to South Asian and Cross-Cultural Studies in Commemoration of Wilhelm Halbfass*, ed. Karin Preisendanz (Vienna: Verlag der Österreichischen Akademie der Wissenschaften, 2007), 473–90. Raffaele Torella, "Studies on Utpaladeva's Īśvarapratyabhijñā-Vivṛti. Part III. Can a Cognition Become the Object of Another Cognition?," in *Mélanges Tantriques à La Mémoire d'Hélène Brunner*, ed. Dominic Goodall and Andre Padoux (Pondicherry, India: Institut Français de Pondichéry/École Française d'Extrême-Orient, 2007), 475–84. Raffaele Torella, "Studies on Utpaladeva's Īśvarapratyabhijñā-Vivṛti. Part II: What Is Memory?," in *Indica et Tibetica. Festschrift für Michael Hahn Zum 65. Geburtstag von Freunden Und Schülern Überreicht*, ed. K. Klaus and J. U. Hartmann (Vienna: Arbeitskreis für tibetische und buddhistische Studien Universität Wien, 2007), 539–63. Torella, "A Fragment of Utpaladeva's Isvarapratyabhijna-Vivrti." Raffaele Torella, "Studies on Utpaladeva's Īśvarapratyabhijñā-Vivṛti. Part IV. Light of the Subject, Light of the Object," in *Pramāṇakīrtiḥ. Papers Dedicated to Ernst Steinkellner on the Occasion of His 70th Birthday*, ed. Birgit Kellner et al. (Vienna: Arbeitskreis für tibetische und buddhistische Studien Universität Wien, 2007), 925–40. Raffaele Torella, "Studies in Utpaladeva's Īśvarapratyabhijñā-Vivṛti. Part V: Selfawareness and Yogic Perception," in *Devadattīyam. Johannes Bronkhorst Felicitation Volume*, ed. Francois Voegli et al. (Bern: Peter Lang, 2012), 275–300. Ratie has also published on these discovered texts in Isabelle Ratie, "Some Hitherto Unknown Fragments of Utpaladeva's Vivṛti (II): Against the Existence of External Objects," in *Śaivism and Tantric Traditions: Essays in Honour of Alexis G.J.S. Sanderson*, ed. Dominic Goodall, Shaman Hatley, Harunaga Isaacson, and Srilata Raman (Leiden: Brill, 2020), 106–43.
29. Lynn White, "The Historical Roots of Our Ecological Crisis," *Science* 155 (1967): 1203–7.
30. *Oxford English Dictionary*, Third Edition (New York: Oxford University Press, 2018), Entry 239421, https://www-oed-com.colorado.idm.oclc.org/view. The quote that the OED gives is: "*Resurgence* Jan. 24/3 The environmental era challenges our theology to be more and more panentheistic." The OED gives the following definition for panentheism: "The theory

or belief that God encompasses and interpenetrates the universe but at the same time is greater than and independent of it. Frequently contrasted with *pantheism*."

31. I think we can profitably compare the panentheist impetus to contain both the world and the divine in Tantric terms with the pervasive Tantric dictum of "*bhukti-mukti*," that Tantra promises both enjoyment of the world *and* the transcendence of the world that comes with enlightenment.
32. We can keep in mind that he and his predecessor, Utpaladeva, modify the initial pantheism presented at the start of this philosophical lineage by Somānanda, as John Nemec points out, in John Nemec, "Evidence for Somānanda's Pantheism," *Journal of Indian Philosophy* 42 (2014): 99–114.
33. The concept of comparative studies of religion, particularly in terms of the idea of comparison and not simply between two different religious traditions, but comparing across secular disciplines and nonreligious categories, has been recently vitalized by Jeffrey Kripal's groundbreaking work in the last two decades. This project has been deeply influenced by this innovative and trailblazing scholarship, including, for instance: Jeffrey Kripal, *Authors of the Impossible: The Paranormal and the Sacred* (Chicago: University of Chicago Press, 2011). See also: Jeffrey Kripal, *Flip: Epiphanies of Mind and the Future of Knowledge* (New York: Bellevue Literary Press, 2019) and Jeffrey Kripal, *Mutants and Mystics: Science Fiction, Superhero Comics, and the Paranormal* (Chicago: University of Chicago Press, 2015).
34. A shorter version of this chapter has already been published in Loriliai Biernacki, "Subtle Body: Rethinking the Body's Subjectivity through Abhinavagupta," in *Transformational Embodiment in Asian Religions: Subtle Bodies, Spatial Bodies*, ed. George Pati and Katherine Zubko (London: Routledge, 2019), 108–27.
35. Loriliai Biernacki, "Connecting Consciousness to Physical Causality: Abhinavagupta's Phenomenology of Subjectivity and Tononi's Integrated Information Theory," *Religions* 7 (2016): 87 https://doi.org/10.3390/rel7070087.

Chapter 1

1. Leviathan, p. 678, in Stephen Shapin and Simon Schaffer, *Leviathan and the Air-Pump: Hobbes, Boyle, and the Experimental Life* (Princeton, NJ: Princeton University Press, 2011), 94.
2. Crush empires, but also give rise to new ones, as we see in the vast amount of wealth gained by certain sectors, IT, and pharma, in the wake of the pandemic. Here we might also consider human action as well as playing into the power of the virus as Latour's conception of collective; virus agency is impacted as well by human agency, wearing masks, and so on.
3. Stephen Buhner, *Herbal Antivirals: Natural Remedies for Emerging Resistant and Epidemic Viral Infections* (North Adams, MA: Storey Publishing, 2013), 12.
4. Abhinavagupta, *Īśvara Pratyabhijñā Vivṛti Vimarśinī*, ed. Paṇḍit Madhusudan Kaul Śāstrī, vol. 3 (Delhi: Akay Reprints, 1985), 260.: "Māyīyānāṃ kīṭāntānāṃ svakāryakaraṇāvasare yat kāryaṃ purā hṛdaye sphurati." See also footnote 67 below, which discusses the distinction Nemec sees between Somānanda and Utpaladeva.
5. Rene Descartes, *Discourse on the Method of Rightly Conducting the Reason, and Seeking Truth in the Sciences*, ed. Ilana Newby, Greg Newby, and Al Haines, trans. John Veitch,

EBook 59 (Project Gutenberg, 1637), Section V, https://www.gutenberg.org/files/59/59-h/59-h.htm.

6. I think it is fair to understand Abhinavagupta's use of the wall here as being quite comparable to Jeffrey Kripal's astute analysis of the image of the movie screen as a contemporary metaphor for nondualism. Kripal not only offers a fascinating analysis of popular culture's use of the movie screen for demonstrating a nondualist transcendence, but also traces it to Plato's use of the wall in the cave as a way of playing with the ideas of truth and illusion, for our purposes Māyā. See Elizabeth Krohn and Jeffrey Kripal, *Changed in a Flash: One Woman's Near-Death Experience and Why a Scholar Thinks It Empowers Us All* (Berkeley, CA: North Atlantic Books, 2018), 148–51. For our use here, we will visit the image of the wall below; we also saw this in the Introduction. Here is the quote from Abhinavagupta: "The category called *Śiva* is itself the body of all things. 'On the wall [of the world which is itself *Śiva*] the picture of all beings appears, shining forth—This statement indicates the way that all these appear." In Abhinavagupta, *Ipvv*, 1985, 3:257: śivatattvaṃ hi sarva padārthānām vapuḥ. Tad bhitta pṛṣṭhe ca sarva bhāva citra nirbhāsa.
7. Abhinavagupta and Utpaladeva, *Isvarapratyabhijnavimarsini, Adhikaras 1-4. Based on the following edition: Īśvara-pratyabhijñā-Vimarśinī of Abhinavagupta: Doctrine of Divine Recognition, Sanskrit Text with the Commentary Bhāskarī.*, ed. K. C. Pandey and K. A. Subramania-Iyer (Delhi: Motilal Banarsidass, digital on Goettingen Register of Electronic Texts in Indian Languages, 1986), ad 1.6.3, line 1237, http://gretil.sub.uni-goettingen.de/gretil/1_sanskr/6_sastra/3_phil/saiva/abhiprvu.htm. "citsvabhāvo 'sau ghaṭaḥ." See footnote 101 below for the context and complete quote.
8. Certainly, Jane Bennett offers this perspective; see Jane Bennett, *Vibrant Matter: A Political Ecology of Things* (Durham, NC: Duke University Press, 2010). But also Karen Barad, even as she veers more toward what might be construed as a Buddhist-oriented interdependency with her intra-action, nevertheless also presents a perspective from the view of quantum particle agency, in Karen Barad, *Meeting the Universe Halfway: Quantum Physics and the Entanglement of Matter and Meaning* (Durham, NC: Duke University Press, 2007). I discuss Barad's work in greater detail in Loriliai Biernacki, "Material Subjects, Immaterial Bodies: Abhinavagupta's Panentheist Matter," in *Entangled Worlds: Religion, Science and the New Materialisms*, ed. Catherine Keller and Mary-Jane Rubenstein (New York: Fordham University Press, 2017), 182–202.
9. Jeffrey Kripal argues a similar point in relation to his work on the paranormal. See, for instance, Krohn and Kripal, *Changed in a Flash*, 136.
10. Loriliai Biernacki, "Connecting Consciousness to Physical Causality: Abhinavagupta's Phenomenology of Subjectivity and Tononi's Integrated Information Theory," *Religions* 7 (2016), 6–7. nos. https://doi.org/10.3390/rel7070087.
11. In Abhinavagupta, *Parātrīśikavivaraṇa*, downloaded from GRETIL: Gottingen Register of Electronic Texts in Indian Languages: http://gretil.sub.uni-goettingen.de/gretil/1_sanskr/6_sastra/3_phil/saiva/partrvpu.htm, p. 212: "sarvaṃ hi sarvātmakam iti. narātmāno jaḍā api tyaktatatpūrvarūpāḥ śāktaśaivarūpabhājo bhavanti, śṛṇuta grāvāṇaḥ [\cf Mahābhāṣya 3.1.1; \cf Vākyapadīya 3 Puruṣasamuddeśa 2], meruḥ śikhariṇām ahaṃ bhavāmi" [Bhagavadgītā 10.23].
12. Rodney Dietart, *Human Superorganism: How the Microbiome Is Revolutionizing the Pursuit of a Healthy Life* (New York: Dutton, Penguin Books, 2016), 9.
13. Julie Livingston and Jasbir Puar, "Interspecies," *Social Text* 29, no. 1 (2011): 10. This is also reflected in political rhetoric, with Trump labeling himself a wartime president.

14. Perhaps we see this in another way as well; the Defund the Police movement also shares with a New Materialism the insight that terrain is key. Support for a diversely dispersed economic model, with funds going not just to policing but also to an infrastructure of habitat, food, and medical support, is akin to the notion that support for a diverse biome makes for health. Every element of a system is interdependent and agential in the outcome of its various components.
15. Lynn Margulis, *Symbiotic Planet* (New York: Basic Books, 1998), 75.
16. Buhner, *Herbal Antivirals*, 11.
17. Dietart, *Human Superorganism*, 13. Dietart points out that the ratio of microbial cells to our human mammalian cells is ten to one. However, in terms of genetic material, human mammalian genes number about 22,000, whereas our microbiome genetic material entails about 10 million microbial genes (in Dietart, 44).
18. Trevor Marshall, *Microbiome and Disease: St. Petersburg State University Address* (St. Petersburg, Russia: St. Petersburg State University, 2013), 18:36, https://www.youtube.com/watch?v=e7PfrkhsKEc.
19. Stephen Buhner, *Healing Lyme: Natural Healing of Lyme Borreliosis and the Coinfections Chlamydia and Spotted Fever Rickettsioses* (Boulder, CO: Raven Press, 2015), 438–39.
20. Jessica Riskin, *Restless Clock: A History of the Centuries-Long Argument over What Makes Things Tick* (Chicago: University of Chicago Press, 2016), 338.
21. Riskin, *Restless Clock*, 358.
22. This, too, is precisely the point that Latour makes in his third lecture of the Gifford series, where he invokes Lovelock's controversial Gaia Thesis, in Bruno Latour, *Facing Gaia: A New Enquiry into Natural Religion*, Gifford Lectures, 2013, https://www.giffordlectures.org/lecturers/bruno-latour. Earlier, Latour traced the roots of our current ecological crisis to the early transitions into a scientific worldview, with its displacement of religious sentiment by a mechanistic science that views matter as lifeless, inert, mere environment, in Bruno Latour, *We Have Never Been Modern* (Cambridge, MA: Harvard University Press, 1993), 50–51. Raymond Martin and John Barresi also skillfully track the origins of this 17th-century transformation into an idea of nature mechanized, in Raymond Martin and John Barresi, *Rise and Fall of Soul and Self: An Intellectual History of Personal Identity* (New York: Columbia University Press, 2008), especially 123–25. As Latour points out, this logically extends to the notion that we humans also are simply objects, subject to the impersonal forces all around us; nothing, not even humans, truly possesses agency or subjectivity. This notion, of course, plays out in the progress of 20th-century science, in the ascendancy of Skinner's Behaviorism in the mid-20th century, and today as well in a thinker like Daniel Dennett, who argues that consciousness is a mere epiphenomenon. Latour instead turns this idea on its head, proposing in his recent Gifford Lectures that there is no such thing as the agent within an inert environment, but rather that the environment itself is agential, rife with myriad agents, each not only adapting to their environment, but all also shaping what they find around them. in Latour, *Facing Gaia*.
23. Stuart Kauffman, *Investigations* (New York: Oxford University Press, 2000), x, 8.
24. Riskin, *Restless Clock*, 347.
25. Rick Nevin, "How Lead Exposure Relates to Temporal Changes in IQ, Violent Crime, and Unwed Pregnancy," *Environmental Research* 83 (n.d.): 1–22.
26. One would hope that recognition of the debilitating agency of lead might prompt the use of another seemingly inert agent, the chelating agent dimercaptosuccinic acid, FDA-approved, to shift the chemistry of bodies and hence the emotions and minds of those poisoned in

Flint, Michigan, in recent years. Given that this agent is FDA-approved for the removal of lead, I find it puzzling that in all the literature discussing the event, there appears to be no suggestion that the situation can be repaired through this fairly well-known procedure for reducing body lead load. See S.J.S. Flora and Shruti Agrawal, "Arsenic, Cadmium, and Lead," in *Reproductive and Developmental Toxicology*, ed. Ramesh Gupta. Second Edition. (North Andover, MA: Elsevier Academic Press, 2017), 537–66, https://www.sciencedirect.com/book/9780128042397/reproductive-and-developmental-toxicology.

27. Bennett, *Vibrant Matter*, 24–25.
28. Likewise, Mel Chen's thoughtful autobiographical description of her altered subjectivity under the effects of another bit of dead matter, the chemical element mercury, Hg, comes to mind. She weaves together both the social psychological and the biological effects of this seemingly inert agent on her altered biological functioning. This prompts us to see how deeply entangled our mental selves are with a wider social narrative and for our purposes here, how a simple metal element, mercury, atomic weight 200.59, can so consistently shape human thought and emotion in Mel Chen, *Animacies: Biopolitics, Racial Mattering and Queer Affect* (Durham, NC: Duke University Press, 2012), 197–200.
29. "Marie Kondo," in *Wikipedia*, accessed May 17, 2020, https://en.wikipedia.org/wiki/Marie_Kondo#cite_note-oz-11.
30. Diana Coole and Samantha Frost, eds., *New Materialisms: Ontology, Agency, and Politics* (Durham, NC: Duke University Press, 2010), 7.
31. Bennett, *Vibrant Matter*, 91.
32. Latour, *We Have Never Been Modern*, 50–53.
33. Coole and Frost, *New Materialisms*.
34. Steven Shapin and Simon Schaffer, *Leviathan and the Air-Pump: Hobbes, Boyle, and the Experimental Life* (Princeton, NJ: Princeton University Press, 2011).
35. See Bennett, *Vibrant Matter*. Also, Barad, *Meeting the Universe Halfway* and William Connolly, *World of Becoming* (Durham, NC: Duke University Press, 2011).
36. See for instance, David Chalmers, *The Conscious Mind: In Search of a Fundamental Theory. New York: Oxford University Press, 1996* (New York: Oxford University Press, 1996). Also: Thomas Nagel, *Mind and Cosmos: Why the Materialist Neo-Darwinian Conception of Nature Is Almost Certainly False* (New York: Oxford University Press, 2012). Also, among much else, see: Philip Goff, *Consciousness and Fundamental Reality* (New York: Oxford University Press, 2017). Galen Strawson, "Physicalist Panpsychism," in *Blackwell Companion to Consciousness*. Second Edition (Oxford: John Wiley, 2017), 374–90. A recent anthology also attests to the growing importance of panpsychism: Godehard Bruntrup, Ludwig Jaskolla, and Benedikt Paul Göcke, eds., *Panentheism and Panpsychism: Philosophy of Religion Meets Philosophy of Mind* (Leiden: Brill Mentis, 2020). For a counterargument, also see Philip Goff, "Why Panpsychism Doesn't Help Us Explain Consciousness," *Dialectica* 63, no. 3 (2009): 289–311, https://doi.org/10.1111/j.1746-8361.2009.01196x.
37. Similarly, Karen Barad's use of Niels Bohr also matches rather neatly when compared to Buddhist conceptions of interdependence (*pratītyasamutpāda*). See Barad, *Meeting the Universe Halfway*. In any case, it is important to keep in mind that New Materialist thought in any case represents varied formulations across the spectrum of what we might loosely understand as conceptions of religiosity or spirituality.
38. Bennett, *Vibrant Matter*, 4–5.
39. Diana Eck, *Darshan: Seeing the Divine Image in India*, Third Edition (New York: Columbia University Press, 1998).

40. We should not forget that temple icons, mūrtis, have the legal juristic status of persons in India, as the recent Ayodhya case demonstrates.
41. Jeffrey Long nicely tracks this influence from India in Jeffrey Long, *Hinduism in America* (London: Bloomsbury Academic, 2020).
42. Walt Whitman, "Song of Myself" (Poetry Foundation), 5.16–17, accessed May 24, 2020, https://www.poetryfoundation.org/poems/45477/song-of-myself-1892-version.
43. Taittirīya, *Taittirīya Mantrakośaḥ: Prathamo Bhagaḥ*, ed. Ramakrishna Maṭh (Mylapore, Madras: Ramakrishna Math Printing Press, n.d.), 73.
44. Taittirīya, *Taittirīya Mantrakośaḥ*, 73.
45. Taittirīya, 73.
46. Taittirīya, 67.
47. Taittirīya, 69: "kapardine ca vyuptakeśāya ca."
48. Taittirīya, 71: "namaḥ śuṣkyāya ca harityāya ca."
49. Taittirīya, 70: "namaḥ kūpyāya cāvaṭyāya ca namo varṣyāya cāvarṣyāya ca."
50. I place Whitman here as panpsychist; however, I think it is fair to argue, as Catherine Keller does, that Whitman might be classed as an apophatic panentheist whose apophatic orientation invokes a sense of wonder, in Catherine Keller, *Cloud of the Impossible: Negative Theology and Planetary Entanglement* (New York: Columbia University Press, 2014), 213.
51. I am thinking especially of Kripal's astute analysis in Jeffrey Kripal, *Flip: Epiphanies of Mind and the Future of Knowledge* (New York: Bellevue Literary Press, 2019). In a similar vein, Kripal points out as well the deep influence of Indian religious traditions, and especially Tantra on the New Age religions in the United States. These, I suggest, really mark the same phenomenon, with American Transcendentalism feeding into what later became the New Age movement. See Kripal's brilliant work on Esalen, in Jeffrey Kripal, *Esalen: The Religion of No Religion* (Chicago: University of Chicago Press, 2008). See also the links these offer with the sciences in David Kaiser, *How the Hippies Saved Physics: Science, Counterculture and the Quantum Revival* (New York: W. W. Norton, 2012).
52. Indeed, the idea of mind itself for much of the Indian tradition, relying on the early and foundational Sāṃkhya template, equates mentality, including the idea of mind (*manas*) with the material realm.
53. Daya Krishna, *Indian Philosophy: A Counter Perspective* (New Delhi: Satguru Publications, 2006), 436–37.
54. See, for instance, Karen Barad's posthumanist articulation via her work on quantum physics in Barad, *Meeting the Universe Halfway*, 136. Also, to get a sense of this issue framed in the context of New Materialisms, see Coole and Frost, *New Materialisms*, 20.
55. Coole and Frost, *New Materialisms*, 8.
56. Viveiros de Castro nicely articulates the philosophical groundwork in this linkage, in Eduardo Viveiros de Castro, *Cannibal Metaphysics*, trans. Peter Skafish (Minneapolis: Univocal, 2014).
57. See Sthaneshwar Timalsina's wonderfully rich description of different species of subtle beings in relation to paradigms of healing within Tantric medieval textual sources in Sthaneshwar Timalsina, "Body, Self, and Healing in Tantric Ritual Paradigm," *Journal of Hindu Studies* 5 (2012): 30–52.
58. Loriliai Biernacki, "Body and Mind in Medieval Hinduism," in *A Cultural History of Hinduism in the Post-Classical Age, 800–1500 CE* (Routledge, 2023).
59. For instance, in the Kashmiri Somadeva's Kathāsaritsāgara, the tree spirit (yakṣa) takes on a lion's body due to his bad karma and laments the change of body as a downgrade,

indicating a hierarchy of species, in Somadeva, *Kathāsaritsāgara* (Nirnaya-Sagar Press in GRETIL, 1915), 1.6.99, http://gretil.sub.uni-goettingen.de/gretil/1_sanskr/5_poetry/4_narr/sokss_pu.htm.

60. For instance, see Jane Bennett's discussion of leveling the playing field as a corrective to an entrenched human hubris in Bennett, *Vibrant Matter*, ix.
61. William Harman makes a similar point in his discussion of object-oriented philosophy in William Harman, "Critical Animal with a Fun Little Post," *Object-Oriented Philosophy* (blog), October 17, 2011, https://doctorzamalek2.wordpress.com/2011/10/17/critical-animal-with-a-fun-little-post/.
62. Viveiros de Castro, *Cannibal Metaphysics*, 57.
63. David Lawrence, "Remarks on Abhinavagupta's Use of the Analogy of Reflection," *Journal of Indian Philosophy* 33 (2005): 592.
64. "Madātmanā ghaṭo vetti vedmyahaṃ vā ghaṭātmanā" in Somānanda, *Śivadṛṣṭi with the Vṛtti of Utpaladeva*, ed. Madhusūdana Kaula Śāstrī, Muktabodha Indological Research, vol. 54 (Srinagar, Kashmir: Kashmir Series of Texts and Studies, 1934), 5.105, https://etexts.muktabodha.org/DL_CATALOG_USER_INTERFACE/dl_user_interface_create_utf8_text.php?hk_file_url=..%2FTEXTS%2FETEXTS%2FsivadrstiHK.txt&miri_catalog_number=M00081.
65. As John Nemec points out, even with a notion of divinity as ultimately without a form, a body (*amūrtā*), Somānanda is able to maintain a quality of diversity, variegation in the experience of the world, namely, through identifying the agent of action (*ātman*, *ātmadravya*) with the action itself (*karman*) in John Nemec, "Influences on and Legacies of Somānanda's Conception of Materiality," in *Around Abhinavagupta: Aspects of the Intellectual History of Kashmir from the Ninth to the Eleventh Century*, ed. Eli Franco and Isabelle Ratie (Berlin: Lit Verlag, 2016), 344.
66. Nemec, "Influences on and Legacies of Somānanda's Conception of Materiality," 341.
67. Nemec also points out that Somānanda differs from Utpaladeva in that Somānanda affords will and desire to quotidien objects, like clay pots, whereas Utpaladeva tends to locate will in Śiva and in Śiva's creative power Māyā, but not in ordinary objects like pots, in John Nemec, *Ubiquitous Śiva: Somānanda's Śivadṛṣṭi and His Tantric Interlocutors* (New York: Oxford University Press, 2011), 32. Hence, terms like eagerness (*aunmukhya*) do not show up in Utpaladeva's work. I suggest that Abhinavagupta recovers some of this agency when he figures the idea of desire arising first in the heart of even a worm.
68. Nemec, "Influences on and Legacies of Somānanda's Conception of Materiality," 362.
69. Coole and Frost, *New Materialisms*, 7.
70. Mary-Jane Rubenstein, *Pantheologies: Gods, Worlds, Monsters* (New York: Columbia University Press, 2018), 58. Note also that Danowski and Viveiros de Castro point out this convergence of pluralism and monism. They write, "PLURALISM = MONISM," the magical formula sought by Deleuze and Guattari (1987: 20) can also be written, when read by a Tardean sorcerer or an Amerindian shaman, as "Pan-psychism = Materialism," in Deborah Danowski and Eduardo Viveiros de Castro, *Ends of the World* (Malden, MA: Polity Press, 2016), 113.
71. Abhinavagupta, *Ipvv*, 1985, 3:312: "He responds, "it [the *puruṣa*, the Person] is associated with Nature" [*Māyā* here]. The words "the state of *puruṣa*" in this way function like a crow's eye [crows are supposed to have one eyeball which moves from one eye socket to the other, so here the words "the state of *puruṣa*" in the *Vṛtti* text connect with the previous idea ending in "lord, master," as the *puruṣa* is considered a *pati*,

master in *Sāṃkhya* philosophy etc., and it also connects with the following phrase, where the *puruṣa* is considered the bound soul]. By stating the idea in this way [the *puruṣa*] is approached from the perspective of Nature and there its existence is from and in the world. So it is [presented] in this way, that is to say, [as one socket for the crow's eye]." "Puṃstvāvasthayaiva" iti kākākṣivat, tena tayā eva uktayā anyad upagamyaṃ pradhānād āgataṃ tatra ca bhavaṃ viśvam ity evaṃ" I am indebted to the late Hemadrinath Cakravarty for explaining this understanding of the crow's eye to me.

72. Abhinavagupta, 3:257: "śivatattvaṃ hi sarva padārthānām vapuḥ. Tad bhitta pṛṣṭhe ca sarva bhāva citra nirbhāsa iti tad abhidhānam eva teṣām upapādanopakramaḥ. Āgamasya ca samastasya tātparyeṇa śivatattvameva artha iti."
73. Abhinavagupta says, "Here [the *tattvas*] are conceived of and exist as essences. A *tattva* is the state of a thing which causes a unification, making the various forms of different classes into one genre called a universal. So, mud, stone, wood, bone, flesh, etc., all [come under the rubric of the *tattva*] earth (*pṛthivī*), a flowing stream, a well, a river, ocean, etc., are water in Abhinavagupta, 3:264: "Etad uktaṃ bhavati iha tasya bhāvastattvam iti vargāṇāṃ viśeṣarūpāṇām ekīkaraṇanimittaṃ sāmānyam ucyate mṛtpāṣāṇadarvasthimāṃsādīnāṃ pṛthivī, saritkūpasaraḥsamudrādīnāṃ jalam iti."
74. I want to stress here again Pandey's initial pioneering and comprehensive work in K. C. Pandey, *Abhinavagupta: An Historical and Philosophical Study*. Second Enlarged Edition (Varanasi: Chowkhamba Sanskrit Series, 1963). Also see David Lawrence's innovative and insightful comparative work in David Lawrence, *Rediscovering God with Transcendental Argument: A Contemporary Interpretation of Monistic Kashmiri Śaiva Philosophy* (Rochester: State University of New York Press, 1999). For an especially influential interpretation of Abhinavagupta's writing slanted toward reading him as an idealist, see particularly Jaidev Singh's many early translations and studies (some of which have been critiqued by later scholarship), for instance, Abhinavagupta, *Trident of Wisdom: Translation of Parātrīśikāvivaraṇa*, trans. Jaidev Singh, Suny Series in Tantric Studies (Rochester: State University of New York Press, 1989). Also see notes 5, 6, 18, and 22, in the introduction for more on Abhinavagupta.
75. Pandey, *Abhinavagupta*, 320.
76. Nemec also notes that Abhinavagupta goes against Somānanda's conception of a disembodied transcendence (*amūrtā*), saying that forms, physical entities, do exist and that they depend on the *ātmadravya* in Nemec, "Influences on and Legacies of Somānanda's Conception of Materiality," 367.
77. Abhinavagupta, *Īśvara Pratyabhijñā Vivṛti Vimarśinī*, ed. Paṇḍit Madhusudan Kaul Śāstrī, vol. 2 (Delhi: Akay Reprints, 1985), 255, https://archive.org/details/in.ernet.dli.2015.326570/page/n1/mode/2up. "otaprotam sakalam viddhvā svarasena śivamayīkurute."
78. Abhinavagupta, *Ipvv*, 1985, 3:255: "Viśva prameyīkaraṇe hi tāvat prameya padottīrṇā tāvad antaḥkaraṇa pratilabdha pūrṇa bhāvā satya pramātṛtā hṛdayaṅgamīkṛtā bhavet."
79. Rubenstein, *Pantheologies*, xx.
80. Rubenstein, 194 n.29.
81. Abhinavagupta, *Ipvv*, 1985, 3:260: "Māyīyānāṃ kīṭāntānāṃ svakāryakaraṇāvasare yat kāryaṃ purā hṛdaye sphurati."
82. Rubenstein, *Pantheologies*, 85.
83. Rubenstein, 86.
84. Torella notes this practice with the nomenclature "sarvasarvātmavāda," "the doctrine that everything has the nature of everything else," in Raffaele Torella, *Īśvarapratyabhijñ*

ākārikā of Utpaladeva with the Author's Vṛtti: Critical Edition and Annotated Translation (Delhi: Motilal Banarsidass, 2002), xv–xvi.

85. This dictum works ritually precisely because it entails the magical concept of resemblance as a way of influencing the material world.
86. Nemec, 345. Nemec discusses this in detail in relation to Somānanda's conception of immateriality of consciousness.
87. Nemec, "Influences on and Legacies of Somānanda's Conception of Materiality," 345.
88. Catherine Keller, *Intercarnations: Exercises in Theological Possibility* (New York: Fordham University Press, 2017), 69.
89. Diana Coole, "Inertia of Matter and the Generativity of Flesh," in *New Materialisms: Ontology, Agency and Politics*, ed. Diana Coole and Samantha Frost (Durham, NC: Duke University Press, 2010), 92.
90. Keller, *Cloud of the Impossible*, 183.
91. John Nemec, "Evidence for Somānanda's Pantheism," *Journal of Indian Philosophy* 42 (2014): 104.
92. Nemec, *Ubiquitous Śiva*, 48. See also Jaidev Singh, *Vijñāna Bhairava or Divine Consciousness*, reprint (Delhi: Motilal Banarsidass, 2003), 94–95. This text was popularized for a Western audience in the late 1950s in a translation collected under the title *Zen Flesh, Zen Bones*, in Paul Reps, *Zen Flesh, Zen Bones: A Collection of Zen and Pre-Zen Writings* (North Clarendon, VT: Tuttle Publishing, 1957).
93. Nemec, *Ubiquitous Śiva*, 124.
94. Nemec, 124.
95. Bill Brown, "Thing Theory," *Critical Inquiry* 28, no. 1 (Autumn 2001): 1–22.
96. But note here that Utpaladeva does not make use of this terminology to any extent in his own work on Recognition, as John Nemec points out in Nemec, *Ubiquitous Śiva*, 32.
97. Abhinavagupta, *Ipvv*, 1985, 3:274: "Tathā hi vedyadaśām aṅgīkṛtavatām api ata eva ucitena idantāparāmarśena parāmṛśyānāṃ bodha eva prakāśātmā sāraṃ vastu, prakāśaś ca ananyonmukhāhaṃ vimarśamayaḥ." Here again Abhinava indulges in a play on words where *parāmarśa* means both touching the "other" and touching the highest. And again he playfully contrasts this with the word *vimarśa*, the supreme power of active awareness, the "touching" of the Lord.
98. Abhinavagupta derives this dual-aspect monism from Utpaladeva's writings; clearly present in Utpaladeva's work, it is less clear in Somānanda's writings.
99. Recall our earlier quote of Abhinavagupta describing how the seemingly lifeless mountain also can claim a subjectivity.
100. Abhinavagupta, *Ipvv*, 1985, 3:262: "abhyantaracinmātrāpekṣayā antarbahirbhāvasya sadbhāvaḥ, māyīye tu sarge >bhyantareśvaravṛddhyādyapekṣayā bahuśākho >sau."
101. Abhinavagupta and Utpaladeva, *IPV*, ad 1.6.3, line 1237. "tadavikalpadaśāyāṃ citsvabhāvo 'sau ghaṭaḥ cidvadeva viśvaśarīraḥ pūrṇaḥ." See here also Catherine Prueitt's extended discussion of this passage relating this to the concept of *apoha*, differentiation as delimitation in Catherine Prueitt, "Shifting Concepts: The Realignment of Dharmakīrti on Concepts and the Error of Subject/Object Duality in Pratyabhijñā Śaiva Thought," *Journal of Indian Philosophy* 45 (2017): 21–47. https://doi.org/DOI 10.1007/s10781-016-9297-8.
102. Abhinavagupta, *Ipvv*, 1985, 3:292: "Abhedaprakāśanaṃ tu anastamitam eva śavaśarīraghaṭādav api, iti na tatkṛto laukiko >yaṃ jaḍājaḍavibhāgaḥ iti yāvat." Lyne

Bansat-Boudon, working from different sources, comes to a similar appraisal of Abhinavagupta's perspective, writing, "In this manner it is demonstrated that insentient objects do not exist, at least not really, or not absolutely," in Lyne Bansat-Boudon, "On Śaiva Terminology: Some Key Issues of Understanding," *Journal of Indian Philosophy* 42, no. 1 (March 2014): 68.

103. This text is a commentary on Utpaladeva's text, *The Commentary on the Verses on Recognition(Īśvara Pratyabhijñā Vivṛti)*. As a commentary, Abhinavagupta glosses specific words from the text he is explaining. I keep in quotations here words that Abhinavagupta draws directly from the text on which he is commenting.

104. Abhinavagupta, *Ipvv*, 1985, 3:292: "'Cit' ity ādi grāhakāt bhinnam iti yāvat. Arthāntarāt grahyāntarāt vilakṣaṇam; tata eva avibhaktam api grāhakagrāhyābhyāṃ vibhāgamāpāditam, tathābhāve >pi 'svayam' iti svena rūpeṇa saṃvinmātramayatāṃ prakāśamānatvena anujjhad api nīlādi jaḍam ucyate. Kutaḥ. Padārthāntarāṇāṃ viviktatayā bhedena yat saṃvedanavaicitryaṃ, tatra asamarthatvāt. Tatra ca hetuḥ 'idantā' ity ādinā uktaḥ."

105. Other earlier and contemporary forms of dualist Śaivism in Kashmir take this transcendent form of deity, Sadāśiva, to be the highest manifestation of divinity. So this cosmology also functions as a polemic. See Alexis Sanderson's extensive delineation of this history, especially in Alexis Sanderson, "Śaivism and the Tantric Traditions," in *Śaivism and the Tantric Traditions*, ed. Stewart Sutherland et al. (London: Routledge, 1988), 660–704.

106. Abhinavagupta, *Ipvv*, 1985, 3:271–72: "acidbhāgo >pi vedyātmā tacchaktir eva Sadāśivarūpeti."

107. Note that Torella points out that objects are real in the inner sphere of the subject whether or not they are externalized. When they are externalized, then they have a kind of causal functionality, by virtue of being separated from the subject in Torella, *Īśvarapratyabhijñā kārikā of Utpaladeva with the Author's Vṛtti: Critical Edition and Annotated Translation*, 149. Similarly we see this in Pandey's translation of the *Īśvarapratyabhijñāvimarśinī*, in K.C. Pandey, *Iśvara Pratyabhijñā of Utpaladeva with the Vimarśinī*, reprint edition, vol. 3 (Delhi: Butala and Company, 1984), 3: 115.

108. Abhinavagupta, "Isvarapratyabhijnavimarsini," Adhikaras 1–4. Based on the following edition: Īśvara-pratyabhijñā-Vimarśinī of Abhinavagupta: doctrine of divine recognition," ed. K. A. Subramania Iyer and K. C. Pandey (Muktabodha Indological Research Institute, 1986), ad 1.5.14: tacca uktanītyā jaḍānāṃ cetanam, tasyāpi prakāśātprakatvam, tasyāpi vimarśaśaktiḥ iti. Torella also points out this idea that the insentient rests in the sentient, in Torella, *Īśvarapratyabhijñākārikā of Utpaladeva with the Author's Vṛtti*, 87.

109. See for instance Sāṃkhya Kārikā, 54 in Gerald Larson, *Classical Sāṃkhya: An Inerpretation of Its History and Meaning*, Reprint (Delhi: Motilal Banarsidass, 1998), 272.

110. Abhinavagupta, *Ipvv*, 1985, 3:350: brahmādikīṭāntamanantakaṃ yallokatraye vedakacakravālam.

111. Somānanda, *Śivadṛṣṭi with the Vṛtti of Utpaladeva*, ed. Madhusūdana Kaula Śāstrī, Muktabodha Indological Research, vol. 54 (Srinagar, Kashmir: Kashmir Series of Texts and Studies, 1934), 5.105. Utpaladeva's verse is not explicit in its demarcation, with "*sarvasya jīvataḥ*" "of all living things" and "*sarvasya*" "everything" in his autocommentary, Torella translating as "the presence of the power to know and create everything is evident in everyone" in Torella, *Īśvarapratyabhijñākārikā of Utpaladeva with the Author's Vṛtti*, 135. Abhinavagupta on the other hand gives us "*sarvasya brahmāderapi kīṭaparyantasya*," "of

everything beginning with Brahmā and ending with a worm, insect" in Abhinavagupta, *Ipvv*, 1985, 2:336.

112. Abhinavagupta, *Ipvv*, 1985, 3:284: "'Tayoś ca'" iti nirdhāraṇapadena pūrvakasya eva arthasya idaṃ sphuṭīkaraṇam iti darśitam."
113. So much so that a widespread practice of invading armies was to mutilate statues of gods, particularly cutting off the noses, so as to cut off the flow of numinosity attached to the images.
114. Abhinavagupta quotes Kṛṣṇa in the *Bhagavad Gītā*, understanding himself to reflect the totality of the cosmos in Abhinavagupta *Parātrīśikavivaraṇa*, downloaded from GRETIL: Gottingen Register of Electronic Texts in Indian Languages: http://gretil.sub.uni-goettingen.de/gretil/1_sanskr/6_sastra/3_phil/saiva/partrvpu.htm, p. 212: sarvaṃ hi sarvātmakam iti. narātmāno jaḍā api tyaktatatpūrvarūpāḥ śāktaśaivarūpabhājo bhavanti, śṛṇuta grāvāṇaḥ [cf Mahābhāṣya 3.1.1; cf Vākyapadīya 3 Puruṣasamuddeśa 2], meruḥ śikhariṇām ahaṃ bhavāmi [Bhagavadgītā 10.23].
115. Keller, *Cloud*, 331 n.52.
116. We might see this as a sort of loose quantum metaphor: by seeing the object, we call it into existence.
117. Bennett, *Vibrant Matter*, 61.
118. Bennett, 2.
119. Ratie observes that Abhinavagupta points to Sāṃkhya, saying that matter has agency for the Sāṃkhya system, that it just doesn't have consciousness. She points out Abhinavagupta's argument that only consciousness has the special power of being both unified and differentiated in Isabelle Ratie, "Śaiva Interpretation of the Satkāryavāda: The Sāṃkhya Notion of Abhivyakti and Its Transformation in the Pratyabhijñā Treatise," *Journal of Indian Philosophy*, no. 42 (March 2014): 154–55 n.94.
120. George Cardona, "Pāṇini's Kārakas: Agency, Animation and Identity," *Journal of Indian Philosophy* 2 (1972): 240–47.
121. Cardona, "Pāṇini's Kārakas," 267.
122. Bruno Latour, "Collective of Humans and Nonhumans," in *Technology and Values: Essential Readings* (Malden, MA: Wiley-Blackwell, 2010), 156–67.
123. Cardona, "Pāṇini's Kārakas," 272–73.
124. Cardona, 273–74.
125. Bansat-Boudon also notes the association between action, agency, and a concommitant sentiency in Bansat-Boudon, "On Śaiva Terminology," 67.
126. Sthaneshwar Timalsina, "Self, Causation, and Agency in the Advaita of Śaṅkara," in *Free Will, Agency, and Selfhood in Indian Philosophy*, ed. Matthew Dasti and Edwin Bryant (New York: Oxford University Press, 2013), 197.
127. As David Lawrence points out, "Utpala thus describes the Pratyabhijñā philosophy as leading to liberation through the contemplation of one's status as the agent of the universe," in David Lawrence, "Proof of a Sentient Knower: Utpaladeva's Ajaḍapramātṛsiddhi with the Vṛtti of Harabhatta Shastri," *Journal of Indian Philosophy* 37 (2009): 632. https://doi.org/10.1007/s10781-009-9074-z.
128. Abhinavagupta, *Ipvv*, 1985, 3:315: "svātantryāṃśena bodharūpasya, na tu saṃvedanāśena jñeyatvasya asaṃvidrūpatvedantātmano 'napahastanāt.'"
129. Abhinavagupta, 3:323: However the "I-ness" which is the nature of pure freedom when being covered over becomes distinct, in this way becomes separated off, that is, characterized by division, is broken asunder. In this way it takes such form as "he enjoys," "he

does," and becoming dependent on another, which is defined by the notion that "I do this in this way by the grace, the kindness of another" and so because it does not manifest, the "I"s" freedom, it is obstructed. It is excluded from freedom... From this [we understand] that, when the "I" which is self-shining is in this portion, it pushes aside its true form, becomes obstructed, is made to manifest by the light of another. It is reduced to the state of being object. That is stated as the condition of nonawareness ("ahantā tu śuddhasvātantryarūpā āropyamāṇā sphuṭaiva vyatiriktatvasya vicchinnatālakṣaṇasya bhuṅkte karotīty evaṃ rūpasya pāratantryasya ca parānugrahād evaṃ karomīty evaṃ lakṣaṇasya svātantryaviruddhasya anavabhāsāt . . .tato 'ham ity aṃśe yā svaprakāśatā; sā viruddhaparaprakāśyatāmakavedyatāpahastitasvarūpeti abodhatā uktā").

130. Abhinavagupta, 3:315: "'Na kvacit' iti 'anāropitasvātantrye 'pi ghaṭādau cidrūpatā sannihitā prakāśaikasāratvāt, sā katham āropitasvātantryeṇa bhaviṣyati. Tad āha 'viśeṣaṇa' iti."
131. Abhinavagupta, 3:258: "Bodhaikarūpasya pramātur yad adhikamabodharūpaṃ, tat nirmātavyapakṣe nikṣipyate iti tasya yat nijam śaktirūpaṃ dharmaḥ."
132. Isabelle Ratie, "The Dreamer and the Yogin: On the Relationship between Buddhist and Śaiva Idealisms," *Bulletin of the School of Oriental and African Studies* 73, no. 3 (October 2010): 469.
133. Isabelle Ratie, "Pāramārthika or Apāramārthika? On the Ontological Status of Separation According to Abhinavagupta," in *Puṣpikā: Tracing Ancient India through Texts and Traditions*, ed. P. Mirning, P.-D. Szanto, and M. Williams (Havertown, UK: Oxbow Books, 2014), 388.
134. Bansat-Boudon, "On Śaiva Terminology," 43–44.
135. Bansat-Boudon, 43.
136. Abhinavagupta, *Ipvv*, 1985, 3:272: "citiśaktir viśvarūpā bhavati na cādhikyaṃ spṛśati" iti sambandhaḥ. Cetanā atidurghaṭakāritvādinā adbhutatāṃ vyanakti. Etat saṃkṣipya ghaṭayati "yo hi" iti "idantābhāk" iti.
137. Rubenstein, *Pantheologies*, 56–57.
138. Rubenstein, 5.
139. Rubenstein, 2.
140. So Abhinavagupta tells us: "This is because of the mutual inseparability of *jñāna*, Knowledge and *kriyā*, Activity which have the respective natures of expansive Light (prakāśa) and Active Awareness (vimarśa)" "tato hetor anyonyam aviyukte jñānakriye prakāśa vimarśātmike" in Abhinavagupta, *Ipvv*, 1985, 3:257.
141. Abhinavagupta, 3:321: "nityavyāpakabodhamātrarūpo hi ahaṃ bhedena nirbhāse iti; tatas teṣāṃ yukta eva anyonyaṃ bhedo grāhyebhyo grāhakāntarebhyaś ca." The context here is Abhinavagupta's explanation of why we find differences among a certain class of very advanced beings called *vijñānākalās*, who have attained a certain level of enlightenment. This differentiation ultimately derives from the freedom that the Lord, *Śiva*, has to generate plurality. Here we see the theism of his panentheism.
142. John Searle, "Can Information Theory Explain Consciousness?," *New York Times Review of Books*, January 10, 2013, 57.
143. Biernacki, "Connecting Consciousness to Physical Causality."
144. Abhinavagupta and Utpaladeva, *IPV*, commentary ad 2.4.19: "bhāsamāno'pi bhedo bādhitaḥ, iti cet, abhedo'pi evam bhedabhāsanena tasya bādhāt." "Bheda" is usually translated as "duality," a term that has a specific philosophical valence. However, the sense here is that multiplicity is a feature of our world, and the term *duality* loses the valence of meaning

for a contemporary audience. In any case, I suspect this type of view is more widely steeped in an Indian cultural perspective than is acknowledged. Ajay Skaria attributes this perspective to Gandhi, though without any connection to Abhinavagupta, in Ajay Skaria, *Unconditional Equality: Gandhi's Religion of Resistance* (Minneapolis: University of Minnesota Press, 2016), 177. Even though I do not address the political ramifications Abhinavagupta's perspective might have for a New Materialism, this is one avenue one might take to parse this out.

145. Abhinavagupta's idea of panentheism as a cosmopsychism is more akin to Schaffer's priority monism (in Jonathan Schaffer, "Monism: The Priority of the Whole," in *Spinoza on Monism* (London: Palgrave Macmillan, 2012), 9–50.), rather than Horgan and Potrc's "blobjectivism" (in Terry Horgan and Matjaz Potrc, "Existence Monism Trumps Priority Monism," in *Spinoza on Monism*, ed. Philip Goff (London: Palgrave Macmillan, 2012), 51–76.), where Horgan and Potrc's model might be aligned with the absolute monism of Advaita Vedanta in contrast to the variety that Abhinavagupta's Tantric model of monism admits.
146. Cognates of *vimarśa* also appear, such as *parāmarśa*, *āmarśa* and so on.
147. Abhinavagupta, *Ipvv*, 1985, 3:314: aham iti camatkārātmano vimarśasya
148. Abhinavagupta, 3:319: saṃvinmātraparamārthā api aham iti svātmaviśrāntilakṣaṇasvāta ntryaparamārthānandacamatkāra
149. Abhinavagupta, 3:251: camatkāramātrātmā yo vimarśastadeva svātantryaṃ
150. Ratie makes this point as well on a variety of occasions, in Ratie, "The Dreamer and the Yogin," 467; also in Isabelle Ratie, "Some Hitherto Unknown Fragments of Utpaladeva's Vivṛti (II): Against the Existence of External Objects," in *Śaivism and Tantric Traditions: Essays in Honour of Alexis G.J.S. Sanderson* (Leiden: Brill, 2020), 113; and in Isabelle Ratie, "Can One Prove That Something Exists Beyond Consciousness? A Śaiva Criticism of the Sautrāntika Inference of External Objects," *Journal of Indian Philosophy* 39 (2011): 491.
151. Much has been written on the "combination problem" and alternatively, the "decombination problem" for cosmopsychism. Briefly, the decombination problem is that if one has a single nondualism cosmic consciousness, the problem then becomes how might a singular cosmic subject separate itself out into the many different voices that make up a plural universe. A couple of good articulations of the problem and possible solutions are Itay Shani, "Cosmopsychism: A Holistic Approach to the Metaphysics of Experience," *Philosophical Papers* 44, no. 3 (2015): 389–437, https://doi.org/10.1080/05568641.2015.1106709. Also see Freya Mathews, "Panpsychism as Paradigm," in *Mental as Fundamental: New Perspectives on Panpsychism*, ed. Michael Blamauer (Frankfurt: Ontos Verlag, 2011), 141–56. And also see Godehard Bruntrup and Ludwig Jaskolla, eds., *Panpsychism: Contemporary Perspectives* (New York: Oxford University Press, 2016).
152. Sthaneshwar Timalsina, "Brahman and the Word Principle (Śabda): Influence of the Philosophy of Bhartṛhari on Maṇḍana's Brahmasiddhi," *Journal of Indian Philosophy* 37 (2009): 194, https://doi.org/10.1007/s10781-009-9065-0.
153. Perhaps this capacity to partake of "This-ness" offers a way in to the kind of mutually sustaining multiplicity that Catherine Keller proposes with a god that does not take over the whole, but works rather toward "negating divine ultimacy" in Keller, *Cloud*, 188.
154. Even if a neo-Darwinism, as Dawkins, for instance, outlines in Richard Dawkins, *Selfish Gene* (London: Oxford University Press, 1976)., results as well in an overarching telos, run by genetic imperatives to reproduce.

155. On this topic, see here Sthaneshwar Timalsina's recent (2020) article addressing Abhinavagupta's conception of the "I" (*aham*). In discussing the idea of "I" in relation to Lacan's conception of ego, he argues for the kind of panentheism I suggest here, which is capable of entertaining both transcendence and immanence, writing, "the consciousness identified in terms of parāmarśa encapsulates both the immanent and transcendent forms of experiences." In Sthaneshwar Timalsina, "Aham, Subjectivity, and the Ego: Engaging the Philosophy of Abhinavagupta," *Journal of Indian Philosophy* 48, no. 4 (September 2020): 779, https://doi.org/10.1007/s10781-020-09439. In this interesting article, he tends to merge the conception of ego with that of the idea of self, a move that I tend to eschew, particularly insofar as I think Abhinavagupta is at pains to point out a subjectivity that transcends egoic identity. On Timalsina's behalf, I suspect he interchanges concepts of subjectivity with that of ego, in part to create a bridge to discuss contemporary Western ideas and in particular the 20th-century thinker Lacan. This interchangeability between ego and the "I" facilitates this discussion for a Western audience, even as I suggest we can find definitional nuance between *ahaṁkāra* as ego and *ahantā* as subjectivity. I only became aware of this article after this book had been written; yet I think it deserves mentioning here.
156. Interestingly, there may be something about the medieval world here more generally. In Carol Walker Bynum's address on wonder, she notes that for medieval Europe "wonder" was associated with diversity and its opposite, "solitum" was associated with the general, in Caroline Walker Bynum, "Presidential Address: Wonder," *American Historical Review* 102, no. 1 (February 1997): 7.
157. Raffaele Torella, "How Is Verbal Signification Possible: Understanding Abhinavagupta's Reply," *Journal of Indian Philosophy* 32 (2004): 178.
158. Apart from Keller's deliberations on Nicholas of Cusa's *complicatio*, I am reminded here as well of her masterful exegesis of the tehomic pleroma, the generative "silence vibrant with the unspoken Word," as akin to the idea of phonemes of language compressed within the unity of supreme consciousness. See Catherine Keller, *Face of the Deep: A Theology of Becoming* (New York: Routledge, 2003), 4.
159. Torella, "How Is Verbal Signification Possible," 178.
160. Torella, 178.
161. Torella, 178. Torella talks about this in terms of succession, *krama*; language conveys meaning through its temporal unfolding in time.
162. Harman, "Critical Animal with a Fun Little Post."
163. Timothy Morton, *Hyperobjects: Philosophy and Ecology after the End of the World* (Minneapolis: University of Minnesota Press, 2013), 15.
164. Bennett, *Vibrant Matter*, 15–16.
165. I discuss the 20th-century Tantric thinker and practitioner Gopinath Kaviraj's explanation of the phenomenon of yogically entering into objects in relation to contemporary sports experience in Loriliai Biernacki, "Transcendence in Sports: How Do We Interpret Mysticism in Sports? Tantra and Cognitive Science Perspectives," *Journal for the Study of Religious Experience* 4 (2018): 24–39.
166. Torella, *Īśvarapratyabhijñākārikā of Utpaladeva with the Author's Vṛtti*, 108. See also Isabelle Ratie, "Otherness in the Pratyabhijñā Philosophy," *Journal of Indian Philosophy* 35 (2007): 321 n.16.
167. Arindam Chakrabarti, "Arindam Chakrabarti. "Arguing from Synthesis to the Self: Utpaladeva and Abhinavagupta Respond to Buddhist No-Selfism," in *Hindu and*

Buddhist Ideas in Dialogue: Self and No-Self, ed. Jonardon Ganeri, Irina Kuznetsova, and Chakravarthi Ram-Prasad (Burlington, VT: Ashgate, 2012), 212.

168. The other side of this penetrabilility of things does indeed show up as the darker side of Tantric magic, *siddhis*, where skilled practitioners, humans as well as nonphysical subtle-bodied beings, penetrate, possessing others in shamanistic-like practices. For a brilliant and all-encompassing analysis of this phenomenon, see Fred Smith's magisterial study, in Frederick Smith, *Self Possessed: Deity and Spirit Possession in South Asian Literature and Civilization* (New York: Columbia University Press, 2006).
169. Abhinavagupta, *Ipvv*, 1985, 3:315: "Nanu evaṃ ghate 'pi yadi cidrūpatām kaścit paśyet, tarhi kim abhrānta eva asau."
170. Abhinavagupta, 3:315: "svātantryāṃśena bodharūpasya, na tu saṃvedanāśena jñeyatvasya asaṃvidrūpatvedantātmano 'napahastanāt."
171. Here Abhinavagupta tells us that "what is intended here is the ordinary form of all knowing Subjects in the world, comprising the specific activity of the hands and feet, etc., of the agent, because this idea is generally accepted in the world." In Abhinavagupta, 3:258: "laukika sarva pramātṛ sādhāraṇa rūpa saṃpādakakara caraṇādi vyāpāra viśeṣa paryantībhūtam eva abhipretaṃ tathā laukikānāṃ prasiddheḥ."
172. Abhinavagupta tells us that, "it is through [examining] the subjectivity of the *Māyā*-bound knowing Subject that the principle of subjectivity is explained, yet still the host of worlds and Archetypes are not created by this [lower] *Māyā*-bound Subject. Even then the Archetype which is the *Māyā*-bound Subject also is at base just the Archetype of *Śiva*. By a two-fold method, by analogy and through being coessential, because of its universality and because of its having one single form ultimately the [*Māyā*-bound subject and the knowing subjectivity of the absolute Śiva] rest in the one principle." In Abhinavagupta, 3:258: "Yadyapi Māyīya pramātṛ mukhena pramātṛtattvaṃ vyākhyātam, tasya ca na tattvabhuvanavargo nirmeyas tathāpi māyāpramātṛtattvaṃ śivatattva eva prakāradvayena sāmānyāt tad ekarūpatvāc cety evaṃ paryavasāyayiṣyati."
173. Abhinavagupta, 3:258: "ātmānam eva pramātṛ saṃjñaṃ karmabhāvena kartṛbhāvena ca avalambamānā kriyā karmasthatvena kartṛsthatveva vā." Abhinavagupta also makes the important point in this section that the limited knower, like us, does not actually create the external world. These are functions of the *tattvas*, which present a world already given to the subject. That is, the limited Māyā-bound person like us does not create the world; this is not an idealism. This creation occurs on a deeper level of subjectivity, akin to that of higher, more aware beings, not gods in this case per se but lords of mantras. See Abhinavagupta, 3:326, 350.
174. Abhinavagupta continues in this paragraph: "When *kriyā*—action—is analyzed, [we see] it as the locus of the object of action or as the locus of the doer of action, *kriyā* itself in fact maintaining a single base, being itself one alone," in Abhinavagupta, *Ipvv*, 1985, 3:258: "avalambamānā kriyā karmasthatvena kartṛsthatveva vā vivicyamānā ekāśrayaiva bhavantī vastuta ekaiva."
175. Lawrence, "Proof of a Sentient Knower," 640.
176. The impure here is a direct translation of *aśuddha*. It refers to entities under the influence of Māyā; that is, having lost an essential awareness of subjectivity, entities at this level conceive themselves as different from others. It is "impure" because one is trapped in a conception of being an object.
177. Abhinavagupta, *Ipvv*, 1985, 3:304: "Iyat tu iha tātparyam—dharādyābhāsā eva miśrībhūya ghātādisvalakṣaṇībhūtāḥ karmendriyair janitāś ca upasarpitāś ca,

buddhīndriyair ālocitāḥ, antaḥkaraṇena saṁkalpanābhimananāniścayanaparyantatāṁ nītāḥ, aśuddhavidyā-vivecitāḥ, kalādibhiḥ pramātāram upadadhadbhir anurañjitāḥ, māyāpramātari viśrāntidvāreṇa abhinnā api santo 'yady apy arthasthitiḥ. . . . |' (A. Pra. Si. 20) iti nyāyena satyapramātari eva bhedavigalanatāratam yena vigalitasvakabhedāḥ prakāśavimarśaparamārthatayā eva viśrāmyantīti Śivam."

178. Abhinavagupta, 3:315: "śaktyā śuddhavidyārūpayā hi ayaṃ samyag iti jaḍarūpatānyakkriyayā cidrūpatāprādhānyena āveśaḥ āsamantāt svarūpapraveśaḥ ity arthaḥ. Yad āha
   'tṛṇāt parṇāt . . . |" '
   iti. Udgamanaṃ hi acidrūpatāyā nyakkāraḥ.
   'aṣṭamūrte kim ekasyām . . . |'
   ity atra tu sa eva toṣaḥ."
179. Abhinavagupta quotes Kṛṣṇa in the *Bhagavad Gītā*, understanding himself to reflect the totality of the cosmos in Abhinavagupta *Parātrīśikavivaraṇa*, downloaded from GRETIL: Gottingen Register of Electronic Texts in Indian Languages: http://gretil.sub.uni-goettingen.de/gretil/1_sanskr/6_sastra/3_phil/saiva/partrvpu.htm, p. 212: "sarvaṃ hi sarvātmakam iti. narātmāno jaḍā api tyaktatatpūrvarūpāḥ śāktaśaivarūpabhājo bhavanti, śṛṇuta grāvāṇaḥ" [cf. Mahābhāṣya 3.1.1; cf. Vākyapadīya 3 Puruṣasamuddeśa 2], meruḥ śikhariṇām ahaṃ bhavāmi [Bhagavadgītā 10.23].
180. Bennett, *Vibrant Matter*, ix, 4, 10, passim.
181. Taittirīya, *Taittirīya Mantrakośaḥ: Prathamo Bhagaḥ*, 74: "Ayam me hasto bhagavānayaṃ me bhagavattaraḥ| ayaṃ me viśvabheśajo ^yagṃ śivābhimarśanaḥ."
182. Whitman, "Song of Myself," 5:11.
183. Abhinavagupta, *Ipvv*, 1985, 3:255: "Viśva prameyīkaraṇe hi tāvat prameya padottīrṇā tāvad antaḥkaraṇa pratilabdha pūrṇa bhāvā satya pramātṛtā hṛdayaṅgamīkṛtā bhavet."

Chapter 2

1. https://www.ted.com/talks/anil_seth_how_your_brain_hallucinates_your_conscious_reality/transcript accessed, October 10, 2017.
2. Of course, the understanding of this breaks down into a variety of similar, but differently nuanced positions, such as the Eliminativism of Paul and Patricia Churchland and the Epiphenomenalism of Daniel Dennett, among others.
3. This is Chalmers's "hard problem." See David Chalmers, *The Conscious Mind: In Search of a Fundamental Theory* (New York: Oxford University Press, 1996).
4. He rightly locates his idea in the lineage of Copernicus and Darwin, displacing the ego, the self, from its central role, thus establishing his position, laying out his cards, so to speak, as a secularist and materialist scientist.
5. Listed in a notable quotes list of Sagan's pithy statements on science: https://todayinsci.com/S/Sagan_Carl/SaganCarl-Quotations.htm
6. https://blogs.scientificamerican.com/guest-blog/10-sublime-wonders-of-science, accessed October 17, 2017.
7. Michael Shermer (March 2004). "The Major Unsolved Problem in Biology," *Scientific American* 290 (3): 103. DOI:10.1038/scientificamerican0304-103.
8. I am reminded of the technique the Buddha prescribes in the *Lotus Sūtra*. Describing the father who lures his children out of a burning house with the promise of toys that

will never materialize, the Buddha then asks his audience if the father's false promise for a greater good was justified. We might ask, does the consolation of wonder justify the brave new paradigm that these scientists urge us to adopt? We can keep in mind here that Buddhism also boldly set out on a program to disabuse its listeners of clinging to a false idea of self (*anātma*), just as Seth does.

9. Lorraine Daston and Katharine Park, *Wonders and the Order of Nature* (New York: Zone Books, 1998).
10. See Daston and Park, *Wonders and the Order of Nature*, p. 319, for a series of drawings of wonder as physically represented in a human body by a gaping open mouth, without speech.
11. Mary Jane Rubenstein points to its early links to praxis as thaumaturgy in Mary-Jane Rubenstein, *Strange Wonder: The Closure of Metaphysics and the Opening of Awe* (New York: Columbia University Press, 2008), 190.
12. See Mary-Jane Rubenstein, *Strange Wonder: The Closure of Metaphysics and the Opening of Awe* (New York: Columbia University Press, 2008), for the links of wonder with indeterminacy, especially pp. 7, 60, 145. Rubenstein suggests connections of wonder with fear, terror, and astonishment, and also links wonder etymologically with the Sanskrit stupa, in a footnote by J. Onians, in Rubenstein, *Strange Wonder*, 199 n.20. Onians's suggestion, perhaps conjectured based on the homonym of stupor and the Sanskrit *stupa*, looks to be incorrect, based on Monier-Williams's dictionary entry, which details that *stupa* derives from the word meaning head, crown, or crest, and becomes the heap of bricks over the sacred place, often of relics of Buddha. Monier-Williams suggests that *stupa* derives from the root stū or styai in Monier Monier-Williams, *Sanskrit-English Dictionary, Etymlogically and Philologically Arranged with Special Reference to Cognate Indo-European Languages* (New York: Oxford University Press, 1960), 1259–60, https://www.sanskrit-lexicon.uni-koeln.de/monier/.
13. Sophia Vasalou, *Practices of Wonder: Cross-Disciplinary Perspectives* (Cambridge: James Clarke & Co., 2013), 10.
14. Caroline Walker Bynum, "Presidential Address: Wonder," *American Historical Review* 102, no. 1 (February 1997): 24. Martha Nussbaum similarly suggests that in wonder a person is only minimally aware of the utilitarian possilities of the object in Martha Nussbaum, *Upheavals of Thought: The Intelligence of Emotions* (Cambridge: Cambridge University Press, 2001), 54–55.
15. Martha Nussbaum makes this point in Nussbaum, *Upheavals of Thought*, 54.
16. Lorraine Daston and Katharine Park, *Wonders and the Order of Nature* (New York: Zone Books, 1998), 319. See also Rubenstein, *Strange Wonder*, 191.
17. Bynum, "Presidential Address: Wonder." Vasalou also makes this point for our contemporary understanding of wonder in Vasalou, *Practices of Wonder*, 17.
18. Daston and Park, *Wonders and the Order of Nature*.
19. Daston and Park, 14. See also Derek Matravers, "Wonder and Cognition," in *Practices of Wonder: Cross-Disciplinary Perspectives* (Cambridge: James Clarke & Co., 2013), 166–78.
20. Daston and Park, *Wonders and the Order of Nature*, 13. Similarly, I suggest, Tulasi Srinivas's recent work on wonder in India operates along congruent lines. Its anthropological reclamation of wonder as an emotion for hope pinned to the miraculous focuses on how wonder as emotion changes our mental analysis of the world, in Tulasi Srinivas, *Cow in the Elevator: An Anthropology of Wonder* (Durham, NC: Duke University Press, 2018).

21. Rubenstein, *Strange Wonder*, 3. Though I might suggest that Rubenstein's argument that wonder as the ground of thinking also renders thinking ungrounded begins to approximate Abhinavagupta's conception of wonder as intimately linked to the will (*icchā*). The comparison may map generally, as part of the phenomenology of wonder, and also quite directly, in Abhinavagupta's cosmological scheme of the *tattvas*, the categories mapping existence, the will, *icchā*, linked to *ahaṁkāra*, egoism, is the direct ground of the mind (*manas*).
22. This, perhaps most flamboyantly, gets articulated in well-known rituals like the sex rite. However, we also see this in ritual practices such as *nyāsa*, where the practitioner places mantras on the body as a way of transforming the body. An extensive amount of work has been done on this subject. A few good starting point is Alexis Sanderson's discussion, in Alexis Sanderson, "Śaivism and the Tantric Traditions," in *Śaivism and the Tantric Traditions*, ed. Stewart Sutherland et al. (London: Routledge, 1988), 660–704. See also Gavin Flood, *Tantric Body: The Secret Tradition of HIndu Religion* (New York: I. B. Tauris, 2006). Also see Loriliai Biernacki, *Renowned Goddess of Desire: Women, Sex and Speech in Tantra* (New York: Oxford University Press, 2007).
23. One important point to note here in relation to wonder as an emotion: regarding the idea of wonder as a *sthayibhāva*, one of the ten *rasas* of *rasa* theory, the Indian literary aesthetic theory of emotions uses the word "*adbhuta*," not "*camatkāra*." We might parse out the distinction, with *adbhuta* veering toward the marvelous and miraculous precisely as an emotional sentiment, but not the refined experience of *rasa*. While *camatkāra* at times is linked to *adbhuta*, Abhinavagupta, a keen writer on *rasa* theory, especially with his *Dhvanyālokalocana*, tends to use *camatkāra* in his later philosophical work rather precisely as part of his formulation of subjectivity and sentience, and not as interchangeable with the emotion of marveling, *adbhuta* in this formulation. We can see a linguistic echo of this even in Srinivas's contemporary work, with the use of *adbhuta* and *aścarya* for the marvelous—for instance, in Srinivas, *Cow in the Elevator*, 3–4.
24. Michel Hulin, "The Conception of Camatkāra in Indian Aesthetics," in *Practices of Wonder: Cross-Disciplinary Perspectives*, ed. Sophia Vasalou (Cambridge: James Clarke & Co., 2013), 226–30. Sthaneshwar Timalsina also points to the problems of seeing *camatkāra* as mere emotion, suggesting it extends beyond emotion to something above and beyond emotion, in Sthaneshwar Timalsina, "Savoring Rasa: Emotion, Judgement, and Phenomenal Content," in *Bloomsbury Research Handbook of Emotions in Classical Indian Philosophy*, ed. Maria Heim, Chakravarthi Ram-Prasad, and Roy Tzohar (London: Bloomsbury Academic, 2021), 260.
25. We might understand this fusion as panentheist in its thrust since it seeks to tie together transcendence and immanence.
26. Vasalou points to something similar when she suggests that wonder helps to recover a kind of innate subjectivity or life of the thing being wondered at in Vasalou, *Practices of Wonder*, 4–5.
27. Jane Bennett, *Vibrant Matter: A Political Ecology of Things* (Duke University Press, 2010), p. 5.
28. Bennett, *Vibrant Matter*, p. 5.
29. Thomas Nagel, *View from Nowhere* (New York: Oxford University Press, 1986).
30. Raghavan suggests this in Venkatarama Raghavan, *Studies on Some Concepts of the Alamkāra-Shastra*, 33 (Adyar: Adyar Library Series, 1942), 268–69. I draw this from Hulin, "The Conception of Camatkāra in Indian Aesthetics," 227.

31. Abhinavagupta, *Īśvara Pratyabhijñā Vivṛti Vimarśinī*, ed. Paṇḍit Madhusudan Kaul Śāstrī, vol. 3 (Delhi: Akay Reprints, 1985), 251: "camatkāro hi iti svātmani ananyāpekṣe viśramaṇam |evaṃ bhuñjānatārūpaṃ camattvaṃ."
32. Abhinavagupta, 3:251: "akhaṇḍa evavā śabdo nirvighnāsvādanavṛttiḥ." In this passage, Abhinavagupta offers an etymological interpretation of *camatkāra*, wonder. I give the whole of this passage with translation: "camatkāro hi iti svātmani ananyāpekṣe viśramaṇam |evaṃ bhuñjānatārūpaṃ camattvaṃ, tadeva karoti saṃrambhe, vimṛśati na anyatra anudhāvati | camaditi kriyāviśeṣaṇam, akhaṇḍa evavā śabdo nirvighnāsvādanavṛttiḥ | camaditi vā āntaraspandāndolanoditaparāmarśa-mayaśabdanāvyaktānukaraṇam" | "wonder, indeed, rests in its own nature, without depending on some other thing. In this way, it has the form of enjoyment which is the state of tasting. That, in fact generates excitement, zeal. It (wonder) actively intuits, grasps (vimṛśati), it does not pursue in some other manner. The word 'camad' is a particular form of action (*kriyā*). Or taking the word as unbroken (i.e., in the compound *camatkāra*) in this way, it is abiding in a state of enjoyment without any obstacles. Or camad can be understood as resembling the unmanifest word, which consists of the highest active awareness that arises from the oscillation of the inner life vibration *(spanda)*."
33. This is what the tradition would term *vikalpa*, the discursive effect of the mind to create oppositional categories.
34. Arindam Chakrabarty offers a nice image of the sensory quality of eating in reference to the Advaita Vedānta thinker Śaṅkarācarya, where he posits eating as metaphor for the union of subject and object in "I and You," a paper presentation of which he sent me a copy, pp. 7–8.
35. Abhinavagupta, *Īśvara Pratyabhijñā Vivṛti Vimarśinī*, ed. Paṇḍit Madhusudan Kaul Śāstrī, vol. 2 (Delhi: Akay Reprints, 1985), 175. https://archive.org/details/in.ernet.dli.2015.326570/page/n1/mode/2up. "ananyāpekṣatā ca eṣaiva yat svātmīyavimarśe'hamiti bhoktṛtāmaye avicchinne bhuñjānatātmani camatkāre rūḍhiḥ."|
36. Lyne Bansat-Boudan also points to a passage in Abhinavagupta's *Paramārthasāra*, which offers wonder as a particular yogic practice. Here the practice of wonder involves worshipping the Self by imagining one's sense capacities as deities and merging one's awareness in the senses, in Lyne Bansat-Boudon, *An Introduction to Tantric Philosophy: The Paramārthasāra of Abhinavagupta with the Commentary of Yogarāja*, trans. Lyne Bansat-Boudon and Kamaleshadatta Tripathi, Routledge Studies in Tantric Traditions (New York: Routledge, 2011), 256.
37. As we saw in Chapter One, for instance, in John Nemec, "Evidence for Somānanda's Pantheism," *Journal of Indian Philos* 42 (2014): 104.
38. Also, see both Ratie's and Torella's discussions of Īśvara Pratyabhijñā Vimarśinī 1.5.11, where Utpaladeva and Abhinavagupta in his commentary note that the crystal lacks sentience and consequently lacks wonder in Isabelle Ratie, "Remarks on Compassion and Altruism in the Pratyabhijñā Philosophy," *Journal of Indian Philosophy* 37 (2009): 359. And see Raffaele Torella, *Īśvarapratyabhijñākārikā of Utpaladeva with the Author's Vṛtti: Critical Edition and Annotated Translation* (Delhi: Motilal Banarsidass, 2002), 118 n.23.
39. Michel Hulin points out that wonder (*camatkāra*) is not that special or extraordinary a state; the state of wonder is the soul's own natural state. That which is the object cannot have this capacity of wonder, so a wall is not capable of the state of wonder. But something

alive has as its main feature the capacity for wonder in Hulin, "The Conception of Camatkāra in Indian Aesthetics," 229.

40. Abhinavagupta repeats the idea that wonder is not dependent on some other thing, this freedom, in this passage and also in the quote given above in footnote 32.
41. Richard Dawkins, *Selfish Gene* (London: Oxford University Press, 1976).
42. Daniel Dennett, *Consciousness Explained* (New York: Little, Brown, 1991).
43. We examine this in more detail in Chapter Five in relation to Abhinavagupta's exposition of levels of subjectivity through the *tattva* system, which is classical India's cosmological taxonomy.
44. Abhinavagupta, *Ipvv*, 1985, 3:251: "camaditi kriyāviśeṣaṇam." Explaining a word vis-a-vis its etymology is a common philosophical practice for Indian authors. Indeed, one can suggest that this practice in itself entails a philosophical understanding of language as innately, ontologically expressive in that words reveal a deeper, innate truth about reality, and not merely give their meaning through conventionally accepted meanings. Lyne Bansat-Boudon suggests that Italian Indologist Raniero Gnoli inserts an emendation in order to get a reading of *camatkāra* that relates to the root *cam*, "to sip," in alignment with the reading Abhinavagupta gives here. Bansat-Boudon rejects this etymology as doubtful, however; based on this particular passage, it does seem that Abhinavagupta follows this line of thinking. The passage I give here is not cited by Bansat-Boudon and would tend to support Gnoli's reading, even if the etymology is linguistically doubtful. See Bansat-Boudon, *Paramārthasāra*, 320–21.
45. Lyne Bansat-Boudon points out that we first see the connection of wonder to the sense of subjectivity in the aesthetic theory of Ānandavardhana's *Dhvanyāloka* 4.16, on which Abhinavagupta writes a commentary, in Bansat-Boudon, *Paramārthasāra*, 320–21.
46. Edwin Gerow, "Abhinavagupta's Aesthetics as a Speculative Paradigm," *Journal of the American Oriental Society*, 114. no. 2 (1994), pp. 93, 186–208.
47. Michel Hulin, "The Conception of Camatkāra in Indian Aesthetics," p. 226. David Shulman also links wonder to "sensual expansion," in David Shulman, *More Than Real: A History of the Imagination in South India* (Cambridge, MA: Harvard University Press, 2012), 256.
48. Sthaneshwar Timalsina, "Theatrics of Emotion: Self-Deception and Self-Cultivation in Abhinavagupta's Aesthetics," *Philosophy East and West* 66, no. 1 (January 2016): 110.
49. Abhinavagupta, *Ipvv*, 1985, 3:251: "kāvyanāṭyarasādāvapi bhāvicittavṛttyantarodayaniyam ātmakavighnavirahita eva āsvādo rasanātmā camatkāra iti uktamanyatra." Abhinavagupta also links wonder to aesthetic experience in Abhinavagupta, *Ipvv*, 1985, 2:179. Discussing there the fact that we do not see the expression of wonder in insentient objects, he says that "this comes from the taste of sweetness etc., by contact with the object. From that also there is the state of absence of being engaged in [the case of the insentient object] in poetry and dance, etc." "madhurādirasāsvāde tu viṣayasparśavyavadhānam | tato.api kāvyanāṭyādau tadvyavadhānaśūnyatā."
50. David Shulman, "Notes on Camatkāra," In David Shulman, ed., *Language, Ritual and Poetics in Ancient India and Iran: Studies in Honor of Shaul Migron*. (Jerusalem: Israel Academy of Sciences and Humanities, 2010: 255–56). The quote itself is also cited here from Lyne Bansat-Boudon and Kamaeshadatta Tripathi, transl., *An Introduction to Tantric Philosophy*, p. 321.
51. See Daston and Park, *Wonders and the Order of Nature*, p. 319, for a series of drawings of wonder as physically represented in a human body by a gaping open mouth, without speech.

52. Navjivan Rastogi "Rasānubhūti Pratibhāna ke Rūpa Meṃ," in *The Concept of Rasa with Special reference to Abhinavagupta*, ed. S.C. Pande (New Delhi: Aryan Books International, 2009, p. 194). Torella as well, elsewhere discussing Abhinavagupta's relationship to yoga, points to Abhinavagupta's critique of yogic practice that withdraws the senses from objects as useless insofar as it only strengthens bondage by suggesting that consciousness is only in some places and not others, in Raffaele Torella, "Abhinavagupta's Attitude towards Yoga," *Journal of the American Oriental Society* 139, no. 3 (2019), pp. 649–50.
53. Bansat-Boudon and Kamaeshadatta Tripathi, transl., *An Introduction to Tantric Philosophy*, p. 321.
54. Bansat-Boudon, *Paramārthasāra*, 79–80: parāhantācamatkārasāra. See the full quote in the next footnote.
55. Abhinavagupta points out the connection between Nature (*prakṛti*) and materiality elsewhere, saying, "Nature is entirely an object, is all objects. . . . Nature manifests even in dualistic conception in only one form as 'This-ness' with a single flavor throughout. A portion of it shines visibly as the objects we see," in Abhinavagupta, *Ipvv*, 1985, 3:295: "tat sarvaṃ prameyam. . . . Pradhānaṃ tu vikalpe nirbhāsamānam api sākṣād-vedyāṃśaukarūpam eva idantayaikarasatayā bhātīti."
56. Bansat-Boudan, *Paramārthasāra*, pp. 79–80. Sanskrit text, p. 358: "kiṃ—rūpā aṇḍacatuṣṭayasaṃkhyā?—ityāha śaktirmāyā, prakṛtiḥ, pṛthvī ca iti | viśvasya pramātṛprameyarūpasya parāhantācamatkārasārasyāpi svasvarūpāpohanātmākhyātimayī niṣedhavyāpārarūpā yā pārameśvarī śaktiḥ."
57. Even as Abhinavagupta's cosmopsychism locates the multitude of different beings and objects as ultimately just the subjectivity of Śiva, the cosmopsychic divinity that unfurls itself to create a universe, Abhinavagupta also makes a point of acknowledging this plurality as genuine. He notes that not only does consciousness pervade all things, but also that this variety of limited individuals have their own capacities for creation, apart from the powers of Śiva, undoing the theological idealism. Instead, this multiplicity of different beings have their own independent creativity. He tells us, "The lordship which is the form of consciousness associated with [those on the level of *Māyā*] is not any way separate or different from lordship [of the Lord] which has the nature of knowledge and action. This is what the words 'by means of that' refer to [i.e., by means of the very same lordship, which is the Energy of *Māyā*, the power to will (*īcchā śakti*) associated with both the Lord and limited Subjects]. So it is correct to say that even for bound souls, knowledge and action are mutually inseparably present. We read in the *Nareśvara Vivekaḥ*: 'Bound souls are both conscious and unconscious in form. Because of the quality of consciousness the Great Lord is only one. With this [since the Lord is one] there can't be anything at all which is lacking consciousness. How is there any grounds for criticizing?' It may be asked—why doesn't the Lordship of the Lord manifest all the time? He counters this doubt with the word 'blue' and so on. This can also be explained, as it was earlier—by means of the Lordship of the Lord, even those bound in *Māyā* have a capacity for creation. . . . 'Or by his own independence'—accepting the idea that there is creation which is not dependent upon the creation of the Lord," in Abhinavagupta, *Ipvv*, 1985, 3:260: "Tasyāś cito rūpaṃ yad aiśvaryam, na hi jñānakriyātmakaiśvaryātiriktā cit kācit, tanmukhena taddvāreṇa yuktaḥ paśūnām api jñānakriyayor anyonyāviyogaḥ. Yat nareśvaravivekaḥ "aṇavaścidacidrūpāścittvād eko maheśvaraḥ |tena kecid acittvāt tu katham ākṣepabhūmayaḥ ||"iti. Nanu bhagavato >pi sadā kathaṃ na avabhāsanā nirvahati, iti śaṅkāṃ bhinatti "nīla" ity ādinā. Yadi vā yat pūrvaṃ samarthitam īśvarasya, tad aiśvaryamukhena māyāpramātṝṇām api nirmāṇaṃ samarthitam ity ekarasatayaiva

grantho neyaḥ . . . . "Svātantryeṇa vā" iti īśvarasṛṣṭyanapekṣayā. Nirmāṇam iti samarthitam iti sambandhaḥ." Here also, the words in quotes indicate words Abhinavagupta glosses from Utpaladeva's text, and I have put in quotation marks the quote he gives from the *Nareśvaravivekaḥ*.

58. Bansat-Boudon, *Paramārthasāra*, 360: akhaṇḍacamatkāra. See Bansat-Boudon's helpful translation for this passage, in Bansat-Boudon, 90. This is the deity Śiva in this passage, but the goddess as well, as we see below. Similarly, in the passage from Yogarāja given above, n. 56, wonder, which is pure subjectivity, is the essence of the multiplicity of subjects and objects that make up the world, in Bansat-Boudon, 358: "viśvasya pramātṛprameyarūpasya parāhantācamatkārasāra." See also p. 71 for this idea of the plurality of the world contained in subjectivity which is wonder.
59. Curiously, this also recalls Carol Walker Bynum's remark that wonder for medieval Europe was associated with diversity, in Bynum, "Presidential Address: Wonder," 7.
60. This ties into Abhinavagupta's dual-aspect monism, which we look at in greater detail in Chapter Four on *vimarśa*. This dual-aspect monism comprises *vimarśa*, which entails sentience, and *prakāśa*, quite literally, the light of consciousness, which winds up on the side of objects. The logic, I think, follows the idea that it is light that allows objects to appear in space. For this dual-aspect monism, Abhinavagupta tells us that "'Intellect' arises from the portion of *prakāśa*, the expanse of light. In contrast, "*paśyantī*," "the level of speech when it is just beginning to blossom," arises from the portion of *vimarśa*... the process whereby "This-ness" becomes distinct is shown to belong to *prakāśa*, where the material thing becomes distinct" in Abhinavagupta, *Ipvv*, 1985, 3:284: "'Buddhiḥ' iti prakāśabhāgena, "paśyantī" iti vimarśāśena... pūrvakasya eva arthasya idaṃ sphuṭīkaraṇam." Again, I put in quotation marks words that Abhinavagupta takes from Utpaladeva's text. Objects themselves partake of consciousness; however, it is hidden because the capacity for awareness is inwardly focused, in a particular state designated by the category (*tattva*) *Sadāśiva*, as we saw in Chapter One.
61. Note the repeated use of the word "unbroken" (*akhaṇḍa*, *akhaṇḍita*) above and in this passage. I suggest that this points to the phenomenology of wonder—as an experience where the mind stops and does not follow its habitual flitting back and forth on different topics.
62. Torella, *Īśvarapratyabhijñākārikā of Utpaladeva with the Author's Vṛtti: Critical Edition and Annotated Translation*, 73: "Ekaḥ prathamopādeyaturyadaśāyām akhaṇḍitagrāhakākhaṇḍ itagrāhyatan melanācamatkāropabṛmhitaḥ sādhāraṇa eva sarvaprāṇināmātmā viśvarūpo maheśvaraḥ." My translation differs only slightly from Torella's translation and draws from his excellent work, on p. 210. John Nemec also points to the importance of this passage in John Nemec, *Ubiquitous Śiva: Somānanda's Śivadṛṣṭi and His Tantric Interlocutors* (New York: Oxford University Press, 2011), 142 n.323.
63. This is framed theologically for this tradition, though the impetus is perhaps adaptable to a current atheism insofar as it entails a subjectivity at base, as I discuss in Chapter One. Here we see that *Śiva*, "the Self of everything," is one's own state of wonder, which expands outward to make the diversity in the world around us, in Bansat-Boudon, *Paramārthasāra*, 71. Similarly, Abhinavagupta's grand-teacher, Utpaladeva, glossing the *Śiva Dṛṣṭi* of Somānanda, tells us that the expansion of the universe arises from joy that is wonder (*camatkāra*), in Nemec, *Ubiquitous Śiva: Somānanda's Śivadṛṣṭi and His Tantric Interlocutors.*, 114. Indeed, the opening verse of Utpaladeva's commentary praises the god Śiva as the one who generates wondrous (*adbhuta*) things and who creates the universe on his own body in Nemec, 99. Note that *adbhuta* does not function as an almost technical

term in the way that *camatkāra* does. However, Abhinavagupta's disciple Kṣemarāja links the two on a conceptual level in Utpaladeva and Kṣemarāja, *Śivastotrāvalī*, ed. Rai Pramadasa Mitra Bahadur (Benares: Chowkhamba Sanskrit Series, 1902), 8: "paramānan davyāptidāyitvātsamastaviṣayāsvādo jagadānandacamatkāraḥ." ("That one [*Śiva*] possesses the taste (*āsvada*) of the entire collection of objects, due to the capacity to pervade all things with supreme bliss, joy, which is wonder, that is the bliss of the world.")

64. So Abhinavagupta tells us explicitly: "The 'I' which is the nature of pure awareness constantly pervading the whole [is capable of] manifesting with duality," in Abhinavagupta, *Ipvv*, 1985, 3:321: "nityavyāpakabodhamātrarūpo hi ahaṃ bhedena nirbhāse."
65. Abhinavagupta, 3:252: "sarvatra hi camatkāra eva icchā."
66. Abhinavagupta, 3:252: "camatkāritā hi bhuñjānarūpatā svātmaviśrāntilakṣaṇā sarvatra icchā."
67. This is a good part of the argument that Mary Jane Rubenstein makes for wonder in the West, in Rubenstein, *Strange Wonder*, 60, 145.
68. John Nemec points to what we might see as a precursor in Somānanda; however Somānanda connects will to the mind. Nemec translates Somānanda: "Perception would not arise for someone who has no will, i.e., for one who is devoid of intentions, because he would not be guided by the mind. Will is nothing but cognition imbued with one's intentions." See Nemec, "Evidence for Somānanda's Pantheism," 108 n.34.
69. *Ipvv*, vol. 3, p. 260: "Nirmātṛpade" iti. Māyīyānāṃ kīṭāntānāṃ svakāryakaraṇāvasare yat kāryaṃ purā hṛdaye sphurati.
70. Sthaneshwar Timalsina, "Self, Causation and Agency in the Advaita of Śaṅkara," in eds. M. Dasti and E. Bryant, *Free Will, Agency, and Selfhood in Indian Philosophy* (New York: Oxford University Press, 2013), 197. Note also Timalsina's own understanding of consciousness in his poem "Samvit prastara": "caitanyam bhāti viśvātmā mānākāro dvyāśritaḥ," "consciousness shines as the self of all, conceived as a multitude of forms resting on duality" (personal correspondence with the author).
71. Lynne Rudder Baker, *Naturalism and The First-Person Perspective*, 62. Thomas Nagel makes the same point, in Thomas Nagel, *Mind and Cosmos: Why the Materialist Neo-Darwinian Conception of Nature Is Almost Certainly False* (New York: Oxford University Press, 2012), 14.
72. In any case, however, Dennett's scientific eliminative reductionism—which at times has been compared to some forms of Buddhism in its critique of a conception of self—his eliminative attempts to exorcise the demon of a self has not entirely silenced his critics. The phenomenologist Zahavi convincingly argues against Dennett's view, in Dan Zahavi, *Subjectivity and Selfhood: Investigating the First Person Perspective* (Boston: MIT, 2008), pp. 110–12.
73. Baker, *Naturalism and The First-Person Perspective*, 120. Dan Arnold, *Brains, Buddhas and Believing: The Problem of Intentionality in Classical Buddhist and Cognitive-Scientific Philosophy of Mind* (New York: Columbia University Press, 2014), 77. Lynne Rudder Baker notes that Dennett's view only appears to avoid the problem of consciousness, particularly in relation to the first-person. She notes, "Any view that takes persons' persistence conditions to be biological, physical, or somatic leaves out—must leave out—what is distinctive about persons, the robust first-person perspective," in Lynne Rudder Baker, *Naturalism and the First-Person Perspective* (New York: Oxford University Press, 2013), 148.

74. Abhinavagupta, *Tantrasāra*, vol. 17, Kashmir Series of Texts and Studies (Srinagar, Kashmir: Research Department Jammu and Kashmir State in Muktabodha Digital Library, 1918), 1.4: http://muktalib5.org/DL_CATALOG/DL_CATALOG_USER_INTERFACE/dl_user_interface_create_utf8_text.php?hk_file_url=..%2FTEXTS%2FETEXTS%2FtantrasaaraHK.txt&miri_catalog_number=M00153. "And, of that [form of Śiva] freedom (svātantryam) is the power of bliss, wonder is the power of will, the form of visible manifestation is the power of consciousness, the nature of comprehensive awareness is the power of knowledge and the capacity to do everything is the power of action. Thus, these are in this way the primary powers." "tasya ca svātantryam ānandaśaktiḥ taccamatkāra icchāśaktiḥ prakāśarūpatā cicchaktiḥ āmarśātmakatā jñānaśaktiḥ sarvākārayogitvaṃ kriyāśaktiḥ ity evaṃ mukhyābhiḥ śaktibhiḥ."
75. We look at this in greater detail in Chapter Four on *vimarśa*, which addresses how Abhinavagupta links mind and consciousness to matter.
76. Abhinavagupta, *Tantrasāra*, 17:8.69–8.70: "ata eva kāra ity anena kṛtakatvam asya uktaṃ sāṃkhyasya tu tat na yujyate sa hi na ātmano 'haṃvimarśamayatām icchati vayaṃ tu kartṛtvam api tasya icchāmaḥ // tac ca śuddhaṃ vimarśa eva apratiyogi svātmacamatkārarūpo 'ham iti."
77. Here Abhinavagupta refers to a class of very advanced beings called *vijñānākalās*, beings who possess knowledge but lack the power and freedom to act. They are free from having to experience the results of deeds because they are not connected with the attachment, aversion, etc., in Abhinavagupta; see *Ipvv*, 1985, 3:318. However, he also tells us that without the wonder that signals a capacity to do things, they are no better off than something that is nonexistent, "Even existing with this state where knower and object are not separated, that [kind of state] is not any different from being in a state of non-existence, because one's awareness (*vimarśa*)—which is really essentially the breath-taking wonder connected with the "I"—this awareness is obscured," in Abhinavagupta, 3:314: "apṛthagbhāvena bhavad api aham iti camatkārātmano vimarśasya tirodhānād asato na viśiṣyate." Abhinavagupta's critique here is not so dissimiliar to Jonardon Ganeri's critique of Cartesianism: that the problem with Cartesianism is not the mind-body connection but rather how Cartesian minds could be causes at all. See Jonardon Ganeri, *Self: Naturalism, Consciousness, and the First-Person Stance* (New York: Oxford University Press, 2015), 314–15.
78. Abhinavagupta, *Ipvv*, 1985, 3:319: "Ye saṃvinmātraparamārthā api aham iti svātmaviśrāntilakṣaṇa-svātantryaparamārthānandacamatkāratirodhānayogāt na uttamāḥ kartāraḥ."
79. This is precisely the critique Abhinavagupta gives of Advaita Vedanta-type models, which he tells us approximate a doctrine of a quiescent Śiva. They lack any capacity for transformation on the highest level because there is no activity of will or desire (*icchā*) in Abhinavagupta, 3:251: "parimāṇaśūnye paradaśāyāṃ nāsti icchāvyavahāra iti śāntaśivādipravādābhiprāyeṇa."
80. He tells us, "It can not be proved that the relation of cause and effect is grounded within what lacks sentience. But rather the relation of cause and effect lies only with that which is conscious": "jaḍe pratiṣṭhitaḥ kārya kāraṇa bhāvo na upapadyate, api tu cidrūpa eva," in Abhinavagupta, 3:257. This is, in fact, one of the primary points Utpaladeva makes throughout in the previous *Kriyādhikāra* section on action in the *Īśvarapratyabhijñākāri kā*. Cause and effect cannot be located within objects. In Abhinavagupta's system, intentionality is understood as solely the provenance of consciousness and sentiency, that is, being alive (*ajaḍa*) is what enables effects in the material world. This viewpoint is somewhat

akin to Lynne Rudder Baker's argument that intentions are not only causally necessary for artifacts like life preservers and fluorescent light bulbs; they are also ontologically necessary. She notes that if somehow, improbably, a light bulb coalesced in space, it would actually not be a light bulb; the intention of someone making the light bulb for a reason is part of the ontological existence of the light bulb, in Baker, *Naturalism and the First-Person Perspective*, 198.

81. I discuss this matter in greater detail in Loriliai Biernacki, "Material Subjects, Immaterial Bodies: Abhinavagupta's Panentheist Matter," in *Entangled Worlds: Religion, Science and the New Materialisms*, ed. Catherine Keller and Mary-Jane Rubenstein (New York: Fordham University Press, 2017), 182–202.
82. Elsewhere I have written about this strategy of linking materiality to consciousness in contemporary panpsychism, comparing Abhinavagupta's model to Giulio Tononi's integrated information theory 3.0 in Loriliai Biernacki, "Connecting Consciousness to Physical Causality: Abhinavagupta's Phenomenology of Subjectivity and Tononi's Integrated Information Theory," *Religions* 7 (2016), https://doi.org/10.3390/rel7070087. We explore this matter in more detail in Chapter Four, addressing the concept of *vimarśa*, active awareness.
83. Abhinavagupta links our ordinary subjectivity to that of the foundational subjectivity, which is Śiva, saying, "the category (*tattva*) which is the *Māyā*-bound Subject also is at base just the category that is *Śiva*. By a two-fold method, by analogy and through being coessential, because of its universality and because of its having one single form ultimately, the [*Māyā*-bound subject and the knowing subjectivity of the Lord] rest in the one category. . . . With the word "etc.," [he indicates] the collection of bodies and jars and so on to be manifested by the *Māyā*-bound knowing subject. The words "belonging to the self" in the *Vṛtti* refer to the categories (*tattvas*) and worlds etc. [They belong to the self] because they are [essentially] not different from the knowing subject, which has been pointed out." In Abhinavagupta, *Ipvv*, 1985, 3:258: "tathāpi māyāpramātṛtattvaṃ śivatattva eva prakāradvayena sāmānyāt tad ekarūpatvāc cety. . . . Ādipadena ca māyāpramātravabhāsanīyaghaṭa-śarīrādisaṃgrahaḥ. 'Ātmanaḥ' iti vṛttau tattvabhuvanādayo >rthāḥ pramātravyatiriktatvāt yato nirdiṣṭāḥ."
84. This resembles the type of cosmopsychism we find in a thinker like Philip Goff. See Philip Goff, *Consciousness and Fundamental Reality* (New York: Oxford University Press, 2017).
85. Earlier in this extended passage he tells us that "wonder is said to be the supreme joy" using this same word for joy, *nirvṛti*, in Abhinavagupta, *Ipvv*, 1985, 2:179: "parāmarśaḥ paramānando nirvṛtiścamatkāra ucyate."
86. Abhinavagupta, 2:181: "evaṃ pāramārthikamahamiti prakāśasya vimarśātmakaṃ nirvṛtirūpaṃ vapuḥ | tacca yatra āropyate, tadapi nirvṛtimayameva bhāti śarīraprāṇādi | tadāha ahamityapi iti." This passage continues, asking why it is that if subjectivity is simply joy, a person might experience suffering. As Abhinavagupta suggests, even in suffering there is a capacity for joy, which shines beneath even suffering. Isabelle Ratie thoughtfully addresses this latter passage in Ratie, "Remarks on Compassion and Altruism in the Pratyabhijñā Philosophy," 359–60.
87. Abhinavagupta, *Parātriṃśikāvivaraṇa*, In Goettingen Register of Electronic Texts in Indian Languages. URL: http://gretil.sub.uni-goettingen.de/gretil/1_sanskr/6_sastra/3_phil/saiva/partrvpu.htm, p. 204: "prakāśasya hi svābhāvikākṛtrimaparavāṅmantravīryacamat kārātma aham iti / yathoktam prakāśasyātmaviśrāntir ahaṃbhāvo hi kīrtitaḥ iti / tad eva guhyam atirahasyam."

88. Abhinavagupta tells us, "The Energy of Consciousness is in fact all forms, the entire universe and She touches nothing beyond Herself." Consciousness (*citi*) makes manifest a wonder by the force of manifesting that which is extremely difficult. Abhinavagupta summarizes this with the words, [God] "who in fact" "partakes of 'This-ness,'" in Abhinavagupta, *Ipvv*, 1985, 3:272: "citiśaktir viśvarūpā bhavati na cādhikyaṃ spṛśati" iti sambandhaḥ. Cetanā atidurghaṭakāritvādinā adbhutatāṃ vyanakti. Etat saṃkṣipya ghaṭayati "yo hi" iti "idantābhāk" iti.
89. Abhinavagupta, *Ipvv*, 1985, 2:179: "yato vimarśa eva camatkāraḥ, sa evaca ajāḍyaṃ." We address *vimarśa* in Chapter Four.
90. In the context of his nondualist cosmopsychism, which understands everything as a refraction of a foundational subjectivity that is Śiva, he takes pains to make clear that his discourse operates as well on our ordinary understanding of differences, telling us, "what is intended here is the ordinary form of all knowing Subjects in the world, comprising the specific activity of the hands and feet, etc., of the agent, because this idea is generally accepted in the world," in Abhinavagupta, *Ipvv*, 1985, 3:258: "laukika sarva pramātṛ sādhāraṇa rūpa saṃpādakakara caraṇādi vyāpāra viśeṣa paryantībhūtam eva abhipretaṃ tathā laukikānāṃ prasiddheḥ."
91. I address this possibility in Chapter Four on *vimarśa*.
92. In addition to the examples I gave in the previous chapter, a couple more to illustrate the point include: 1) Abhinavagupta, *Iśvara Pratyabhijñā Vivṛti Vimarśinī*, ed. Paṇḍit Madhusudan Kaul Śāstrī, reprint, vol. 1 (Delhi: Akay Reprints, 1985), 8, https://archive.org/details/IshvaraPratyabhijnaVivritiVimarshiniAbhinavaguptaPart1KashmirSanskrit/mode/2up. "pūrṇāhambhāvasya vā yā camatkārāpattiḥ" "the attainment of wonder which is the state of full subjectivity" and 2) Abhinavagupta, *Ipvv*, 1985, 2:181: "ahamitica matkārādhyāsaṃ" "placing wonder, which is the 'I';" also, 3).

    Abhinavagupta, *Ipvv* 2:435: "ahamiticamatkārātmanā," "with the essence of wonder, which is the 'I.'" These are a few examples of Abhinavagupta's linkage of wonder with the "I," but not exhaustive.
93. Nagel, *View from Nowhere*.
94. Jayaratha, in his 12th-century commentary on Abhinavagupta's *Tantrāloka* (Light on Tantra), gestures toward the experiential component of this expansive subjectivity, explaining subjectivity as "shining abundantly in everything, as the dense wonder of supreme joy which takes on simply the form of one's own experience," "etat svānubhūtimātra-rūpaparānandacamatkāraghanatvena sarvātiśāyi bhāsate." In Abhinavagupta and Jayaratha. *Tantrālokaviveka*, 2:31. Srinagar: Kashmir Series of Texts and Studies volumes 23, 28, 30, 36, 35, 29, 41, 47, 59, 52, 57 and 58. Digitally accessed in Muktabodha Indological Research Institute. URL: http://muktalib5.org/DL_CATALOG/DL_CATALOG_USER_INTERFACE/dl_user_interface_create_utf8_text.php?hk_file_url=..%2FTEXTS%2FETEXTS%2FTantraloka-1-14-HK.txt&miri_catalog_number=M00092. Accessed on December 1, 2018.
95. Even as we see subjectivity to a singular cosmopsychism, it still manifests in a multiplicity of agents with different goals. As Abhinavagupta tells us, "In terms of agency, which in reality everywhere belongs to *Śiva* alone, because of the ego which arises out of what is made by *icchā*/will of that, agency is ascribed to others also," in Abhinavagupta, *Ipvv*, 1985, 3:261: "Sarvatra ca vastutaḥ śivasyaiva kartṛtve >pi tadicchākṛtād abhimānato >nyasya kartṛtvam ucyate."

96. Īśvara Pratyabhijñā Vivṛti Vimarśinī, vol. 3, p. 251: "camatkāro hi iti svātmani ananyāpekṣe viśramaṇam." This is part of the passage I quoted earlier. In note 32, I give the whole of this passage.
97. Abhinavagupta, *Tantrasāra*, vol. 17, Kashmir Series of Texts and Studies (Srinagar, Kashmir: Research Department Jammu and Kashmir State in Muktabodha Digital Library, 1918), 8.68–8.70: "ahaṃkāro yena buddhipratibimbite vedyasamparke kaluṣe puṃprakāśe anātmani ātmābhimānaḥ śuktau rajatābhimānavat // ata eva kāra ity anena kṛtakatvam asya uktaṃ . . . tac ca śuddhaṃ vimarśa eva apratiyogi svātmacamatkārarūpo 'ham iti." http://muktalib5.org/DL_CATALOG/DL_CATALOG_USER_INTERFACE/dl_user_interface_create_utf8_text.php?hk_file_url=..%2FTEXTS%2FETEXTS%2FtantrasaaraHK.txt&miri_catalog_number=M00153.
98. Nagel, *Mind and Cosmos*, 91.
99. Nagel, 91.
100. The issue particularly focuses on the question of how to bring in something new without some external teleology to kickstart some new element into the system. As Harvey Alper points out, wonder for Abhinavagupta also points to the possibility of something new, for an immanent self to bring in some new thing, surprising itself, in Harvey Alper, "Judgement as a Transcendental Category in Utpaladeva's Śaiva Theology, The Evidence of the Pratyabhijñākārikāvṛtti," *Adyar Library Bulletin* 51 (1987): 201. Sthaneshwar Timalsina also suggests that we can connect *camatkāra*, the idea of wonder, as linked to a kind of emergentism, though hedging his bets he notes, "It is in finding *camatkāra* that a new property emerges that makes savoring possible. And by 'emergence' I only mean 'manifestation' (*abhivyakti*) of the properties that were not visible in the causal categories; there is no implication that I am committed to any specific causal account comparable to those in contemporary physicalisms." In Timalsina, "Savoring Rasa: Emotion, Judgement, and Phenomenal Content," 259. In any case, Abhinavagupta can by no means be understood to support anything like the emergentism that a New Materialist thinker like Connolly proposes. As David Lawrence points out, Abhinavagupta says the "new" just means what was already in the secret texts and concealed, in David Lawrence, *Rediscovering God with Transcendental Argument: A Contemporary Interpretation of Monistic Kashmiri Śaiva Philosophy* (Rochester: State University of New York Press, 1999), 43. This goes against the idea of "new" as evolutionary emergence. On the other hand, Indian conceptions of transformation, *pariṇāma*, not an absolute change, but a transformation of latent elements, do resonate with Connolly's idea of preadaptive tendencies, in William Connolly, *World of Becoming* (Durham, NC: Duke University Press, 2011), 19. Jonardon Ganeri discusses the idea of Emergentism within Indian traditions in Jonardon Ganeri, "Emergentisms: Ancient and Modern," *Mind*, 2011. https://doi.org/10.1093/mind/fzr038.
101. Connolly, *World of Becoming*, 37–39. Also see William Connolly, "Materialities of Experience," in *New Materialisms: Ontology, Agency and Politics* (Durham, NC: Duke University Press, 2010), 178–200.
102. I suspect this in part centers around the slippage between a nondualism and the problems of theodicy. We also find the term *līlā* used as well, both translated as play, with *līlā* connoting a sense of amorousness as well.
103. Nemec, *Ubiquitous Śiva: Somānanda's Śivadṛṣṭi and His Tantric Interlocutors.*, 137–38.
104. Abhinavagupta, *Ipvv*, 1985, 3:393.

105. Nemec, *Ubiquitous Śiva: Somānanda's Śivadṛṣṭi and His Tantric Interlocutors*, 138.
106. Abhinavagupta, *Ipvv*, 1985, 3:251: camaditi vā āntaraspandāndolanoditaparāmarśamayaśabdanāvyaktānukaraṇam. I give this passage in full, earlier in note 32.
107. See Catherine Keller, *Intercarnations: Exercises in Theological Possibility* (New York: Fordham University Press, 2017).
108. These include (1) *prāṇa*, the outgoing breath, (2) *apāna*, the downgoing, in-breath, (3) *samāna*, the equalizing breath, (4) *udāna*, the up-breath, and (5) *vyāna*, the breath that pervades everywhere. Note that Abhinavagupta's schematic differs in an important way from most discussions in yoga in that the *prāṇa* is translated as the in-breath and *apāna* is translated as the outbreath in almost all contemporary discourses on yoga; in any case, the scheme of five breaths is quite old.
109. Here is the passage: "In this way the *prāṇa* situated in the heart [i.e. the *prāṇa* called *samāna*] rests in the middle channel [the Suṣumna], having attained an equilibrium. Then when it quits flowing in the channels on the sides [the *iḍa* and *piṅgala*], it, by that action, then flows upward by the path of the hollow reed [the *suṣumna* channel]. Then due to this upward flow in the central path becoming stabilized, it is called the *udāna*. And that [*udāna*] has the nature of fire, burning up division, duality. Consequently, it is the basis of the Fourth state." In Abhinavagupta, *Ipvv*, 1985, 3:349: "Prāṇa eva hṛdayabhuvi madhyasthāne viśrāntaḥ samānatāṃ pratipadya yadā pārśvapravāhavicchedāt tena eva ūrdhvaṃ suṣiramārgeṇa pravahati, tadā ūrdhvamā smantādanitīti udānaḥ. Sa ca bhedaṃ dahann agnikalpaḥ. Tata eva sa turyabhūmau."
110. Abhinavagupta, 3:348: "Aham ity ekarasena anuvedye tu yadā idantā ācchāditā bhavati bhāvanāsātmyādīśvara-sadāśivasaṃvidi iva turyadaśāyāṃ rasaviddhatāmrakanakanyāyena." Here *Sadāśiva* and *Īśvara* refer to the third and fourth archetypes, respectively, in descending order. These are also the names of deities, but Abhinavagupta tells us that these two states are not the gods referred to. Rather, they are just principles (*tattvas*): "this is a two-fold principle separate from the governing deities who have just the same name as these two Archetypes," in Abhinavagupta, 3:274: "Adhiṣṭhātṛdevatāvyatiriktam eva tatsanāmakam etat tattvadvayam." This type of transcendence also entails retention of an essential subject–object division.
111. Abhinavagupta, *Ipvv*, 1985, 3:349: sa eva tu samastaṃ dehavartitattvabhuvanādi yadā vyāpya ā samantādan iti, tadā paramaśivasvabhāvasturyātītarūpatayā paraḥ pūrṇo vyānaḥ iti.
112. Abhinavagupta links these five breaths as well to the Tantric-based practice involving awakening the kuṇḍalinī, a body-based energy conceived of as a goddess residing at the base of the spine, which then rises up the spine in a process that eventually gives magical powers and enlightenment. Again, we see the importance of the body. Abhinavagupta says, "In this way the *prāṇa* situated in the heart [i.e., the *prāṇa* called *samāna*] rests in the middle channel [the Suṣumna], having attained an equilibrium. Then when it quits flowing in the channels on the sides [the *iḍa* and *piṅgala*], it, by that action, then flows upward by the path of the hollow reed [the *suṣumna* channel]. Then due to this upward flow in the central path becoming stabilized, it is called the *udāna*, the upward breath," in Abhinavagupta, 3:349: "prāṇa eva hṛdayabhuvi madhyasthāne viśrāntaḥ samānatāṃ pratipadya yadā pārśvapravāhavicchedāt tena eva ūrdhvaṃ suṣiramārgeṇa pravahati, tadā ūrdhvamā samantādanitīti udānaḥ."
113. It seems to me rather interesting and, indeed, telling—and perhaps also not surprising—that a thinker like Connolly, articulating a New Materialism, also gestures toward a shift

to subjectivity. He relies on a Nietzschean philosophy, with its contours of subjectivity emphasized—albeit a softer, more Whiteheadian subjectivity—to articulate his theory of immanence capable of bringing in the new, in Connolly, *World of Becoming*, 30, and passim. While only implicit in Connolly, and somewhat oblique, still I suggest we can read in his appeal to immanence contours we find already in Abhinavagupta, specifically a shift to a subjectivity-oriented philosophy. Immanence, particularly of a materialist variety, has a hard time filling the shoes of transcendence, pulling the new in and offering something outside the confines of egoic identity. I suspect that Connolly leans on subjectivity intuitively, sensible of the links between transcendence and the third-person perspective. And curiously, when Connolly offers strategies for generating a mundane transcendence, the activities he recommends "start by meditating, or taking a walk in the woods, or reviewing a problem in clearing your mind of trivia before going to sleep," pointing to an idea of "reflexive intelligence," in Connolly, 75–76. These entail just the sort of engagement that we saw Abhinavagupta link to the self in a state of wonder: "the 'I' actively reflecting on its own self as the one who enjoys; this gives rise to wonder, which is the nature of unbroken sensory enjoyment," in Abhinavagupta, *Ipvv*, 1985, 2:175: "ananyāpekṣatā ca eṣaiva yat svātmīyavimarśe'hamiti bhoktṛtāmaye avicchinne bhuñjānatātmani camatkāre rūḍhiḥ."

114. Keeping a notion of time is key to any conception of immanence, as Connolly suggests as well, in Connolly, *World of Becoming*, 20–21.

115. I give this rich passage in full here, which begins with a quote from Somānanda's *Śivadṛṣṭi*: "When however the creation of the Lord happens, delight spreads open in a glorious consciousness, resulting in a variety of effects in a multi-colored design, then there exists the mind-stuff poised, just about to [act]. That intent of the will is the first instant of time" (*Śivadṛṣṭi* 1/7–1/8). Even the highest Reality, *Śiva*, the energy of bliss—which is that form where unfolding is just about to happen—that energy of bliss has priority, that is, primacy and prior existence with regard to the energy of will, [i.e., there *is* sequence here as well]. The word "*tuṭi*" is explained as a unit of time. Otherwise, in the absence of sequence, how could there be states of priority and posterity? However, with reference to those who are to be instructed and to those limited souls who are completely within [the grip of *Māyā*]. There [the notion of a lack of sequence] is appropriate. [This section goes against those who want to put the absolute completely beyond the reach of time. Abhinava says this is acceptable as a teaching for bound souls, but it is not the truth]. You may protest that it says here in this verse that limited souls which are created have sequence; [since they exist within time], but the *Śiva* archetype does not. In reply he says "because of the universality of the Subject. [I.e., the Subject, who resides in the limited *Māyā*-bound individual is the same as the Subject which is *Śiva*, so if the limited Subject can manifest sequence, surely the *Śiva* Archetype has the capacity to also contain sequence]. There also, in fact, the presence of sequence is proved. So [the text] says "that, in this way." Alternatively, he says, "Or perhaps" these souls, these *Māyā*-bound souls do not at all [have sequence either] here viewing them from the perspective of the ultimate reality." In Abhinavagupta, *Ipvv*, 1985, 3:263: "yadā tu tasya ciddharmavibhavāmodajṛmbhayā |vicitraracanānānākāryasṛṣ ṭipravartane || bhavaty unmukhatā cittā secchāyāḥ prathamā tuṭiḥ | (2/8) iti. paramaśive >pi bhagavati Aunmukhyarūpāyā ānandaśakterīcchāśakty apekṣayā prathamatvaṃ pūrvabhāvitvaṃ, tuṭir iti kālāṃśarūpatvaṃ tad upapadyate; anyathā kramābhāve kathaṃ pūrvāparībhāvavyavahāraḥ, kintu, upadeśyāpekṣayā antargatamāyīyapramātrapekṣayā ca yukto >sāv iti. Nanu atra sūtre kramavanto māyāpramātāraḥ sṛṣṭāḥ, na tu śivatattvam. Āha 'pramātṛsāmānyāt' iti. Tatrāpi hi upapāditā kramasthitiḥ. Ata eva uktaṃ 'tad evam'

iti. Te vā na kecid iti vāstavaṃ pakṣamāha 'athavā' iti. ||" We might note his alternative as well—if the divine itself is free of time, then we might suggest that viewed from this perspective ordinary beings are as well.

116. George Dreyfus, "Self and Subjectivity: A Middle Way Approach" (New York: Oxford University Press, 2013), 135.
117. Elizabeth Krohn and Jeffrey Kripal, *Changed in a Flash: One Woman's Near-Death Experience and Whay a Scholar Thinks It Empowers Us All* (Berkeley, CA: North Atlantic Books, 2018), 193.
118. See note 109 above for the full passage and its translation.
119. Krohn and Kripal, *Changed in a Flash*.
120. This fullness of subjectivity is the principle or category of Śiva, the Śiva *tattva* in Abhinavagupta, *Ipvv*, 1985, 3:257: "śivatattvaṃ hi sarva padārthānām vapuḥ."
121. In this way, fate is never entirely determined, but only partially, by the web of sheaths that usually overlay our awareness, including, time, a limited sense of knowledge, limited capacity to do, desire, and fate (*niyati*). By accessing this inner subjectivity, we can be not constrained by these layers of time, desire, limited knowledge, and fate. This means a freedom to change destiny is somewhat accessible, to the extent we can embrace a stance of subjectivity. In keeping with Kripal's model, I would conjecture, this is why a person like Elizabeth Krohn sometimes gets it right and sometimes not. However, this is not to say that Kripal's notion of the human as two, like the two birds in the tree in the *Maṇḍukya Upaniṣad* 3.1.1, one part of us embedded here in our world of change and the other above untouched—this is not to say that this still does not operate. I suggest, rather, a different interpretation. We might interpret it instead as a subjectivity that can both recognize its fullness and be embedded in the world, the fifth state of consciousness, in place of a duality of transcendence and immanence.
122. Abhinavagupta tells us, " 'Or by his own independence'—accepting the idea that there is creation which is not dependent upon the creation of the Lord," in Abhinavagupta, *Ipvv*, 1985, 3:260: "Svātantryeṇa vā" iti īśvarasṛṣṭyanapekṣayā. Nirmāṇam iti samarthitam iti sambandhaḥ."
123. Baker, *Naturalism and the First-Person Perspective*, 140.
124. Baker, 162, 164.
125. Torella, 2002, 108. Somdev Vasudev also points this out, Siddhis article, p. 23, as does Isabelle Ratie. Here the argument is focused primarily on a Buddhist philosophical argument of whether one cognition can be the object of another cognition. However, its implications for the first-person perspective are salient.
126. Abhinavagupta says, "Here it's because the limited souls who are to be taught are associated with duality. And they partake of time and sequence." In Abhinavagupta, *Īśvara Pratyabhijñā Vivṛti Vimarśinī*, ed. Paṇḍit Madhusudan Kaul Śāstrī, vol. 3 (Delhi: Akay Reprints, 1985), 262: "Iha dvaitavanto māyīyāḥ pramātāra upadeśyāḥ, te ca kālakramabhājaḥ." And after all, a cosmopsychism, where everything is the subjectivity of divinity pretty much makes moot the whole notion of a god that can intervene in human affairs. This of course points to the paucity of our images of divinity; the notion of divinity itself may not be the fault line.
127. Bansat-Boudon, *Paramārthasāra*, 256. Abhinavagupta suggests this practice as well in his *Tantrasāra*, where he describes sprinkling the earth with the flavor of wonder (*kṛtvādhāradharāṃ camatkṛtirasaprokṣākṣaṇakṣālitām*) as the process of worshiping

the deity within the temple of one's own body (dehadevasadane), in Abhinavagupta, *Tantrasāra*, 17:20.14–20.15.

Chapter 3

1. My translation draws from and modifies Olivelle's translation (Patrick Olivelle, *Upaniṣads*. Translated by Patrick Olivelle. New York: Oxford University Press, 1996), 64.
2. Rodney Dietart, *Human Superorganism: How the Microbiome Is Revolutionizing the Pursuit of a Healthy Life* (New York: Dutton, Penguin Books, 2016), 24.
3. This chapter has been published as "Subtle Body: Rethinking the body's subjectivity through Abhinavagupta," in *Transformational Embodiment in Asian Religions: Subtle Bodies, Spatial Bodies*. ed. George Pati and Katherine Zubko (New York: Routledge Press, 2019), 108–27.
4. In Richard Dawkins, *River Out of Eden: A Darwinian View of Life* (New York: Basic Books, Reprint Edition, 1996), 95.
5. Rodney Dietart points to the genome project as a primary factor in upending this idea that we might be individuals marked off from others by the boundary of our skin, in Dietart, *Human Superorganism*, 26.
6. Kathleen McAuliffe, *This Is Your Brain on Parasites* (Boston: Mariner Books, Houghton Mifflin Harcourt, 2016), 57–82.
7. Emese Prandovsky, Elizabeth Gaskell, Heather Martin, J. P. Dubey, Joanne P. Webster, and Glenn McConkey. "The Neurotropic Parasite Toxoplasma Gondii Increases Dopamine Metabolism," *PLoS One*, 5, No. 9 (2011): e23866.
   Published online September 21, 2011. doi: 10.1371/journal.pone.0023866
8. McAuliffe, *This Is Your Brain on Parasites*, 63. Sapolsky notes 3–4 times more likely in his interview with Edge TV (R. Sapolsky n.d.).
9. McAuliffe, *This Is Your Brain on Parasites*, 75.
10. What I will not do here is articulate for this context of the subtle body the helpful and well-trod understanding of construction of a self through its engagement with an external social world. Much has been written about how identity, agency, and desires are enacted via the social world we inhabit, through advertising (I'm thinking of Pierre Bourdieu's work particularly, though much else is certainly available) through cultural expectations of gender (I think of Judith Butler here), and through our understandings of self in relation to others as a kind of interbeing with others (I think of Catherine Keller's brilliant work here). This understanding has also been followed in relation to ideas of the subtle body (I'm thinking of Gavin Flood's work, in Gavin Flood, *The Tantric Body: The Secret Tradition of Hindu Religion* (New York: I. B. Tauris 2006).
11. Rick Nevin, "How Lead Exposure Relates to Temporal Changes in IQ, Violent Crime, and Unwed Pregnancy," *Environmental Research* 83 (n.d.): 1–22.
12. Here Freud's monochromatic Darwinian deterministic drives as everything just the id is replaced by an expansive multiplicity.
13. See Fred Smith's excellent and expansive treatment of the various spirits that possess humans, for instance, p.194, in Frederick Smith, *Self Possessed: Deity and Spirit Possession in South Asian Literature and Civilization* (New York: Columbia University Press, 2006).
14. This, of course, is Richard Dawkins's provocative thesis in Richard Dawkins, *Selfish Gene* (London: Oxford University Press, 1976).

15. (Sapolsky, Stanford Lectures, lecture 25 2010) Stanford Lectures. Sapolsky addresses the problem of free will in Lecture 25, beginning 3:09 minutes, especially 5:34 minutes, 25:38 minutes. On this topic also see, (Sapolsky, Sapolsky on Free Will 2018), beginning 0:40 minutes.
16. See Alexis Sanderson's seminal article on this nomenclature: Alexis Sanderson, "Saivism and the Tantric Traditions," in *World's Religions*, ed. Stewart Sutherland, L. Houlden, P. Clarke, and F. Hardy (London: Routledge, 1988).Also, Gavin Flood points out that Tantric conceptions of the body rely on a notion of an emanationist cosmology which is implicitly and often explicitly pluralistic, in Flood, *Tantric Body*, 29.
17. See Geoffrey Samuel, "Subtle-Body Processes: towards a Non-reductionist Understanding," in *Religion and the Subtle Body in Asia and the West: Between Mind and Body*, ed. Geoffrey Samuel and Jay Johnston (New York: Routledge, 2013); Jay Johnston, "Subtle Subjects and Ethics: The Subtle Bodies of Post-Structuralist and Feminist Philosophy," in *Religion and the Subtle Body in Asia and the West: Between Mind and Body*, ed. Geoffrey Samuel and Jay Johnston (New York: Routledge, 2013), 239–48; and Dory Heilijgers-Seelen, *The System of Five Cakras in Kubjikamatatantra, 14–16* (Leiden: Brill, 1994).
18. What is known as the *antaḥkaraṇa*, in Ayon Maharaj, "Panentheistic Cosmopsychism: Swami Vivekananda's Sāṃkhya-Vedāntic Solution to the Hard Problem of Consciousness," in *Panentheism and Panpsychism: Philosophy of Religion Meets Philosophy of Mind*, ed. Ludwig Jaskolla, Godehard Brüntrup, and Benedikt Paul Göcke (Paderborn: Mentis Brill, 2019), 276.
19. Abhinavagupta, *Ipvv*, vol. 3, p. 257: "Tad eva ca sarvabhāvānām pāramārthikam vapuḥ." The "tad" here refers to the "tat" in the verse a few lines earlier on which Abhinavagupta comments, referencing "matur," "belonging to the subject." The subject Abhinavagupta refers to is conscious, since as Abhinavagupta notes immediately in his commentary that causality cannot be attributed to insentient objects, but only to consciousness and only to that which is sentient: "jaḍe pratiṣṭhitaḥ kārya kāraṇa bhāvo na upapadyate, api tu cidrūpa eva."
20. *Ipvv*, vol. 3, p. 257: "Tad bhitta pṛṣṭhe ca sarva bhāva citra nirbhāsa iti."
21. *Ipvv*, vol. 3, p. 257: "śivatattvaṃ hi sarva padārthānām vapuḥ."
22. Abhinavagupta, *Parātriṃśikāvivaraṇa*, downloaded from S. D. Vasudeva's Indology E-text webpage: http://homepage.mac.com/somadevah/etx/PaTriViv.txt, p. 212: "narātmāno jaḍā api tyaktatatpūrvarūpāḥ śāktaśaivarūpabhājo bhavanti, śṛṇuta grāvāṇaḥ" [cf. Mahābhāṣya 3.1.1 and Vākyapadīya 3 Puruṣasamuddeśa 2], "meruḥ śikhariṇām ahaṃ bhavāmi" [Bhagavadgītā 10.23].
23. We see this idea in the *Bṛhadaraṇyaka Upaniṣad* 4.4.4, in Patrick Olivelle, *Upaniṣads, Trans. from the Original Sanskrit* (New York: Oxford University Press, 1996). Here the dead person takes on a better body, that of a celestial being (*gandharva*, *pitṛ*), just as a goldsmith takes a piece of gold and molds it into a more beautiful shape. Here, like Abhinavagupta, however, we still keep an idea of the body.
24. *Ipvv*, vol. 3, p. 282: "Tena aham bhāvena ajñatā sarvathaiva tirodhīyate iti punar api nīlam idam iti na prarohet. Tatas tādṛgaparo >ham bhāvo >tra niṣektavyo yas tatra jñatāṃ nirmalatayātiraskartuṃ na śaktaḥ."
25. He tells us this in the specific context of discussing the subtle body *(puryaṣṭaka)*. Note that Torella points to Utpaladeva's conception of two types of self-awareness (*aham pratyavamarśa*), a pure one related to ascertainment of "I" as pure consciousness creating the field, and an impure one that relates the "I" to its manifestation as object, as subtle body

(puryaṣṭaka) as *prāṇa* or breath, and as the body *(deha)* in Raffaele Torella, *Īśvarapratyabhi jñākārikā of Utpaladeva with the Author's Vṛtti: Critical Edition and Annotated Translation* (Delhi: Motilal Banarsidass, 2002), 132, v.1.6.4.

26. See Wilhelm Halbfass's extensive discussion of karma in the context of transmigration, in *Tradition and Reflection: Explorations in Indian Thought* (New York: State University of New York Press, 1991), especially pp. 291–346.
27. Śaṅkara and Bṛhadaraṇyaka, *Bṛhadaraṇyaka Upaniṣad with Śaṅkara's commentary*, Kanva recension with the commentary ascribed to Śaṅkara, 2020, 4.4.2, http://gretil.sub.uni-goe ttingen.de/gret_utf.htm#BrhUp. "ekībhavati na paśyatīty āhuḥ |ekībhavati na jighratīty āhuḥ |ekībhavati na rasayatīty āhuḥ |ekībhavati na vadatīty āhuḥ |ekībhavati na śṛṇotīty āhuḥ |ekībhavati na manuta ity āhuḥ|ekībhavati na spṛśatīty āhuḥ |ekībhavati na vijānātīty āhuḥ." Following speech, he does not hear, does not think, does not touch, does not comprehend. See also Olivelle (*Upaniṣads*. p. 64), who translates this differently as "he is sinking," and S. Radhakrishnan, *The Principle Upaniṣads* (London: Unwin Human, 1989), p. 270, with whose translation of "ekībhavati" as "becoming one" I concur.
28. Śaṅkara and Bṛhadaraṇyaka, 4.4.2: "ekībhavati karaṇajātaṃ svena liṅgātmanā . . . tathā ghrāṇadevatānivṛttau ghrāṇamekībhavati liṅgātmanā tadā na jighratītyāhuḥ."
29. Śaṅkara and Bṛhadaraṇyaka, 4.4.3: "tad yathā tṛṇajalāyukā tṛṇasyāntaṃ gatvānyam ākramam ākramyātmānam upasaṃharati |evam evāyam ātmedaṃ śarīraṃ nihatyāvidyāṃ gamayitvānyam ākramam ākramyātmānam upasaṃharati."
30. Matthew Dasti and Stephen Phillips, *Nyāya Sutra: Selections with Early Commentaries*. Translated by Matthew Dasti and Stephen Phillips (Indianapolis: Hackett Publishing Co., 2017). 88.
31. Halbfass, *Tradition and Reflection*, 304; also Ashok Aklujkar, "Can the Grammarians "Dharma" Be a "Dharma" for All?" *Journal of Indian Philosophy* (Spring) 32 (2004): 705.
32. Smith, *Self Possessed*, 208.
33. Alex Watson, "The Self as a Dynamic Constant. Rāmakaṇṭha's Middle Ground Between a Naiyāyika Eternal Self-Substance and a Buddhist Stream of Consciousness-Moments." *Journal of Indian Philosophy* 42 (2014), 176.
34. Gerlad Larson, *Classical Sāṃkhya: An Interpretation of its History and Meaning* (Delhi: Motilal Banarsidass, 1969), 272.
35. Gopī Nātha Kavirāja, ed., *Tripurā Rahasya: Jñāna Khaṇḍa*, vol. 15 (Varanasi: Princess of Wales Saraswati Bhavana Texts, 1927), 12.72–96. See also the translation by Saraswathi, Swami Sri Ramanananda. *Tripura Rahasya or the Mystery Beyond the Trinity*. Translated by Swami Sri Ramanananda Saraswathi. Tiruvanamalai: Ramanamasramam, 2006, 104–6.
36. David White, *Sinister Yogis* (Chicago: University of Chicago Press, 2011), 153–56, also talks about this phenomenon of one person entering another person's body, where the yogi is capable of directing the entered body like a puppet.
37. Mādhava Vidyāraṇya, *Śaṅkaradigvijaya* (Śrīraṅgam: Śrīvaṇivilasamudranālayaḥ, 1972), 10.104b: "mahipasya varṣma guruyogabalo 'aviśadātivāhikaśarīrayutaḥ." See also Madhava-Vidyaranya, *Sankara-Dig-Vijaya: The Traditional Life of Sri Sankaracharya*, trans. Swami Tapasyananda (Madras: Ramakrishna, n.d.).
38. See a discussion of the process as described in the writings of the 20th-century Tantric thinker Gopinath Kaviraj in Loriliai Biernacki, "Transcendence in Sports: How Do We Interpret Mysticism in Sports? Tantra and Cognitive Science Perspectives." *Journal for the Study of Religious Experience*, 2018: 24–40. Interestingly, when I described this story of

Śaṅkara to my undergraduate students, they overwhelmingly felt that he had broken his vows of celibacy, even though he had sex in a different body.

39. James Hartzell. *Tantric Yoga* (Ann Arbor, MI: UMI Dissertation, 1997), p. 574, in Suśruta 3.1.16, also 569–70. Note that he contradicts Surendranath Dasgupta here, who says there is no connection.
40. Hartzell. *Tantric Yoga*, 559.
41. Hartzell, 573.
42. I cannot help but think of Jim Tucker's fascinating work on birthmarks as physical manifestations of experience that carry over from one life to the next. Thus, a person who died from a crushed limb in a previous life has that limb debilitated in their current life. See Jim Tucker and Ian Stevenson, *Life before Life: Children's Memories of Previous Lves* (London: St. Martin's Griffin, 2008).
43. Joseph Alter also notes that hatha yoga postulates a theory of the body where "even the most subtle sheath is constituted of matter." See "Sex, Askesis and the Athletic Perfection of the Soul: Physical Philosophy in the Ancient Mediterranean and South Asia," in *Religion and the Subtle Body in Asia and the West* (New York: Routledge, 2015), 138.
44. Fred Smith also points out that the Indian conception of self includes an idea of fluidity, divisibility and penetrability as features of personhood (Smith, *Self Possessed*, 37).
45. Never mind that ideas of the subtle suggest that it departs with death so that by the time the Swamiji recovered the corpse from the river, the subtle body with its *cakras* would have already departed on its journey to the next world.
46. Perhaps not so unlike Kumārila's *apūrva*.
47. Sanderson, "Sarvāstivāda and Its Critics," 38–39.
48. Antonio Damasio, *Self Comes to Mind: Constructing the Conscious Brain* (New York: Pantheon, 2010), 8.
49. Mark Siderits, "Buddhism and Techno-Physicalism: Is the Eightfold Path a Program?" *Philosophy East and West*. 51 (July 2001): 311. See also Dan Arnold's critique of the notion in *Brains, Buddhas, and Believing: The Problem of Intentionality in Classical Buddhist and Cognitive-Scientific Philosophy of Mind* (New York: Columbia University Press, 2014), 4, 246 n. 11.
50. Thomas Metzinger,"Why Are Out-of-Body Experiences Interesting for Philosophers? The Theoretical Relevance of OBE Research." *Cortex* 45 (2009): 257.
51. Metzinger, "Why Are Out-of-Body Experiences Interesting," 257.
52. Metzinger, 257.
53. See Sthaneshwar Timalsina's insightful understanding of the assimilation of two levels of reality within subjectivity of the self through a Kashmiri model, using Abhinavagupta's work on rasa theory to understand how an actor can occupy two-tiers of absolute and ordinary, both at the same time in "Theatrics of Emotion: Self-Deception and Self-Cultivation in Abhinavagupta's Aesthetics." *Philosophy East and West* 66, no. 1 (January 2016): 104–21.
54. Christian Coseru, "Freedom from Responsibility: Agent-Neutral Consequentialism and the Bodhisattva Ideal," in *Buddhist Perspectives on Free Will: Agentless Agency?*, ed. Rick Repetti (London: Routledge, 2016), *passim*, especially 102.
55. Samuel, "Subtle-body Processes," 251.
56. Johnston, Subtle Subjects and Ethics, 240
57. Abhinavagupta, *Ipvv*, vol. 3, 310: "śūnyapuryaṣṭakasaṃkucitasaṃvitsvabhāvaḥ, saṃsaraṇaśilaḥ."

58. Abhinavagupta, *Ipvv*, vol. 3, 286–87: "Rudrādes tulanam" ity ādau ca 'so >ham' iti tāvat saṃskārapūrṇa eva aham iti parāmarśāt garvakopādyudayā yuktāḥ. Svakṛtasaṃkocasaṃskāravatī yā cit, tanmayatayā pralīnam apasāritaśabdādirūpa viśeṣam ekam iti puryaṣṭakāntarāder bhinnam."
59. Taken from the *Iśa Upaniṣad*, verse 16 (Olivelle, *Upaniṣads*, pp. 80–81).
60. Abhinavagupta, *Ipvv*, vol. 3, pp. 335–36: "śūnyāhantām ākṣipya vartamānaḥ puryaṣṭakaḥ iti uktaḥ. . . . Yad āhuḥ 'līnaśūnyasamādhāvapyāste liṅgaśarīraḥ |' iti. 'Tathā ca' iti yata evaṃ, tata evaṃ yojanā sā śūnye 'hantā prāṇādiprerikā akṣavṛttirūpā puryaṣṭakātmiketi."
61. Abhinavagupta, *Ipvv*, vol. 3, p. 334: "Ubhayor api ca ayaṃ yonyantarasañcārī puryaṣṭakaśabdavācyo yato 'tra prāṇādipañcakam indriyavargau dvau niścayātmikā ca tṛtīyā svīkṛtāntaḥkaraṇāntarā dhīrvyajyate."
62. Abhinavagupta, *Ipvv*, vol. 3, p. 306: "puryaṣṭakātmatātyantasūkṣmadeha eva vā." In the text he is quoting Utpaladeva's commentary, and he links the subtle body here, as we saw earlier, to Emptiness.
63. Abhinavagupta, *Ipvv*, vol. 3, p. 306: "kālaviśeṣeṇa ca śarīrivat niyatena pārimityabhājā yo 'vacchedas tadrahitaḥ; sāmānyakālayogas tu tasya api asty eva. . . . Puryaṣṭakasya dehatā asty eva mahābhūtaiḥ samanvayād iti tad api iha na vacanīyam iti mohavyapohanāya śaṅkodbhāvanārthaṃ dehagrahaṇam."
64. Abhinavagupta, *Ipvv*, vol. 3, p. 307: "tayor astu prameyatā, tābhyāṃ tu anyat pramīyate ghaṭādi bāhyaśarīreṇa asamparke bhogasaṃpādakatvāyogāt." "Ata eva" iti yato 'nyat na pramīyate tābhyāṃ, tataḥ.
65. Abhinavagupta, *Ipvv*, vol. 3, p. 336: "Yatas tanmātrapañcakamantaḥkaraṇaṃ ceti kecana puryaṣṭakam āhuḥ sparśatanmātreṇa prāṇādisvīkārāt, tata eva atra pakṣavaicitrye vastuno na vaicitryam iti."
66. Quoting Utpaladeva, he tells us: "in the creation of objects the expansion and unfoldment of the objective world belongs to the prāṇa, while the dissolution of the world is a process belonging to the subject alone." Abhinavagupta, *Ipvv*, vol. 3, vol. 3, p. 344: "arthānāṃ sarge 'pi asau prāṇasya pravṛttiḥ pramātuḥ pralaya eva." Lakṣmanjoo also notes this reversal of function for *prāṇa* and *apāna*. This reversal is in keeping with Olivelle's translation of the *Upaniṣad*, where he also translates *prāṇa* as out-breath (p. 100).
67. Abhinavagupta, *Ipvv*, vol. 3, p. 337.
68. Abhinavagupta, *Ipvv*, vol. 3, pp. 335–36.
69. Abhinavagupta, *Ipvv*, vol. 3, p. 349.
70. Abhinavagupta, *Ipvv*, vol. 3, p. 309.
71. Dominic Wujastyk, "Interpreting the Image of the Human Body in Premodern India." *International Journal of Hindu Studies* 13, no. 2 (2009): 200.
72. Flood, *Tantric Body*, 13.
73. My translation of the well-known name for this portion of the text called *laghu nyāsa*.
74. Taittirīya, *Taittirīya Mantrakośaḥ: Prathamo Bhagaḥ*, ed. Ramakrishna Maṭh (Madras: Ramakrishna Math Printing Press, n.d.), 3.10.4–3.10.9: Agnir me vāci śritaḥ| Vāghṛdaye| Hṛdayaṃ mayi| Ahamamṛte| Amṛtaṃ brahmaṇi|| My translation of this basic formula which substitutes a different deity for each verse.
75. We also see hints of this above in Śaṅkara's depiction of the five sensory functions like smell collecting in the subtle body, even as Śaṅkara's adherence to his nondualism tends toward precluding a sensibility of various deities.

76. Gavin Flood points out that Tantric conceptions of the body rely on a notion of an emanationist cosmology, which is implicitily and often explicitly pluralistic. See Flood, *Tantric Body*, 29.
77. Alexis Sanderson suggests that this text is not actually authored by Abhinavagupta, since the mental worship of Ānandabhairava and his consort Ānandabhairavī surrounded by the eight mothers has no parallel in Abhinavagupta's other works, in Alexis Sanderson, "Śaiva Exegesis of Kashmir," in *Mélanges Tantriques a La Mémoire d'Helene Brunner/ Tantric Studies in Memory of Helene Brunner*, ed. Dominic Goodall and Andre Padoux, vol. 106, Collection Indoogie (Pondicherry, India: Institut Francais d'Indologie /Ecole Francaise d'Extreme-Orient, 2007), 381. I am grateful to John Nemec for pointing this reference out to me.
78. Abhinavagupta, *Dehasthadevata*, vs. 1. See also Flood, *Body and Cosmology in Kashmir Śaivism* (San Francisco: Mellen Research University Press, 1993), 305–8. My translation alters these two only slightly.
79. There is not an exact correspondence. The subtle body, for instance, is composed of the five breaths, whereas in this hymn, Abhinavagupta only mentions the *prāṇa* and *apāna* breaths.
80. See note 77 above.
81. Abhinavagupta, *Ipvv*, vol. 3, p. 309: "Tata eva brahmahṛdayo viṣṇukaṇṭho rudratālur Īśvarabhrūmadhyāḥ Sadāśivoudhvabrahmarandhro 'nāśritātmakaśaktisopānoparipad aḥ kāraṇaṣaṭkavigrahaḥ parameśvaraḥ iti hṛdayādisvarūpābhidhānena sūcita āgamiko 'rthaḥ.'"
82. Merlin Donald, *Mind So Rare: The Evolution of Human Consciousness* (New York: W. W. Norton & Company, 2002).
83. George Lakoff and Marc Johnson, *Philosophy in the Flesh* (New York: Basic Books, 1999).
84. Brian Massumi, "The Autonomy of Affect." *Cultural Critique*, no. 31 (1995): 83–109, https://doi.org/, no. 31 (1995): 10.2307/1354446.
85. Damasio, *Self Comes to Mind*, 37.
86. Patrick McNamara, *Neuroscience of Religious Experience* (New York: Cambridge University Press, 2014), 37.
87. Timothy Morton, *Hyperobjects: Philosophy and Ecology after the End of the World* (Minneapolis: University of Minnesota Press, 2013), 139.
88. Abhinavagupta, *Ipvv*, vol. 3, p. 281: "Nanu adarśanayogyaṃ puryaṣṭakādi prakāśamānatayā nāma saṃbhāvyatāṃ ghaṭādivadeva, tasya tu kim ahaṃ pratītyā adhikayā yena uktaṃ 'pratītau' iti. Āha 'tasyaiva' iti. 'Kevalam' iti iyadadhikamavaśyam aṅgīkāryam. Ahaṃ pratītyabhāve hi sa eva 'śuddhājñatvasahita' iti ātmatayāyo na dṛśyate bhāvavargo nīlādiḥ, sa naiva prakāśeta, prakāśate ca asau."
89. Abhinavagupta, *Ipvv*, vol. 3, p. 309: "pravibhajyātmanātmānaṃ sṛṣṭvā bhāvān pṛthag vidhān |sarveśvaraḥ sarvamayaḥ svapne bhoktā pravartate." Quote taken from Bhartṛhari's *Vākyapadīya* 1.140.

Chapter 4

1. In John Wheeler, "Not Consciousness but the Distinction between the Probe and the Probed as Central to the Elemental Quantum Act of Observation," in *Role of Consciousness in the Physical World*, ed. R.G. Jahn (Boulder, CO: Westview, 1981), 94.

2. Hawking told the BBC: "The development of full artificial intelligence could spell the end of the human race." URL: http://www.bbc.com/news/technology-30290540, accessed 4/15/17.
3. Daniel Fagella, *AI Future Outlook* (blog), November 28, 2018. https://emerj.com/ai-future-outlook/elon-musk-on-the-dangers-of-ai-a-catalogue-of-his-statements.
4. Nick Bostrom, *Superintelligence: Paths, Dangers, Strategies* (New York: Oxford University Press, 2014), 129.
5. Perhaps it is not surprising that a wing of Musk's SpaceX company is named after the infamous corporation Cyberdyne that develops Skynet, the human-killing AI in the *Terminator* movies.
6. Loriliai Biernacki, "Connecting Consciousness to Physical Causality: Abhinavagupta's Phenomenology of Subjectivity and Tononi's Integrated Information Theory," *Religions* 7 (2016). https://doi.org/10.3390/rel7070087.
7. Philip Goff's work on cosmopsychism offers similarities. See Philip Goff, "Cosmopsychism, Micropsychism, and the Grounding Relation," in *The Routledge Handbook of Panpsychism*, ed. William Seager (Leiden: Routledge, 2019). Also, perhaps even more similar to Abhinavagupta's model involving a dual-aspect of externalized physicality and internalized subjectivity is Itay Shani's cosmopsychism. This extends even to Shani's use of language like "appearance," Shani, 412, which also functions as a key idea for Abhinavagupta's concept of *bhāsa*, often translated as "appearance." On the notion of "appearance," see Isabelle Ratie, "The Dreamer and the Yogin: On the Relationship between Buddhist and Śaiva Idealisms," *Bulletin of the School of Oriental and African Studies* 73, no. 3 (October 2010): 465. Abhinavagupta's model also bears resemblance to Shaffer's priority monism in Jonathan Schaffer, "Monism: The Priority of the Whole," in *Spinoza on Monism* (London: Palgrave Macmillan, 2012), 9–50.
8. See David Lawrence's insightful and groundbreaking comparative study in David Lawrence, *Rediscovering God with Transcendental Argument: A Contemporary Interpretation of Monistic Kashmiri Śaiva Philosophy* (Rochester: State University of New York Press, 1999). Also see especially for the early categorization of Abhinavagupta's thought: K. C. Pandey, *Abhinavagupta: An Historical and Philosophical Study*, 2nd Enlarged Edition (Varanasi: Chowkhamba Sanskrit Series, 1963).
9. See Chakravarthi Ram-Prasad, *Indian Philosophy and Consequences of Knowledge: Themes in Ethics, Metaphysics and Soteriology* (Burlington, VT: Ashgate, 2007), 53–55.
10. Harald Atmanspacher, "20th Century Variants of Dual-Aspect Thinking," *Mind and Matter* 12, no. 2 (2014): 246. Atmanspacher points to Thomas Nagel, David Chalmers, Gilles Deleuze, and William James among many others.
11. Rosi Braidotti, *Posthuman* (Cambridge: Polity Press, 2013), 56. Jane Bennett also invokes Spinoza as part of her philosophical lineage, for instance, Jane Bennett, "Powers of the Hoard: Further Notes on Material Agency," ed. Jeffrey Cohen (New York: Punctum Books, 2012), 238. We see Spinoza as well, front and center, in Jane Bennett, *Vibrant Matter: A Political Ecology of Things* (Durham, NC: Duke University Press, 2010), x, passim.
12. As Douglas Duckworth points out, there are a variety of panpsychisms: a strong form, sometimes referred to as animistic panpsychism, which imputes some form of mentality to all matter, even electrons, and weaker forms, which amount to a unified structural monism, in Douglas Duckworth, "The Other Side of Realism: Panpsychism and Yogācāra," in *Buddhist Philosophy: A Comparative Approach*, ed. Steven Emmanuel (Hoboken, NJ: John

Wiley, 2018), 29–30. Abhinavagupta's panentheist monism readily approximates the weak version, and at times a case might be made toward a strong version.

13. Giulio Tononi, "Why Scott Should Stare at a Blank Wall and Reconsider (or, the Conscious Grid," *Shtetl-Optimized: The Blog of Scott Aaronson* (blog), accessed April 13, 2016. http://www.scottaaronson.com/blog/?p=1823.
14. Here Abhinavagupta's panentheism does operate as a cosmopsychism, in a model that approximates Goff's conception of a cosmopsychism. See Goff, "Cosmopsychism, Micropsychism, and the Grounding Relation."
15. Abhinavagupta, *Īśvara Pratyabhijñā Vivṛti Vimarśinī*, ed. Paṇḍit Madhusudan Kaul Śāstrī, vol. 3 (Delhi: Akay Reprints, 1985), 315: Nanu evaṃ ghate 'pi yadi cidrūpatām kaścit paśyet, tarhi kim abhrānta eva asau. Om ity āha "jaḍasya tu" iti "Yukta eva" iti ucita. We address this quote in greater detail in Chapter One and Chapter Five.
16. Abhinavagupta, 3:315: jaḍarūpatānyakkriyayā cidrūpatāprādhānyena āveśaḥ ā samantāt svarūpapraveśaḥ.
17. Christof Koch, "When Computers Surpass Us," *Scientific American Mind* 26, no. 5 (October 2015): 26–29.
18. Biernacki, "Connecting Consciousness to Physical Causality."
19. Philip Goff, *Consciousness and Fundamental Reality* (New York: Oxford University Press, 2017).
20. Goff.
21. K. C. Pandey, *Iśvara Pratyabhijñā of Utpaladeva with the Vimarśinī*, reprint edition, vol. 3 (Delhi: Butala and Company, 1984), 188. This is Pandey's translation of "tena maheśvara eva bhagavān viśvakartā," line 2260. This line concludes Abhinavagupta's description of God who becomes the universe of jars and so on, out of God's own freedom.
22. As I have suggested, Abhinavagupta's panentheism is probably close to Goff's idea of cosmopsychism, and while Abhinavagupta's system easily configures to Goff's cosmopsychism, still his theism retains the notion of *Śiva* (not to mention other deities as well) as supernatural agent, even if his panentheism can be construed, tinkered with minimally to avoid the problems Goff points to within dualist theistic systems.
23. Thomas Nagel, *Mind and Cosmos: Why the Materialist Neo-Darwinian Conception of Nature Is Almost Certainly False* (New York: Oxford University Press, 2012).
24. This indeed is behind the push toward a bottom-up emergentism in Tononi and Koch's IIT 3.0. See Masafumi Oizumi, Larissa Albantakis, and Giulio Tononi, "From the Phenomenology to the Mechanisms of Consciousness: Integrated Information Theory 3.0," *PLOS: Computational Biology*, May 8, 2014. http://journals.plos.org/ploscompbiol/article?id=10.1371/journal.pcbi.1003588. Abhinavagupta's panentheism as a cosmopsychism does certainly derive from above, from *Śiva*, yet his use of a first-person perspective that embeds consciousness all the way through undermines the idea of transcendence, as we saw in the discussion of transcendence in Chapter Two.
25. Mary-Jane Rubenstein, *Pantheologies: Gods, Worlds, Monsters* (New York: Columbia University Press, 2018).
26. Rubenstein, *Pantheologies*, 5.
27. Rubenstein, 6.
28. John Nemec, "Evidence for Somānanda's Pantheism," *Journal of Indian Philosophy* 42 (2014): 99–114.
29. Tononi is decidedly an emergentist; I discuss this in Chapter Five, note 7. Abhinavagupta, as Isabelle Ratie points out, is not. I agree with Ratie's perspective on this issue, even

as Sthaneshwar Timalsina proposes that we can find a type of emergentism within Abhinavagupta's thought. Keep in mind that Timalsina also rearticulates the concept of emergence so as to not entail a gulf between consciousness and matter. See Sthaneshwar Timalsina, "Aham, Subjectivity, and the Ego: Engaging the Philosophy of Abhinavagupta," *Journal of Indian Philosophy* 48, no. 4 (September 2020): 785. https://doi.org/10.1007/s10781-020-09439. See also a not yet published article, Sthaneshwar Timalsina, "Vimarśa: The Concept of Reflexivity in the Philosophy of Utpala and Abhinavagupta," *Acta Orientalia" Claus Peter Zoller and Hong Luo (Eds.)*, no. LXXX (Special Issue) Proceedings of "Sanskrit in China 2019: Sanskrit on Paths (forthcoming). See also Isabelle Ratie, "Śaiva Interpretation of the Satkāryavāda: The Sāṃkhya Notion of Abhivyakti and Its Transformation in the Pratyabhijñā Treatise," *Journal of Indian Philosophy*, no. 42 (March 2014): 171. See also Timothy O'Connor, "Emergent Properties," in *Stanford Encyclopedia of Philosophy* (Stanford University, August 10, 2020). https://plato.stanford.edu/entries/properties-emergent. Additionally, see Philip Clayton and Paul Davies, eds., *Re-Emergence of Emergence: The Emergentist Hypothesis from Science to Religion* (New York: Oxford University Press, 2008).

30. We can see this, for instance, in the 8th-century thinker Śaṅkara's understanding of the absolute as being-**consciousness**-bliss (*satcidānanda*).
31. Ram-Prasad's discussion of Śāntarakṣita via Buddhist Studies scholar Paul Williams' understanding of reflexivity gets at the typology that I discuss in Abhinavagupta; see Ram-Prasad, *Indian Philosophy*, 58.
32. There is much current philosophy of mind literature that parses out ideas of consciousness in terms of "access consciousness" in contrast to "phenomenal consciousness," as Chalmers and others have pointed out. For our present purposes, to place Abhinavagupta's idea in conversation with contemporary conceptions of neuroscience, we might understand *vimarśa* as pointing to something akin to access consciousness, while *cit* and *saṃvid* point to a broader sense of consciousness as a field of awareness, though not quite the phenomenal awareness that Chalmers or Dan Zahavi point to as being akin to the qualia of experience. See in particular Mark Siderits, Dan Zahavi, and Evan Thompson, eds., *Self, No Self?: Perspectives from Analytical, Phenomenological, and Indian Traditions* (New York: Oxford University Press, 2013).
33. Anil Seth, *Neuroscience of Consciousness with Anil Seth* (London: Royal Institute, 2017), 1:05. https://www.youtube.com/watch?v=xRel1JKOEbI.
34. John Searle, *Mystery of Consciousness* (New York: New York Review, 1997), 5.
35. Antonio Damasio, *Self Comes to Mind: Constructing the Conscious Brain* (New York: Pantheon, 2010), 8.
36. Gerald Edelman, *Wider than the Sky: The Phneomenal Gift of Consciousness* (New Haven, CT: Yale University Press, 2005), 4.
37. *Ipvv*, vol. 3, p. 338: "sādhāraṇyaṃ sthairyādyavabhāsāntarasaṃbhinne vimarśasthairyānuvṛtter jāgratpade bādhanāt vibhramarūpatā."
38. Abhinavagupta, *Ipvv*, 3:268: "idam ity asya vicchinnavimarśasya . . . |" (A. Pr. Si. 15). Here is the longer passage: Even in that state [of dissolution or deep sleep] in which knowable objects are retained, the withdrawal takes the form of dormant impressions floating in the inner organs [mind, intellect and ego] of the Subject caught in *Māyā*. That also, really, accurately, [is the state of "this," not the "I"]. The *Ajaḍa Pramātṛ Siddhi* says: 'In the state of "this" one's active awareness is discontinuous.' (*Ajaḍa Pramātṛ Siddhi* 15). Logically then, resting within the state of "I" [the awareness of the Lord] touches "I-this," which is the state of just only *Sadāśiva* alone. However, when the Principle of "I-ness" is in a form

which contains dormant impressions, then the state is not *Sadāśiva* alone, but *Sadāśiva* mixed with "This-ness." "tasyāṃ savedyāvasthāyām api yo māyīyagrāhakāntaḥkaraṇa-parivartanasaṃskārarūpo nimeṣaḥ, so >pi tattvataḥ "idam ityasya vicchinnavimarśasya . . . |" (A. Pr. Si. 15) "iti nyāyena aham iti pade viśrāmyann aham idam iti Sadāśivatām eva spṛśati. Yadā tu saṃskārarūpatve >sya ahantaiva tattvaṃ, tadā pramukha eva Sadāśivatā idantayā."

39. Pandey, IPV, vol. 3, 70: "svabhāvamavabhāsasya vimarśaṃ viduranyathā / prakāśo'rthoparakto'pi sphaṭikādijaḍopamaḥ" // Ipk_1,5.11 // taken from *Īśvara Pratyabhijñā Vimarśinī* in Muktabodha Digital library. See also Raffaele Torella, *Īśvara pratyabhijñākārikā of Utpaladeva with the Author's Vṛtti: Critical Edition and Annotated Translation* (Delhi: Motilal Banarsidass, 2002), 118.

40. Abhinavagupta, *Īśvara Pratyabhijñā Vivṛti Vimarśinī*, ed. Paṇḍit Madhusudan Kaul Śāstrī, vol. 2 (Delhi: Akay Reprints, 1985), 435. https://archive.org/details/in.ernet.dli.2015.326570/page/n1/mode/2up. galvarkamaṇeriva avimṛṣṭaṃ.

41. See Somānanda, *Śivadṛṣṭi*, 5.106: "The clay pot knows by means of my self and I know by means of the self of the clay pot."

42. John Nemec, "The Body and Consciousness in Early Pratyabhijñā Philosophy: Amūrtatva in Somāananda's Śivadṛṣṭi," in *Tantrapuṣpāñjali: Tantric Traditions and Philosophy of Kashmir: Studies in Memory of Pandit H.N. Chakravarty* (New Delhi: Indira Gandhi National Centre for the Arts, 2018), 215–25.

43. John Nemec, *Ubiquitous Śiva: Somānanda's Śivadṛṣṭi and His Tantric Interlocutors* (New York: Oxford University Press, 2011), 59–62. Dyczkowski also notes that the terms *vimarśa* and *prakāśa* do not appear in the Āgama scriptural literature. He cites just two occurrences and points out that these two terms are mostly absent; they are not present in the *Śiva Sūtras* or in the *Spandakārikā*, in Mark Dyczkowski, *The Doctrine of Vibration: An Analysis of the Doctrines and Practices of Kashmir Shaivism* (Albany: State University of New York Press, 1986), 233, nn.101, 26. Accordingly, Lyne Bansat-boudan translates *vimarśa* as a nontechnical term, meaning "notion"/"concept," in Lyne Bansat-Boudon, *An Introduction to Tantric Philosophy: The Paramārthasāra of Abhinavagupta with the Commentary of Yogarāja*, trans. Lyne Bansat-Boudon and Kamaleshadatta Tripathi, Routledge Studies in Tantric Traditions (New York: Routledge, 2011), 170.

44. Īśvara Pratyabhijñā Vivṛti Vimarśinī Abhinavagupta comm on 1.5.11, line 991: "nirvimarśatvāt jaḍam / sarvatra vastuto vimarśātmakapramātṛsvabhāvatādātmyāha ṃparāmarśaviśrānteḥ ajaḍatvameva."

45. See Biernacki, "Connecting Consciousness to Physical Causality."

46. See also David Lawrence's work on *vimarśa* (Lawrence, *Rediscovering God*, 1999) Rediscovering God) and Douglas Duckworth, "From Yogācāra to Philosophical Tantra in Kashmir and Tibet," *Sophia*, no. 57 (2017): 611–23, https://doi.org/DOI 10.1007/s11841-017-0598-5, which works from Lawrence's conceptualization, both insightful treatments of *vimarśa* which address this concept from a different angle than my treatment here.

47. For our modern Western condition, sight eclipses all the other senses. In contrast, Ganganath Jha, in his introduction to the *Nyāyasūtra*, alerts us to *Nyāyasūtra* 3.1.52 where he points out that early Sāṁkhya and Nyāya have only one sense: *tvāk*, touch, and that all other senses derive from touch, and "relative consciousness is only available when there is contact between *manas* [mind] and *tvāk* [touch]," in Ganganath Jha, *Nyāya: Gautama's Nyāyasūtras with Vātsyāyana-Bhāṣya*, Poona Oriental Series (Poona: Poona Oriental Book Agency, 1959), x.

48. David Lawrence remarks that *vimarśa* is about recognition, awareness in contrast to *prakāśa* as unconscious reflection. See David Lawrence, "Remarks on Abhinavagupta's Use of the Analogy of Reflection," *Journal of Indian Philosophy* 33 (2005): 586–88. Raffaele Torella translates it as "reflective awareness" in Raffaele Torella, *Ipk of Utpaladeva* (Delhi: Motilal Banarsidass 2002), p. 152 and elsewhere. Bansat-boudan translates *vimarśa* on p. 170 of the Paramarthasara as a nontechnical term, meaning "notion"/ "concept." Isabelle Ratie translates it as "grasping." See Isabelle Ratie, "A Five-Trunked, Four-Tusked Elephant Is Running in the Sky": How Free Is Imagination According to Utpaladeva and Abhinavagupta?," *Asiatische Studien: Zeitschrift Der Schweizerischen Gesellschaft Für Asienkunde = Études Asiatiques: Revue de La Société Suisse D'études Asiatiques* 64, no. 2 (2010): 341–85, http://dx.doi.org/10.5169/seals-147851. She translates it as "realization" more recently in Isabelle Ratie, "An Indian Debate on Optical Reflections and Its Metaphysical Implications: Śaiva Nondualism and the Mirror of Consciousness," in *Indian Epistemology and Metaphysics* (London: Bloomsbury, 2017), 212. Alper translates it as "judgment," in Harvey Alper, "Judgement as a Transcendental Category in Utpaladeva's Śaiva Theology, The Evidence of the Pratyabhijñākārikāvṛtti," *Adyar Library Bulletin* 51 (1987): 176–241. Kerry Skora also notes its connections with touch in Kerry Skora, "The Pulsating Heart and Its Divine Sense Energies: Body and Touch in Abhinavagupta's Trika Śaivism," *Numen* 54, no. 4 (2007): 420–58.
49. See also where Alper describes *vimarśa* and *prakāśa* as two foundational modalities of the Pratyabhijñā system in Harvey Alper, "Judgement as a Transcendental Category in Utpaladeva's Śaiva Theology, The Evidence of the Pratyabhijñākārikāvṛtti," *Adyar Library Bulletin* 51 (1987): 31. Michel Hulin points to *vimarśa* as active and *prakāśa* as passive, in Michel Hulin, *Le Principe de l'Ego dans la Pensée Indienne Classique: la Notion d'Ahaṃkāra*, vol. 44 (Paris: Publications de l'Institut de Civilisation Indienne, 1978), 243.
50. Abhinavagupta, *Ipvv*, vol. 3, p. 257: "tato hetor anyonyam aviyukte jñānakriye prakāśa vimarśātmike." We find this also in Abhinavagupta, "Isvarapratyabhijnavimarsini, Adhikaras 1-4. Based on the following edition: Īśvara-pratyabhijñā-Vimarśinī of Abhinavagupta: doctrine of divine recognition," ed. K. A. Subramania Iyer and K. C. Pandey (Muktabodha Indological Research Institute, 1986), ad 4.4.
51. Torella also notes that *vimarśa* is activity and *prakāśa* is knowledge, in Raffaele Torella, *Īśv arapratyabhijñākārikā of Utpaladeva with the Author's Vṛtti: Critical Edition and Annotated Translation* (Delhi: Motilal Banarsidass, 2002), 211. Pandey also points to *vimarśa* as action, in Pandey, *Iśvara Pratyabhijñā of Utpaladeva with the Vimarśinī*, 3:222.
52. Ram-Prasad offers a cogent analysis of various Indian philosophical approaches to it, Ram-Prasad, *Indian Philosophy*. See also David Lawrence's extensive and insightful work on *prakāśa*, especially, Lawrence, "Remarks on Abhinavagupta's Use of the Analogy of Reflection." and David Lawrence, "Proof of a Sentient Knower: Utpaladeva's Ajaḍapramātṛsiddhi with the Vṛtti of Harabhatta Shastri," *Journal of Indian Philosophy* 37 (2009): 627–53. https://doi.org/10.1007/s10781-009-9074-z. Also see Ratie's insightful work, especially Isabelle Ratie, "Pāramārthika or Apāramārthika? On the Ontological Status of Separation According to Abhinavagupta," in *Puṣpikā: Tracing Ancient India through Texts and Traditions*, ed. P. Mirning, P.-D. Szanto, and M. Williams (Havertown, UK: Oxbow Books, 2014), 381–405. Also see Ratie's Isabelle Ratie, "Can One Prove That Something Exists Beyond Consciousness? A Śaiva Criticism of the Sautrāntika Inference of External Objects," *Journal of Indian Philosophy* 39 (2011): 479–501.

53. Abhinavagupta, *Ipvv*, 1985, 3:359: "kriyājñānaśaktī vimarśaprakāśamayyau." "The energies of action and knowledge consist of *vimarśa* and *prakāśa*." Also, Abhinavagupta tells us, "the lord, whose own form is the form of the whole world, indeed pervading everywhere. That which is light (*prakāśa*) and active awareness (*vimarśa*) are in this way the innate forms of awareness, as twofold, knowledge and action" ("viśvarūpasya bhagavataḥ svarūpabhūta eva viśvatra yaḥ prakāśo yaśca vimarśaḥ, te tāvajjñānakriye svarūpadvayaparāmarśa eva), in Abhinavagupta, "IPV," 4.4 commentary.
54. *Ipvv*, vol. 3, p. 262: "Īśvara Pratyabhijñā Vivṛti Vimarśinī: Tataḥ sā śaktir antaravabhāsmānasvabhāvatayā jñānaśaktir ucyate, bahirbhāvarūpeṇa tu kramopabṛṃhitena vimarśadārḍhyena upalakṣitā kriyāśaktir."
55. Bennett, *Vibrant Matter*, 55.
56. See also Sthaneshwar Timalsina's thoughtful discussion linking kriyā to the idea of power particular in linguistic terms in Sthaneshwar Timalsina, "Linguistic and Cosmic Powers: The Concept of Śakti in the Philosophies of Bhartṛhari an Abhinavagupta," in *Classical and Contemporary Issues in Indian Studies: Essays in Honor of Trichur S. Rukmani* (Delhi: D. K. Printworld, 2013), 217.
57. Andre Padoux, *Hindu Tantric World: An Overview* (Chicago: University of Chicago Press 2017), p. 89. Padoux also notes the connection that the feminine has with speech and the word. We should keep in mind that the word "*vimarśa*" itself is masculine in gender.
58. Abhinavagupta, *Ipvv*, 1985, 3:257: "tām antarbahirātmatām kramikāvabhāsām kriyā śaktim." Here Abhinavagupta uses his commentary to expand the range of action, *kriyā śakti*, to extend it beyond its typical confinement to just matter and the external world. His move is to also incorporate within action a capacity to be internal, to connect it to a sense of subjectivity. He also connects the idea of time as well to this sense of the subject and awareness as internal (the *kramikāvabhāsām* in the quote), though in the interests of space, I do not take up this point here but do discuss the idea of time in relation to transcendence in Chapter Two.
59. Abhinavagupta, *Ipvv*, vol. 3, p. 257: "tato hetor anyonyam aviyukte jñānakriye prakāśa vimarśātmike. Tad eva ca sarvabhāvānām pāramārthikam vapuḥ."
60. Again, note the difference here between this formulation and that of his predecessor Somānanda, who opts for a bodiless (*amūrtatva*) conception of consciousness, in John Nemec, "Influences on and Legacies of Somānanda's Conception of Materiality," in *Around Abhinavagupta: Aspects of the Intellectual History of Kashmir from the Ninth to the Eleventh Century*, ed. Eli Franco and Isabelle Ratie (Berlin: Lit Verlag, 2016), 341–74. See also Lynne Bansat-Boudan's discussion of Abhinavagupta's use of the cosmic body in Bansat-Boudon, *Paramārthasāra*, 152–53.
61. James Batten first pointed this out to me, personal communication.
62. Abhinavagupta, *Ipvv*, 1985, 3:343: "Anayoḥ" iti prāṇo 'vabhāsanena dehādiriktīkurvann eva viṣayaṃ prakāśayan sūrya iti tatkālo dinaṃ, apāno vimarśanena antarviśrāntyānandadāyī dehādipramātṛbhāvamāpyāyayatīti candras tatkālo niśeti pramātrapekṣāpradhānatayā evaṃ vibhajyate."
63. Alper, "Judgement as a Transcendental Category in Utpaladeva's Śaiva Theology," 10.
64. Alper, "Judgement as a Transcendental Category," 33.
65. Raffaele Torella also references this feature of *vimarśa* as capturing the particularity of life; translating *vimarśa* as "determinate awareness" and "determinate reflective awareness"; and noting that every concrete object of knowledge is mixed with space and time and that *vimarśa* also entails these distinctions of time and place, in Torella, *Īśvarapra*

tyabhijñākārikā of Utpaladeva with the Author's Vṛtti: Critical Edition and Annotated Translation, 171. At times, Torella also translates *vimarśa* as simply "reflective awareness."

66. Ratie, "An Indian Debate on Optical Reflections and Its Metaphysical Implications: Śaiva Nondualism and the Mirror of Consciousness," 212. Sthaneshwar Timalsina makes a similar point in a soon to be published article which he kindly sent me, that is, that *vimarśa* enables a capacity for multiplicity, in Timalsina, "Vimarśa: The Concept of Reflexivity in the Philosophy of Utpala and Abhinavagupta."
67. Ratie, "An Indian Debate on Optical Reflections and Its Metaphysical Implications," 212.
68. Alper, "Judgement as a Transcendental Category in Utpaladeva's Śaiva Theology," 21.
69. Alper, 10.
70. Jaidev Singh, *Vijñāna Bhairava or Divine Consciousness*, reprint (Delhi: Motilal Banarsidass, 2003), 68, vs 71.
71. Singh, *Vijñāna Bhairava or Divine Consciousness*, 68, vs 72.
72. Singh, 105, vs 118.
73. The idea of cosmopsychism might also be understood as what Atmanspacher calls "holistic dual-aspect monism," where the holism entails that the diversity we see here is a result of a decomposition of an originary substratum, which is neither (or both) mind and matter, in Atmanspacher, "20th Century Variants of Dual-Aspect Thinking."
74. See Goff's discussion of the distinctions between micro-panpsychism and the macro-panpsychism that makes for cosmopsychism in Goff, "Cosmopsychism, Micropsychism, and the Grounding Relation."
75. The philosophical relevance of an idea of cosmopsychism is also entertained by contemporary Western philosphers, Goff, as we have seen, and also Itay Shani and Joachim Keppler's proposal for engaging the problem of subjective phenomenal experience withn NCC brain research and with a causal explanatory model in Itay Shani and Joachim Keppler, "Cosmsopsychism and Consciousness Research: A Fresh View on the Causal Mechanisms Underlying Phenomenal States," *Frontiers in Psychology* 11.371 (March 5, 2020): 1–7. https://doi.org/10.3389/fpsyg.2020.00371.
76. Abhinavagupta, *Ipvv*, 1985, 3:257: "śivatattvaṃ hi sarva padārthānām vapuḥ. Tad bhitta pṛṣṭhe ca sarva bhāva citra nirbhāsa iti tad abhidhānam eva teṣām upapādanopakramaḥ. Āgamasya ca samastasya tātparyeṇa śivatattvameva artha iti." See also Ratie's discussion of the notion of the wall as a canvas, consciousness containing the variegation of the world in Ratie, "Pāramārthika or Apāramārthika? On the Ontological Status of Separation According to Abhinavagupta."
77. Pandey, *Abhinavagupta: An Historical and Philosophical Study*, 326.
78. Karen Barad, *Meeting the Universe Halfway: Quantum Physics and the Entanglement of Matter and Meaning* (Durham, NC: Duke University Press, 2007), 181–82.
79. Goff, "Cosmopsychism, Micropsychism, and the Grounding Relation."
80. Abhinavagupta, *Īśvara Pratyabhijñā Vivṛti Vimarśinī*, ed. Paṇḍit Madhusudan Kaul Śāstrī, reprint, vol. 1 (Delhi: Akay Reprints, 1985), 190. https://archive.org/details/IshvaraPratyabhijnaVivritiVimarshiniAbhinavaguptaPart1KashmirSanskrit/mode/2up. ya āsvādaścamatkāro nijābhogaparāmarśātmā. "The self which is wonder, relishing the awareness of its own enjoyment." The full quote is given in note 82.
81. Abhinavagupta, *Ipvv*, 1985, 2:179: "yato vimarśa eva camatkāraḥ, sa evaca ajāḍyaṃ." With this, as we saw in Chapter Two, Abhinavagupta captures an astute intuition in the phenomenology of wonder. Not precisely or simply an emotion, wonder stops the mind. In

doing so, it pushes awareness into something more vital than a rote rehearsal of thought. This might be conceived as stopping the mind by stopping the mind's propensity toward dichotomizing thought (*vikalpa*).

82. Abhinavagupta, *Ipvv*, 1985, 1:190. "anunmiṣitagrāhyagrāhakādivaicitryā, ata eva bhagavataḥ svābhogaṃ prati ya āsvādaścamatkāro nijābhogaparāmarśātmā yadāha . . . . .viśvamāmṛśasi rūpamāviśan | (u. sto. 13|15) iti." The word *āviśan*, which comes from the root *viś*, is frequently used in the sense of possession. See Fred Smith's masterful work on possession, in Frederick Smith, *Self Possessed: Deity and Spirit Possession in South Asian Literature and Civilization* (New York: Columbia University Press, 2006).
83. Abhinavagupta, *Ipvv*, 1985, 1:190: "Naca kadācidapi parameśvara evaṃ tadrūpaśūnyaḥ | yadāhuḥ parameṣṭhipādāḥ: śānte śivatvaṃ sthūle'pi śivatvaṃ." It might be argued that Abhinavagupta shifts Somānanda's original meaning. On this score, see particularly John Nemec's translation of the verse by Somānanda in Nemec, *Ubiquitous Śiva*, 246–47.
84. Alper, "Judgement as a Transcendental Category in Utpaladeva's Śaiva Theology," 33. This, interestingly, leaves us with an uncanny image of a cosmopsychism with a personality.
85. Lawrence, *Rediscovering God with Transcendental Argument*, 115. K. C. Pandey also cites Berkeley's philosophy as akin to the Pratyabhijñā.
86. This article by Timalsina is not yet published, and I did not have the opportunity to read it until after the present book had been completed. He kindly sent me a copy of the article in September 2021, and I think it bears relevance to the topic at hand, precisely in that this paper supports my argument for understanding *vimarśa* as underlying both a subjective and an objective perspective. The publication data is Timalsina, "*Vimarśa*: The Concept of Reflexivity in the Philosophy of Utpala and Abhinavagupta." I quote from p. 4 of the copy he sent me.
87. In terms of the idea of emergence, Timalsina hedges his position, arguing for emergence, but qualifying it, as he quotes Amṛtānanda, "Emergence here means the vivification of the effect that is already there in the cause." In Timalsina, "Aham, Subjectivity, and the Ego: Engaging the Philosophy of Abhinavagupta," 787. As I mention earlier, my own argument is that *vimarśa* ties together the materiality of the world with consciousness not through creating something new, and not through an act of transcendence but rather like a mobius strip, in its linkage of consciousness embedded within materiality and tied to the activity and dynamism of the world.
88. Pandey, *Abhinavagupta*, 320.
89. Ratie, "Can One Prove That Something Exists beyond Consciousness? A Śaiva Criticism of the Sautrāntika Inference of External Objects," 481 n.4. Note also that Ratie also references the idealism in this system in Ratie, "An Indian Debate on Optical Reflections and Its Metaphysical Implications," 216. Ratie makes a similar case for reading Abhinavagupta against an idealist perspective in Ratie, "Pāramārthika or Apāramārthika."
90. Lawrence, *Rediscovering God with Transcendental Argumen*, 115. Ratie also points to this component of Utpaladeva's and Abhinavagupta's thought, in Ratie, "Can One Prove That Something Exists Beyond Consciousness?," 491–92. Additionally, Dyczkowski also points to this, saying that *prakāśa* is "absolute consciousness understood as the unchanging ontological ground of all appearing," in Dyczkowski, *The Doctrine of Vibration*, 59.
91. Evan Thompson, *Waking, Dreaming, Being: Self and Consciousness in Neuroscience, Meditation and Philosophy* (New York: Columbia University Press, 2015), 98–100.

92. Lawrence, *Rediscovering God with Transcendental Argument*, 159–65. For Lawrence's purposes, this idealism offers a way of thinking through a contemporary argument for God.
93. Thompson, *Waking, Dreaming, Being*, 104–5.
94. For an analogous comparison of the contrasting use of subject and selfhood in relation to objects, see Catherine Prueitt's thoughtful article on the Buddhist Dharmakīrti and Utpaladeva's Pratyabhijñā reconfiguration of Dharmakīrti, in Catherine Prueitt, "Shifting Concepts: The Realignment of Dharmakīrti on Concepts and the Error of Subject/Object Duality in Pratyabhijñā Śaiva Thought," *Journal of Indian Philosophy* 45 (2017): 21–47, https://doi.org/DOI 10.1007/s10781-016-9297-8.
95. Lawrence, *Rediscovering God with Transcendental Argument*, 115–16, 120–21. See also Lawrence's discussion on language in the Internet Encylopedia of Philosophy in David Lawrence, "Kashmiri Shaiva Philosophy," in *Internet Encyclopedia of Philosophy*, 2005. https://iep.utm.edu/kashmiri/. Torella also points to the identity of *vimarśa* with *śabdana*, that is, connecting *vimarśa* to the capacity for sound and speech in Torella, *Īśv arapratyabhijñākārikā of Utpaladeva with the Author's Vṛtti*, 163. Navjivan Rastogi also addresses this in various writings, including Navjivan Rastogi, "Rasānubhūti Pratibhāna ke Rūpa Meṃ," in *The Concept of Rasa with Special reference to Abhinavagupta*, ed. S.C. Pande (New Delhi: Aryan Books International, 2009), 185–205. He also specifically discusses this in Navjivan Rastogi, "Vak as Pratyavamarsa: Bhartrhari from Abhinavan Perspective," in *Bhartrhari—Language, Thought and Reality*, ed. Mithilesh Chaturvedi (New Delhi: Motilal Banarsidass, 2009), 301–42; pdf separate pagination, www.svabhinava.org/abhinava/NavjivanRastogi/VakPratyavamarsa.pdf. K. C. Pandey points this out in his work on Utpaladeva and Abhinavagupta in Pandey, *Iśvara Pratyabhijñā of Utpaladeva with the Vimarśinī*, 3:149. Padoux notes this as well in Andre Padoux, *Hindu Tantric World: An Overview* (Chicago: University of Chicago Press, 2017), 89.
96. Torella, *Īśvarapratyabhijñākārikā of Utpaladeva with the Author's Vṛtti*, 125–27. See also Raffaele Torella, "From an Adversary to the Main Ally: The Place of Bhartrhari in the Kashmirian Saiva Advaita," in *Bhartrhari—Language, Thought and Reality*, ed. Mithilesh Chaturvedi (New Delhi: Motilal Banarsidass, 2009), 343–54. Torella also notes that Abhinavagupta's philosophical school understands the element of language as word as having primacy and importance over the object to which the word refers, in contrast to some other Tantric schools such as the Siddhantins, in "The Word in Abhinavagupta's Bṛhadvimarśinī," 854.
97. Nemec, *Ubiquitous Śiva*, 161 n.100.
98. He makes this suggestion in a not yet published article, in Timalsina, "Vimarśa: The Concept of Reflexivity in the Philosophy of Utpala and Abhinavagupta," 8.
99. Rastogi, "Vak as Pratyavamarsa: Bhartrhari from Abhinavan Perspective," 13-pdf pagination. Navjivan Rastogi also connects *vimarśa*'s capacity to relate objects to the subject, noting that it constitutes the essential power of speech in Rastogi, "Rasānubhūti Pratibhāna ke Rūpa Meṃ," 189. Here he equates *vimarśa* to language, "vāk (yā vimarśa)."
100. Torella discusses *madhyamā*, citing Abhinavagupta as the purview of thought when the mind, the intellect, and the ego bring about discursive thought as imagination, deliberation, and ego-reference. This happens on the level of *madhyamā* because *vimarśa* is acting through the subtle body (*puryaṣṭaka*) in "The Word in Abhinavagupta's Bṛhadvimarśinī," 858.

101. This stage of language, the third of four for Abhinavagupta, is free from mental discursive thought, which creates distinctions (*vikalpa*) and is connected with the power of will (*icchā śakti*). See Torella, "The Word in Abhinavagupta's Bṛhadvimarśinī," 861.
102. For a wonderful overview, see particularly Andre Padoux, *Vāc: The Concept of the Word in Selected Hindu Tantras* (Albany: State University of New York Press, 1990).
103. Nemec, *Ubiquitous Śiva: Somānanda's Śivadṛṣṭi and His Tantric Interlocutors*, 161 n.100.
104. Abhinavagupta, *Ipvv*, 1985, 2:203: sarveṇa hi rūpeṇa saṃvidvimarśo bhavati.
105. Abhinavagupta, "IPV," line 1165, commentary on 1.5.19. "atra tu darśane viṣayasyāpi vimarśamayatvāt abhilāpamayatvameva vastutaḥ." Here I use Pandey's translation with only minimal modifications, Pandey, *Iśvara Pratyabhijñā of Utpaladeva with the Vimarśinī*, 3:82.
106. Barad, *Meeting the Universe Halfway*, 206.
107. Īśvara Pratyabhijñā Vivṛti Vimarśinī Abhinavagupta comm on 1.5.11, line 991: sarvatra vastuto vimarśātmakapramātṛsvabhāva . . . ajaḍatvameva.
108. Torella, *Īśvarapratyabhijñākārikā of Utpaladeva with the Author's Vṛtti: Critical Edition and Annotated Translation*, 186–87. The word that Torella translates as desire, "bubhūṣāyogena," is linked to a desire to be, translated literally. Ratie also makes this point, that desire (*icchā*) is intrinsic to consciousness, in Isabelle Ratie, "The Dreamer and the Yogin: On the Relationship between Buddhist and Śaiva Idealisms," *Bulletin of the School of Oriental and African Studies* 73, no. 3 (October 2010): 463.
109. Abhinavagupta *Parātrīśikavivaraṇa*, downloaded from GRETIL: Gottingen Register of Electronic Texts in Indian Languages: http://gretil.sub.uni-goettingen.de/gretil/1_sanskr/6_sastra/3_phil/saiva/partrvpu.htm, p. 212: narātmāno jaḍā api tyaktatatpūrvarūpāḥ śāktaśaivarūpabhājo bhavanti, śṛṇuta grāvāṇaḥ [\cf Mahābhāṣya 3.1.1; \cf Vākyapadīya 3 Puruṣasamuddeśa 2], meruḥ śikhariṇām ahaṃ bhavāmi [Bhagavadgītā 10.23].
110. Abhinavagupta, *Ipvv*, 1985, 3:320: "yo hi tathā bubhūṣur na pratihanyate, sa svatantraḥ. Etac ca bhagavata eva asti tasya eva sarvapūrṇatvena 'svāminaḥ . . . |' (1/5/10)ity uktanayena bubhūṣālakṣaṇayā icchayā yogāt."
111. Theology aside, the notion of value, particularized desire as a foundational feature of a cosmopsychism, does nothing to alleviate human fears in relation to computer sentience. Known as the AI alignment problem, as Bostic points out, there is no guarantee that when computers become superintelligent, their goals will align with human goals. This he exemplifies with the paperclip scenario, to point out how the goals that AI might set will conceivably have little to do with human values.
112. Bansat-Boudan notes the connection between action and the ideas of freedom and agency; quoting from Utpaladeva's *Śivadṛṣṭivṛtti*, we see the freedom of *Śiva*, the lord is "a capacity that itself consists in agency; and that [capacity for being an agent, which stems from Will itself] is but the "energy of Action," in Lyne Bansat-Boudon, "On Śaiva Terminology: Some Key Issues of Understanding," *Journal of Indian Philosophy* 42, no. 1 (March 2014): 70.
113. He links *prakāśa*, light, with *saṃvit*, an expansive fabric of consciousness that looks like a panpsychism.
114. *Ipvv*, vol. 3, p. 323: "bodhasya yato 'yam ahaṃ vimarśa ātmā sārabhūtas tatas tatra āropite svabhāvino 'pi āropo jāta eva. Etad eva ca yuktam iti."
115. I think that what we see here is Abhinavagupta's formulation of what Chalmers calls phenomenal consciousness and psychological consciousness. In this case, Abhinavagupta proposes that the contents, the psychological component of awareness, are a natural

extension of phenomenal awareness. This is key for Abhinavagupta to bridge the gap between consciousness and body, his solution to the "hard problem," which was no less a problem for his philosophical context than for ours. In this understanding, phenomenal awareness allows itself to be shaped and to give rise to the contents of consciousness. See David Chalmers, *The Conscious Mind: In Search of a Fundamental Theory* (New York: Oxford University Press, 1996).

116. *Ipvv*, vol. 3, p. 262: "Tataḥ sā śaktir antaravabhāsmānasvabhāvatayā jñānaśaktir ucyate, bahirbhāvarūpeṇa tu kramopabṛṃhitena vimarśadārḍhyena upalakṣitā kriyāśaktir."
117. *Ipvv*, vol. 3, p. 316: "Yato 'ham iti vimarśamayatvam ātmana upapāditam, tad eva kartṛtvam uktaṃ."
118. It makes some sense to read the Sāṃkhyan *puruṣa* as akin to Chalmers's conception of phenomenal experience; in both cases, all contents are bracketed off as a separate instantiation of consciousness.
119. *Ipvv*, vol. 3, p. 317: "Evaṃ ca kāryarūpaṃ jagat puruṣam ayam eva. Yat śrutiḥ 'puruṣa evedaṃ sarvam' iti." He cites Ṛg Veda *Puruṣa* Sūktam 10.90.2.
120. Abhinavagupta, *Ipvv*, 1985, 3:316: "tataḥ kartṛtvaṃ vyatirikte kārye na upapadyate."
121. Translation modified slightly from Pandey, *Iśvara Pratyabhijñā of Utpaladeva with the Vimarśinī*, 3:72. Ipv commentary on 1.5.12, line 1021, in Muktabodha IPV: citkriyā ātmā ucitaḥ citikartṛtā ca iti pṛthageva / evaṃ tu na kvacit paṭhitam //12//
122. For this verse, see also John Nemec's thoughtful article, which traces this notion of the self as capable of action through Utpaladeva and his teacher, Somānanda, where Somānanda explicitly defines the self in large measure against the realist schools of the Nyāya and Vaiśeṣika, in Nemec, "Influences on and Legacies of Somānanda's Conception of Materiality," 358–61.
123. See also Bansat-Boudan's interesting contextualization of the idea of pure consciousness (*śāntabrahmavāda*), critiqued as insensible; pure consciousness is insentient (*mūḍhabhāva*) because it lacks *vimarśa*, in Bansat-Boudon, *Paramārthasāra*, 155.
124. For the relationship between Buddhism and the Pratyabhijñā, see especially Raffaele Torella, "The Pratyabhijñā and the Logical-Epistemological School of Buddhism," in *Ritual and Speculation in Early Tantrism: Studies in Honor of André Padoux*, ed. Teun Goudriaan (New York: State University of New York Press, 1992), 327–45. Also see Ratie, "The Dreamer and the Yogin: On the Relationship between Buddhist and Śaiva Idealisms."
125. Pandey, *Iśvara Pratyabhijñā of Utpaladeva with the Vimarśinī*, 3:72. Commenting on this idea of making action the basis of the self, he continues: "this understanding is not found anywhere." This also is a slight modification of Pandey's translation, taken from Ipv commentary on 1.5.12, line 1021, in Muktabodha IPV: evaṃ tu na kvacit paṭhitam //12//
126. Ipv commentary to 1.5.15–16: Line 1129: "sarvāḥ śaktoḥ kartṛtvaśaktiḥ aiśvaryātmā samākṣipati / sā ca vimarśarūpā iti yuktam asyā eva prādhānyam."
127. Dan Arnold, *Brains, Buddhas and Believing: The Problem of Intentionality in Classical Buddhist and Cognitive-Scientific Philosophy of Mind* (New York: Columbia University Press, 2014), 21, and passim. Also, Torella, "The Pratyabhijñā and the Logical-Epistemological School of Buddhism." See also Douglas Duckworth's interesting analysis of the exchange through Dharmakīrti to Utpaladeva, to later Tibetan thinkers, in Douglas Duckworth, "From Yogācāra to Philosophical Tantra in Kashmir and Tibet," *Sophia*, no. 57 (2017): 615. https://doi.org/DOI 10.1007/s11841-017-0598-5. For a useful discussion of Abhinavagupta's knowledge of Buddhist philosophers including Dharmakīrti, see also Lawrence McCrea, "Abhinavagupta as Intellectual Historian of Buddhism," in *Around*

Abhinavagupta:Aspects of the Intellectual History of Kashmir from the Ninth to the Eleventh Century, ed. Eli Franco and Isabelle Ratie (Berlin: Lit Verlag, 2016), 263–86. Galen Strawson also points to this notion of causality as indicative of real things, "to be concretely real is to be capable of having an effect on something else," in Galen Strawson, "Physicalist Panpsychism," in *Blackwell Companion to Consciousness*, 2nd ed. (Oxford: John Wiley & Sons, 2017), 379.

128. See Giulio Tononi, *Phi: A Voyage from the Brain to the Soul* (New York: Pantheon, 2012). See also Biernacki, "Connecting Consciousness to Physical Causality."
129. We see this also in Advaita Vedānta, as Ram-Prasad points out in his astute analysis of Citsukha's *Tattvapradīpikā*, Ram-Prasad, *Indian Philosophy*, 78.
130. Abhinavagupta, "IPV," line 1642, commentary on 1.8.10: viṣayaprakāśa eva saṃvit ucyate.
131. John Searle, "Can Information Theory Explain Consciousness?," *New York Times Review of Books*, January 10, 2013.
132. Biernacki, "Connecting Consciousness to Physical Causality: Abhinavagupta's Phenomenology of Subjectivity and Tononi's Integrated Information Theory."
133. Abhinavagupta, "IPV," line 1644, commentary on 1.8.11: "api tu sadaiva vimṛśyamānarūpaḥ, iti vimṛśadrūpatvam."
134. Abhinavagupta, line 1644, commentary on 1.5.11: "sarvathā tu vimarśa eva jñānaṃ tena vinā hi jaḍabhāvo 'sya syāt."
135. Abhinavagupta, line 2287, commentary on verse 3.1.1: "jñānaṃ vimarśānuprāṇitam, vimarśa eva ca kriyeti."
136. He tells us as well, "So the process whereby 'This-ness' becomes distinct is shown to belong to the former, *prakāśa*, where the material thing becomes distinct." Here is the passage: "'Intellect' [arises from the] portion of *prakāśa*, the expanse of light. In contrast, '*paśyantī*' the level of speech when it is just beginning to blossom" [arises from the] portion of *vimarśa*, Active Awareness [the two aspects of the Lord, *prakāśa* and *vimarśa*]. Consequently the state of being an object and the state of being something that can be spoken about were earlier separately talked about [since they are two very different things]. The words, "and of the two" [being an object and being something capable of being spoken about] he explains with the words, "one of the two is selected out." So the process whereby "This-ness" becomes distinct is shown to belong to the former, *prakāśa*, where the material thing becomes distinct [and not that which is capable of being spoken of]." In Abhinavagupta, *Ipvv*, 1985, 3:284: "Buddhiḥ" iti prakāśabhāgena, "paśyantī" iti vimarśāśena. Tata eva prameyatā vācyatā ca prāk pṛthag uktā. "Tayoś ca" iti nirdhāraṇapadena pūrvakasya eva arthasya idaṃ sphuṭīkaraṇam iti darśitam.
137. Alper, "Judgement as a Transcendental Category in Utpaladeva's Śaiva Theology," 28.
138. Atmanspacher, "20th Century Variants of Dual-Aspect Thinking."
139. Strawson, "Physicalist Panpsychism."
140. Strawson, 374.
141. This ever-present availability can be seen as precisely what distinguishes Tantric models from other Indian nondualisms that suggest full enlightenment can only be had outside of a physical body. See Andy Fort's study of *jivanmukti*, in Andrew Fort, *Jīvanmukti in Transformation: Embodied Liberation in Advaita and Neo-Vedanta* (Rochester, NY: State University of New York Press, 1998).
142. Abhinavagupta, *Ipvv*, 1985, 3:255: this is Abhinavagupta's "samasta saṃpat."

143. Abhinavagupta, 3:272: "citiśaktir viśvarūpā bhavati na cādhikyaṃ spṛśati" iti sambandhaḥ. Cetanā atidurghaṭakāritvādinā adbhutatāṃ vyanakti. Etat saṃkṣipya ghaṭayati "yo hi" iti "idantābhāk" iti.
144. Abhinavagupta, *Ipvv*, 1985, 1:180: "etadeva svātantryaṃ yadatidurghaṭakāritvam | durghaṭaṃ ca tat niyatiśaktikṛtādeva māyādaśāyāṃ." Elsewhere Abhinavagupta describes *niyati śakti* as the power to individuate; it is what makes the mud that forms a clay jar separate from a piece of wood, in Abhinavagupta, *Ipvv*, 1985, 3:270: "In fact, the categories of earth and so on are only just forms of the Energy of the Supreme Lord. That being so, because it is directed by the will of the Lord, the mud comes to exist also through the action of *niyati*, the Archetype of fate [as a limitation in its material form—made of mud and not wood]. And so the pot is said to have a separate cause. [i.e., the mud, though, in reality, this is simply a form of the Lord's *Śakti*]." "Tathā hi mṛdādiḥ padārthaḥ parameśvaraśaktirūpa eva saṃstad icchāvaśāt ghaṭakāraṇatayā api niyatau nirbhāsamānaḥ pṛthak kāraṇam ucyate."
145. As a cosmopsychism, it also avoids the combinatory problem endemic to micropanpsychisms.
146. Brooke Jarvis, "Insect Apocalypse Is Here," *New York Times Magazine*, November 27, 2018. https://www.nytimes.com/2018/11/27/magazine/insect-apocalypse.html.

Chapter 5

1. James Gleick, *Information: A History, A Theory, A Flood* (New York: Pantheon, 2011), 8.
2. Richard Dawkins, *River Out of Eden: A Darwinian View of Life*, Reprint (New York: Basic Books, 1996), 95.
3. Michael Pollan, "The Intelligent Plant Scientists Debate a New Way of Understanding Flora," *New Yorker*, December 15, 2013.
4. Pollan, "The Intelligent Plant Scientists Debate a New Way of Understanding Flora," 3.
5. Loriliai Biernacki, "Connecting Consciousness to Physical Causality: Abhinavagupta's Phenomenology of Subjectivity and Tononi's Integrated Information Theory," *Religions* 7 (2016), https://doi.org/10.3390/rel7070087.
6. Diana Coole traces out a genealogy of this mentality to Descartes. The world here is a great cosmic machine whose divine creator vacated it, "leaving behind a mechanism that is amenable to the calculations and deductions of reason." In Diana Coole, "Inertia of Matter and the Generativity of Flesh," in *New Materialisms: Ontology, Agency and Politics*, ed. Diana Coole and Samantha Frost (Durham, NC: Duke University Press, 2010), 95.
7. Tononi's model follows an emergentist model. He arrives at the emergent new property through a process of accretion. He describes the process poetically for us in his *PHI: A Journey from the Brain to the Soul*, in an imagined conversation between Galileo and a German baron, who references the philosopher Leibniz. Galileo reasons about "which mechanisms would one have to add in order to augment the lowly photodiode and make it like Galileo's brain?" In order to get, as Tononi puts it, "meaning out of mechanism," the Baron tells Galileo, "By piling one mechanism on top of another, that's how it's done! . . . One mechanism alone—things are this way and not another way—generates hardly any information: one nondescript bit. But if you pile them up, so that one builds upon another, not only side-by-side, but each standing on the shoulders of the others, as it were, they generate far more information, bits multiply." With enough nested circuitry

one can make the jump from the mere mechanism of a manufactured mechanical device, a photodiode, to the wonder of consciousness. This notion of meaning from mechanism is precisely at issue for philosophers like Thomas Nagel, who argues for the need for alternative models beyond reductive materialism. Whether his emergentism genuinely overcomes the problem of meaning out of mechanism is not quite clear. I discuss the idea of meaning further below. See Giulio Tononi, *Phi: A Voyage from the Brain to the Soul* (New York: Pantheon, 2012), 199–203.

8. Philip Goff, *Consciousness and Fundamental Reality* (New York: Oxford University Press, 2017). And Abhinavagupta's system also shares some features with the type of cosmopsychism that Ayon Maharaj attributes to the early 20th-century figure Vivekananda; namely, it offers a nondualism that does not reject the materiality of the world. See Ayon Maharaj, "Panentheistic Cosmopsychism: Swami Vivekananda's Sāṃkhya-Vedāntic Solution to the Hard Problem of Consciousness," in *Panentheism and Panpsychism: Philosophy of Religion Meets Philosophy of Mind*, ed. Ludwig Jaskolla, Godehard Brüntrup, and Benedikt Paul Göcke (Paderborn: Mentis Brill, 2019).
9. Abhinavagupta, *Īśvara Pratyabhijñā Vivṛti Vimarśinī*, ed. Paṇḍit Madhusudan Kaul Śāstrī, vol. 3 (Delhi: Akay Reprints, 1985), 255, https://archive.org/details/in.ernet.dli.2015.485473/mode/2up. otaprotam sakalam viddhvā svarasena śivamayīkurute |yo >nuttara dhāmnyudayan svayam amṛta niṣecanam tam asmi nataḥ ||. We saw this briefly in Chapter One.
10. These are the *tattvas*, and this section of the *Īśvara Pratyabhijñā Vivṛti Vimarśinī* explicates this model of thirty-six categories, arranged hierarchically from the highest as the absolute *Śiva* down to the five elements of space, air, fire, water, and earth. The lower twenty-five of these categories are inherited from the earlier Sāṃkhya system. Abhinavagupta's Tantric tradition adds five additional categories to encompass what is known as the "pure creation" from the category *Śiva* to Pure Knowledge (*śuddhavidyā*) and an additional six categories to incorporate the ideas of *Māyā*, which generates a sense of duality, along with the coverings that include time, limited knowledge and limited ability to do things, fate, and attachment.
11. This seeming contradiction is the wondrous deed that consciousness, *citi*, can do, as we saw in Chapter One: "the Energy of Consciousness is in fact all forms, the entire universe and She touches nothing beyond Herself." Consciousness (*citi*) makes manifest a wonder by the force of doing that which is extremely difficult. This he summarizes with the words, [*Śiva*/*Citi*] "who in fact" "partakes of 'This-ness,'" in Abhinavagupta, *Ipvv*, 1985, 3:272: "citiśaktir viśvarūpā bhavati na cādhikyaṃ spṛśati" iti sambandhaḥ. Cetanā atidurghaṭakāritvādinā adbhutatāṃ vyanakti. Etat saṃkṣipya ghaṭayati "yo hi" iti "idantābhāk" iti.
12. We also saw this pattern in Tononi's articulation of *Phi*, in Biernacki, "Connecting Consciousness to Physical Causality."
13. This is known as the decombination problem. For a cogent articulation of the problem, see Itay Shani and Joachim Keppler, "Beyond Combination: How Cosmic Consciousness Grounds Ordinary Experience," *Journal of the American Philosophical Association* 4, no. 3 (2018): 390–410, https://doi.org/10.1017/apa.2018.30.
14. As I mention in the Introduction, I draw from the KSTS publication of the Sanskrit (listed in the bibliography), which has not yet been translated, so my notes include the Sanskrit and my translations, and the Sanskrit notes for this chapter are extensive.

15. The idea of a cosmopsychism unfolding to create the world offers, as well, a different emotional flavor; Abhinavagupta's map of the tattvas stresses the interconnection of the whole. He tells us, "The purport of this section is to show the interconnection, all through, from highest to lowest, of this whole creation." In Abhinavagupta, *Ipvv*, 1985, 3:256: "samasto> pi ayam sarga otaprota iti prakaraṇa tātparyam." Rather than as basis a Darwinian bottom-up multiplicity of forces mutually warring, a cosmopsychism with its outflow of subjectivity suggests instead an organicism, a mutual interconnectivity.
16. Daniel Dennett, *Information, Evolution, and Intelligent Design* (London: Royal Institution, 2015), 20:38, https://www.youtube.com/watch?v=AZX6awZq5Z0.
17. Nevermind the uncanny structural resemblance to Derrida's well-known aim of deconstruction, implosion from within. As Freud put it, the ego is not sovereign in its own house.
18. Fred Smith's brilliant and comprehensive study of the phenomenon of possession illustrates this amply. See Frederick Smith, *Self Possessed: Deity and Spirit Possession in South Asian Literature and Civilization* (New York: Columbia University Press, 2006).
19. Berit Brogaard, "In Search of Mentons: Panpsychism, Physicalism and the Missing Link," in *Panpsychism: Contemporary Perspectives* (New York: Oxford University Press, 2017), 150.
20. Brogaard, "In Search of Mentons," 139.
21. Rosi Braidotti, *Posthuman Knowledge* (New York: Polity Press, 2019), 22.
22. See particularly Jeffrey Kripal, *Flip: Epiphanies of Mind and the Future of Knowledge* (New York: Bellevue Literary Press, 2019). We also see this especially in the snippets of his brilliant, forthcoming *The Superhumanities: Historical Precedents, Moral Objections, New Realities* (Kripal, forthcoming.)
23. Gleick, *Information: A History, A Theory, A Flood*, 358–59.
24. Or perhaps the *ātman* is the proper analogy, as Krishna tells Arjuna that the *ātman*, the Self, is not destroyed when the body is burned in *Bhagavad Gītā* 2.23
25. I discuss this more in Loriliai Biernacki "AI Immortality: The Problem with Ray Kurzweil's Downloadable Consciousness and a Fermentation Model of Self" (forthcoming).
26. Douglas Hofstadter, *Godel, Escher, Bach: An Eternal Golden Braid*, 20th Anniversary Edition (New York: Basic Books, 1999), 4. https://www.academia.edu/39721656/G%C3%B6del_Escher_Bach_An_Eternal_Golden_Braid_20th_Anniversary_Edition_by_Douglas_R._Hofstadter?email_work_card=view-paper.
27. *Consciousness Is a Mathematical Pattern: Max Tegmark at TEDxCambridge 2014* (Cambridge: TedX, 2014). https://www.youtube.com/watch?v=GzCvlFRISIM.
28. Abhinavagupta *Parātrīśikavivaraṇa*, downloaded from GRETIL: Gottingen Register of Electronic Texts in Indian Languages. http://gretil.sub.uni-goettingen.de/gretil/1_sanskr/6_sastra/3_phil/saiva/partrvpu.htm, p. 212: sarvaṃ hi sarvātmakam iti.
29. See Biernacki, "Connecting Consciousness to Physical Causality."
30. *Max Tegmark at TEDxCambridge 2014*, 10:36.
31. *Max Tegmark at TEDxCambridge 2014*, 15:23.
32. Śivadatta Miśra Śāstrī, ed., *Bṛhatstotraratnākara* (Varanasi: Jyotiṣa Prakāśana, 1997), 258. "Mahālakṣmyaṣṭaka Stotram," 4b: "Mantra mūrte sadā devi."
33. Abhinavagupta, *Ipvv*, 1985, 3:v.3, 283. "Na hi ete śabdanarūpavat saṃvedanagāminaḥ iti saṃvidaṃ saṃkocayanto nibiḍatamam āvṛṇvate nanu. Evaṃ śabdanaśarīro mantrātmā hṛdayākāśe vimarśarūpatayā viparivartamānaḥ."
34. Abhinavagupta, 3:298: "vācaka-śabdasya nādātmano vicitra-samaya-sahiṣṇu-śābda-vṛtta-mūlāneka-varṇa-grāma-bīja-bhūtasya yato 'neka-vācyādhyāsavataḥ sarvāvakāśa-dāna-kṣamateti ekaḥ prakāraḥ, vācako vā astu avācako vā khaṭa-khaṭādir api śabdaḥ

sarvāvakāśasahaḥ sparśa-sahacāritā-rahito mūrtatābhāvād apratighātako yata iti aparaḥ prakāraḥ. Tan nirūpayati "nādātmā" ity."

35. Abhinavagupta, *Īśvara Pratyabhijñā Vivṛti Vimarśinī*, ed. Paṇḍit Madhusudan Kaul Śāstrī, vol. 2 (Delhi: Akay Reprints, 1985), 298: "pṛthivyādīnāṁ tāvad avakāśa-dātṛtā naiva sambhāvyate kathaṁcit, dṛśyamānā api na teṣāṁ sā svabhāvaḥ; api tu tat sahacāriṇa ākāśasya evety arthaḥ."
36. Abhinavagupta, *Ipvv*, 1985, 3:298: "It has a 'portion of grossness' means that space alone by its quality of being entered into, has the inherent nature of hollowness, [and this is a gross quality]. But this is not the subtle element [sound]. The quality of sound has a form which consists of agitation and which is not entered into [by other elements such as earth]." "'Sthaulya-bhāga' iti yo 'sau sanniveśātmanā suṣira-svabhāvaḥ, tad ākāśam eva; na tu tanmātram, yat tu asan-niveśātmakaṁ kṣobha-mayaṁ rūpaṁ, sa śabdo guṇa iti abhiprāyaḥ."
37. It is important to remember that delinking information from meaning arises particularly with Shannon's stipulation that in order to use the patterns in information, one needs to ignore the component of meaning. This kickstarts the identification of information as objective data divorced from a subjective meaningful stance. On this score, see particularly N. Katherine Hayles, *How We Became Posthuman: Virtual Bodies in Cybernetics, Literature, and Informatics* (Chicago: University of Chicago Press, 1999).
38. Abhinavagupta, *Ipvv*, 1985, 3:v.3, 284: "śarīrādau māyāpramātṝṇāṃ paramāsthā bandhasthānatvena bhāti samastānāṃ tad bhaṅgabhīrusvabhāvatvāt."
39. Though the robot body, which is attached to his downloaded consciousness-information, this metallic body will share the fate of earth, dust to dust, with no better durability or freedom from fear. I discuss this in Biernacki, "AI Immortality" (forthcoming).
40. Erwin Schrodinger, *What Is Life? The Physical Aspect of the Living Cell* (Dublin: Dublin Institute for Advanced Studies: Trinity College Dublin, 1944), 31. https://duckduckgo.com/?q=schrodinger+what+is+life&t=ffab&atb=v108-1&ia=web.
41. Christof Koch, "Future of Consciousness: Future of Biology" (Schrodinger at 75, Dublin: Trinity College Dublin, 2018). https://www.youtube.com/watch?v=luGE5e2_xKM.
42. Thomas Metzinger, "Out-of-Body Experiences as the Origin of the Concept of a 'Soul,'" *Mind and Matter* 3, no. 1 (2005): 81.
43. Elizabeth Krohn and Jeffrey Kripal, *Changed in a Flash: One Woman's Near-Death Experience and Why a Scholar Thinks It Empowers Us All* (Berkeley, CA: North Atlantic Books, 2018), 227–30. For the link between quantum physics and subtle bodies, see also Ed Kelly, Paul Marshall, and Adam Crabtree, eds., *Beyond Physicalism: Toward Reconciliation of Science and Spirituality (New York: 2015* (New York: Rowman and Littlefield, 2015).
44. John Wheeler, "Information, Physics, Quantum: The Search for Links" (3rd International Symposium Foundations of Quantum Mechanics, Tokyo: Plus magazine, 1989), 311/ https://plus.maths.org/content/it-bit-0.
45. Wheeler, "Information, Physics, Quantum," 320.
46. See Biernacki, "Connecting Consciousness to Physical Causality." Wheeler writes this, of course, long before we see New Materialism, pointing to the role 20th-century quantum physics has played in modeling information away from anthropocentrism.
47. Abhinavagupta, *Ipvv*, 1985, 3:258: "Bodhaikarūpasya pramātur yad adhikamabodharūpaṃ, tat nirmātavyapakṣe nikṣipyate iti tasya yat nijam śaktirūpaṃ dharmaḥ."

48. Here Abhinavagupta also points out that this creation is two-fold, that is containing the dual-aspect qualities of both knowledge (*jñāna*) as inwardness and action (*kriyā*) as materiality in Abhinavagupta, 3:262: "abhyantaracinmātrāpekṣayā antarbahirbhāvasya sadbhāvaḥ, māyīye tu sarge >bhyantareśvaravṛddhyādyapekṣayā bahuśākho >sau. Sa eṣa dvayo >pi sargaḥ paramaśivasya bhagavataḥ śaktivijṛmbhā. Tataḥ sā śaktir antaravabhāsmānasvabhāvatayā jñānaśaktir ucyate, bahirbhāvarūpeṇa tu kramopabṛṃhitena vimarśadārḍhyena upalakṣitā kriyāśaktir iti vyapadiśyate."
49. Biernacki, "Connecting Consciousness to Physical Causality."
50. Abhinavagupta, *Ipvv*, 1985, 3:v.3, 266: "viśvaṃ nimiṣitaṃ ced ekarasaiva ahantā."
51. This is the well-known *tattva* system. Its basis derives from early Sāṃkhya cosmology with twenty-five principles. See Gerald Larson, *Classical Sāṃkhya: An Interpretation of Its History and Meaning*, Reprint (Delhi: Motilal Banarsidass, 1998).
52. Abhinavagupta, *Ipvv*, 1985, 3:267: "Yadā tu sā praśānty upalakṣitā dhyāmalatvena asphuṭā saṃpadyate, tadā vedya yoge >pi śivatāyā unmajjanāt sarveṇa kalanāprakāreṇa śivateti Sadāśivatā ucyate. Sā ca māyāpadavyavasthitānāṃ bhūtānāṃ grāhakagrāhyarūpāṇāṃ pralayaḥ sarvathaiva māyīyarūparadhvaṃsāt. Māyātattve ca tadā bhūtāni nidhīyante, tac ca parameśaśaktirūpaṃ Sadāśivapade idam ity aṃśasparśena viśrāmyatīti nimeṣaḥ Sadāśivatā."
53. Abhinavagupta, 3:264: "Tatra śuddhacaitanyavargasya mantramaheśvarākhyasya yat bhāvacakram asmadādyantaḥkaraṇavedyabhāvarāśisadṛśaṃ dhyāmalaprāyamunmīlitam ātracitrakalpaṃ prathamasṛṣṭau."
54. Abhinavagupta, 3:v.3, 263: "Ata āntaryā jñānarūpāyā daśāyā udrekāvabhāsane."
55. Abhinavagupta, 3:v.3, 265: "bāhyatvasphuṭatāvidhāyi yat viśvasya caitanyasāmarthyam īśvaratattvaṃ."
56. Here I take "*pūrṇacitrapratime*" as a *bahuvrīhi* modifying "*bahiṣkaraṇavedyasadṛśi*."
57. Abhinavagupta, *Ipvv*, 1985, 3:264: "mantreśvarādirūpasya tu bahiṣkaraṇavedyasadṛśi pūrṇacitrapratime sthityavasthā īśvaratattvam."
58. John Wheeler, "Not Consciousness but the Distinction between the Probe and the Probed as Central to the Elemental Quantum Act of Observation," in *Role of Consciousness in the Physical World*, ed. R.G. Jahn (Boulder, CO: Westview, 1981), 92.
59. Elsewhere Wheeler uses the metaphor of smoke to precisely stop in its tracks the inference to something like the interconnectedness faster than the speed of light implied in quantum entanglement. This he does specifically as a plea to prevent the acknowledgment of psi and the paranormal in an appendix titled "Where There's Smoke, There's Smoke" in Wheeler, 101–6.
60. Wheeler, "Information, Physics, Quantum: The Search for Links," 320.
61. Wheeler, 320. I discuss Tononi and Koch in Biernacki, "Connecting Consciousness to Physical Causality."
62. Wheeler, "Information, Physics, Quantum: The Search for Links," 320.
63. Wheeler, 320.
64. Tegmark points to this when he says, "consciousness is the way information feels," as we saw above, in *Max Tegmark at TEDxCambridge 2014*, 10:36.
65. Wheeler, "Information, Physics, Quantum: The Search for Links," 320.
66. Wheeler, 320.
67. Wheeler, "Not Consciousness but the Distinction between the Probe and the Probed as Central to the Elemental Quantum Act of Observation," 97.

68. John Nemec, "Evidence for Somānanda's Pantheism," *Journal of Indian Philos* 42 (2014): 108.
69. Vivieros de Castro points to seeing nonhuman animals as persons, as subjects in a gesture that can encompass more than simply nonhuman animals, in Eduardo Vivieros de Castro, *Cannibal Metaphysics*, trans. Peter Skafish (Minneapolis: Univocal, 2014), p. 62.
70. Karen Barad, *Meeting the Universe Halfway: Quantum Physics and the Entanglement of Matter and Meaning* (Durham, NC: Duke University Press, 2007), 283.
71. See also the recent quantum physics theoretical work that undermines altogether ideas of causality in Natalie Wolchover, "Quantum Mischief Rewrites the Laws of Cause and Effect," *Quanta Magazine*, March 11, 2021. https://www.quantamagazine.org/quantum-mischief-rewrites-the-laws-of-cause-and-effect-20210311.
72. Here Abhinavagupta is arguing against Sāṃkhya in particular, which relegates causality to the realm of *prakṛti*, matter, which is understood as insentient, unlike *puruṣa*, which is the sentient, enlivening spirit in Abhinavagupta, *Ipvv*, 1985, 3:267: jaḍe pratiṣṭhitaḥ kārya kāraṇa bhāvo na upapadyate, api tu cidrūpa eva.
73. Indeed, as Diana Coole points out, the problem is that matter is understood to be inherently "devoid of agency or meaning" in Coole, "Inertia of Matter and the Generativity of Flesh," 92.
74. Abhinavagupta, *Ipvv*, 1985, 3:315: Nanu evaṃ ghate 'pi yadi cidrūpatām kaścit paśyet, tarhi kim abhrānta eva asau. We saw this in Chapter Four.
75. Not to mention, the ethical implications are staggering.
76. See Biernacki, "Connecting Consciousness to Physical Causality." Abhinavagupta gives us a little more to work with on this panentheist or panpsychist vision. It is not a simple case of consciousness spread out over all matter, like a "thin layer of jam," as we see with John Searle's critique of Tononi's panpsychism. This is also in effect the same critique of monisms that William James offers in his *Pluralistic Universe* in William James, *A Pluralistic Universe*, Hibbert Lectures and Manchester College (New York: Longmans, Green and Co., 1909). https://archive.org/details/pluralisticunive00jamerich/page/n5. How does one differentiate between things when the essence of everything is the same, that is, to invoke Hegel, in a night in which all cows are black? Abhinavagupta's dual-aspect panentheism addresses the problem through the idea that subjectivity allows an innate consciousness to appear as the awareness we conceive of as consciousness, as we saw in Chapter Four discussing *vimarśa*. For Abhinavagupta, one's place on the spectrum is determined by the extent of the embrace of subjectivity, and various levels throughout entail an interrelationality between subjects and objects. This connectivity between subjects and objects is interesting for our purposes here, as it hints toward something like the kind of interactive relationality that Wheeler contemplates with his "so many participant-observers" exchanging bits of information to create the world. Subjectivity is not equally distributed, and it is a process—as we saw earlier: "removing the form which is insentient, we allow the form which is sentient, the conscious, to take predominance" in Abhinavagupta, *Ipvv*, 1985, 3:315: "jaḍarūpatānyakkriyayā cidrūpatāprādhānyena āveśaḥ āsamantāt."
77. Robert Wright, *Quantifying Consciousness: Robert Wright & Christof Koch*, Wright Show (MeaningofLife.tv, 2016), 7:34. https://www.youtube.com/watch?v=B_YnBIXK6QU.
78. This is Giulio Tononi's "difference that makes a difference," in Tononi, *Phi*. See Biernacki, "Connecting Consciousness to Physical Causality."
79. Ṛg Veda *Puruṣa* Sūktam 10.90.2.

80. Abhinavagupta, *Ipvv*, 1985, 3:317: "tataḥ kartṛtvaṃ vyatirikte kārye na upapadyate tādṛśasya kāryakāraṇabhāvasya vitatya dūṣitatvāt. Evaṃ ca kāryarūpaṃ jagat puruṣam ayam eva. Yat śrutiḥ 'puruṣa evedaṃ sarvam' iti."
81. See Masafumi Oizumi, Larissa Albantakis, and Giulio Tononi, "From the Phenomenology to the Mechanisms of Consciousness: Integrated Information Theory 3.0," *PLOS: Computational Biology*, May 8, 2014. http://journals.plos.org/ploscompbiol/article?id=10.1371/journal.pcbi.1003588. See also my discussion of their panpsychism in Biernacki, "Connecting Consciousness to Physical Causality."
82. See John Searle, "Can Information Theory Explain Consciousness?," *New York Times Review of Books*, January 10, 2013. Also see Tononi, *Phi*, 199–203. See also note 7 above. Elsewhere Tononi specifies the cutoff point. Tononi suggests that there is a grain: the grain is 100–200 milliseconds and the physical size is groups of neurons. This is the level where Tononi proposes one gets maximum *phi*—which is what is needed for consciousness. Quantum spaces should have more information because there are more possible states, but because the indeterminism and degeneracy prevent the information from being accessed, he suggests one gets higher *Phi* at the level of neurons. See his talk at FQXI panel on consciousness: FQXi, *The Physics of Information: FQXi's 4th International Conference* (Vieques Island, Puerto Rico, 2014), https://www.youtube.com/watch?v=MtUZw3PkKYg. This occurs for those combinations that work through recursive feedback loops.
83. See Coleman's thoughtful critique of the problems with panpsychism in an emergentist model in Sam Coleman, "The Real Combination Problem: Panpsychism, Micro-Subjects, and Emergence," *Erkenntnis* 79 (2014): 36–37. https://doi.org/10.1007/s10670-013-9431-x.
84. Abhinavagupta, *Ipvv*, 1985, 3:315: "Om ity āha 'jaḍasya tu' iti 'Yukta eva' iti ucita." We also saw this in Chapter Four.
85. We saw this in Chapter One, where the problem for the type of cosmopsychism that Abhinavagupta proposes is the reverse of the combination problem; rather, the problem involves how a cosmopsychism might actually partake of limited awareness. This is, Abhinavagupta tells us, the wonder that consciousness performs: "Consciousness (*citi*) makes manifest a wonder by the force of doing that which is extremely difficult. This he summarizes with the words, [*Śiva/Citi*] 'who in fact' 'partakes of This-ness.'" In Abhinavagupta, 3:272: "citiśaktir viśvarūpā bhavati na cādhikyaṃ spṛśati" iti sambandhaḥ. Cetanā atidurghaṭakāritvādinā adbhutatāṃ vyanakti. Etat saṃkṣipya ghaṭayati 'yo hi' iti 'idantābhāk' iti."
86. See especially Larson's discussion of the Sāṃkhya categories, in Larson, *Classical Sāṃkhya: An Inerpretation of Its History and Meaning*. *Puruṣa* is classically male, and it literally means the man, however, I translate it in gender-neutral terms, in keeping with our contemporary general shift toward understanding the term *man* in the texts of previous centuries to point to humanity as a whole.
87. *Buddhi* is the term for the individual; the idea of an intellectual awareness on a cosmic level is referenced in the term *mahat*.
88. The five senses include our familiar ones—sight, hearing, taste, smell, and touch. The five organs of action are speaking, grasping, moving, procreating, and eliminating.
89. Yes, it never quite loses a consciousness lying within, but this is hidden, not displayed.
90. Wheeler, "Not Consciousness but the Distinction between the Probe and the Probed as Central to the Elemental Quantum Act of Observation," 97.
91. Quoting from the *Spanda Kārika*, Abhinavagupta tells us: "The *Śiva* Archetype alone is the body of all things, On the wall [of the world which is itself *Śiva*] the picture of all

beings appear, shining forth" in Abhinavagupta, *Ipvv*, 1985, 3:257: "śivatattvaṃ hi sarva padārthānām vapuḥ. Tad bhitta pṛṣṭhe ca sarva bhāva citra nirbhāsa iti."

92. At the same time, I suggest that for Abhinavagupta, we might also see these categories as a phenomenology of the process of thought; the unfolding to make a cosmos mirrors the process consciousness takes as thought in the (human) mind, aligned with what we experience here.
93. The term used here, *ābhāsa*, refers to the idea that the world appears as differentiated even as it is derived from a singular cosmopsychism. For more on this term, see David Lawrence's thoughtful and influential analysis, in David Lawrence, "Remarks on Abhinavagupta's Use of the Analogy of Reflection," *Journal of Indian Philosophy* 33 (2005): 583–99. Also see K. C. Pandey, *Abhinavagupta: An Historical and Philosophical Study*, 2nd Enlarged Edition (Varanasi: Chowkhamba Sanskrit Series, 1963).
94. Abhinavagupta, *Ipvv*, 1985, 3:271–72: "Ye >pi pratibimbarūpā grāhakās teṣāṃ cidbhāgaḥ śiva eveti upapādya acidbhāgo >pi vedyātmā tacchaktir eva Sadāśivarūpeti upapādayati 'grāhakā api' iti." Other earlier and contemporary forms of dualist Śaivism in Kashmir take this transcendent form of deity, *Sadāśiva*, to be the highest manifestation of divinity. So this cosmology also functions as a polemic. See Alexis Sanderson's extensive delineation of this history, especially in Alexis Sanderson, "Śaivism and the Tantric Traditions," in *Śaivism and the Tantric Traditions*, ed. Stewart Sutherland et al. (London: Routledge, 1988), 660–704.
95. Abhinavagupta's dual-aspect model aligns with the type of dual-aspect model that Harald Atmaspacher points to as being capable of bridging the mind–body distinction, particularly on two counts. First, as Atmanspacher points out, it makes sense to have gradations from the base all throughout as we see in Abhinavagupta as well. See Harald Atmanspacher, "20th Century Variants of Dual-Aspect Thinking," *Mind and Matter* 12, no. 2 (2014): 254–55. Second, Atmanspacher points to another feature, "Ordering factors which may be regarded as ontic relative to the perspective of the mind–matter distinction, can be seen epistemic relative to the *unus mundus*," in Atmanspacher, 255. Atmanspacher explores this relative onticity in Atmanspacher, 287. And again he addresses it in relation to Bohm's physics in Atmanspacher, 284. Abhinavagupta also points to a concept similar to this idea of "relative onticity" stating, "On the level of the process of knowledge the state of *Sadāśiva* is in fact the state of maintenance, but on the level of the thing, the object, the state of *Sadāśiva* is the state of dissolution in Abhinavagupta, *Ipvv*, 1985, 3:272: "Pramāṇabhūmau sadāśivapada eva sthitiḥ, vastubhūmau tu pralaya."
96. The term here for this individual, *Māyāpramātṛ*, indicates a sentient knower situated on the level of *Māyā*, that is, trapped in duality. *Pramātṛ* is literally the one who measures, curiosly evoking again Wheeler's conception of the world coming to exist by questions that delimit and measure it.
97. Abhinavagupta, *Ipvv*, 1985, 3:265–66: "aham iti ananyonmukhaḥ prakāśavimarśaḥ, idam iti anyonmukhaḥ. . . . Māyāpramātari ca tau grāhakagrāhyalakṣaṇe pṛthag adhikaraṇe siddhau."
98. Commenting on this verse defining the fifth *tattva*, Abhinavagupta describes as *śuddhavidyā*, pure: "When 'I' and 'this' function identically, when they both refer to the same entity, this is called '*sadvidyā*', the state of 'real wisdom' || 3 || When this occurs the wisdom, the science is pure (śuddhavidyā). The impure wisdom which later comes out from that is something else," in Abhinavagupta, 3:265: "Sāmānādikaraṇyaṃ ca

sadvidyāhamidaṃ dhiyoḥ ||3|| Satī śuddhā vidyā; aśuddhavidyā tato >nyaiveti avāntarasya arthaḥ."

99. This is Śaṅkara's well-known description of *Māyā* as *anirvācanīya*, incapable of being described.

100. Abhinavagupta tells us, "The Archetype of *Māyā*, is not accepted merely as the material cause in the body and as separate [from the Lord, as is the case in *Sāṃkhya* with *Prakṛti*], but rather is considered as the inseparable Energy (*śakti*) of the Supreme Lord. In fact the categories of earth and so on are only just forms of the Energy of the Supreme Lord." In Abhinavagupta, *Ipvv*, 1985, 3:270: "Māyātattvaṃ dehe na upādānakāraṇamātratvena pṛthaktvena saṃmatam, api tu parameśvaraśaktitayā. Tathā hi mṛdādiḥ padārthaḥ parameśvaraśaktirūpa eva." This means as well that humans and other limited knowers are subject to limitations like the grip of time, but not so with *Māyā*, as Abhinavagupta tells us: "There is connection with the divisions of time for the entities in *Māyā*, but not for *Māyā* herself, as a form of the energy of *Parameśvara*, the supreme Lord," in Abhinavagupta, 3:274: "Māyīyānāṃ kālabhedasaṃgatiḥ, na tu parameśvaraśaktirūpāyā māyāyāḥ."

101. That is: "For this very reason, because of this contraction, the bound soul is in every way Small and limited. This is connected with the statement, "Because of the control of that impurity belonging to *Māyā*, the division into object and Subject occurs, and that is the Small, limited individual," in Abhinavagupta, *Ipvv*, 1985, 3:274: "Tata eva sarvataḥ saṃkocād aṇuḥ. "So >nur yadvaśād bhinnavedyavedakas tanmāyīya."

102. Abhinavagupta, 3:292: "aniruddhaṃ satatānāvṛtaṃ, tatra kim abhivyañjanenety āśaṅkya satyam evaṃ paramārthacaitanye, bhinnaviṣayakalpitacaitanyacarcā punar iyaṃ vartate ity āśayena āh 'caitanyaṃ ca' iti. 'Iha' iti puṃstattve."

103. He tells us, "The words, 'in the category of *karma*' means that [the *Puruṣa*] is being illuminated through dependence on some thing other than itself," in Abhinavagupta, 3:292: "Karmakakṣyām iti pāratantryeṇa prakāśyamānatām."

104. Abhinavagupta: "Isvarapratyabhijnavimarsini, Adhikaras 1–4. Based on the following edition: Īśvara-pratyabhijñā-Vimarśinī of Abhinavagupta: doctrine of divine recognition," ed. K. A. Subramania Iyer and K. C. Pandey (Muktabodha Indological Research Institute, 1986), ad 4.5: "tatra ca saṃkucitacinmātrasvabhāvaḥ puruṣo."

105. Abhinavagupta, *Ipvv*, 1985, 3:292: "Cit ity ādi grāhakāt bhinnam iti yāvat. Arthāntarāt grahyāntarāt vilakṣaṇam; tata eva avibhaktam api grāhakagrāhyābhyāṃ vibhāgamāpāditam, tathābhāve >pi 'svayam' iti svena rūpeṇa saṃvinmātramayatāṃ prakāśamānatvena anujjhad api nīlādi jaḍam ucyate."

106. There are the *tattvas* in the pure creation; then *Māyā* and Abhinavagupta lists the remaining thirty, to make thirty-six: "The word 'thirty' [in Utpaladeva' text] refers to the twenty categories including the gross and subtle elements, the sense organs and organs of action, along with the Archetypes of mind, ego, intellect, Nature, the Person Archetype (*Puruṣa*), attachment, fate (*niyati*), science (*vidyā*), limitation as a part (*kalā*), and time." In Abhinavagupta, 3:269–70: "Triṃśat iti bhūtatanmātrabuddhikarmendriyaviṃśakaṃ mano >hambuddhiprakṛtipuruṣarāganiyatividyākalākālāś ceti."

107. So we see: "The nature of the limited subject as perceiver is affected dependent upon the objects perceived. Although the Energies of time etc., [including also the *tattvas* of *niyati*, individuation, *kalā*, limitation of action, *vidyā*, limitation of knowledge and *rāga*, attachment] affect the object, nevertheless they do so in a general way, not in a particular

way. On the other hand, the Energies of the organs of action and those of the organs of sense perception, the eye, etc., affect the object in a particular way as something [specific] to be known and to be done." In Abhinavagupta, 3:271: "Grāhyāyattatvāt grāhakatāyā yadyapi kālādiśaktayo >pi grāhyam spṛśanti, tathāpi sāmānyata eva na viśeṣataḥ; buddhikarmendriyaśaktayas tu jñeyatayā kāryatayā ca viśeṣata eva grāhyaṃ spṛśanti."

108. Abhinavagupta describes it: "In reality the Lord alone creates things so they exist in some particular way. This being the case, a sprout does not revert back to a seed, nor is the jar the material cause out of which mud arises. Equally, both are incapable of [generating what belongs to the other]. Similarly, by virtue of being experienced in a common way, universally by all Subjects, they are said to manifest in just this one particular way—that the seed is the material cause of the sprout, while clay is not. And likewise, that clay is the material cause of the pot; the seed is not. . . . That attribute, in reality, is only within the Subject, not in the object perceived." Abhinavagupta also construes these as universals. In Abhinavagupta, 3:290: "Tataś ca ayam arthaḥ vastuto bhagavān eva tathā nirbāsate iti sthite na bījasya aṅkuraṃ prati ghaṭaṃ vā upādānatāpi mṛda iti tulyam asāmarthyaṃ dvayoḥ, tathāpi sarvapramātṛsādhāraṇyena evam ābhāti bījam upādānam aṅkurasya, na mṛt; sā tu ghaṭasya, na bījam . . . sa vastutaḥ pramātari eva, na prameye."

109. Abhinavagupta, 3:289: "rāgeṇa rañjitātmāsau kālena kalitaḥ priye |niyatyā yam ito bhūyaḥ puṃbhāvenopabṛṃhitaḥ ||kalodvalitacaitanyo vidyādarśitagocaraḥ."

110. Abhinavagupta states, "In fact, these sheaths are mutually entwined, mutually enhancing each other, like the flavors in a milk sweet . . . 'like the layers / sheaths on the pith of the banana tree stem, like the flavors in a milk-sweet and so on, like the balls within the *kadamba* flower, the sheaths, [attachment, *niyati*, *vidyā* etc.] arise intertwined in a various fluctuating sequence.'" In Abhinavagupta, 3:292–93: "Etāni hi kañcukāni modakaras avadanyonyānugrahalakṣaṇamelanavṛttini. . . . . . kadalīgarbhadalavanmodakādirasādivat |kadambagolavaccitrāt kramāt kañcukasambhavaḥ."

111. Abhinavagupta, 3:270–71: "Kālādayo grāhakatve upayujyante. Adhunā na kiṃcit karomi jānannabhiṣvakto >ham iti hi kālakalāvidyārāgānuviddha eva aṇur niyatyanuprāṇito grāhaka ucyate."

112. Abhinavagupta also counsels us against a merely mental projection of a state of enlightenment, telling us that saying, "and 'I am that [*Brahman*, Self]', [is fine, but] to the extent that the latent residual impressions remains fully [operative], it is reasonable that pride and anger, etc., will still arise. Consciousness, which here possesses latent traces, herself creates limitation. Consciousness is one alone, yet has a specific form where it consists of sound [form, taste] etc. which flow down and are absorbed [in consciousness in the form of residual traces] and from this the subtle body (*puryaṣṭaka*) is separated from [full consciousness.]" In Abhinavagupta, 3:287: "ca 'so >ham' iti tāvat saṃskārapūrṇa eva aham iti parāmarśāt garvakopādyudayā yuktāḥ. Svakṛtasaṃkocasaṃskāravatī yā cit, tanmayatayā pralīnam apasāritaśabdādirūpa viśeṣam ekam iti puryaṣṭakāntarāder bhinnam." See as well Chapter Three on the subtle body, *puryaṣṭaka*, literally the "City of Eight," consisting of mind, ego, vital air, and so on. The subtle body carries the karmas that define us from one life to the next.

113. He links these five sheaths to linguistic expressions affirming their essential inherence within the subject, not outside the subject, saying, "So time with its dual flow of direction is joined with the Person, the *Puruṣa*, as a sheath covering him. This has been duly pointed out in the scriptural texts. [The other sheaths], *niyati*, the force which determines

restriction, fate, and the other three follow along [being joined to the Person] in the same manner. The expressions and the interjections, 'In this way,' 'oh no,' 'somewhat,' 'yesterday,' and 'oh!' are a form of this highest Awareness (*vimarśa*), expressions with the essential nature of one of the sheaths, respectively, of fate, attraction, limitation of action, time, and limitation of knowledge. They occur in pure consciousness, not within the object. The purport of this is that the collection [of the five sheaths] are not independent, nor are they, by their being universally present, qualities of objects." In Abhinavagupta, 3:288: "pravahadvayaḥ kālaḥ sa puṃsa eva kañcukatvena yukta ity āgameṣu tathā nirdiṣṭaḥ. Niyatyāder eṣa eva nayaḥ. 'Eva' iti 'vata vata' iti 'kiṃcit' iti 'hyaḥ' iti 'āsa' iti hi vimarśā niyatirāgakalākālavidyātmānaḥ saṃvidi eva, na vedye. Tad ayaṃ vargo na svatantraḥ, nāpi sāmānyena prameyadharmaḥ."

114. Abhinavagupta, 3:289: "tato hetoḥ kālādīnām ābhāsanakriyāmukhena pravṛttānāṃ kathaṃ pramātṛpratīter bahir bhāvaḥ."

115. Abhinavagupta, 3:289: " 'Kālasya' iti sarvasāmānyam api viśiṣyata iti yāvat." Abhinavagupta continues this passage, saying, "In fact, with the word 'merely', [Utpaladeva] refutes the idea that time is truly common to all Subjects. So in this connection he says, time is 'also a Reflection, a manifestation and manipulation of form which is not reality, but conditional.' To that extent, from afar time performs the activity of delimitation and being remote is another one of its functions. Even the Appearance of time is not external and separate, common to all separately, in the way that a stick is. One may see [first] jasmine flower, then mango, then citron, then kuṭaja, then lotus and then white-flowered jasmine in continued sequence, but the form of time, this sequence does not exist externally, separately from the thing it modifies in the way that a stick does." In Abhinavagupta, 3:289: "Mātrapadena sarvapramātṛsādhāraṇyaṃ nirākṛtam. Ata eva āha "ābhāso >pi" iti. Dūrata eva tāvad avacchedanakriyā, dūre ca arthakriyāntaram. Ābhāsanam api daṇḍavat na kālasya pṛthak sarvasādhāraṇyena bahir asti. Kundacūtamallikākuṭajakamalamālatīsantānam hi kramikaṃ paśyet, na tu tatpratīter bahirbhūtam daṇḍam iva kālaṃ kramarūpam."

116. Abhinavagupta, *Ipvv*, 1985, 3:290: "tataḥ pramātur dharmaḥ kālaḥ." He follows this with the familiar use of etymology to reinforce the argument, where the Sanskrit reveals a pun: "The Subject is indeed driven by time, so we say, he is forced to act by time." In Abhinavagupta, 3:290: "Pramātā hi kalitaḥ san kalayitā kālena kalita iti uktaḥ."

117. Abhinavagupta says, "In deep sleep and in dissolution, negation, and in the meditation *samādhi* state called 'non-existence' the form of that which is not the Self appears, as it were, in the image of space. Then calling to mind that object [the negation] through his free will, he contemplates it as the Self and becomes devoted to it, conceiving it to be the real 'I.' " In Abhinavagupta, *Ipvv*, 1985, 3:280: "'Suṣupte pralaye vā' iti 'na' iti abhāvasamādhau ca yat vyomakalpamanātmarūpam iva ābhāti, tad anusmaryamāṇatvena vedyaṃ sadaham iti ātmatvena svātantryeṇa abhiniviśyate."

118. Abhinavagupta, 3:280: "Ucchvasimi, niḥśvasimi, ity atra prāṇo vāyukalpaḥ, bubhukṣe, pipāssāmi, iti pratyaye manyuprajvalanādau ca sa eva tejaḥ samupabṛṃhitaḥ. Antaraham vedmi sukhī duḥkhī mūḍho >ham, ity ādyavasthāsu svacchasalilāśayasadṛśī buddhiḥ, kṛśaḥ sthūlo gauro >ham, ity ādau śarīram eva pṛthvīprāyam." He continues this section, saying, "And here even though in reality pure consciousness alone exists, when it appears as some external object, [like the body as earth, or hunger as fire] then it is said to be the first type of misapprehension caused by *Māyā*. However, when that which clearly exists in the open as an object, which is even insentient—when that is taken as the Self, the

'I'—that is the second type of delusion caused by *Māyā*." In Abhinavagupta, 3:280: "Atra ca cinmātratāparamārthe >pi yat vedyatābhāsanam, etad ādyaṃ viparyāsaṃ māyīyam; atiraskṛtavedyabhāvam eva tu tat jaḍam api sat yad aham iti ātmatayā bhāti, tat dvitīyam."

119. Barad, *Meeting the Universe Halfway*, 320.
120. Rene Descartes, *Discourse on the Method of Rightly Conducting the Reason, and Seeking Truth in the Sciences*, trans. John Veitch (Chicago: Open Court Publishing Company, 1913), 59–62, https://archive.org/details/in.ernet.dli.2015.1762/page/n3.
121. Abhinavagupta, *Ipvv*, 1985, 3:311: "Yo 'sau mukta uktaḥ, sa bhāvān svāṅgavat pramimīte."

Bibliography

Introduction

Abhinavagupta. *Īśvara-Pratyabhijñā-Vimarśinī of Abhinavagupta: Doctrine of Divine Recognition: Sanskrit Text with the Commentary Bhāskarī*. Edited by K. A. Subramania Iyer and K. C. Pandey. 3 vols. New Delhi: Motilal Banarsidass, 1986.

Abhinavagupta. *Īśvara Pratyabhijñā Vivṛti Vimarśinī*. Edited by Paṇḍit Madhusudan Kaul Śāstrī. Vol. 3. Delhi: Akay Reprints, 1985. https://archive.org/details/in.ernet.dli.2015.485473/mode/2up.

Alper, Harvey. "Judgement as a Transcendental Category in Utpaladeva's Śaiva Theology, The Evidence of the Pratyabhijñākārikāvṛtti." *Adyar Library Bulletin 51* (1987): 176–241.

Ānandavardhana, and Abhinavagupta. *Dhvanyāloka of Ānandavardhana with the Locana of Abhinavagupta*. Translated by Daniel Ingalls, Jeffrey Masson, and M. V. Patwardhan. Harvard Oriental Series. Cambridge, MA: Harvard University Press, 1990.

Baker, Lynne Rudder. *Naturalism and the First-Person Perspective*. New York: Oxford University Press, 2013.

Biernacki, Loriliai. "Connecting Consciousness to Physical Causality: Abhinavagupta's Phenomenology of Subjectivity and Tononi's Integrated Information Theory." *Religions 7* (2016): 87. https://doi.org/10.3390/rel7070087.

Biernacki, Loriliai. "Subtle Body: Rethinking the Body's Subjectivity through Abhinavagupta." *In Transformational Embodiment in Asian Religions: Subtle Bodies, Spatial Bodies*, edited by George Pati and Katherine Zubko, 108–27. London: Routledge, 2019.

Biernacki, Loriliai. "Words and Word-Bodies: Writing the Religious Body." *In Words. Religious Language Matters*, edited by Ernst van den Hemel and Asja Szafraniec, 70–83. New York: Fordham University Press, 2016.

Biernacki, Loriliai, and Philip Clayton, eds. *Panentheism across the World's Traditions*. New York: Oxford University Press, 2014.

Chakrabarti, Arindam. "Arguing from Synthesis to the Self: Utpaladeva and Abhinavagupta Respond to Buddhist No-Selfism." *In Hindu and Buddhist Ideas in Dialogue: Self and No-Self*, edited by Jonardon Ganeri, Irina Kuznetsova, and Chakravarthi Ram-Prasad, 199–216. Burlington, VT: Ashgate, 2012.

Chakravarty, H. N. *Tantrasāra of Abhinavagupta*. Edited by Boris Marjanovic. New Delhi: Rudra Press, 2012.

Douglas Duckworth. "From Yogācāra to Philosophical Tantra in Kashmir and Tibet." *Sophia*, no. 57 (2017): 611–23. https://doi.org/DOI 10.1007/s11841-017-0598-5.

Dyczkowski, Mark. *The Doctrine of Vibration: An Analysis of the Doctrines and Practices of Kashmir Shaivism*. Albany: State University of New York Press, 1986.

Flood, Gavin. *Tantric Body: The Secret Tradition of Hindu Religion*. New York: I. B. Tauris, 2006.

Griffin, David Ray. *Panentheism and Scientific Naturalism: Rethinking Evil, Morality, Religious Experience, Religious Pluralism, and the Academic Study of Religion*. Claremont, CA: Process Century Press, 2014.

Halbfass, Wilhelm. *Tradition and Reflection: Explorations in Indian Thought*. New York: State University of New York Press, 1991.

Hartshorne, Charles, and William Reese, eds. *Philosophers Speak of God*. Chicago: University of Chicago Press, 1953.

Keller, Catherine. *Cloud of the Impossible: Negative Theology and Planetary Entanglement*. New York: Columbia University Press, 2014.

Keller, Catherine. *Intercarnations: Exercises in Theological Possibility*. New York: Fordham University Press, 2017.

Kripal, Jeffrey. *Authors of the Impossible: The Paranormal and the Sacred*. Chicago: University of Chicago Press, 2011.

Kripal, Jeffrey. *Flip: Epiphanies of Mind and the Future of Knowledge*. New York: Bellevue Literary Press, 2019.

Kripal, Jeffrey. *Mutants and Mystics: Science Fiction, Superhero Comics, and the Paranormal*. Chicago: University of Chicago Press, 2015.

Lawrence, David. "Proof of a Sentient Knower: Utpaladeva's Ajaḍapramātṛsiddhi with the Vṛtti of Harabhatta Shastri." *Journal of Indian Philosophy* 37 (2009): 627–53. https://doi.org/10.1007/s10781-009-9074-z.

Lawrence, David. *Rediscovering God with Transcendental Argument: A Contemporary Interpretation of Monistic Kashmiri Śaiva Philosophy*. Rochester: State University of New York Press, 1999.

Lidke, Jeffrey. "A Thousand Years of Abhinavagupta." *Sutra Journal* (January 2016). http://www.sutrajournal.com/a-thousand-years-of-abhinavagupta-by-jeffrey-lidke.

Nemec, John. "Evidence for Somānanda's Pantheism." *Journal of Indian Philosophy 42* (2014): 99–114.

Nemec, John. "Influences on and Legacies of Somānanda's Conception of Materiality." *In Around Abhinavagupta: Aspects of the Intellectual History of Kashmir from the Ninth to the Eleventh Century*, edited by Eli Franco and Isabelle Ratie, 341–74. Berlin: Lit Verlag, 2016.

Nemec, John. "The Two Pratyabhijñā Theories of Error." *Journal of Indian Philosophy 40*, no. 2 (2012): 225–57.

Osborne, Arthur. *Teachings of Bhagavan Sri Ramana Maharshi in His Own Words*. Eighth Edition. Tiruvannamalai: Sri Ramanasramam, 2002.

Oxford English Dictionary. Third Edition. New York: Oxford University Press, 2018. https://www-oed-com.colorado.idm.oclc.org/view.

Padoux, Andre. *Vāc: The Concept of the Word in Selected Hindu Tantras*. Albany: State University of New York Press, 1990.

Pandey, K. C. *Abhinavagupta: An Historical and Philosophical Study*. Second Enlarged Edition. Varanasi: Chowkhamba Sanskrit Series, 1963.

Pandey, K. C. *Īśvarapratyabhijñāvimarśinī in the Light of the Bhāskarī with an Outline of History of Saiva Philosophy*. Vol. *84*. Sarastībhavana-Granthamālā. Varanasi: Sampurnand Sanskrit University, 1996.

Prueitt, Catherine. "Shifting Concepts: The Realignment of Dharmakīrti on Concepts and the Error of Subject/Object Duality in Pratyabhijñā Śaiva Thought." *Journal of Indian Philosophy 45* (2017): 21–47. https://doi.org/10.1007/s10781-016-9297-8.

Raghavan, Venkatarama. *Abhinavagupta and His Works*. Varanasi: Chaukhamba Orientalia, 1981.

Rastogi, Navjivan. *Introduction to the Tantrāloka*. New Delhi: Motilal Banarsidass, 1987.

Rastogi, Navjivan. "Rasānubhūti Pratibhāna ke Rūpa Meṃ." In *The Concept of Rasa with Special reference to Abhinavagupta*, edited by S.C. Pande, 185–205. New Delhi: Aryan Books International, 2009.

Ratie, Isabelle. "The Dreamer and the Yogin: On the Relationship between Buddhist and Śaiva Idealisms." *Bulletin of the School of Oriental and African Studies 73*, no. 3 (October 2010): 437–78.

Ratie, Isabelle. *Le Soi et l'Autre: Identité, Différence et Altérité Dans La Philosophie de La Pratyabhijñā*. Leiden: Brill, 2011.

Ratie, Isabelle. "Otherness in the Pratyabhijñā Philosophy." *Journal of Indian Philosophy 35* (2007): 313–70.

Ratie, Isabelle. "Pāramārthika or Apāramārthika? On the Ontological Status of Separation According to Abhinavagupta." *In Puṣpikā: Tracing Ancient India through Texts and Traditions*, edited by P. Mirning, P.-D. Szanto, and M. Williams, 381–405. Havertown, PA: Oxbow Books, 2014.

Ratie, Isabelle. "Some Hitherto Unknown Fragments of Utpaladeva's Vivṛti (II): Against the Existence of External Objects." *In Śaivism and Tantric Traditions: Essays in Honour of Alexis G.J.S. Sanderson*, edited by Dominic Goodall, Shaman Hatley, Harunaga Isaacson, and Srilata Raman, 106–43. Leiden: Brill, 2020.

Ratie, Isabelle. "Utpaladeva and Abhinavagupta on the Freedom of Consciousness." In *Oxford Handbook of Indian Philosophy*, edited by Jonardon Ganeri, 437–68. New York: Oxford University Press, 2016. https://doi.org/10.1093/oxfordhb/9780199314621.013.27.

Rubenstein, Mary-Jane. *Pantheologies: Gods, Worlds, Monsters*. New York: Columbia University Press, 2018.

Rubenstein, Mary-Jane. *Strange Wonder: The Closure of Metaphysics and the Opening of Awe*. New York: Columbia University Press, 2008.

Sanderson, Alexis. "Śaiva Exegesis of Kashmir." In *Mélanges Tantriques a La Mémoire d'Helene Brunner/ Tantric Studies in Memory of Helene Brunner*, edited by Dominic Goodall and Andre Padoux, *106*:231–442 and 551–82. Collection Indologie. Pondicherry, India: Institut Francais d'Indologie/Ecole Francaise d'Extreme-Orient, 2007.

Sanderson, Alexis. "Śaivism and the Tantric Traditions." *In Śaivism and the Tantric Traditions*, edited by Stewart Sutherland, F Hardy, L. Houlden, and P. Clarke, 660–704. London: Routledge, 1988.

Silburn, Lilian. *Kuṇḍalinī: The Energy of the Depths: A Comprehensive Study Based on the Scriptures of Nondualistic Kasmir Saivism*. Translated by Jacques Gontier. Suny Series in the Shaiva Traditions of Kashmir. Rochester: State University of New York, 1988.

Singh, Jaidev. *Pratyabhijñāhṛdayaṃ: The Secret of Self-Recognition*. Delhi: Motilal Banarsidass, 1977.

Singh, Jaidev. *Vijñāna Bhairava or Divine Consciousness*. Reprint. Delhi: Motilal Banarsidass, 2003.

Skora, Kerry. "The Pulsating Heart and Its Divine Sense Energies: Body and Touch in Abhinavagupta's Trika Śaivism." *Numen 54*, no. 4 (2007): 420–58.

Timalsina, Sthaneshwar. "Body, Self, and Healing in Tantric Ritual Paradigm." *Journal of Hindu Studies 5* (2012): 30–52.

Timalsina, Sthaneshwar. *Language of Images: Visualization and Meaning in Tantras*. Asian Thought and Culture 71. New York: Peter Lang, 2015.

Timalsina, Sthaneshwar. "Reconstructing Abhinavagupta's Philosophy of Power." In *Navin Doshi Felicitation Volume*, 85–104. South Asian Studies Association Volume, 2020.

Timalsina, Sthaneshwar. "Self, Causation, and Agency in the Advaita of Śaṅkara." *In Free Will, Agency, and Selfhood in Indian Philosophy*, edited by Matthew Dasti and Edwin Bryant, 186–209. New York: Oxford University Press, 2013.

Timalsina, Sthaneshwar. *Tantric Visual Culture: A Cognitive Approach*. New York: Routledge, 2015.

Timalsina, Sthaneshwar. "Theatrics of Emotion: Self-Deception and Self-Cultivation in Abhinavagupta's Aesthetics." *Philosophy East and West 66*, no. 1 (January 2016): 104–21.

Torella, Raffaele. "Abhinavagupta as an Aristocrat." In *Archaeologies of the Written: Indian, Tibetan, and Buddhist Studies in Honour of Cristina Scherrer-Schaub*, edited by Vincent Tournier, Vincent Eltschinger, and Marta Sernesi, 843–56. Universitá Degli Studi Di Napoli

"L'orientale" École Française D'extrême-Orient Université De Lausanne 89. Napoli: Unior Press, 2020.

Torella, Raffaele. "A Fragment of Utpaladeva's Isvarapratyabhijna-Vivrti." *East and West 38* (1988): 137–74.

Torella, Raffaele. *Īśvarapratyabhijñākārikā of Utpaladeva with the Author's Vṛtti: Critical Edition and Annotated Translation*. Delhi: Motilal Banarsidass, 2002.

Torella, Raffaele. *Philosophical Traditions of India: An Appraisal*. Varanasi: Indica Books, 2011.

Torella, Raffaele. "Studies in Utpaladeva's Īśvarapratyabhijñā-Vivṛti. Part V: Selfawareness and Yogic Perception." *In Devadattīyam. Johannes Bronkhorst Felicitation Volume*, edited by Francois Voegli, Vincent Eltschinger, Danielle Feller, and Bogdan Diaconescu, 275–300. Bern: Peter Lang, 2012.

Torella, Raffaele. "Studies on Utpaladeva's Īśvarapratyabhijñā-Vivṛti. Part I: Anupalabdhi and Apoha in a Śaiva Garb." *In Expanding and Merging Horizons. Contributions to South Asian and Cross-Cultural Studies in Commemoration of Wilhelm Halbfass*, edited by Karin Preisendanz, 473–90. Vienna: Verlag der Österreichischen Akademie der Wissenschaften, 2007.

Torella, Raffaele. "Studies on Utpaladeva's Īśvarapratyabhijñā-Vivṛti. Part II: What Is Memory?" In *Indica et Tibetica. Festschrift für Michael Hahn Zum 65. Geburtstag von Freunden und Schülern Überreicht*, edited by K. Klaus and J. U. Hartmann, 539–63. Vienna: Arbeitskreis für tibetische und buddhistische Studien Universität Wien, 2007.

Torella, Raffaele. "Studies on Utpaladeva's Īśvarapratyabhijñā-Vivṛti. Part III. Can a Cognition Become the Object of Another Cognition?" *In Mélanges Tantriques à La Mémoire d'Hélène Brunner*, edited by Dominic Goodall and Andre Padoux, 475–84. Pondicherry, India: Institut Français de Pondichéry/École Française d'Extrême-Orient, 2007.

Torella, Raffaele. "Studies on Utpaladeva's Īśvarapratyabhijñā-Vivṛti. Part IV. Light of the Subject, Light of the Object." *In Pramāṇakīrtiḥ. Papers Dedicated to Ernst Steinkellner on the Occasion of His 70th Birthday*, edited by Birgit Kellner et al., 925–40. Vienna: Arbeitskreis für tibetische und buddhistische Studien Universität Wien, 2007.

Vogel, Gretchen. "Where Have All the Insects Gone?" *Science*, 356 (May 10, 2017): 576–79. https://doi.org/10.1126/science.aal1160.

Vyas, Suryaprakaś. *Siddhitrayi*. Varanasi: Chowkhamba Sanskrit Series, 1989.

Wallis, Christopher. *Tantra Illuminated: The Philosophy, History and Practice of a Timeless Tradition*. San Rafael, CA: Mattamayura Press, 2013.

White, David. *Tantra in Practice. Princeton Readings in Religions*. Princeton, NJ: Princeton University Press, 2000.

White, Lynn. "The Historical Roots of Our Ecological Crisis." *Science 155* (1967): 1203–7.

Chapter 1

Abhinavagupta. *Īśvara Pratyabhijñā Vivṛti Vimarśinī*. Edited by Paṇḍit Madhusudan Kaul Śāstrī. Vol. 3. Delhi: Akay Reprints, 1985.

Abhinavagupta. *Īśvara Pratyabhijñā Vivṛti Vimarśinī*. Edited by Paṇḍit Madhusudan Kaul Śāstrī. Vol. 2. Delhi: Akay Reprints, 1985. https://archive.org/details/in.ernet.dli.2015.326570/page/n1/mode/2up.

Abhinavagupta. "*Isvarapratyabhijnavimarsini, Adhikaras 1-4. Based on the following edition: Īśvara-pratyabhijñā-Vimarśinī of Abhinavagupta: doctrine of divine recognition.*" Edited by K.A. Subramania Iyer and K.C. Pandey. Muktabodha Indological Research Institute, 1986.

Abhinavagupta. *Trident of Wisdom: Translation of Parātrīśikāvivaraṇa*. Translated by Jaidev Singh. Suny Series in Tantric Studies. Rochester: State University of New York Press, 1989.

Abhinavagupta and Utpaladeva. *Isvarapratyabhijnavimarsini, Adhikaras 1-4. Based on the following edition: Īśvara-pratyabhijñā-Vimarśinī of Abhinavagupta: doctrine of devine recognition, Sanskrit Text with the commentary Bhāskarī*. Edited by K.C. Pandey and K.A. Subramania-Iyer. Delhi: Motilal Banarsidass, digital on Goettingen Register of Electronic Texts in Indian Languages, 1986. http://gretil.sub.uni-goettingen.de/gretil/1_sanskr/6_sastra/3_phil/saiva/abhiprvu.htm.

Bansat-Boudon, Lyne. "On Śaiva Terminology: Some Key Issues of Understanding." *Journal of Indian Philosophy 42*, no. 1 (March 2014): 39–97.

Barad, Karen. *Meeting the Universe Halfway: Quantum Physics and the Entanglement of Matter and Meaning*. Durham, NC: Duke University Press, 2007.

Bennett, Jane. *Vibrant Matter: A Political Ecology of Things*. Durham, NC: Duke University Press, 2010.

Biernacki, Loriliai. "Body and Mind in Medieval Hinduism." *In A Cultural History of Hinduism in the Post-Classical Age, 800–1500 CE*, edited by Karen Pechilis. Routledge, Forthcoming 2023.

Biernacki, Loriliai. "Connecting Consciousness to Physical Causality: Abhinavagupta's Phenomenology of Subjectivity and Tononi's Integrated Information Theory." *Religions 7* (2016). https://doi.org/10.3390/rel7070087.

Biernacki, Loriliai. "Material Subjects, Immaterial Bodies: Abhinavagupta's Panentheist Matter." *In Entangled Worlds: Religion, Science and the New Materialisms*, edited by Catherine Keller and Mary-Jane Rubenstein, 182–202. New York: Fordham University Press, 2017.

Biernacki, Loriliai. "Transcendence in Sports: How Do We Interpret Mysticism in Sports? Tantra and Cognitive Science Perspectives." *Journal for the Study of Religious Experience 4* (2018): 24–39.

Brown, Bill. "Thing Theory." *Critical Inquiry 28*, no. 1 (Autumn 2001): 1–22.

Bruntrup, Godehard, and Ludwig Jaskolla, eds. *Panpsychism: Contemporary Perspectives*. New York: Oxford University Press, 2016.

Bruntrup, Godehard, Ludwig Jaskolla, and Benedikt Paul Göcke, eds. *Panentheism and Panpsychism: Philosophy of Religion Meets Philosophy of Mind*. Leiden: Brill Mentis, 2020.

Buhner, Stephen. *Healing Lyme: Natural Healing of Lyme Borreliosis and the Coinfections Chlamydia and Spotted Fever Rickettsioses*. Boulder, CO: Raven Press, 2015.

Buhner, Stephen. *Herbal Antivirals: Natural Remedies for Emerging Resistant and Epidemic Viral Infections*. North Adams, MA: Storey Publishing, 2013.

Bynum, Caroline Walker. "Presidential Address: Wonder." *American Historical Review 102*, no. 1 (February 1997): 1–17.

Cardona, George. "Pāṇini's Kārakas: Agency, Animation and Identity." *Journal of Indian Philosophy 2* (1972): 231–306.

Chakrabarti, Arindam. "Arindam Chakrabarti. "Arguing from Synthesis to the Self: Utpaladeva and Abhinavagupta Respond to Buddhist No-Selfism." *In Hindu and Buddhist Ideas in Dialogue: Self and No-Self*, edited by Jonardon Ganeri, Irina Kuznetsova, and Chakravarthi Ram-Prasad, 199–216. Burlington, VT: Ashgate, 2012.

Chalmers, David. *The Conscious Mind: In Search of a Fundamental Theory*. New York: Oxford University Press, 1996.

Chen, Mel. *Animacies: Biopolitics, Racial Mattering and Queer Affect*. Durham, NC: Duke University Press, 2012.

Connolly, William. *World of Becoming*. Durham, NC: Duke University Press, 2011.

Coole, Diana. "Inertia of Matter and the Generativity of Flesh." In *New Materialisms: Ontology, Agency and Politics*, edited by Diana Coole and Samantha Frost, 92–115. Durham, NC: Duke University Press, 2010.

Coole, Diana, and Samantha Frost, eds. *New Materialisms: Ontology, Agency, and Politics*. Durham, NC: Duke University Press, 2010.

Danowski, Deborah, and Eduardo Viveiros de Castro. *Ends of the World*. Malden, MA: Polity Press, 2016.

Dawkins, Richard. *Selfish Gene*. London: Oxford University Press, 1976.

Descartes, Rene. *Discourse on the Method of Rightly Conducting the Reason, and Seeking Truth in the Sciences*. Edited by Ilana Newby, Greg Newby, and Al Haines. Translated by John Veitch. EBook 59. Project Gutenberg, 1637. https://www.gutenberg.org/files/59/59-h/59-h.htm.

Dietart, Rodney. *Human Superorganism: How the Microbiome Is Revolutionizing the Pursuit of a Healthy Life*. New York: Dutton, Penguin Books, 2016.

Eck, Diana. *Darshan: Seeing the Divine Image in India*. 3rd ed. New York: Columbia University Press, 1998.

Flora, S. J. S., and Shruti Agrawal. "Arsenic, Cadmium, and Lead." In *Reproductive and Developmental Toxicology*, edited by Ramesh Gupta, 2nd ed., 537–66. North Andover, MA: Elsevier Academic Press, 2017. https://www.sciencedirect.com/book/9780128042397/reproductive-and-developmental-toxicology.

Goff, Philip. *Consciousness and Fundamental Reality*. New York: Oxford University Press, 2017.

Goff, Philip. "Why Panpsychism Doesn't Help Us Explain Consciousness." *Dialectica 63*, no. 3 (2009): 289–311. https://doi.org/10.1111/j.1746-8361.2009.01196x.

Harman, William. "Critical Animal with a Fun Little Post." *Object-Oriented Philosophy* (blog), October 17, 2011. https://doctorzamalek2.wordpress.com/2011/10/17/critical-animal-with-a-fun-little-post.

Horgan, Terry, and Matjaz Potrc. "Existence Monism Trumps Priority Monism." In *Spinoza on Monism*, edited by Philip Goff, 51–76. London: Palgrave Macmillan, 2012.

Kaiser, David. *How the Hippies Saved Physics: Science, Counterculture and the Quantum Revival*. New York: W. W. Norton, 2012.

Kauffman, Stuart. *Investigations*. New York: Oxford University Press, 2000.

Keller, Catherine. *Cloud of the Impossible: Negative Theology and Planetary Entanglement*. New York: Columbia University Press, 2014.

Keller, Catherine. *Face of the Deep: A Theology of Becoming*. New York: Routledge, 2003.

Keller, Catherine. *Intercarnations: Exercises in Theological Possibility*. New York: Fordham University Press, 2017.

Kripal, Jeffrey. *Esalen: The Religion of No Religion*. Chicago: University of Chicago Press, 2008.

Kripal, Jeffrey. *Flip: Epiphanies of Mind and the Future of Knowledge*. New York: Bellevue Literary Press, 2019.

Krishna, Daya. *Indian Philosophy: A Counter Perspective*. New Delhi: Satguru Publications, 2006.

Krohn, Elizabeth, and Jeffrey Kripal. *Changed in a Flash: One Woman's Near-Death Experience and Whay a Scholar Thinks It Empowers Us All*. Berkeley, CA: North Atlantic Books, 2018.

Larson, Gerald. *Classical Sāṃkhya: An Inerpretation of Its History and Meaning*. Reprint. Delhi: Motilal Banarsidass, 1998.

Latour, Bruno. "Collective of Humans and Nonhumans." In *Technology and Values: Essential Readings*, edited by Craig Hanks, 156–67. Malden, MA: Wiley-Blackwell, 2010.

Latour, Bruno. *Facing Gaia: A New Enquiry into Natural Religion*. Gifford Lectures, 2013. https://www.giffordlectures.org/lecturers/bruno-latour.

Latour, Bruno. *We Have Never Been Modern*. Cambridge, MA: Harvard University Press, 1993.

Lawrence, David. "Proof of a Sentient Knower: Utpaladeva's Ajaḍapramātṛsiddhi with the Vṛtti of Harabhatta Shastri." *Journal of Indian Philosophy 37*, no. 6 (2009): 627–53. https://doi.org/10.1007/s10781-009-9074-z.

Lawrence, David. *Rediscovering God with Transcendental Argument: A Contemporary Interpretation of Monistic Kashmiri Śaiva Philosophy*. Rochester: State University of New York Press, 1999.

Lawrence, David. "Remarks on Abhinavagupta's Use of the Analogy of Reflection." *Journal of Indian Philosophy* 33 (2005): 583–99.

Livingston, Julie, and Jasbir Puar. "Interspecies." *Social Text 29*, no. 1 (2011): 3–14.

Long, Jeffrey. *Hinduism in America*. London: Bloomsbury Academic, 2020.

Margulis, Lynn. *Symbiotic Planet*. New York: Basic Books, 1998.

"Marie Kondo." In *Wikipedia*. Accessed May 17, 2020. https://en.wikipedia.org/wiki/Marie_Kondo#cite_note-oz-11.

Marshall, Trevor. *Microbiome and Disease: St. Petersburg State University Address*. St. Petersburg State University, 2013. https://www.youtube.com/watch?v=e7PfrkhsKEc.

Martin, Raymond, and John Barresi. *Rise and Fall of Soul and Self: An Intellectual History of Personal Identity*. New York: Columbia University Press, 2008.

Mathews, Freya. "Panpsychism as Paradigm." *In Mental as Fundamental: New Perspectives on Panpsychism*, edited by Michael Blamauer, 141–56. Frankfurt: Ontos Verlag, 2011.

Morton, Timothy. *Hyperobjects: Philosophy and Ecology after the End of the World*. Minneapolis: University of Minnesota Press, 2013.

Nagel, Thomas. *Mind and Cosmos: Why the Materialist Neo-Darwinian Conception of Nature Is Almost Certainly False*. New York: Oxford University Press, 2012.

Nemec, John. "Evidence for Somānanda's Pantheism." *Journal of Indian Philos 42* (2014): 99–114.

Nemec, John. "Influences on and Legacies of Somānanda's Conception of Materiality." *In Around Abhinavagupta: Aspects of the Intellectual History of Kashmir from the Ninth to the Eleventh Century*, edited by Eli Franco and Isabelle Ratie, 341–74. Berlin: Lit Verlag, 2016.

Nemec, John. *Ubiquitous Śiva: Somānanda's Śivadṛṣṭi and His Tantric Interlocutors*. New York: Oxford University Press, 2011.

Nevin, Rick. "How Lead Exposure Relates to Temporal Changes in IQ, Violent Crime, and Unwed Preganancy." *Environmental Research 83*, no. 1 (2000): 1–22.

Pandey, K. C. *Abhinavagupta: An Historical and Philosophical Study*. Second Enlarged Edition. Varanasi, India: Chowkhamba Sanskrit Series, 1963.

Pandey, K. C. *Iśvara Pratyabhijñā of Utpaladeva with the Vimarśinī*. Reprint edition. Vol. 3. Delhi: Butala and Company, 1984.

Prueitt, Catherine. "Shifting Concepts: The Realignment of Dharmakīrti on Concepts and the Error of Subject/Object Duality in Pratyabhijñā Śaiva Thought." *Journal of Indian Philosophy 45* (2017): 21–47. https://doi.org/DOI10.1007/s10781-016-9297-8.

Ratie, Isabelle. "Can One Prove That Something Exists beyond Consciousness? A Śaiva Criticism of the Sautrāntika Inference of External Objects." *Journal of Indian Philosophy 39* (2011): 479–501.

Ratie, Isabelle. "Otherness in the Pratyabhijñā Philosophy." *Journal of Indian Philosophy 35* (2007): 313–70.

Ratie, Isabelle. "Pāramārthika or Apāramārthika? On the Ontological Status of Separation According to Abhinavagupta." *In Puṣpikā: Tracing Ancient India through Texts and Traditions*, edited by P. Mirning, P.-D. Szanto, and M. Williams, 381–405. Havertown, UK: Oxbow Books, 2014.

Ratie, Isabelle. "Śaiva Interpretation of the Satkāryavāda: The Sāṃkhya Notion of Abhivyakti and Its Transformation in the Pratyabhijñā Treatise." *Journal of Indian Philosophy 42*, no. 1 (March 2014): 127–72.

Ratie, Isabelle. "Some Hitherto Unknown Fragments of Utpaladeva's Vivṛti (II): Against the Existence of External Objects." *In Śaivism and Tantric Traditions: Essays in Honour of Alexis G.J.S. Sanderson*, edited by Dominic Goodall, Shaman Hatley, Harunaga Isaacson, and Srilata Raman, 106–43. Leiden: Brill, 2020.

Ratie, Isabelle. "The Dreamer and the Yogin: On the Relationship between Buddhist and Śaiva Idealisms." *Bulletin of the School of Oriental and African Studies 73*, no. 3 (October 2010): 437–78.

Reps, Paul. *Zen Flesh, Zen Bones: A Collection of Zen and Pre-Zen Writings*. North Clarendon, VT: Tuttle Publishing, 1957.

Riskin, Jessica. *Restless Clock: A History of the Centuries-Long Argument over What Makes Things Tick*. Chicago: University of Chicago Press, 2016.

Rubenstein, Mary-Jane. *Pantheologies: Gods, Worlds, Monsters*. New York: Columbia University Press, 2018.

Sanderson, Alexis. "Śaivism and the Tantric Traditions." *In Śaivism and the Tantric Traditions*, edited by Stewart Sutherland, F. Hardy, L. Houlden, and P. Clarke, 660–704. London: Routledge, 1988.

Schaffer, Jonathan. "Monism: The Priority of the Whole." *In Spinoza on Monism*, edited by Philip Goff, 9–50. London: Palgrave Macmillan, 2012.

Searle, John. "Can Information Theory Explain Consciousness?" *New York Times Review of Books*. January 10, 2013, 53–58. https://www.nybooks.com/articles/2013/01/10/can-information-theory-explain-consciousness/.

Shani, Itay. "Cosmopsychism: A Holistic Approach to the Metaphysics of Experience." *Philosophical Papers* 44, no. 3 (2015): 389–437. https://doi.org/10.1080/05568641.2015.1106709.

Shapin, Steven, and Simon Schaffer. *Leviathan and the Air-Pump: Hobbes, Boyle, and the Experimental Life*. Princeton, NJ: Princeton University Press, 2011.

Singh, Jaidev. *Vijñāna Bhairava or Divine Consciousness*. Reprint. Delhi: Motilal Banarsidass, 2003.

Skaria, Ajay. *Unconditional Equality:Gandhi's Religion of Resistance*. Minneapolis: University of Minnesota Press, 2016.

Smith, Frederick. *Self Possessed: Deity and Spirit Possession in South Asian Literature and Civilization*. New York: Columbia University Press, 2006.

Somadeva. *Kathāsaritsāgara*. Nirnaya-Sagar Press in GRETIL, 1915. http://gretil.sub.uni-goettingen.de/gretil/1_sanskr/5_poetry/4_narr/sokss_pu.htm.

Somānanda. *Śivadṛṣṭi with the Vṛtti of Utpaladeva*. Edited by Madhusūdana Kaula Śāstrī. Muktabodha Indological Research. Vol. *54*. Srinagar, Kashmir: Kashmir Series of Texts and Studies, 1934. https://etexts.muktabodha.org/DL_CATALOG_USER_INTERFACE/dl_user_interface_create_utf8_text.php?hk_file_url=..%2FTEXTS%2FETEXTS%2FsivadrstiHK.txt&miri_catalog_number=M00081.

Strawson, Galen. "Physicalist Panpsychism." *In Blackwell Companion to Consciousness*. Second Edition, edited by Susan Schneider and Max Velmans, 374–90. Oxford: John Wiley, 2017.

Taittirīya. *Taittirīya Mantrakośaḥ: Prathamo Bhagaḥ*. Edited by Ramakrishna Maṭh. Mylapore, Madras: Ramakrishna Math Printing Press, n.d.

Timalsina, Sthaneshwar. "Aham, Subjecitivity, and the Ego: Engaging the Philosophy of Abhinavagupta." *Journal of Indian Philosophy 48*, no. 4 (September 2020): 767–89. https://doi.org/10.1007/s10781-020-09439.

Timalsina, Sthaneshwar. "Body, Self, and Healing in Tantric Ritual Paradigm." *Journal of Hindu Studies 5* (2012): 30–52.

Timalsina, Sthaneshwar. "Brahman and the Word Principle (Śabda): Influence of the Philosophy of Bhartṛhari on Maṇḍana's Brahmasiddhi." *Journal of Indian Philosophy 37* (2009): 189–206. https://doi.org/10.1007/s10781-009-9065-0.

Timalsina, Sthaneshwar. "Self, Causation, and Agency in the Advaita of Śaṅkara." *In Free Will, Agency, and Selfhood in Indian Philosophy*, edited by Matthew Dasti and Edwin Bryant, 186–209. New York: Oxford University Press, 2013.

Torella, Raffaele. "How Is Verbal Signification Possible: Understanding Abhinavagupta's Reply." *Journal of Indian Philosophy 32* (2004): 173–88.

Torella, Raffaele. *Īśvarapratyabhijñākārikā of Utpaladeva with the Author's Vṛtti: Critical Edition and Annotated Translation*. Delhi: Motilal Banarsidass, 2002.

Viveiros de Castro, Eduardo. *Cannibal Metaphysics*. Translated by Peter Skafish. Minneapolis: Univocal, 2014.

Whitman, Walt. "*Song of Myself*." Poetry Foundation. Accessed May 24, 2020. https://www.poetryfoundation.org/poems/45477/song-of-myself-1892-version.

Chapter 2

Abhinavagupta. *Īśvara Pratyabhijñā Vivṛti Vimarśinī*. Edited by Paṇḍit Madhusudan Kaul Śāstrī. Vol. *3*. Delhi: Akay Reprints, 1985.

Abhinavagupta. *Īśvara Pratyabhijñā Vivṛti Vimarśinī*. Edited by Paṇḍit Madhusudan Kaul Śāstrī. Vol. *2*. Delhi: Akay Reprints, 1985. https://archive.org/details/in.ernet.dli.2015.326570/page/n1/mode/2up.

Abhinavagupta. *Īśvara Pratyabhijñā Vivṛti Vimarśinī*. Edited by Paṇḍit Madhusudan Kaul Śāstrī. Reprint. Vol. *1*. Delhi: Akay Reprints, 1985. https://archive.org/details/IshvaraPratyabhijnaVivritiVimarshiniAbhinavaguptaPart1KashmirSanskrit/mode/2up.

Abhinavagupta. *Tantrasāra*. Edited by Paṇḍit Mukund Rām Shāstrī, Vol. *17*. Kashmir Series of Texts and Studies. Srinagar, Kashmir: Research Department Jammu and Kashmir State in Muktabodha Digital Library, 1918. http://muktalib5.org/DL_CATALOG/DL_CATALOG_USER_INTERFACE/dl_user_interface_create_utf8_text.php?hk_file_url=..%2FTEXTS%2FETEXTS%2FtantrasaaraHK.txt&miri_catalog_number=M00153.

Alper, Harvey. "Judgement as a Transcendental Category in Utpaladeva's Śaiva Theology, The Evidence of the Pratyabhijñākārikāvṛtti." *Adyar Library Bulletin 51* (1987): 176–241.

Baker, Lynne Rudder. *Naturalism and the First-Person Perspective*. New York: Oxford University Press, 2013.

Bansat-Boudon, Lyne. *An Introduction to Tantric Philosophy: The Paramārthasāra of Abhinavagupta with the Commentary of Yogarāja*. Translated by Lyne Bansat-Boudon and Kamaleshadatta Tripathi. Routledge Studies in Tantric Traditions. New York: Routledge, 2011.

Biernacki, Loriliai. "Connecting Consciousness to Physical Causality: Abhinavagupta's Phenomenology of Subjectivity and Tononi's Integrated Information Theory." *Religions 7* (2016): 1–11. https://doi.org/10.3390/rel7070087.

Biernacki, Loriliai. "Material Subjects, Immaterial Bodies: Abhinavagupta's Panentheist Matter." *In Entangled Worlds: Religion, Science and the New Materialisms*, edited by Catherine Keller and Mary-Jane Rubenstein, 182–202. New York: Fordham University Press, 2017.

Biernacki, Loriliai. *Renowned Goddess of Desire: Women, Sex and Speech in Tantra*. New York: Oxford University Press, 2007.

Bynum, Caroline Walker. "Presidential Address: Wonder." *American Historical Review 102*, no. 1 (February 1997): 1–17.

Connolly, William. "Materialities of Experience." *In New Materialisms: Ontology, Agency and Politics*, edited by Diana Coole and Samantha Frost, 178–200. Durham, NC: Duke University Press, 2010.

Connolly, William. *World of Becoming*. Durham, NC: Duke University Press, 2011.

Daston, Lorraine, and Katharine Park. *Wonders and the Order of Nature*. New York: Zone Books, 1998.

Dawkins, Richard. *Selfish Gene*. London: Oxford University Press, 1976.

Dennett, Daniel. *Consciousness Explained*. New York: Little, Brown and Co., 1991.

Dreyfus, George. "*Self and Subjectivity: A Middle Way Approach*," 114–56. New York: Oxford University Press, 2013.

Flood, Gavin. *Tantric Body: The Secret Tradition of HIndu Religion*. New York: I. B. Tauris, 2006.

Ganeri, Jonardon. "Emergentisms: Ancient and Modern." *Mind 120*, no. 479 (2011): 671–703. https://doi.org/10.1093/mind/fzr038.

Ganeri, Jonardon. *Self: Naturalism, Consciousness, and the First-Person Stance*. New York: Oxford University Press, 2015.

Goff, Philip. *Consciousness and Fundamental Reality*. New York: Oxford University Press, 2017.

Hulin, Michel. "The Conception of Camatkāra in Indian Aesthetics." *In Practices of Wonder: Cross-Disciplinary Perspectives*, edited by Sophia Vasalou, 225–34. Cambridge: James Clarke & Co., 2013.

Keller, Catherine. *Intercarnations: Exercises in Theological Possibility*. New York: Fordham University Press, 2017.

Krohn, Elizabeth, and Jeffrey Kripal. *Changed in a Flash: One Woman's Near-Death Experience and Why a Scholar Thinks It Empowers Us All*. Berkeley, CA: North Atlantic Books, 2018.

Lawrence, David. *Rediscovering God with Transcendental Argument: A Contemporary Interpretation of Monistic Kashmiri Śaiva Philosophy*. Rochester: State University of New York Press, 1999.

Matravers, Derek. "Wonder and Cognition." *In Practices of Wonder: Cross-Disciplinary Perspectives*, edited by Sophia Vasalou, 166–78. Cambridge, UK: James Clarke & Co., 2013.

Monier-Williams, Monier. *Sanskrit-English Dictionary, Etymlogically and Philologically Arranged with Special Reference to Cognate Indo-European Languages*. New York: Oxford University Press, 1960. https://www.sanskrit-lexicon.uni-koeln.de/monier.

Nagel, Thomas. *Mind and Cosmos: Why the Materialist Neo-Darwinian Conception of Nature Is Almost Certainly False*. New York: Oxford University Press, 2012.

Nagel, Thomas. *View from Nowhere*. New York: Oxford University Press, 1986.

Nemec, John. "Evidence for Somānanda's Pantheism." *Journal of Indian Philosophy 42* (2014): 99–114.

Nemec, John. *Ubiquitous Śiva: Somānanda's Śivadṛṣṭi and His Tantric Interlocutors*. New York: Oxford University Press, 2011.

Nussbaum, Martha. *Upheavals of Thought: The Intelligence of Emotions*. Cambridge: Cambridge University Press, 2001.

Raghavan, Venkatarama. *Studies on Some Concepts of the Alamkāra-Shastra*. Adyar Library Series, 33. Adyar: Adyar Library and Research Center, 1942.

Ratie, Isabelle. "Remarks on Compassion and Altruism in the Pratyabhijñā Philosophy." *Journal of Indian Philosophy 37*, no. 4 (2009): 349–66.

Rubenstein, Mary-Jane. *Strange Wonder: The Closure of Metaphysics and the Opening of Awe*. New York: Columbia University Press, 2008.

Sanderson, Alexis. "Śaivism and the Tantric Traditions." *In Śaivism and the Tantric Traditions*, edited by Stewart Sutherland, F Hardy, L. Houlden, and P. Clarke, 660–704. London: Routledge, 1988.

Shulman, David. *More Than Real: A History of the Imagination in South India*. Cambridge, MA: Harvard University Press, 2012.

Srinivas, Tulasi. *Cow in the Elevator: An Anthropology of Wonder*. Durham, NC: Duke University Press, 2018.

Timalsina, Sthaneshwar. "Savoring Rasa: Emotion, Judgement, and Phenomenal Content." *In Bloomsbury Research Handbook of Emotions in Classical Indian Philosophy*, edited by Maria Heim, Chakravarthi Ram-Prasad, and Roy Tzohar, 255–75. London: Bloomsbury Academic, 2021.

Timalsina, Sthaneshwar. "Theatrics of Emotion: Self-Deception and Self-Cultivation in Abhinavagupta's Aesthetics." *Philosophy East & West 66*, no. 1 (January 2016): 104–21.

Torella, Raffaele. "Abhinavagupta's Attitude towards Yoga." *Journal of the American Oriental Society 139*, no. 3 (2019): 647–60.

Torella, Raffaele. *Īśvarapratyabhijñākārikā of Utpaladeva with the Author's Vṛtti: Critical Edition and Annotated Translation*. Delhi: Motilal Banarsidass, 2002.

Utpaladeva, and Kṣemarāja. *Śivastotrāvalī*. Edited by Rai Pramadasa Mitra Bahadur. Benares: Chowkhamba Sanskrit Series, 1902.

Vasalou, Sophia. *Practices of Wonder: Cross-Disciplinary Perspectives*. Cambridge: James clarke & Co., 2013.

Chapter 3

Abhinavagupta. *Īśvara Pratyabhijñā Vivṛti Vimarśinī*. Edited by Paṇḍit Madhusudan Kaul Shāstrī. Vol. *3*. Delhi: Akay Reprints, 1985.

Abhinavagupta. *Dehasthadevatācakrastrotram*. http://www.abhinavagupta.net/hymns/track-5-dehasta-devata-cakra-strotra, New Delhi: Ishwar Ashram Trust, accessed September 22, 2018.

Aklujkar, Ashok. "Can the Grammarians 'Dharma' Be a 'Dharma' for All?" *Journal of Indian Philosophy* (Spring) *32* (2004): 687–732.

Alper, Harvey. "Judgement as a Transcendental Category in Utpaladeva's Śaiva Theology, The Evidence of the Pratyabhijñākārikāvṛtti." *Adyar Library Bulletin 51* (1987): 176–241.

Alter, Joseph. "Sex, Askesis and the Athletic Perfection of the Soul: Physical Philosophy in the Ancient Mediterranean and South Asia." In *Religion and the Subtle Body in Asia and the West*, edited by Geoffrey Samuel and Jay Johnston, 120–48. New York: Routledge, 2015.

Arnold, Dan. *Brains, Buddhas, and Believing: The Problem of Intentionality in Classical Buddhist and Cognitive-Scientific Philosophy of Mind*. New York: Columbia University Press, 2014.

Bṛhadaraṇyaka. "Bṛhadaraṇyaka Upaniṣad with Śankara's commentary." *Brhadaranyaka-Upanisad (Brhadaranyakopanisad), Kanva recension with the commentary ascribed to Samkara*. Edited by V. P. Limaye and R. D. Vadekar. *Prod. Input by members of the Sansknet* project. Poona: Vaidika Saṁśodhana Mandala, 2020 [1958].

Baker, Lynne Rudder. *Naturalism and the First-Person Perspective*. New York: Oxford University Press, 2013.

Bering, Jesse. "One Last Goodbye: The Strange Case of Terminal Lucidity." *Scientific American*, November 25, 2014. https://blogs.scientificamerican.com/bering-in-mind/one-last-goodbye-the-strange-case-of-terminal-lucidity/.

Bhartṛhari. *Vākyapadīya*. Based on the edition by Wilhelm Rau. Gottingen: Gottingen Register of Electronic Texts in Indian Languages, 1977.

Biernacki, Loriliai. "Transcendence in Sports: How Do We Interpret Mysticism in Sports? Tantra and Cognitive Science Perspectives." *Journal for the Study of Religious Experience 4*, no. 1 (2018): 24–39.

Coseru, Christian. "Freedom from Responsibility: Agent-Neutral Consequentialism and the Bodhisattva Ideal." In *Buddhist Perspectives on Free Will: Agentless Agency?*, edited by Rick Repetti, 92–105. London: Routledge, 2016.

Coseru, Christian. *Perceiving Reality: Consciousness, Inentionality and Cognition in Buddhist Philosophy*. New York: Oxford University Press, 2012.

Coseru, Christian. "Taking the Intentionality of Perception Seriously: Why Phenomenology Is Inescapable." *Philosophy East and West 65*, no. 1 (2015): 227–48.

Damasio, Antonio. *Self Comes to Mind: Constructing the Conscious Brain*. New York: Pantheon, 2010.

Dasti, Matthew, and Stephen Phillips. *Nyāya Sutra: Selections with Early Commentaries*. Translated by Matthew Dasti and Stephen Phillips. Indianapolis: Hackett Publishing Co., 2017.

Donald, Merlin. *Mind So Rare: the Evolution of Human Consciousness*. New York: W. W. Norton, 2002.

Flood, Gavin. *Body and Cosmology in Kashmir Śaivism*. San Francisco: Mellen Research University Press, 1993.

Flood, Gavin. *Tantric Body: The Secret Tradition of Hindu Religion*. New York: I. B. Tauris, 2006.

Franco, Eli, and Eigner, Dagmar. *Yogic Perception, Meditation and Altered States of Consciousness*. Wien: Austrian Academy of Sciences Press, 2009.

Ganeri, Jonardon. "Self-Intimation, Memory and Personal Identity." *Journal of Indian Philosophy, 27* (1999): 469–83.

Ganeri, Jonardon. *Self: Naturalism, Consciousness, and the First-Person Stance*. New York: Oxford University Press, 2015.

Halbfass, Wilhelm. *Tradition and Reflection: Explorations in Indian Thought*. New York: State University of New York Press, 1991.

Hartzell, James. *Tantric Yoga*. Ann Arbor, MI: UMI Dissertation, 1997.

Heilijgers-Seelen, Dory. *The System of Five Cakras in Kubjikamatatantra, 14–16*. Leiden: Brill, 1994.

Johnston, Jay. "Subtle Subjects and Ethics: The Subtle Bodies of Post-Structuralist and Feminist Philosophy." In *Religion and the Subtle Body in Asia and the West: Between Mind and Body*, edited by Geoffrey Samuel and Jay Johnston, 239–48. New York: Routledge, 2013.

Kavirāja, Gopī Nātha. *Tripurā Rahasya (Jñāna Khaṇḍa)*. Edited by Gopī Nātha Kavirāja. Vol. 15. Varanasi: Princess of Wales Saraswati Bhavana Texts, 1927.

Lakoff, George, and Marc Johnson. *Philosophy in the Flesh*. New York: Basic Books, 1999.

Larson, Gerald. *Classical Sāṃkhya: An Inerpretation of its History and Meaning*. Delhi: Motilal Banarsidass, 1969.

Maas, Philip. "The So-called Yoga of Suppression in the Pātāñjala Yogaśāstra." *In Yogic Perception, Meditation and Altered States of Consciousness*, edited by Eli Franco and Dagmar Eigner, 263–82. Wien: Austria Academy of Sciences, 2009.

Madhava-Vidyaranya. *Sankara-Dig-Vijaya: The Traditional Life of Sankaracharya*. Madras: Ramakrishna Math, n.d.

McAuliffe, Kathleen. *This is your Brain on Parasites*. Boston: Mariner Books, Houghton Miflin Harcourt, 2016.

McNamara, Patrick. *Neuroscience of Religious Experience*. New York: Cambridge University Press, 2014.

Metzinger, Thomas. "Why Are Out-of-Body Experiences Interesting for Philosophers? The Theoretical Relevance of OBE Research." *Cortex 45* (2009): 256–58.

Morton, Timothy. *Hyperobjects: Philosophy and Ecology after the End of the World* . Minneapolis: University of Minnesota Press, 2013.

Olivelle, Patrick. *Upaniṣads*. Translated by Patrick Olivelle. New York: Oxford University Press, 1996.

Radhakrishnan, S. *The Principle Upaniṣads*. Translated by S. Radhakrishnan. London: Unwin Hyman, 1989.

Ratie, Isabelle. "Can One Prove That Something Exists beyond Consciousness? A Śaiva Criticism of the Sautrāntika Inference of External Objects." *Journal of Indian Philosophy 39* (2011): 479–501.

Ratie, Isabelle. "Otherness in the Pratyabhijñā Philosophy." *Journal of Indian Philosophy 35* (2007): 313–70.

Samuel, Geoffrey. "Subtle-body Processes: towards a Non-redutionist Understanding." In *Religion and the Subtle Body in Asia and the West: Between Mind and Body*, edited by Geoffrey Samuel and Jay Johnston, 249–66. New York: Routledge, 2013.

Sanderson, Alexis. "Śaivism and the Tantric Traditions." In *World's Religions*, edited by Stewart Sutherland, L. Houlden, P. Clarke and F. Hardy, 660–704. London: Routledge, 1988.

Sanderson, Alexis. "Sarvāstivāda and Its Critics: Anātmavāda and the Theory of Karma." In *Buddism into the Year 2000*, edited by Dhammakāya Foundation, 33–48. Bangkok: Dhammakaya, 1994.

Sapolsky, Robert. *Sapolsky on Free Will*. PAU Talks, Stanford, Palo Alto, CA, July 4, 2018. https://www.youtube.com/watch?v=ihhVe8dKNSA, accessed August 21, 2018.

Sapolsky, Robert. "Stanford Lectures, lecture 25." 2010. https://www.youtube.com/watch?v=-PpDq1WUtAw&index=25&list=PL150326949691B199, accessed June 18, 2018.

Sapolsky, Robert. "Robert Sapolsky Interview: Toxoplasmosis." *Edge TV*. Edge TV. https://www.youtube.com/watch?v=m3x3TMdkGdQ, accessed August 25, 2018.

Saraswathi, Swami Sri Ramanananda. *Tripura Rahasya or the Mystery Beyond the Trinity.* Translated by Swami Sri Ramanananda Saraswathi. Tiruvanamalai: Ramanamasramam, 2006.

Siderits, Mark. "Buddhism and Techno-Physicalism: Is the Eightfold Path a Program?" *Philosophy East and West. 51* (July 2001): 307–14.

Siderits, Mark, Zahavi, Dan and Thompson, Evan, ed. *Self, No Self?: Perspectives from Analytical, Phenomenological, and Indian Traditions.* New York: Oxford University Press, 2013.

Smith, Frederick. *Self Possessed: Deity and Spirit Possession in South Asian Literature and Civilization.* New York: Columbia University Press, 2006.

Sarma, Subramania, ed. "Taittirīya Brāhmaṇa." *Yajurveda: Krishna Yajurveda Works of the Taittiriya Shaka.* http://www.sanskritweb.net/yajurveda. Accessed September 24, 2018.

Timalsina, Sthaneshwar. "Theatrics of Emotion: Self-Deception and Self-Cultivation in Abhinavagupta's Aesthetics." *Philosophy East and West 66*, no. 1 (January 2016): 104–21.

Torella, Raffaele. *Īśvarapratyabhijñākārikā of Utpaladeva with the Author's Vṛtti: Critical Edition and annotated translation.* Delhi: Motilal Banarsidass, 2002.

Torella, Raffaele. *Philosophical Traditions of India: An Appraisal.* Varanasi: Indica Books, 2011.

Torella, Raffaele. "Utpaladeva's Lost Vivṛti on the Īśvarapratyabhijñā-Kārikā." *Journal of Indian Philosophy 42*, no. 1 (2014): 115–26.

Vasudev, Somdev. "The Unconscious Experiencer: Bhoktṛtva in the Pramātṛbheda of the Trika." *Journal of Indological Studies 24 and 25* (2012–2013): 204–30.

Vidyāraṇya, Mādhava. *Śaṅkaradigvijaya*. Śrīraṅgam: Śrīvaṇivilasamudranālayaḥ, 1972.

Watson, Alex. "The Self as a Dynamic Constant. Rāmakaṇṭha's Middle Ground between a Naiyāyika Eternal Self-Substance and a Buddhist Stream of Consciousness-Moments." *Journal of Indian Philosophy 42* (2014): 173–93.

White, David. *Sinister Yogis.* Chicago: University of Chicago Press, 2011.

Wujastyk, Dominic. "Interpreting the Image of the Human Body in Premodern India." *International Journal of HIndu Studies 13*, no. 2 (2009): 189–298.

Zahavi, Dan. *Subjectivity and Selfhood: Investigating the First-Person Perspective.* Boston: MIT Press, 2005.

Chapter 4

Abhinavagupta. *Īśvara Pratyabhijñā Vivṛti Vimarśinī.* Edited by Paṇḍit Madhusudan Kaul Śāstrī. Vol. *3*. Delhi: Akay Reprints, 1985.

Abhinavagupta. *Īśvara Pratyabhijñā Vivṛti Vimarśinī.* Edited by Paṇḍit Madhusudan Kaul Śāstrī. Vol. *2*. Delhi: Akay Reprints, 1985. https://archive.org/details/in.ernet.dli.2015.326570/page/n1/mode/2up.

Abhinavagupta. *Īśvara Pratyabhijñā Vivṛti Vimarśinī.* Edited by Paṇḍit Madhusudan Kaul Śāstrī. Reprint. Vol. *1*. Delhi: Akay Reprints, 1985. https://archive.org/details/IshvaraPratyabhijnaVivritiVimarshiniAbhinavaguptaPart1KashmirSanskrit/mode/2up.

Abhinavagupta. "*Isvarapratyabhijnavimarsini, Adhikaras 1–4. Based on the following edition: Īśvara-pratyabhijñā-Vimarśinī of Abhinavagupta: doctrine of divine recognition.*" Edited by K.A. Subramania Iyer and K.C. Pandey. Muktabodha Indological Research Institute, 1986.

Alper, Harvey. "Judgement as a Transcendental Category in Utpaladeva's Śaiva Theology, The Evidence of the Pratyabhijñākārikāvṛtti." *Adyar Library Bulletin 51* (1987): 176–241.

Arnold, Dan. *Brains, Buddhas and Believing: The Problem of Intentionality in Classical Buddhist and Cognitive-Scientific Philosophy of Mind.* New York: Columbia University Press, 2014.

Atmanspacher, Harald. "20th Century Variants of Dual-Aspect Thinking." *Mind and Matter 12*, no. 2 (2014): 245–88.

Bansat-Boudon, Lyne. *An Introduction to Tantric Philosophy: The Paramārthasāra of Abhinavagupta with the Commentary of Yogarāja*. Translated by Lyne Bansat-Boudon and Kamaleshadatta Tripathi. Routledge Studies in Tantric Traditions. New York: Routledge, 2011.

Bansat-Boudon, Lyne. "On Śaiva Terminology: Some Key Issues of Understanding." *Journal of Indian Philosophy 42*, no. 1 (March 2014): 39–97.

Barad, Karen. *Meeting the Universe Halfway: Quantum Physics and the Entanglement of Matter and Meaning*. Durham, NC: Duke University Press, 2007.

Bennett, Jane. "*Powers of the Hoard: Further Notes on Material Agency*." Edited by Jeffrey Cohen, 237–72. New York: Punctum Books, 2012.

Bennett, Jane. *Vibrant Matter: A Political Ecology of Things*. Durham, NC: Duke University Press, 2010.

Biernacki, Loriliai. "Connecting Consciousness to Physical Causality: Abhinavagupta's Phenomenology of Subjectivity and Tononi's Integrated Information Theory." *Religions 7* (2016): 1–11. https://doi.org/10.3390/rel7070087.

Bostrom, Nick. *Superintelligence: Paths, Dangers, Strategies*. New York: Oxford University Press, 2014.

Braidotti, Rosi. *Posthuman*. Cambridge: Polity Press, 2013.

Chalmers, David. *The Conscious Mind: In Search of a Fundamental Theory. New York: Oxford University Press, 1996*. New York: Oxford University Press, 1996.

Clayton, Philip, and Paul Davies, eds. *Re-Emergence of Emergence: The Emergentist Hypothesis from Science to Religion*. New York: Oxford University Press, 2008.

Damasio, Antonio. *Self Comes to Mind: Constructing the Conscious Brain*. New York: Pantheon, 2010.

Duckworth, Douglas. "From Yogācāra to Philosophical Tantra in Kashmir and Tibet." *Sophia*, no. *57* (2018): 611–23. https://doi.org/DOI 10.1007/s11841-017-0598-5.

Duckworth, Douglas. "The Other Side of Realism: Panpsychism and Yogācāra." *In Buddhist Philosophy: A Comparative Approach*, edited by Steven Emmanuel, 29–43. Hoboken, NJ: John Wiley, 2018.

Dyczkowski, Mark. *The Doctrine of Vibration: An Analysis of the Doctrines and Practices of Kashmir Shaivism*. Albany: State University of New York Press, 1986.

Edelman, Gerald. *Wider than the Sky: The Phneomenal Gift of Consciousness*. New Haven, CT: Yale University Press, 2005.

Fagella, Daniel. *AI Future Outlook* (blog), November 28, 2018. https://emerj.com/ai-future-outlook/elon-musk-on-the-dangers-of-ai-a-catalogue-of-his-statements.

Goff, Philip. *Consciousness and Fundamental Reality*. New York: Oxford University Press, 2017.

Goff, Philip. "Cosmopsychism, Micropsychism, and the Grounding Relation." In *The Routledge Handbook of Panpsychism*, edited by William Seager, 144–56. Leiden: Routledge, 2019.

Hulin, Michel. *Le Principe de l'Ego dans la Pensée Indienne Classique: la Notion d'Ahaṃkāra*. Vol. *44*. Paris: Publications de l"Institut de Civilisation Indienne, 1978.

Jarvis, Brooke. "Insect Apocalypse Is Here." *New York Times Magazine*, December 2, 2018. https://www.nytimes.com/2018/11/27/magazine/insect-apocalypse.html.

Jha, Ganganath. *Nyāya: Gautama's Nyāyasūtras with Vātsyāyana-Bhāṣya*. Poona Oriental Series. Poona: Poona Oriental Book Agency, 1959.

Koch, Christof. "When Computers Surpass Us." *Scientific American Mind 26*, no. 5 (October 2015): 26–29.

Lawrence, David. "Kashmiri Shaiva Philosophy." In *Internet Encyclopedia of Philosophy*, edited by James Fieser and Bradley Dowden, 2005. https://iep.utm.edu/kashmiri/.

Lawrence, David. "Proof of a Sentient Knower: Utpaladeva's Ajaḍapramātṛsiddhi with the Vṛtti of Harabhatta Shastri." *Journal of Indian Philosophy 37* (2009): 627–53. https://doi.org/10.1007/s10781-009-9074-z.

Lawrence, David. *Rediscovering God with Transcendental Argument: A Contemporary Interpretation of Monistic Kashmiri Śaiva Philosophy*. Rochester: State University of New York Press, 1999.

Lawrence, David. "Remarks on Abhinavagupta's Use of the Analogy of Reflection." *Journal of Indian Philosophy 33* (2005): 583–99.

McCrea, Lawrence. "Abhinavagupta as Intellectual Historian of Buddhism." In *Around Abhinavagupta:Aspects of the Intellectual History of Kashmir from the Ninth to the Eleventh Century*, edited by Eli Franco and Isabelle Ratie, 263–86. Berlin: Lit Verlag, 2016.

Nagel, Thomas. *Mind and Cosmos: Why the Materialist Neo-Darwinian Conception of Nature Is Almost Certainly False*. New York: Oxford University Press, 2012.

Nemec, John. "Evidence for Somānanda's Pantheism." *Journal of Indian Philos 42* (2014): 99–114.

Nemec, John. "Influences on and Legacies of Somānanda's Conception of Materiality." *In Around Abhinavagupta: Aspects of the Intellectual History of Kashmir from the Ninth to the Eleventh Century*, edited by Eli Franco and Isabelle Ratie, 341–74. Berlin: Lit Verlag, 2016.

Nemec, John. "The Body and Consciousness in Early Pratyabhijñā Philosophy: Amūrtatva in Somāananda's Śivadṛṣṭi." In *Tantrapuṣpāñjali: Tantric Traditions and Philosophy of Kashmir: Studies in Memory of Pandit H.N. Chakravarty*, edited by Bettina Baumer and Hamsa Stainton, 215–25. New Delhi: Indira Gandhi National Centre for the Arts, 2018.

Nemec, John. *Ubiquitous Śiva: Somānanda's Śivadṛṣṭi and His Tantric Interlocutors*. New York: Oxford University Press, 2011.

O'Connor, Timothy. "Emergent Properties." In *Stanford Encyclopedia of Philosophy*, edited by Edward Zalta. Stanford University, August 10, 2020. https://plato.stanford.edu/entries/properties-emergent/.

Oizumi, Masafumi, Larissa Albantakis, and Giulio Tononi. "From the Phenomenology to the Mechanisms of Consciousness: Integrated InformationTheory 3.0." *PLOS: Computational Biology 10*, no. 5 (May 8, 2014). http://journals.plos.org/ploscompbiol/article?id=10.1371/journal.pcbi.1003588.

Padoux, Andre. *Hindu Tantric World: An Overview*. Chicago: University of Chicago Press, 2017.

Padoux, Andre. *Vāc: The Concept of the Word in Selected Hindu Tantras*. Albany: State University of New York Press, 1990.

Pandey, K. C. *Abhinavagupta: An Historical and Philosophical Study*. 2nd Enlarged. Varanasi: Chowkhamba Sanskrit Series, 1963.

Pandey, K. C. *Iśvara Pratyabhijñā of Utpaladeva with the Vimarśinī*. Reprint edition. Vol. 3. 3 vols. Delhi: Butala and Company, 1984.

Prueitt, Catherine. "Shifting Concepts: The Realignment of Dharmakīrti on Concepts and the Error of Subject/Object Duality in Pratyabhijñā Śaiva Thought." *Journal of Indian Philosophy 45* (2017): 21–47. https://doi.org/DOI 10.1007/s10781-016-9297-8.

Ram-Prasad, Chakravarthi. *Indian Philosophy and Consequences of Knowledge: Themes in Ethics, Metaphysics and Soteriology*. Burlington, VT: Ashgate, 2007.

Rastogi, Navjivan. "Rasānubhūti Pratibhāna ke Rūpa Meṃ." *In The Concept of Rasa with Special reference to Abhinavagupta*, edited by S.C. Pande, 185–205. New Delhi: Aryan Books International, 2009.

Rastogi, Navjivan. "Vak as Pratyavamarsa: Bhartrhari from Abhinavan Perspective." In *Bhartrhari—Language, Thought and Reality*, edited by Mithilesh Chaturvedi, 301–42; pdf separate pagination. New Delhi: Motilal Banarsidass, 2009. www.svabhinava.org/abhinava/NavjivanRastogi/VakPratyavamarsa.pdf.

Ratie, Isabelle. "A Five-Trunked, Four-Tusked Elephant Is Running in the Sky": How Free Is Imagination According to Utpaladeva and Abhinavagupta?" *Asiatische Studien: Zeitschrift Der Schweizerischen Gesellschaft Für Asienkunde = Études Asiatiques: Revue de La Société Suisse D'études Asiatiques 64*, no. 2 (2010): 341–85. http://dx.doi.org/10.5169/seals-147851.

Ratie, Isabelle. "An Indian Debate on Optical Reflections and Its Metaphysical Implications: Śaiva Nondualism and the Mirror of Consciousness." In *Indian Epistemology and Metaphysics*, edited by Joerg Tuske, 207–40. London: Bloomsbury, 2017.

Ratie, Isabelle. "Can One Prove That Something Exists Beyond Consciousness? A Śaiva Criticism of the Sautrāntika Inference of External Objects." *Journal of Indian Philosophy 39* (2011): 479–501.

Ratie, Isabelle. "Pāramārthika or Apāramārthika? On the Ontological Status of Separation According to Abhinavagupta." *In Puṣpikā: Tracing Ancient India through Texts and Traditions*, edited by P. Mirning, P.-D. Szanto, and M. Williams, 381–405. Havertown: Oxbow Books, 2014.

Ratie, Isabelle. "Śaiva Interpretation of the Satkāryavāda: The Sāṃkhya Notion of Abhivyakti and Its Transformation in the Pratyabhijñā Treatise." *Journal of Indian Philosophy 42*, no. 1 (March 2014): 127–72.

Ratie, Isabelle. "The Dreamer and the Yogin: On the Relationship between Buddhist and Śaiva Idealisms." *Bulletin of the School of Oriental and African Studies 73*, no. 3 (October 2010): 437–78.

Rubenstein, Mary-Jane. *Pantheologies: Gods, Worlds, Monsters*. New York: Columbia University Press, 2018.

Schaffer, Jonathan. "Monism: The Priority of the Whole." In *Spinoza on Monism*, edited by Philip Goff, 9–50. London: Palgrave Macmillan, 2012.

Searle, John. "Can Information Theory Explain Consciousness?" *New York Times Review of Books*. January 10, 2013, 53–58. https://www.nybooks.com/articles/2013/01/10/can-information-theory-explain-consciousness/.

Searle, John. *Mystery of Consciousness*. New York: New York Review, 1997.

Seth, Anil. *Neuroscience of Consciousness with Anil Seth*. London: Royal Institution, February 1, 2017. https://www.youtube.com/watch?v=xRel1JKOEbI.

Shani, Itay. "Cosmopsychism: A Holistic Approach to the Metaphysics of Experience." *Philosophical Papers 44*, no. 3 (2015): 389–437. https://doi.org/10.1080/05568641.2015.1106709.

Shani, Itay, and Joachim Keppler. "Cosmsopsychism and Consciousness Research: A Fresh View on the Causal Mechanisms Underlying Phenomenal States." *Frontiers in Psychology 11*.371 (March 5, 2020): 1–7. https://doi.org/10.3389/fpsyg.2020.00371.

Siderits, Mark, Dan Zahavi, and Evan Thompson, eds. *Self, No Self?: Perspectives from Analytical, Phenomenological, and Indian Traditions*. New York: Oxford University Press, 2013.

Singh, Jaidev. *Vijñāna Bhairava or Divine Consciousness*. Reprint. Delhi: Motilal Banarsidass, 2003.

Skora, Kerry. "The Pulsating Heart and Its Divine Sense Energies: Body and Touch in Abhinavagupta's Trika Śaivism." *Numen 54*, no. 4 (2007): 420–458.

Smith, Frederick. *Self Possessed: Deity and Spirit Possession in South Asian Literature and Civilization*. New York: Columbia University Press, 2006.

Strawson, Galen. "Physicalist Panpsychism." *In Blackwell Companion to Consciousness*, 2nd ed., edited by Susan Schneider and Max Velmans, 374–90. Oxford: John Wiley & Sons, 2017.

Thompson, Evan. *Waking, Dreaming, Being: Self and Consciousness in Neuroscience, Meditation and Philosophy*. New York: Columbia University Press, 2015.

Timalsina, Sthaneshwar. "Aham, Subjecitivity, and the Ego: Engaging the Philosophy of Abhinavagupta." *Journal of Indian Philosophy 48*, no. 4 (September 2020): 767–89. https://doi.org/10.1007/s10781-020-09439.

Timalsina, Sthaneshwar. "Linguistic and Cosmic Powers: The Concept of Śakti in the Philosophies of Bhartṛhari an Abhinavagupta." In *Classical and Contemporary Issues in Indian Studies: Essays in Honor of Trichur S. Rukmani*, edited by P. Pratap Kumar and Jonathan Duquette, 211–32. Delhi: D. K. Printworld, 2013.

Timalsina, Sthaneshwar. "Vimarśa: The Concept of Reflexivity in the Philosophy of Utpala and Abhinavagupta." *Acta Orientalia " Claus Peter Zoller and Hong Luo (Eds.)*, Proceedings of "Sanskrit in China 2019: Sanskrit on Paths *80* (2020): 98–121.

Tononi, Giulio. *Phi: A Voyage from the Brain to the Soul*. New York: Pantheon, 2012.

Tononi, Giulio. "Why Scott Should Stare at a Blank Wall and Reconsider (or, the Conscious Grid." *Shtetl-Optimized: The Blog of Scott Aaronson* (blog). Accessed April 13, 2016. http://www.scottaaronson.com/blog/?p=1823.

Torella, Raffaele. "From an Adversary to the Main Ally: The Place of Bhartrhari in the Kashmirian Saiva Advaita." *In Bhartrhari—Language, Thought and Reality*, edited by Mithilesh Chaturvedi, 343–54. New Delhi: Motilal Banarsidass, 2009.

Torella, Raffaele. *Īśvarapratyabhijñākārikā of Utpaladeva with the Author's Vṛtti: Critical Edition and Annotated Translation*. Delhi: Motilal Banarsidass, 2002.

Torella, Raffaele. "The Pratyabhijñā and the Logical-Epistemological School of Buddhism." *In Ritual and Speculation in Early Tantrism: Studies in Honor of André Padoux*, edited by Teun Goudriaan, 327–45. New York: State University of New York Press, 1992.

Wheeler, John. "Not Consciousness but the Distinction between the Probe and the Probed as Central to the Elemental Quantum Act of Observation." *In Role of Consciousness in the Physical World*, edited by R.G. Jahn, 87–111. Boulder, CO: Westview, 1981.

Chapter 5

Abhinavagupta. *Īśvara Pratyabhijñā Vivṛti Vimarśinī*. Edited by Paṇḍit Madhusudan Kaul Śāstrī. Vol. *3*. Delhi: Akay Reprints, 1985. https://archive.org/details/in.ernet.dli.2015.485473/mode/2up.

Abhinavagupta. *Īśvara Pratyabhijñā Vivṛti Vimarśinī*. Edited by Paṇḍit Madhusudan Kaul Śāstrī. Vol. *2*. Delhi: Akay Reprints, 1985. https://archive.org/details/in.ernet.dli.2015.326570/page/n1/mode/2up.

Abhinavagupta. "*Isvarapratyabhijnavimarsini, Adhikaras 1-4. Based on the following edition: Īśvara-pratyabhijñā-Vimarśinī of Abhinavagupta: doctrine of divine recognition.*" Edited by K.A. Subramania Iyer and K.C. Pandey. Muktabodha Indological Research Institute, 1986.

Atmanspacher, Harald. "20th Century Variants of Dual-Aspect Thinking." *Mind and Matter 12*, no. 2 (2014): 245–88.

Barad, Karen. *Meeting the Universe Halfway: Quantum Physics and the Entanglement of Matter and Meaning*. Durham, NC: Duke University Press, 2007.

Biernacki, Loriliai. "Connecting Consciousness to Physical Causality: Abhinavagupta's Phenomenology of Subjectivity and Tononi's Integrated Information Theory." *Religions 7* (2016): 1–11. https://doi.org/10.3390/rel7070087.

Braidotti, Rosi. *Posthuman Knowledge*. New York: Polity Press, 2019.

Brogaard, Berit. "In Search of Mentons: Panpsychism, Physicalism and the Missing Link." In *Panpsychism: Contemporary Perspectives*, edited by Godehart Bruntrup and Ludwig Jaskolla, 130–52. New York: Oxford University Press, 2017.

Coleman, Sam. "The Real Combination Problem: Panpsychism, Micro-Subjects, and Emergence." *Erkenntnis 79* (2014): 19–44. https://doi.org/10.1007/s10670-013-9431-x.

Consciousness Is a Mathematical Pattern: Max Tegmark at TEDxCambridge 2014. Cambridge: TedX, 2014. https://www.youtube.com/watch?v=GzCvlFRISIM.

Coole, Diana. "Inertia of Matter and the Generativity of Flesh." In *New Materialisms: Ontology, Agency and Politics*, edited by Diana Coole and Samantha Frost, 92–115. Durham, NC: Duke University Press, 2010.

Dawkins, Richard. *River Out of Eden: A Darwinian View of Life. Reprint*. New York: Basic Books, 1996.

Dennett, Daniel. *Information, Evolution, and Intelligent Design*. London: Royal Institution, 2015. https://www.youtube.com/watch?v=AZX6awZq5Z0.

Descartes, Rene. *Discourse on the Method of Rightly Conducting the Reason, and Seeking Truth in the Sciences*. Translated by John Veitch. Chicago: Open Court Publishing Company, 1913. https://archive.org/details/in.ernet.dli.2015.1762/page/n3.

FQXi. *The Physics of Information: FQXi's 4th International Conference*. Vieques Island, Puerto Rico, 2014. https://www.youtube.com/watch?v=MtUZw3PkKYg.

Gleick, James. *Information: A History, A Theory, A Flood*. New York: Pantheon, 2011.

Goff, Philip. *Consciousness and Fundamental Reality*. New York: Oxford University Press, 2017.

Hayles, N. Katherine. *How We Became Posthuman: Virtual Bodies in Cybernetics, Literature, and Informatics*. Chicago: University of Chicago Press, 1999.

Hofstadter, Douglas. *Godel, Escher, Bach: An Eternal Golden Braid*. 20th Anniversary Edition. New York: Basic Books, 1999. https://www.academia.edu/39721656/G%C3%B6del_Escher_Bach_An_Eternal_Golden_Braid_20th_Anniversary_Edition_by_Douglas_R._Hofstadter?email_work_card=view-paper.

James, William. *A Pluralistic Universe*. Hibbert Lectures and Manchester College. New York: Longmans, Green and Co., 1909. https://archive.org/details/pluralisticunive00jamerich/page/n5.

Kelly, Ed, Paul Marshall, and Adam Crabtree, eds. *Beyond Physicalism: Toward Reconciliation of Science and Spirituality*. New York: Rowman and Littlefield, 2015.

Koch, Christof. "*Future of Consciousness: Future of Biology*." Dublin: Trinity College Dublin, 2018. https://www.youtube.com/watch?v=luGE5e2_xKM.

Kripal, Jeffrey. *Flip: Epiphanies of Mind and the Future of Knowledge*. New York: Bellevue Literary Press, 2019.

Krohn, Elizabeth, and Jeffrey Kripal. *Changed in a Flash: One Woman's Near-Death Experience and Why a Scholar Thinks It Empowers Us All*. Berkeley, CA: North Atlantic Books, 2018.

Larson, Gerald. *Classical Sāṃkhya: An Inerpretation of Its History and Meaning*. Reprint. Delhi: Motilal Banarsidass, 1998.

Lawrence, David. "Remarks on Abhinavagupta's Use of the Analogy of Reflection." *Journal of Indian Philosophy* 33 (2005): 583–99.

Maharaj, Ayon. "Panentheistic Cosmopsychism: Swami Vivekananda's Sāṃkhya-Vedāntic Solution to the Hard Problem of Consciousness." In *Panentheism and Panpsychism: Philosophy of Religion Meets Philosophy of Mind*, edited by Ludwig Jaskolla, Godehard Brüntrup, and Benedikt Paul Göcke, 273–302. Paderborn: Mentis Brill, 2019.

Metzinger, Thomas. "Out-of-Body Experiences as the Origin of the Concept of a 'Soul.'" *Mind and Matter* 3, no. 1 (2005): 57–84.

Miśra Śāstrī, Śivadatta, ed. *Bṛhatstotraratnākara*. Varanasi: Jyotiṣa Prakāśana, 1997.

Nemec, John. "Evidence for Somānanda's Pantheism." *Journal of Indian Philosophy* 42 (2014): 99–114.

Oizumi, Masafumi, Larissa Albantakis, and Giulio Tononi. "From the Phenomenology to the Mechanisms of Consciousness: Integrated InformationTheory 3.0." *PLOS: Computational Biology 10*, no. 5 (May 8, 2014). http://journals.plos.org/ploscompbiol/article?id=10.1371/journal.pcbi.1003588.

Pandey, K. C. *Abhinavagupta: An Historical and Philosophical Study*. 2nd Enlarged. Varanasi: Chowkhamba Sanskrit Series, 1963.

Pollan, Michael. "The Intelligent Plant Scientists Debate a New Way of Understanding Flora." *New Yorker*, 92-n/a, December 23, 2013. https://colorado.idm.oclc.org/login?url= https://www-proquest-com.colorado.idm.oclc.org/magazines/intelligent-plant/docview/1476389274/se-2.

Sanderson, Alexis. "Śaivism and the Tantric Traditions." In *Śaivism and the Tantric Traditions*, edited by Stewart Sutherland, F Hardy, L. Houlden, and P. Clarke, 660–704. London: Routledge, 1988.

Searle, John. "Can Information Theory Explain Consciousness?" *New York Times Review of Books*. January 10, 2013, 53–58. https://www.nybooks.com/articles/2013/01/10/can-information-theory-explain-consciousness/.

Schrodinger, Erwin. *What Is Life? The Physical Aspect of the Living Cell*. Dublin Institute for Advanced Studies: Trinity College Dublin, 1944. https://duckduckgo.com/?q=schrodinger+what+is+life&t=ffab&atb=v108-1&ia=web.

Shani, Itay, and Joachim Keppler. "Beyond Combination: How Cosmic Consciousness Grounds Ordinary Experience." *Journal of the American Philosophical Association* 4, no. 3 (2018): 390–410. https://doi.org/10.1017/apa.2018.30.

Smith, Frederick. *Self Possessed: Deity and Spirit Possession in South Asian Literature and Civilization*. New York: Columbia University Press, 2006.

Tononi, Giulio. *Phi: A Voyage from the Brain to the Soul*. New York: Pantheon, 2012.

Wheeler, John. "*Information, Physics, Quantum: The Search for Links.*" Tokyo: Plus magazine, 1989. https://plus.maths.org/content/it-bit-0.

Wheeler, John. "Not Consciousness but the Distinction between the Probe and the Probed as Central to the Elemental Quantum Act of Observation." *In Role of Consciousness in the Physical World*, edited by R.G. Jahn, 87–111. Boulder, CO: Westview, 1981.

Wolchover, Natalie. "Quantum Mischief Rewrites the Laws of Cause and Effect." *Quanta Magazine*, March 11, 2021. https://www.quantamagazine.org/quantum-mischief-rewrites-the-laws-of-cause-and-effect-20210311/.

Wright, Robert. *Quantifying Consciousness: Robert Wright and Christof Koch*. Wright Show. MeaningofLife.tv, 2016. https://www.youtube.com/watch?v=B_YnBIXK6QU.

Index

For the benefit of digital users, indexed terms that span two pages (e.g., 52–53) may, on occasion, appear on only one of those pages.

Abhinavagupta, 1–2, 13
  Indian legacy of, 22–23, 33–34, 39
  influence of, 2–3, 156n.9
  methodology of, 8
  scholarship on, 25
  and Somānanda, distinctions between, 31, 41–42
action (*kriyā*)
  as both external and internal, 107
  consciousness and matter connected in, 115–16
  in dual-aspect monism, 97–98
  knowledge and, 136–37
  matter inked to, 135–36
  object creation and, 139
  self defined through, 116–17
  vimarśa linked with, 106–7
  wonder linked with, 49–50, 54
Advaita Vedānta, 4, 133, 158–59n.18
  American Transcendalists and, 20–21
  ātman in, 41–42
  Brahman in, 37
  light in, 97–98, 106
  two-tiered reality in, 83–84
  variety in, 35
  will in, 33–34
aesthetic tradition, 2–3, 54, 55
Āgamādhikāra, 5–7, 25, 127
agency, 141
  in Abhinavagupta's system, 58, 101
  consciousness and, 23
  democracy of, 24
  displacement of human, 72–73, 74
  Indian cosmological view of, 22–23
  in linking wonder to will, 58–59
  of matter, 19, 20–21, 51–52, 60
  New Materialist view of, 22–23
  two-tiered reality and, 83–84
  Western scientific view of, 18
agential realism, 112–13
Agni, 88, 89, 90–91
Alper, Harvey, 108–9, 111, 114
American Transcendentalists, 20–21
analogies and metaphors
  alchemy, 65–66
  caterpillar, 78
  clay pot, 15, 23, 29, 33–34, 41, 100, 137, 145
  crow's eye, 24, 41–42
  glass-block universe, 67
  Russian doll, 30–31, 117, 118–19
  self-as information, 82–83
  wall image (*bhitta*), 13–14, 109–10, 118
Ānandabhairava, 89–90, 91
Ānandabhairavī, 89–90
anātma doctrine, 75–76, 81–82, 176–77n.8
animals, 13, 22–23, 105
animism, 15–16, 19, 36, 45
  and Abhinavagupta, differences between, 61
  medieval European view of, 26–27
  New Materialism and, 22–23
  panpsychism and, 20
  in Tantra, 27–28
anthropocentrism, 13, 15, 17, 22–23, 127–28
Arnold, Dan, 58
artificial intelligence and computers, 35, 105
  Abhinavagupta's panentheism and, 100–1
  alignment problem, 206n.111
  as metaphor for brains, 129–30
  sentience of, 10, 95–96, 99, 110, 113, 121–22
  vimarśa of, 112–13
Arya Samāj, 81
astral travel, 134
atheism, 15–16, 19–21, 96–97, 102, 182–83n.63
Atmanspacher, Harald, 10, 98, 99, 118

avijñapti, 81–82
awareness, 66–67, 77
consciousness linked with, 143–44
drawn within, 137
excess, 135
experience as, 112–13
freedom of, 41
ground of, 111–12
inward-directed, 21–22
levels of, 30, 208n.136
limited, 215n.85
materially based, 116–17
nondual, 29–30, 33–34
nonhuman, 135
reflective, 106, 110, 114
shared, 40
sheaths overlaying, 190n.121
subjectivity and, 38, 67–69
vimarśa and, 108–9, 114–15
See also self-awareness

Bansat-Boudan, Lyne, 35
Barad, Karen, 20, 60, 110, 112–13, 142–43, 153
Bennett, Jane, 18, 19–20, 28, 30–31, 32–33, 40, 44, 50, 56, 98, 107
Berkeley, George, 111
Beyond the Fourth (*turiyātita*), 66, 67
Bhagavad Gita, 20–21, 32–33, 77, 78
Bhartṛhari, 33–34, 39, 94, 112–13
bhūta suddhi, 156n.7
bioethics, 19
biology, 74, 90, 93, 96–97, 110, 145
Block, Ned, 103–4
body
Abhinavagupta's articulation of, 89–92
affective processes of, 91–92
as boundary, 9–10, 71–72, 94
breaking down, 133
consciousness and, 76–77, 98
as gods' abode, 90–91
"I" in, 60–61
importance of, 188n.112
limitations of, 58, 150–51
and mind, connection between, 1–2, 25
nonhuman life and, 17
physical and sound, distinctions between, 131–32
physical and subtle, relationship between, 79–80, 86–87, 88
spirit and, 20–21
in tantra, 2–3
transcendence linked with, 65, 89
wonder and, 55
See also under Tantra
Bohm, David, 118–19
Bohr, Neils, 60, 95, 153, 165n.37
Bostrom, Nick, 95–96, 122
Brahmā, 31, 88, 90–91
Brahman, 37, 58
Brahmaṇī, 89–90
Braidotti, Rosi, 98, 129, 141
brain, 46–47, 61, 82–83, 103–4, 120–21, 129–30, 134
breath (*prāṇa*)
body and, 131–32
five vital, 65, 81, 86, 87–88
Gaṇeśa as, 89–90
prakāśa and *vimsarśa* in, 108, 118
self conceived as, 151
subtle body and, 85–86
Bṛhadaraṇyaka Upaniṣad, 71, 78, 192n.23
Brogaard, Berit, 126, 128–29, 153
Brown, Bill, 28, 30–31
Bruno, Giordano, 26–27
Buddha, 78
Buddhism, 176–77n.8
consciousness in, 111–12
reincarnation in, 78–79, 81–83
self as process in, 116–17
subtle body in, 75–76
Tibetan, 133
two-tiered reality in, 83–84
Buhner, Stephen, 17
Bynum, Caroline Walker, 48–49

cakras, 80, 81, 88, 90–91
Cardona, George, 33–34
causality, 59, 142–44, 150–51, 152, 184–85n.80, 192n.19
Chakrabarti, Arindam, 40
Chalmers, David, 100–1
channels, subtle, 65, 80
"City of Eight," 84–88, 93
cognitive science, 46–47, 81–82, 104, 109
communication, 20–21, 124, 127–28, 141–42
Connelly, William, 20
consciousness, 10–11
all-pervasive, 102–3
body and, 76–77
and brain, neuroscience on, 46–47
choice and, 13

contemporary models of, 102, 109, 119
defining, 103–6
as dense mass (*cidghana*), 35
energy of, 120, 186n.88
freedom and, 34–35
giving birth, 135, 149–50
as information, 129–31, 141–42
inherent in everything, 52–53
and matter, relationships between, 1–2, 3–4, 7–8, 15, 22, 136–37, 138–40, 152
multiplicity of, 109–10
in panentheism's, 100–1
phenomenal and psychological, 206–7n.115
prakāśa and *vimarśa* in, 117
self-aware, 126
subjectivity of, 23
as subtle body, 84, 94
transformation of (matter), 61
translations of term, 10, 99, 102–4
unfolding of, 6, 110, 145–46
universal delight in, 28
as universal field, 37, 126, 128–29, 153
as *vimarśa*, 38
Wheeler's speculation on, 140
See also pure consciousness
Conway, Anne, 27, 29–30
Coole, Diana, 19, 24
Copernicus, 176n.4
Coseru, Christian, 83–84
cosmology, 3–4
contemporary models of, 98–99
ecology and, 7
emanationist, 196n.76
humans in, 8
Indian, 14, 22–23, 74, 75–76, 81, 103–4
Tantric, 127
See also *tattva* system
cosmopsychism, 13–15, 25–26, 197n.7
contemporary models, 96–97, 125
decombination problem of, 38
desire in, 114
divinity in, 181–82n.57
freedom and, 37–38
God and, 36
holist, 126
limitations of, 215n.85
nondualism and, 24, 186n.90
objects in, 15–16, 40
originary, 109, 120, 148
panentheist, 110
shared subjectivity of, 41–42, 43–44
unfolding, 127, 128–29, 153
Covid-19 pandemic, 12–13
creation, 29, 55–56, 88, 101, 106–7, 136–37, 139, 153, 175n.173, 181–82n.57
Cudworth, Ralph, 103–4

Dalai Lama incarnations, 81–82
Damasio, Antonia, 93, 104
Darwin, Charles, 9–11, 39, 71, 94, 123–24, 126, 127–28, 176n.4
Dasti, Matthew, 78–79
Daston, Lorraine, 47–49, 55
Dawkins, Richard, 123
death, 78, 79–80
Dehasthadevatācakrastotram, 89–90, 91
deities
in body, 9–10, 88–94
driving human actions, 74–75
sound bodies of, 131, 138–39
transcendent form, 170n.105
Deleuze, Gilles, 107
Dennett, Daniel, 53, 58, 116, 127–28, 143–44, 164n.22
Derrida, Jacques, 211n.17
Descarte, René, 13, 59, 62–63, 68, 95, 112–13, 143, 144, 150–51, 153, 209n.6
desire, 9–10, 93, 113–14, 149
Dharmakīrti, 117
Dietart, Rodney, 16–17, 71
Digvijaya (Śaṅkara), 82–83
diversity, 3, 5, 10–11
agonistic, 127, 128–29
freedom and, 39
generating, 25, 38–39, 55–56, 119
wonder of, 35–36, 56, 127
divinity, 6, 7–8, 20–21, 56–57, 69, 76–77
Donald, Merlin, 91–92
Donne, John, 1, 7–8
dream states, 104
Dreyfus, George, 67
drops (*bindus*), 80
dual-aspect monism, 10, 118, 120–21, 182n.60
awareness in, 41
consciousness in, 130–31
contemporary models of, 4
holistic, 203n.73
knowledge and activity in, 106, 107
overview, 96–99
parameters of, 114

dual-aspect monism (*cont.*)
Somānanda's, 105
twenty 20th-century models of, 118–20
two poles of, 28–29, 30–31, 37–38, 106, 115
variant understandings of, 111

eagerness (*aunmukhya*), 28
ecological crisis, 12–13, 22–23, 44, 153–54, 164n.22
Edelman, Gerald, 47, 104
ego, 9–10
in materialist science, 176n.4
mind and, 91–92
in Sāṃkhya, 81
self and, distinctions between, 63
in subtle body, 78–79
transcendence and, 63–64
embodiment, 54, 118
emergentism, 102, 144–45, 198n.24, 204n.87
Emerson, Ralph Waldo, 20–21
emotions, 18, 49–50, 88, 178nn.23–24, 203–4n.81
Emptiness, 85–87
endosymbiosis, 93
energy centers, 90
enlightenment, 5, 119–20, 218n.112
ether/space (*akāśa*), 132–33, 151
everything as nature of everything, 27, 31–32

faith, 9–11, 48, 94, 123–24, 126, 127–28
fate, 67–68
Feynman, Richard, 47, 134
first-person perspectives, 8, 42, 152
body and, 93–94
choice in, 117
elements expressed by, 151
freedom and, 39, 58
as grammatical position, 31–32
information as, 125, 138
meaning and, 143
New Materialism and, 14
in panentheism, 3, 99
residue of, 58
and third-person, mixed, 15–16
vimarśa in, 105–6
Whitman's, 8
will as intention in, 60–61
wonder in, 62–63, 64
five elements, 127, 132, 136–37, 151
five primary powers, 58
Flegr, Jaroslav, 71–72
Flood, Gavin, 88
Fourth State (*turya*), 51–52, 56–57, 65–66
freedom
of divinity, 119–20
doctrine of, 117
limitations on human, 53
subjectivity of, 34, 38, 39, 67–68
vimarśa and, 37–38
free will, 9–10, 54, 58, 59, 74, 83–84, 92, 145
Freud, Sigmund, 73, 211n.17
Frost, Samantha, 19, 24

Gaṇeśa, 31–32, 89–90
Gerow, Edwin, 54
God, 71
Abhinavagupta and Spinoza on, comparison, 36
desire in, 114
everyday life and, 109
limitations on, 120
rejecting, 9–11, 123–24, 127–28
teleology and, 63–64
Goff, Philip, 100–1, 110, 114, 125

Halbfass, Wilhelm, 78–79
Harman, William, 15–16, 39–40
Hartzell, James, 80–81
Hawking, Stephen, 10, 95–96, 100, 129–30
Her, 110
Hobbes, Thomas, 12, 19–20
Hoftstadter, Douglas, 129–30
holomovement, 118–19
Hulin, Michel, 49, 54
human exceptionalism, 12–13, 22–23, 53, 96
humanism, 48
humans, decentering, 3, 8, 15

"I," 147
cosmopsychic expressions of, 67–68
as divinity, 60
embodied within materiality, 56–57
as *kartṛ* (agent), 58–59
materially embodied, 98
wonder's role in, 49–50, 51–52, 62–63
idealism, 4, 97–98, 111, 116, 120–21
in Abhinavagupta's system, 5, 13–14, 157n.15, 158–59n.18
ignorance (*avidyā*), 37, 58
immanence, 4, 7–8, 15–16, 36, 37, 66, 69, 102, 118, 188–89n.113

indeterminacy, 137–38
individual responsibility, 83–84
Indrāṇī, 90
"I-ness" (*ahantā*), 94, 128–29, 136–37, 144–45
  body and, 93–94
  in consciousness, 126
  freedom and, 171–72n.129
  sentience linked with, 31
  shared, 40
  subtle body and, 85–86
  See also subjectivity
information
  bodies, 133
  contemporary concepts of, 4, 7–8
  dual role of, 124, 126
  Indian and contemporary views of, connection between, 133–34
  materiality of, 126–27, 151–52
  movement of, 128–29
  as object, 139–40
  transmitting, 10–11, 127–28, 151
  as unifying concept, 124–25, 129–31, 141
  See also under meaning
Integrated Information Theory 3.0, 96–97, 124, 125, 130–31, 141, 144–45
intentionality
  in Abhinavagupta's theism, 101
  of body, 74–75
  of ego, 63
  information and, 141
  language and, 60–61, 65, 112–13
  materiality and, 150–51
  meaning and, 126–27
  time and, 67–69
interdependence, 164n.14, 165n.37
Īśvara Pratyabhijñā Vivṛti Vimarśinī, 5–7, 46, 54–55, 90–91, 125–26, 127
Īśvara tattva, 66, 90, 138–39, 147
"it from bit," 124, 125, 126–27, 134–36, 137–38, 139, 140, 141–42, 143

Jataka tales, 78
Jayaratha, 186n.94
Johnson, Marc, 91–92
Johnston, Jay, 84
Johnston, Mark, 68

karma
  in Buddhism, 81–82
  limitations of, 53, 58, 148
  subjectivity and, 67–68
  subtle body and, 73, 78–79
  traces of, 129–30
karmapuruṣa (action-spirit), 80
Kashmir, 2–3, 5–6, 13
Kashmiri Śaivism, 50, 147, 158–59n.18, 170n.105
Kātyāyana, 33–34
Kauffman, Stuart, 18
Kaumarī, 89–90
Keller, Catherine, 27, 32–33, 39–40, 65
knowledge
  Abhinavagupta's conception of, 135–37
  acquiring, 150
  and action, relationships between, 36, 106, 107
  in dual-aspect monism, 97–98
  genuine, 153
  "I-ness" as, 139
  information and, 10–11, 124–25
  through first-person awareness, 68–69
  transformation of, 138
  vimarśa and, 117, 118
Koch, Christof, 96–97, 100–1, 124, 133, 135, 136–37, 140, 143–44. *See also* Integrated Information Theory 3.0
Kondo, Marie, 19
Kripal, Jeffrey, 20–21, 67, 129, 134, 141
Krishna, Daya, 21–22
kriyā śakti, 107, 202n.58
Kṛṣṇa, 31–32, 77, 211n.24
Kṣemarāja, 182–83n.63
kuṇḍalinī, 188n.112
Kurzweil, Ray, 129–30, 133, 151–52

Lakoff, George, 91–92
Lakṣmī, 90, 131
language
  five sheaths and, 218–19n.113
  intentionality in, 60–61, 65, 112–13
  latent multiplicity of, 39–40
  levels of, 112–13
  of medieval India, 39–40
  philosophical understanding of, 180n.44
  quantum mechanics and, 134
  sound and, 132
latent residual impressions, 85, 111, 129–30, 218n.112
Latour, Bruno, 33–34, 162n.2, 164n.21
Lawrence, David, 23, 42, 111
lead, tetraethyl, 18

light (*prakāśa*), 28
  activity and, 172n.140
  in dual-aspect monism, 31, 97–98, 114
  elements of, 115–16
  freedom and, 35, 37–38
  gendered binary of, 107
  idealism and, 111
  knowledge linked with, 106
  resting in, 42–43
  vimarśa and, 105, 106
limited knowers, 147, 148
limited Subject (*grahaka*), 29–31, 147, 150
Livingston, Julie, 16–17
Lotus Sūtra, 176–77n.8
luminosity, 97–98

macrocosm-microcosm linkage, 89, 90–91
Madhurāja Yogin, 2–3
Maharaj, Ayon, 75–76
Maharshi, Ramana, 4–5
Maṇḍana, 39
Maṇḍukya Upaniṣad, 190n.121
mantra
  Abhinavagupta's theology of, 7–8, 126, 138–39
  deity bodies of, 22–23, 145–46
  as information, 125, 133, 135–36
  mathematical formulas and, 131–32, 152
  wonder and, 46, 60–61
Mantramārga, 75
Margulis, Lynn, 17, 93
Massumi, Brian, 9–10, 92
materialism
  atheist, 14–15
  mechanistic, 69
  nondualist, 83–84
  physicalist, 130–31
  popular views of, 19–20
  scientific, 63–64
materiality
  in Abhinavagupta's panentheism, 4–5, 6, 13–14
  consciousness and, 25, 76–77, 126–27
  subjectivity and, 14, 54, 62–63, 69, 110–11, 152
  transcendence and, 7–8
  vimarśa linked with, 107
  wonder as essence of, 56–57
mathematical patterns, 126, 130–31, 133, 152
matter
  Abhinavagupta's focus on, 7
  action and, 117
  agonistic relation to, 122
  arising from subject, 135
  four classic principles, 55–56
  humility and, 45
  intentionality of, 143
  language capacity in, 112–13
  meaning and consciousness intrinsic to, 144
  negation, 22
  subjectivity in, 98
  vimarśa and, 120–21
  vitality of, 21–22, 32–33
  wonder linked to, 9, 46, 48–50
  See also under consciousness
Maxwell, John, 103–4
Māyā, 13–14
  Abhinavagupta's view of, 148
  duality of, 126–27
  function of, 29, 149
  level of, 120
  operation of, 137
  plurality and, 24
  as principle of matter, 55–56
  trap of, 53, 133
  Utpaladeva's view of, 167n.67
McNamara, Patrick, 93
meaning, 126–27, 153
  causality and, 143
  consciousness and, 138
  information and, 125, 129, 134, 141–42
  matter/materiality and, 133, 142–44, 150–51
  sound and, 132
memory, 40, 44, 88, 91–92
Metzinger, Thomas, 82–83, 133–34
mind
  in Abhinavagupta's system, 9–10, 13–14
  cognitive executive function of, 91–92
  in Indian tradition, 166n.52
  and matter, difference between, 124, 143
  in Sāṃkhya, 81
  silenced by wonder, 52, 203–4n.81
  in subtle body, 78–79
mind-body dualism
  bridging, 216n.95
  problems of, 81, 99, 100–1, 102, 115–16
Miśra, Maṇḍana, 79–80
Mitchell, W.J.T, 32–33
molecular signaling, 17–18
Morton, Timothy, 15–16, 39–40, 93

multiplicity, 3, 8, 40, 77, 84–85, 93–94
Musk, Elon, 10, 95–96
mysticism, 20–21, 61, 130–31, 133, 134

nāda, 132
Nagel, Thomas, 46, 51, 62, 101, 209–10n.7
naming, 44, 139
Nareśvara Vivekaḥ, 181–82n.57
Nature. See *prakṛti* (Nature)
Nāyaiyikas, 78–79
Nemec, John, 24, 27, 65, 105, 112–13, 142
Neo-Darwinism, 18
neuroscience, 9, 10, 46–47, 63, 99, 102–3
Nevin, Rick, 18
New Materialism, 107, 110
  Abhinavagupta's system and, 3–4, 8, 13–15, 24, 40, 60, 153–54
  agency of matter in, 72, 73, 75
  animism and, 27
  atheism in, 15–16
  ecology and, 12–13
  economic model in, 18, 164n.14
  human role in, 22–23, 44
  information and, 10–11, 126
  matter in, 7, 19, 98, 142–44
  panpsychism in, 20
  plurality and freedom linked in, 39
  sentience in, 7–8, 61
  subject-centered perspective in, 69
  third-person perspectives in, 36
  transcendence in, 62
  wonder linked to materiality in, 49, 56
Nicholas of Cusa, 27, 32–33
nonawareness, 171–72n.129
nondualism, 3, 120
  dual-aspect, 37, 142–43
  Indian traditions of, 39
  matter in, 4, 13–14, 115–16
  subjectivity as foundation, 23–24, 25–26
  within theology, 60
  See also dual-aspect monism
nontheism, 19–20
numinosity, 20–21, 28
nyāsa practice, 156n.7, 178n.22
Nyāya Sūtra, 78–79, 200n.47

objects
  agency of, 33–34
  appearance/arising of, 118, 139–40
  delight in, innate, 27–28
  freedom and, 34–35
  grammatical position of, 33–34
  as impenetrable, 40
  inward-directed impulse of, 147
  inwardly withdrawn consciousness of, 30–31
  nonappearance of, 136–37
  personal subjectivities and, 29–30
  śakti of, 135
  sentience of, innate, 15–16, 28
  state of being (*idantā*), 10–11
  status of, 25–26
  and things, distinguishing between, 32–33
  vimarśa of, 112–13
  vitality of, 44, 77
ontology, 25
  hierarchy in, 23
  of New Materialism, 39
  object-oriented, 15–16, 39–40
out-of-body experiences, 82–83, 133–34

Padoux, Andre, 107
pāka śāstra, 52
Pandey, K.C, 2–3, 25–26, 35–36, 111
panentheism, 37, 125
  body in, 9–10, 60
  contemporary applications of, 4
  differentiation in, 128–29
  foundational subjectivity in, 3
  grammatology of, 32
  holism of, 153
  linguistic analysis, 7
  and panpsychism, contemporary, 96–97
  subtle body in, 9–10
  theology of, 75
  See also dual-aspect monism
Pāṇinī, 33–34
panpsychism, 4, 125
  Abhinavagupta's system and, 10, 37, 126
  artificial intelligence and, 100–1
  consciousness's extension in, 144–45
  contemporary, 99, 102
  cosmology of, 20
  materiality and, 107
  mind and matter in, 143
  in New Materialism, 75
  pantheism in, 24
  physicalist, 119
  theism and, 20–21, 25–26, 101
  variety of, 197–98n.12
  Western versions of, 96–97

pantheism, 102
animism and, 26–27
Somānanda's, 24, 28, 41
paperclip apocalypse, 95–96, 122
Paramārthasāra, 55–56, 70
parasites, 71–72, 90, 94, 123–24, 126, 127–28
Park, Katharine, 47–49, 55
Pauli-Jung model, 118–19
person. See *puruṣa* (person)
phenomenal experience, 111–12
Phi, 144–45
Phillips, Stephen, 78–79
physics, 129–30
play (*krīḍa*), 64
pluralism, 15–16, 24
plurality, 35–36, 56, 84–85, 89–90
Poe, Edgar Allan, 132
prakṛti (Nature), 41–42, 55–56, 81, 144
Pratyabhijñā, 171n.127
predetermination, 67–68
Preskill, John, 129–30
projections, 31–33, 77
psychology, contemporary, 63
Puar, Jasbir, 16–17
pure consciousness, 29, 30, 59, 66, 84, 94, 114, 133, 136–37, 149
puruṣa (person), 24, 114, 115–16, 142–44, 149–50, 167–68n.71
Puruṣa Sūkta, 116

quantum mechanics, 134
quantum physics, 134, 142–43, 153
quantum theory, 60, 126–27

Raghavan, Venkatarama, 52
rasa theory, 49, 54, 156n.9, 178n.23
Rastogi, Navjivan, 55–56, 112–13
Ratie, Isabelle, 35, 40, 108–9
Realist Idealism, 25–26, 35–36, 111
Recognition (*Pratyabhijñā*), 5, 25, 171n.127
consciousness in, 103–4, 114
dual-aspect monism of, 105
enlightenment in, 119–20
of one's first-person perspective, 45
wonder in, 49–50
reflexive intelligence, 188–89n.113
reincarnation, 78–83, 86
Riskin, Jessica, 14–15, 18
Rubenstein, Mary Jane, 24, 26–27, 36, 48–49, 102
Rudder-Baker, Lynne, 58, 68
Rudra, 90–91
Rudrapraśna, 12
Russellian neural monism, 118

Sadāśiva, 30–31, 66, 90, 136–37, 138–39, 147, 216n.94
Sagan, Carl, 9, 47
Śaiva tradition, 108
śakti/Śakti, 35, 55–56, 90, 147, 148
Śaṁbhavī, 89–90
Sāṃkhy Kārikā (Īśvarakṛṣṇa), 78–79
Sāṃkhya tradition, 166n.52
Abhinavagupta's reworking of, 136–37, 142–43
body in, 81
causality in, 143
dualism of, 58–59, 76–77
ego (*ahaṃkāra*) in, 63
gendered binary in, 107, 114
matter in, 171n.119
puruṣa in, 115–16, 143–44, 167–68n.71
subtle body in, 78–79
tattvas in, 145–47
saṃskāras, 78–79
Samuel, Geoffrey, 84
Sanderson, Alexis, 81–82
Śaṅkara, 41–42, 58, 78–79, 82–84, 195n.75, 199n.30
Śaṅkaradigvijaya, 79–80
Sanskrit grammatical tradition, 33–34
Sapolsky, Robert, 72, 74, 83–84, 90
Sarasvati, Dayananda, 81
Schaeffer, Simon, 19–20
Schrödinger, Erwin, 133, 142–43
science, Western, 9, 18, 19–20, 153–54. *See also* cognitive science; neuroscience; quantum physics
Scientific America, 47, 48, 54, 62, 69
scientific reductionism, 116
Searle, John, 14–15, 37, 99, 104, 117, 121, 144–45
second-person perspective, 32, 76–77, 144–45
self, 72
Abhinavagupta's view of, 41–42, 115–17
in Advaita Vedānta, 4–5
as all-pervasive, 83
arising of, 93
body and, 211n.24
boundaries of, 126
identification with, 8

limited sense of, 149–50
material embodiment of, 114–15
meaning and, 143–44
in reincarnation, 78–79
tied to matter by wonder, 59
vimarśa and, 105, 115
wonder and ordinary sense of, 47–48
self-awareness, 68–69, 104, 192–93n.25
sense organs, 42–43, 86
senses, 78–79, 89–90
sensory enjoyment, 52–55
sentience, 3–4, 7–8
and all-pervasive consciousness, distinctions between, 102–3
arising through body, 9–10
attaining, 42
freedom as basis of, 34, 59
identification and, 8
insentience and, 15–16, 29–30, 32–33, 52, 61, 121, 145
lack of definiteness in, 41
language capacity and, 112–13
materiality and awareness in, 110
sensory enjoyment and, 53
subject and object mixed in, 51–52
subjectivity and, 9, 14, 15–16
vimarśa linked with, 98, 105
Seth, Anil, 9, 46–47, 48–49, 51, 54, 62, 69, 99, 104
Shapin, Steven, 19–20
Shapiro, James, 18
Shastri, Harabhatta, 42
sheaths (*kañcukas*), 148, 149–51, 190n.121
Shermer, Michael, 47
Shulman, David, 55
Siderits, Mark, 81–83
Śiva, 2–3, 60, 181–82n.57
Abhinavagupta's conception of, 118–19
as cosmopsychism, 110–11, 137–38, 150–51
divine freedom of, 64
as foundational subjectivity, 186n.90
single reality of, 3–4, 24–25, 97–98, 100, 109, 126, 127, 130–31
Somānanda's pantheism and, 24
as state of wonder, 182–83n.63
tattva of, 76–77, 110, 147
Utpaladeva's view of, 167n.67
Śiva/Citī, 36, 215n.85
Smith, Fred, 78–79
Somānanda, 24
Abhinavagupta's development of, 32
on divine freedom, 64
pantheism of, 31, 102
on perception, 142
on sentience, 105
on *Śiva*, 110–11
on time, 67–68
on *vimarśa*, 112–13
on will, 183n.68
soul, 46–47, 102, 134, 179–80n.39, 217n.101
sound, 131–32, 138–39
enjoyment of, 133
materiality of, 125, 152
meaning and, 132–33
spanda (vibration), 65, 67–68
Spanda Kārika, 215n.91
Spinoza, Baruch, 15–16, 36, 38, 98
spirit, 41–42, 74–75, 77, 78–79
spirit-body duality, rejection of, 74–75
spontaneity, 117, 120–21
Śrī Rudrapraśna, 20–21, 44
statues and icons, 31–32, 77
Strawson, Galen, 119
subject and object
dual apprehension of, 148
mixed, 51–52, 56–57, 148, 152
relationship between, 138
subjectivity, 8, 13
in Abhinavagupta's system, 10–11, 35, 36, 40
as body (*vapuḥ*) of everything, 67–69
concentrations of, differing, 130–31
crucial function of, 153–54
epistemology of, 62–63
five sheaths and, 150–51
foundational, 14, 37, 59–61, 67, 69
genuine, goal of, 43
hierarchy in, 23
limited, 41–42, 127
within materiality, 102–3
materially embodied, 122
matter and, 7, 9, 19, 49–50
movement of, 151
of objects, 26–27
other included in, 45
shared, 32–33, 51, 121
state of, 136–37
subtle body as attribute of, 94
transformation of (matter), 61
vimarśa linked with, 98
will and, 57
wonder and, 46, 54, 61–63

subtle body, 3–4, 9–10, 19, 82–83
 Abhinavagupta's distinctions in understanding, 76–77, 81
 breath and, 85–86
 deities composing, 74–75
 function of, 83–84
 in Indian tradition, 22–23, 75–76, 88–89
 intersubjectivity and, 84
 karma and, 129–30
 limitations of, 150–51
 multiplicity of agencies in, 72–73, 90, 92
 quasi-materiality of, 87
 soul as, 134
 in transmigration, 78–79
 variant views of, 74
 See also "City of Eight"
subtle matter, 19
Surya, 89

Taittirīya Brāhmaṇa, 88–89
Tantra, 2–3, 127, 130–31
 animism in, 27–28
 body in, 2–3, 9–10, 49, 75, 88, 196n.76
 enlightenment in, 208n.141
 gender archetypes in, 107
 materiality and transcendence in, 7–8
 multiplicity in, 29
 siddhis of, 40
 subtle body in, 91
Tantrasāra, 58–59
taste (*āsvāda*), 110
tattva system, 3–4, 23, 127
 Abhinavagupta's use of, 6, 10–11, 126, 147–48, 149, 152, 178n.21
 function of, 175n.173
 outline of, 146–47
 Śiva in, 25
Tegmark, Max, 100–1, 126, 130–31, 133, 140, 141, 152
teleology, 15–16
 of New Materialism, 39
 reworkings of, 63–65
Terminator, 95–96, 122
theism
 Abhinavagupta's, 20–21, 96–97, 101–2, 155n.3
 avoiding, 100–1
 Western inheritance of, 102, 127–28
theology, 73
 Abhinavagupta's, 113–14
 agency in, 74–75
 of body, 92
 ecology and, 7
 of freedom, 137–38
 intentionality in, 120
third-person perspectives
 excess of, 29, 30–31
 as grammatical position, 31–32
 modern habit of, 14–15
 problems with, 58, 68
 on telos, 39
 telos and, 64
"this-ness" (*idantā*), 28–29, 30–31, 126, 128–29
 concealing, 66
 differentiation process of, 31, 208n.136
 as external marker, 130–31
 freedom and, 34, 41–42
 God in, 120
 indistinct, 137
 Śiva/Citī and, 36
 See also objects
Thompson, Evan, 111–12
Thoreau, Henry David, 20–21
thoughts, 40, 41–42, 49–50, 57, 87, 216n.92
Timalsina, Sthaneshwar, 33–34, 39, 54, 58, 111
time
 sheath of, 148, 149, 150
 subtle body and, 86–87
 transcendence and, 67–69
Tononi, Giulio, 96–97, 105–6, 117, 124, 135, 136–37, 140, 143–44. *See also* Integrated Information Theory 3.0
Torella, Raffaele, 39–40, 68–69, 112–13
touch, sense of, 106, 110
transcendence, 3–4, 118
 in Abhinavagupta's system, 5, 13–14, 51–52, 65–67
 atheistic, 9
 body's role in, 54
 ego and, 63
 information and, 151–52
 rethinking, 51, 52–53, 62–63, 107
 Western legacy of, 10, 99, 101
 wonder and, 46, 47–51
Tripurarahsya, 79–80
turiyātita. *See* Beyond the Fourth (*turiyātita*)

Utpaladeva, 171n.127
 Ajaḍapramātṛ Siddhi, 42, 104
 on cause and effect, 184–85n.80

on desire, 113
on Fourth State, 65
on freedom, 34–35
Īśvarapratyabhijñākārikā, 5–6
Īśvarapratyabhijñāvivṛti, 5–7
on *krīḍa*, 64
on material form, 110
on objects, 27
panentheism of, 24, 31, 100
on self-awareness, 192–93n.25
theology of, 108–9
on *vimarśa*, 105, 108–9, 112–13, 114
on wonder, 56–57, 182–83n.63
on yogic powers, 68–69

Vasalou, Sophia, 48
Vayu, 88, 89
Vijñāna Bhairava, 27, 109
vijñānākalās, 184n.77
Vijñānavāda idealism, 35
vikalpa, 57, 179n.33, 203–4n.81
vimarśa (active awareness), 42–43, 132
Abhinavagupta's use of term, 96, 102–3, 105, 114–15
activity and, 114, 116–17, 118, 135–36, 172n.140
as Ānandabhairavī, 89–90
as consciousness, 10, 103–5
in dual-aspect monism, 30–31, 97–98
elements of, 115–16
etymology of, 106
everyday experience and, 108–9
linguistic orientation of, 112–13
of objects, 28–29
prakāśa intertwined with, 120–21
sentience and, 3–4, 61
subjectivity and, 38
subtle body and, 81
translations of, 201n.48, 202–3n.65
variant views on, 111
viruses, 16–18, 41, 72
Viṣṇu, 88, 90
vitalism, 50
Viveiros de Castro, Eduardo, 23, 123, 142
Vivekananda, 75–76, 210n.8
volition, 73

Wargo, Eric, 67
war mentality, 16–17
Watson, Alex, 78–79
Webster, Joanne, 71–72
Western modernity, 13
Western philosophy, 57
Wheeler, John Archibald, 1, 124, 125, 126–27, 140, 141–42, 144–45, 152. *See also* "it from bit"
White, Lynn, 7
White, Roger, 46
Whitehead, Alfred North, 27
Whitman, Walt, 8, 15–16, 20–21, 44, 45
will (*icchā)*
arising through body, 9–10
body and, 90
in cells, 93
as desire to be, 113–14
language and, 60–61
in objects, 28, 33–34
wonder linked to, 49, 57–59, 178n.21
See also free will; intentionality
withdrawal, inward, 137
wonder (*camatkāra*), 7–8
Abhinavagupta's use of, 48–51, 62
in aesthetics, 54
capacity for, 122
contemporary sense, 46–48
etymologies (interpretive), 52, 54, 65
as foundational subjectivity, 61
freedom in, 53–54
of immanence, 36
knowledge and actioned linked by, 38
krīDa and, 64
phenomenology of, 47–48, 178n.21
sensory enjoyment of, 52–53
use of term, 3–4, 9
vimarśa and, 110
Wujastyk, Dominik, 88

yoga practice, 40, 87–88, 181n.52
Yogarāja, 35, 55–56, 70
yogic powers, 67, 68–69